Introduction to the philosophy of mind

READINGS FROM DESCARTES TO STRAWSON

Academic Editor: **William K. Frankena**

University of Michigan

Introduction to the philosophy of mind

READINGS FROM DESCARTES TO STRAWSON

Edited by **HAROLD MORICK**

State University of New York at Albany

SCOTT, FORESMAN AND COMPANY

Preface

This book brings under one cover the most influential essays on mind since the advent of modern philosophy.[1] It is intended as a supplemental reader for introductory courses in the problems of philosophy and as a reader for courses in philosophy of mind, metaphysics, and epistemology. Although the selections vary in difficulty, most are easily understood by the college student. Most of the main issues about the mind are dealt with in these essays. Questions about the nature of self and self-knowledge run through all of them.

The book presents a small number of philosophers in selections which tend to be longer than is usual in philosophical anthologies. Thirteen of the sixteen selections are either complete essays or intact chapters or subsections of books.[2] It is an anthology made up of two sections.

The first section, "Modern Philosphers of Mind in Contemporary Perspective," begins with a selection from Descartes, the first modern philospher of mind. The next three modern selections—those from Hume, Kant, and Brentano—mark three turning points in the development of the philosophy of mind. Each of these four selections is followed by contemporary commentaries which in their own right are also major contributions to contemporary philosophy; indeed Ryle, Ayer, Penelhum, Strawson, and Chisholm are mostly concerned more with the philosophical issues than with textual exegesis.

The second section, "Contemporary Philosophers of Mind," begins with the three most influential twentieth-century philosophers of mind—Wittgenstein, Sartre, and Ryle; continues with Malcolm's already classic review of the *Investigations;* and closes with the two current theories of mind most widely discussed, the "identity theory," inaugurated by Place's famous article and Strawson's "Persons" approach.

A word or two now about the character of the introductory essay. The depth and lucidity of this anthology's first selection, Descartes' First, Second, and Sixth Meditations, makes superfluous the usual kind of editor's introduction. Consequently, this introductory essay isn't of the usual kind; it deals with a fairly delimited topic, the privacy of mind. I've focussed it this way because it seems to me that con-

[1] By "modern" I mean postmedieval, and by "contemporary," twentieth century.
[2] The exceptions are the selections from Hume's *Treatise*, Kant's *Critique*, and Sartre's *Transcendence of the Ego*.

fusions about the privacy of inner experience constitute the biggest single obstacle to reaching a clear understanding of the nature of mind. The reader should turn to my essay only when he has read enough of the selections to realize that perplexities about privacy are endemic to philosophical inquiry about mind, and that consequently this topic merits special attention. More pointedly, the essay may be used as an introduction to Wittgenstein's lecture-notes on private experience, one of this anthology's more difficult selections.

Since the essays are dated and arranged in chronological order, the book can be used to trace the main lines of the history of philosophical thinking about mind. But the beginner should leave for last the Kant, Wittgenstein, and Intentionality (Brentano and Sartre) sections because they are the most difficult.

One or two miscellaneous points need to be made. First, the comparative lengths of the selections from the philosophers included is not to be taken as a measure of their comparative worth. Second, although Strawson's "Self, Mind, and Body" makes little reference to Kant, it deals in a more accessible way with substantially the same questions treated in "The Soul"; for this reason I place it before "The Soul."

I wish to express my gratitude to the authors, editors, and publishers who kindly gave permission to reprint the essays below. I am especially indebted to William Frankena, Peter Geach, and Roderick Chisholm for their incisive criticisms of an earlier draft of my brief introductory essay. I want also to thank Jerome Shaffer and E. M. Zemach on this count. I thank Paul Rohe of Scott, Foresman for his patience and very able assistance. And most of all I am grateful to my wife, Sandra, for her generous help and encouragement.

Harold Morick
Albany, New York

Contents

INTRODUCTORY ESSAY:
THE PRIVACY OF PSYCHOLOGICAL PHENOMENA*

I want here to give some characterization of what is psychological or mental, and thereby to locate the subject matter of the philosophy of mind by contrasting the privacy of a person's mind with the publicity of the material world. There are many sorts of privacy which have been attributed to mind, some of which fail to characterize the mental and two of which succeed.

1. Nonobservational Knowledge as a Criterion of the Psychological.

The characteristics a person has and the states and processes he undergoes seem to be of two fundamentally different kinds. Let's say one feels depressed because one is overweight. One knows about one's obesity in essentially the same way that anyone else does—by looking at the spare tire around one's midriff and by putting oneself on the bathroom scale and reading off the bad news. One also knows in essentially the same way as anyone else such other physical characteristics as that one has a darker tan than Jones has and that one has a normal ratio of white to red corpuscles.

On the other hand, a person seems to know about his psychological characteristics in a way very different from the way in which others know about them. Other people learn that he is depressed from his behavior, what he does and says. But that is not the way he knows about his *own* feelings. In fact, speaking of a "way" of knowing one's own feelings seems here to be misleading, for the knowledge accrues to one *directly:* one doesn't need to observe one's own hangdog look and the rest to know that one feels depressed. Simply having that feeling puts one into a position to know what it is that one feels. Thus there would appear to be good reason for the common sense division of a person's characteristics into private and public, into psychological and physical; it seems obvious that mental states, unlike bodily states, are by nature known directly by one and only one person, namely, the person who has them.

"But," the objection might be raised, "isn't this characterization of the mental too narrow? It appears to exclude such psychological

---

*See the fifth paragraph of the preface.

characteristics as capabilities and character traits. One cannot know without observing one's own actions whether or not one can thread needles or do arithmetic. Nor can one so know whether or not one is vain or cowardly. A person has to see himself in action to find out these sorts of things." We may reply that while to be vain is *mainly* to be prone to do things like talk at length about oneself whenever the opportunity arises, to lapse into silence and yawns when the topic isn't oneself, to be unable to pass a mirror without looking at oneself, and so on, it is *also* to be prone to entertain grandiose self-centered thoughts. To assert vanity of someone is to imply that he is an entity which can have a self-conception, which can think about itself. And thinking is essentially an inner happening. Thus concepts such as vanity are psychological or mental *only because* of their inner experience component. We must divide psychological concepts into those which are concepts of essentially inner states (such as thinking to oneself or having a pain) and those which are not (such as being vain or good at arithmetic). It is the former we shall be concerned with here when we speak of psychological concepts and states.

I think there are two objections which are fatal to the claim made above that psychological states, unlike bodily states, are by nature known directly by one and only one person, namely the person who has them. First, some philosophers have denied the contrast with bodily states, have claimed that certain *physical* states are, indeed, known directly only by the person who has them. They remind us that even when one's eyes are closed, one can say what position one's limbs are in and whether or not they are moving. These philosophers ask how one knows these things and suggest that at least sometimes we know them directly, without observing our own limbs. Since their suggestion is intelligible and consistent, it is logically possible that one and only one person can know certain *physical* states directly—without observation.

Second, it is at least conceivable that *other* people could have non-observational knowledge of one's thoughts and feelings, namely by mental telepathy. Whatever may turn out to be the truth about the hypothesis that there are some people, mental telepathists, who can read other people's minds, the idea of mental telepathy is neither unintelligible nor self-contradictory. Since it is logically possible that someone else could directly know one's own thoughts and feelings, it cannot be a *defining* characteristic of one's thoughts and feelings that they are directly accessible to oneself alone.

Thus we have seen that there are two objections which invalidate the claim that a defining characteristic of the mental is that only the subject of a state of consciousness can have direct knowledge of it. I shall now propose an alternative characterization of mind which can meet the above objections because it is correct, and which preserves the basic intuition that direct knowledge somehow distinguishes mental from physical phenomena.

Even if it be granted that a person has the knack of directly knowing the movements and positions of his limbs, there is no contradiction in saying that he could lose this knack and have to rely on observations of his own limbs in the way that the rest of us learn these things about his limbs. Similarly, even if there were telepathists who could read other people's minds, there would be no contradiction in saying that they could lose this extraordinary talent and have to go back to observing other people's behavior to figure out what others are thinking and feeling. On the other hand, it is self-contradictory to say that a person *who understands* first person, present tense psychological sentences such as "I'm in pain" and "I'm thinking to myself" might lose the knack of knowing his thoughts and feelings directly and have to go back to observing his own behavior to find out what his thoughts and feelings are—that, for instance, in order to know that he is in pain he might have to look at himself in a mirror; or that in order to know what he is thinking about, he might have to wait and listen to his own testimony! Thus the notion of direct knowledge does after all provide a unique characteristic of states of consciousness, namely that these states *must* be known directly by the person who has them at the time he has them if he is to know about them at all at the time he has them, but they needn't be so known about by other people. No nonpsychological property must be known *only* in this way. In other words, a statement S reports a current, psychological state of a person P provided that:

P is the only person of whom it is self-contradictory to say that he knows S is true on the basis of observation. [1]

It is not self-contradictory to say that Jones can know by observation that his legs are crossed. Nor is it self-contradictory to say that anybody other than Jones, even a telepathist, can know by observation that Jones is in pain. But it *is* self-contradictory to say that Jones can know by observation that he is in pain.

It is important to note that while this criterion establishes a funda-

[1] This criterion can be reformulated to satisfy those philosophers who claim that it "makes no sense" to speak of *any* kind of first person knwoledge of the immediate contents of consciousness. See My "Cartesian Privilege and the Strictly Mental," *Philosophy and Phenomenological Research*, forthcoming.

mental difference between the characteristic of being a psychological state and that of being a bodily state, it does not show that persons are anything other than a species of material body. The fact that the properties of being a thought process and of being an electrochemical process are *very* different no more shows that both properties couldn't be properties of one thing—the brain, say—than the fact that the properties of being white and being expensive and being holy are *very* different shows that all three couldn't be properties of the very same thing—a robe, say. What we would have to show, and may now provide the basis for showing by proposing another criterion of the mental, is that some thoughts and feelings possess a property which is *incompatible* with a property which is a defining property of matter.

2. Final Epistemic Authority as a Criterion of the Psycholocigal.

The discussion which led to our first criterion of the psychological took as its starting point the intuition that one's thoughts and feelings are private in that they are known with a certain *immediacy* by one and only one person, namely, oneself. The following discussion takes as its starting point another intuition: one's thoughts and feelings are private in that they are known with a certain *ultimacy* by one and only one person, namely, oneself.

Matter, including the human body of course, seems to be public in the sense that no one's knowledge claims about it are in principle any better than anyone else's. One isn't, for example, in a uniquely advantageous position to know whether or not it is true that one is overweight or that one's brain is gray and furrowed. Are states of mind also public in this sense? Certainly public are those personal characteristics which essentially consist of outward behavior and circumstance. Other people are in at least as good a position as I am to know if I am vain, lazy, or scatterbrained. On the other hand, in regard to knowledge claims about those states whose essence consists of what happens inwardly—what we have been referring to simply as "psychological states"—it would appear to be absurd for a person to accept anybody else's word over his own. It seems evident that no one's word may be accepted over a person's honest testimony that he feels tired and cold, has an image of a sunset, is daydreaming about a Cadillac, or is entertaining the thought that tomorrow is Washington's birthday or that the first line on the oculist's chart which looks fuzzy to him is the next to last line.

It should be noted that a person should not be granted this final epistemic authority about his *past* states of consciousness. He need not have the last word about what he *was* thinking or feeling, for the passage of time cancels whatever authority he had. For instance, yesterday a man may have absently divulged to us that he was daydreaming about lying on the beach, and yet today he fails to remember either the daydream or the avowal. We must also note that having the last word about the immediate contents of one's consciousness doesn't in itself imply infallibility on this subject any more than infallibility about occurrences in the ballpark is implied by the final authority of the baseball umpire. On any given occasion what the umpire says might be false: the pitch which he called a strike was actually slightly above the batter's shoulders. A similar point was made about final *legal* authority by Supreme Court Justice Robert Jackson: "We are not final because we are infallible, but we are infallible only because we are final."

"But surely," one might say, "we have this final authority only because science does not as yet know enough about our brains. Isn't it just a matter of time before scientists will be able to use instruments like electroencephalographs to determine exactly what our thoughts and feelings are?" No one in 1969 can reasonably deny that this is a possibility. Even now scientists have discovered striking correlations between a person's states of consciousness and his bodily states and occurrences. For example, they have discovered that when people dream their eyes move rapidly. Sometimes the correlations are of quite a specific nature: the eye movements of a man who dreamt he was climbing a flight of stairs were precisely of the kind one makes when actually climbing stairs. Now let us suppose for a moment that science becomes ever more successful in this line so that in the twenty-fifth century each different conscious state is correlated uniquely with a particular state of the brain. (When and only when John entertains the thought that tomorrow is Washington's birthday is he in brain-state *A;* and when and only when he thinks that tomorrow is Lincoln's birthday is he in brain-state *B;* and so forth.) "If all this came about," one might well reason, "people would no longer have final authority about their thoughts and feelings; there could be cases in which we would justifiably say that a person is mistaken. Suppose that a particular person honestly believes that he is seeing a green afterimage while his brain-state is of the kind found correlated with red afterimages. Surely it would be unreasonable for scientists to accept this single report as falsifying what by our hypothesis is a well established psychophysical law."

It must be granted that this objection shows that some day it *could* happen that scientists might justifiably override a subject's own testimony. And this seems to show that having final epistemic authority about our thoughts and feelings is by no means a necessary feature of human nature. But, in fact, it doesn't. The scientists of the twenty-fifth century could legitimately override or perhaps "explain away" the subject's testimony because it conflicted with a well established psychophysical law. But, we must ask, how could this law have been established in the first place? Only through correlating epistemically privileged reports with brain-states. That is, since there is no behavior which we think of as uniquely characterizing having an afterimage, the only way that investigating scientists could determine what brain-state, if any, *is* constantly and exclusively conjoined with the having of any kind of afterimage whatsoever is by asking people to *tell* them what they are experiencing. (This is the way in which the dream investigators discovered the relation between up-and-down eye movements and the dream content of walking up the staircase.) In short, it is true that a person's report of his current, psychological states could be overriden; but only on the basis of some psychophysical law which itself could only have been established on the basis of *other* such first person psychological reports.

An analogy may make this point clearer. It is quite possible that we shall come to treat the viewing of an event on television—the murder of a presidential assassin, say—as of equal informational weight with eyewitness reports; and in the case of conflict even override the eyewitness report on the basis of what we see on the television set. If we did this, it would appear that we were denying that eyewitness reports have a ground level position in our knowledge of physical occurrences. If we remind ourselves, however, of how we come to know that television sets show the world as it really is, we realize that the eyewitness report of the murder would be, and could only be overridden on the ultimate basis of *other* eyewitness reports.

We may say then that a person's psychological states alone are private in the sense that whenever there is a doubt or dispute about their existence and character, his word is final in the following way. A statement S reports a current psychological state of a person *P* provided that:

> *P's* sincere testimony that S is true cannot possibly be overridden by any evidence which is independent of other self-testimony.

Doesn't this imply that a person's word is also the final authority about whether or not his testimony is sincere, about whether or not he's lying? No, we don't always take another person's word on this, and there is no logical reason why we ought to. In any case, the details of how one determines another person's sincerity are not to the point. For if a person honestly maintains that he is daydreaming about lying on the beach—however "publicly" his honesty be determined (by a lie-detector perhaps)—his testimony has a unique ultimate authority; whereas his honest claim that he weighs 171 pounds is in principle no better than anybody else's claim about his weight.

Final epistemic authority about psychological, but not bodily, states provides, then, a second way of showing that these two kinds of states are fundamentally different. But it may establish something more; namely, that persons are not material bodies. The concept of a person is the concept of an entity which necessarily has psychological attributes. But it would seem that we cannot possibly ascribe these attributes to material bodies, or to any part of them, such as a brain. For a *defining* characteristic of matter appears to be that matter is public in the sense that no one's knowledge claims about what attributes matter does and does not have are in principle better than anyone else's. If this is a defining characteristic, it would follow that anyone who claimed that a person is nothing but a particular kind of material object would have to, if he is to avoid ascribing incompatible characteristics to a species of material bodies (the bodies of human beings), deny that there are any states of consciousness at all. In other words, he would have to deny that there are things which necessarily have thoughts and feelings: he would have to deny that there are any such things as persons! Thus our second criterion of the psychological seems to lead to the conclusion that persons and material bodies are two different kinds of entities.

3. *Two Other Sorts of Privacy Which Are Often Claimed to Be Criteria of the Psychological.*

In another sense something is private to a given person if he alone can know that it exists and what characteristics it has. Does this furnish us with another criterion of the psychological? That is, are states of consciousness alone private in this way? This raises important and intricate questions about the conditions of knowledge which cannot be dealt with here. However, we may say a word or two about the inference which typically leads people to conclude that thoughts and feelings are private in this way: "one cannot know what another person is really thinking or feeling because one cannot think another's thoughts nor feel his feelings."

First, the conclusion must not be confused with the claim that we have final epistemic authority about our own inner experiences. It is one thing to conclude that each person is in the *best* position to know what he is thinking and feeling, as we have concluded above, and it is quite another thing to conclude that he is the *only* one who can know.

Second, saying I can't *feel* someone else's feelings simply means I can't *have* them. "I feel a toothache" and "I have a toothache" are just two ways of saying the same thing. What misleads people here is that there is another sense of "feel" where "I feel . . . " and "I have . . . " don't at all mean the same thing. Clearly, "I feel a cavity" says something different from "I have a cavity." Similarly, "I can't *see* his afterimages, *dream* his dreams, or *think* his thoughts" are other ways of saying, respectively, "I can't *have* his afterimages, *have* his dreams, or *have* his thoughts." So in a clearer way of speaking, the inference in question is that one cannot possibly know what another person's inner experiences are because one cannot have them.

Third, is the given premise of the inference true? Is it really true that people cannot have the same feeling? When, for example, we truly empathize with the slain man's widow, don't we share her grief? If someone asks this kind of question, the chances are that he is unaware of the ambiguity of "same" and of "identical."

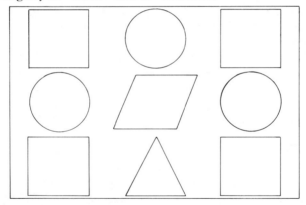

If one says that the figure in the lower right-hand corner of this diagram is the same as the figure which has a triangle to the left of it and a circle above it—then one is using "the same" to speak of *numerical* identity; while if one says that the figure in the lower right-hand corner of the diagram is the same as the figure in the upper left-hand corner—then one is using "the same" to speak of *qualitative* identity.[2] When the son and daughter share the widow's grief, numerically there are three feelings which are qualitatively the same; numerically so because

---

[2]The example is due to P. F. Strawson.

states of consciousness, like all other states, owe their numerical identity to the thing whose states they are. So we see that the given premise, properly construed in terms of numerical identity, is true: we cannot have *numerically the same* feeling as another.

On the other hand, there is no reason to think that the remaining (tacit) premise is true. The inference in question is enthymematic. It presupposes that one must be able to have another person's thoughts and feelings if one is to have knowledge of the existence and character of another person's thoughts and feelings. And there is no more reason to believe this than there is to believe that one must be able to have another person's smiles if one is to have knowledge of the existence and character of another person's smiles.

Now we also see that privacy of ownership cannot be a criterion of the psychological since physical states and processes are also private in this way.

In this essay I have distinguished four different sorts of privacy which might serve as a criterion of the mental. In one sense something is private to someone if he is the only person whose knowledge of its existence and character must be nonobservational knowledge. In another sense a subject matter would be private to him if in some fundamental way he is the final authority concerning its existence and character. Similar to this sense of "private" is a third, which we get by replacing "final authority" with "sole authority." Finally, according to a fourth sense something would be private to a person if it could not possibly belong to anyone else.

Of these criteria only the first and second are satisfied by all psychological states and by no bodily states. Thus, we have established that there are at least two basic differences between the characteristic of being a psychological state and the characteristic of being a bodily state. The fourth criterion is indeed satisfied by all states of consciousness, but it is also satisfied by physical states and events as well (this piece of dynamite cannot have that stick's explosion). And as for the third criterion, I can in this essay only assert that there is no reason to think that it is satisfied by anything at all.

PART I

Modern Philosophers of Mind in Contemporary Perspective

1

René Descartes

MEDITATIONS I, II, & VI[1]

Meditation I.

Of the things which may be brought within the sphere of the doubtful.
It is now some years since I detected how many were the false beliefs
that I had from my earliest youth admitted as true, and how doubtful
was everything I had since constructed on this basis; and from that
time I was convinced that I must once for all seriously undertake to
rid myself of all the opinions which I had formerly accepted, and com-
mence to build anew from the foundation, if I wanted to establish any
firm and permanent structure in the sciences. But as this enterprise
appeared to be a very great one, I waited until I had attained an age
so mature that I could not hope that at any later date I should be better
fitted to execute my design. This reason caused me to delay so long that
I should feel that I was doing wrong were I to occupy in deliberation
the time that yet remains to me for action. To-day, then, since very
opportunely for the plan I have in view I have delivered my mind from
every care [and am happily agitated by no passions] and since I have
procured for myself an assured leisure in a peaceable retirement, I
shall at last seriously and freely address myself to the general upheaval
of all my former opinions.

Now for this object it is not necessary that I should show that all
of these are false—I shall perhaps never arrive at this end. But inasmuch as reason already persuades me that I ought no less carefully
to withhold my assent from matters which are not entirely certain
and indubitable than from those which appear to me manifestly to be
false, if I am able to find in each one some reason to doubt, this will
suffice to justify my rejecting the whole. And for that end it will not be
requisite that I should examine each in particular, which would be an
endless undertaking; for owing to the fact that the destruction of the
foundations of necessity brings with it the downfall of the rest of the
edifice, I shall only in the first place attack those principles upon which
all my former opinions rested.

[1]From René Descartes, *Meditations on First Philosophy*, trans. Elizabeth Haldane and
G. R. T. Ross (London: Cambridge Univ. Press, 1931). Reprinted by permission of the
publisher. First published in Latin in 1641. Expressions in brackets are from a French
translation of the Latin which Descartes approved.

All that up to the present time I have accepted as most true and certain I have learned either from the senses or through the senses; but it is sometimes proved to me that these senses are deceptive, and it is wiser not to trust entirely to any thing by which we have once been deceived.

But it may be that although the senses sometimes deceive us concerning things which are hardly perceptible, or very far away, there are yet many others to be met with as to which we cannot reasonably have any doubt, although we recognise them by their means. For example, there is the fact that I am here, seated by the fire, attired in a dressing gown, having this paper in my hands and other similar matters. And how could I deny that these hands and this body are mine, were it not perhaps that I compare myself to certain persons, devoid of sense, whose cerebella are so troubled and clouded by the violent vapours of black bile, that they constantly assure us that they think they are kings when they are really quite poor, or that they are clothed in purple when they are really without covering, or who imagine that they have an earthenware head or are nothing but pumpkins or are made of glass. But they are mad, and I should not be any the less insane were I to follow examples so extravagant.

At the same time I must remember that I am a man, and that consequently I am in the habit of sleeping, and in my dreams representing to myself the same things or sometimes even less probable things, than do those who are insane in their waking moments. How often has it happened to me that in the night I dreamt that I found myself in this particular place, that I was dressed and seated near the fire, whilst in reality I was lying undressed in bed! At this moment it does indeed seem to me that it is with eyes awake that I am looking at this paper; that this head which I move is not asleep, that it is deliberately and of set purpose that I extend my hand and perceive it; what happens in sleep does not appear so clear nor so distinct as does all this. But in thinking over this I remind myself that on many occasions I have in sleep been deceived by similar illusions, and in dwelling carefully on this reflection I see so manifestly that there are no certain indications by which we may clearly distinguish wakefulness from sleep that I am lost in astonishment. And my astonishment is such that it is almost capable of persuading me that I now dream.

Now let us assume that we are asleep and that all these particulars, e.g. that we open our eyes, shake our head, extend our hands, and so on, are but false delusions; and let us reflect that possibly neither our hands nor our whole body are such as they appear to us to be. At the same time we must at least confess that the things which are represented to us in sleep are like painted representations which can only have been formed as the counterparts of something real and true, and that in this way those general things at least, i.e. eyes, a head, hands, and a whole body, are not imaginary things, but things really existent. For, as a matter of fact, painters, even when they study with the greatest skill to represent sirens and satyrs by forms the most strange and extraordinary, cannot give them natures which are entirely new, but merely make a certain medley of the members of different animals; or if their imagination is extravagant enough to invent something so novel that nothing similar has ever before been seen, and that then their work represents a thing purely fictitious and absolutely false, it is certain all the same that the colours of which this is composed are necessarily real. And for the same reason, although these general things, to wit, [a body], eyes, a head, hands, and such like, may be imaginary, we are bound at the same time to confess that there are at least some other objects yet more simple and more universal, which are real and true; and of these just in the same way as with certain real colours, all these images of things which dwell in our thoughts, whether true and real or false and fantastic, are formed.

To such a class of things pertains corporeal nature in general, and its extension, the figure of extended things, their quantity or magnitude and number, as also the place in which they are, the time which measures their duration, and so on.

That is possibly why our reasoning is not unjust when we conclude from this that Physics, Astronomy, Medicine and all other sciences which have as their end the consideration of composite things, are very dubious and uncertain; but that Arithmetic, Geometry and other sciences of that kind which only treat of things that are very simple and very general, without taking great trouble to ascertain whether they are actually existent or not, contain some measure of certainty and an element of the indubitable. For whether I am awake or asleep, two and three together always form five, and the square can never have more than four sides, and it does not seem possible that truths so clear and apparent can be suspected of any falsity [or uncertainty].

Nevertheless I have long had fixed in my mind the belief that an all-powerful God existed by whom I have been created such as I am. But how do I know that He has not brought it to pass that there is no earth, no heaven, no extended body, no magnitude, no place, and that nevertheless [I possess the perceptions of all these things and that] they seem to me to exist just exactly as I now see them? And, besides, as I sometimes imagine that others deceive themselves in the things which they think they know best, how do I know that I am not deceived every time that I add two and three, or count the sides of a square, or judge of things yet simpler, if anything simpler can be imagined? But possibly God has not desired that I should be thus deceived, for He is said to be supremely good. If, however, it is contrary to His goodness to have made me such that I constantly deceive myself, it would also appear to be contrary to His goodness to permit me to be sometimes deceived, and nevertheless I cannot doubt that He does permit this.

There may indeed be those who would prefer to deny the existence of a God so powerful, rather than believe that all other things are uncertain. But let us not oppose them for the present, and grant that all that is here said of a God is a fable; nevertheless in whatever way they suppose that I have arrived at the state of being that I have reached—whether they attribute it to fate or to accident, or make out that it is by a continual succession of antecedents, or by some other method—since to err and deceive oneself is a defect, it is clear that the greater will be the probability of my being so imperfect as to deceive myself ever, as is the Author to whom they assign my origin the less powerful. To these reasons I have certainly nothing to reply, but at the end I feel constrained to confess that there is nothing in all that I formerly believed to be true, of which I cannot in some measure doubt, and that not merely through want of thought or through levity, but for reasons which are very powerful and maturely considered; so that henceforth I ought not the less carefully to refrain from giving credence to these opinions than to that which is manifestly false, if I desire to arrive at any certainty [in the sciences].

But it is not sufficient to have made these remarks, we must also be careful to keep them in mind. For these ancient and commonly held opinions still revert frequently to my mind, long and familiar custom having given them the right to occupy my mind against my inclination and rendered them almost masters of my belief; nor will I ever lose the habit of deferring to them, or of placing my confidence in them, so long as I consider them as they really are, i.e. opinions in some measure doubtful, as I have just shown, and at the same time highly probable, so that there is much more reason to believe in than to deny them. That is why I consider that I shall not be acting amiss, if, taking of set purpose a contrary belief, I allow myself to be deceived, and for a certain time pretend that all these opinions are entirely false and imaginary, until at last, having thus balanced my former prejudices with my latter [so that they cannot divert my opinions more to one side than to the other], my judgment will no longer be dominated by bad usage or turned away from the right knowledge of the truth. For I am assured that there can be neither peril nor error in this course, and that I cannot at present yield too much to distrust, since I am not considering the question of action, but only of knowledge.

I shall then suppose, not that God who is supremely good and the fountain of truth, but some evil genius not less powerful than deceitful, has employed his whole energies in deceiving me; I shall consider that the heavens, the earth, colours, figures, sound, and all other external things are nought but the illusions and dreams of which this genius has availed himself in order to lay traps for my credulity; I shall consider myself as having no hands, no eyes, no flesh, no blood, nor any senses, yet falsely believing myself to possess all these things; I shall remain obstinately attached to this idea, and if by this means it is not in my power to arrive at the knowledge of any truth, I may at least do what is in my power [i.e. suspend my judgment], and with firm purpose avoid giving credence to any false thing, or being imposed upon by this arch deceiver, however powerful and deceptive he may be. But this task is a laborious one, and insensibly a certain lassitude leads me into the course of my ordinary life. And just as a captive who in sleep enjoys an imaginary liberty, when he begins to suspect that his liberty is but a dream, fears to awaken, and conspires with these agreeable illusions that the deception may be prolonged, so insensibly of my own accord I fall back into my former opinions, and I dread awakening from this slumber, lest the laborious wakefulness which would follow the tranquillity of this repose should have to be spent not in daylight, but in the excessive darkness of the difficulties which have just been discussed.

Meditation II.

Of the Nature of the Human Mind; and that it is more easily known than the Body.

The Meditation of yesterday filled my mind with so many doubts that it is no longer in my power to forget them. And yet I do not see in what manner I can resolve them; and, just as if I had all of a sudden fallen into very deep water, I am so disconcerted that I can neither make certain of setting my feet on the bottom, nor can I swim and so support myself on the surface. I shall nevertheless make an effort and follow anew the same path as that on which I yesterday entered, i.e. I shall proceed by setting aside all that in which the least doubt could be supposed to exist, just as if I had discovered that it was absolutely false; and I shall ever follow in this road until I have met with something which is certain, or at least, if I can do nothing else, until I have learned for certain that there is nothing in the world that is certain. Archimedes, in order that he might draw the terrestrial globe out of its place, and transport it elsewhere, demanded only that one point should be fixed and immoveable; in the same way I shall have the right to conceive high hopes if I am happy enough to discover one thing only which is certain and indubitable.

I suppose, then, that all the things that I see are false; I persuade myself that nothing has ever existed of all that my fallacious memory represents to me. I consider that I possess no senses; I imagine that body, figure, extension, movement and place are but the fictions of my mind. What, then, can be esteemed as true? Perhaps nothing at all, unless that there is nothing in the world that is certain.

But how can I know there is not something different from those things that I have just considered, of which one cannot have the slightest doubt? Is there not some God, or some other being by whatever name we call it, who puts these reflections into my mind? That is not necessary, for is it not possible that I am capable of producing them myself? I myself, am I not at least something? But I have already denied that I had senses and body. Yet I hesitate, for what follows from that? Am I so dependent on body and senses that I cannot exist without these? But I was persuaded that there was nothing in all the world, that there was no heaven, no earth, that there were no minds, nor any bodies: was I not then likewise persuaded that I did not exist? Not at all; of a surety I myself did exist since I persuaded myself of something [or merely because I thought of something]. But there is some deceiver or other, very powerful and very cunning, who ever employs his ingenuity in deceiving me. Then without doubt I exist also if he deceives me, and let him deceive me as much as he will, he can never cause me to be nothing so long as I think that I am something. So that after having reflected well and carefully examined all things, we must come to the definite conclusion that this proposition: I am, I exist, is necessarily true each time that I pronounce it, or that I mentally conceive it.

But I do not yet know clearly enough what I am, I who am certain that I am; and hence I must be careful to see that I do not imprudently take some other object in place of myself, and thus that I do not go astray in respect of this knowledge that I hold to be the most certain and most evident of all that I have formerly learned. That is why I shall now consider anew what I believed myself to be before I embarked upon these last reflections; and of my former opinions I shall withdraw all that might even in a small degree be invalidated by the reasons which I have just brought forward, in order that there may be nothing at all left beyond what is absolutely certain and indubitable.

What then did I formerly believe myself to be? Undoubtedly I believed myself to be a man. But what is a man? Shall I say a reasonable animal? Certainly not; for then I should have to inquire what an animal is, and what is reasonable; and thus from a single question I should insensibly fall into an infinitude of others more difficult; and I should not wish to waste the little time and leisure remaining to me in trying to unravel subtleties like these. But I shall rather stop here to consider the thoughts which of themselves spring up in my mind, and which were not inspired by anything beyond my own nature alone when I applied myself to the consideration of my being. In the first place, then, I considered myself as having a face, hands, arms, and all that system of members composed of bones and flesh as seen in a corpse which I designated by the name of body. In addition to this I considered that I was nourished, that I walked, that I felt, and that I thought, and I referred all these actions to the soul: but I did not stop to consider what the soul was, or if I did stop, I imagined that it was something extremely rare and subtle like a wind, a flame, or an ether, which was spread throughout my grosser parts. As to body I had no manner of doubt about its nature, but thought I had a very clear knowledge of it; and if I had desired to explain it according to the notions that I had then formed of it, I should have described it thus: By the body I understand all that which can be defined by a certain figure: something which can be confined in a certain place, and which can fill a given space in such a way that every other body will be excluded from it; which can be perceived either by touch, or by sight, or by hearing, or by taste, or by smell: which can be moved in many ways not, in truth, by itself, but by something which is foreign to it, by which it is touched [and from which it receives impressions]: for to have the power of self-movement, as also of feeling or of thinking, I did not consider to appertain to the nature of body: on the contrary, I was rather astonished to find that faculties similar to them existed in some bodies.

But what am I, now that I suppose that there is a certain genius which is extremely powerful, and, if I may say so, malicious, who employs all his powers in deceiving me? Can I affirm that I possess the least of all those things which I have just said pertain to the nature of body? I pause to consider, I revolve all these things in my mind, and I find none of which I can say that it pertains to me. It would be tedious to stop to enumerate them. Let us pass to the attributes of soul and see if there is any one which is in me? What of nutrition or walking [the first mentioned]? But if it is so that I have no body it is also true that I can neither walk nor take nourishment. Another attribute is sensation. But one cannot feel without body, and besides

I have thought I perceived many things during sleep that I recognised in my waking moments as not having been experienced at all. What of thinking? I find here that thought is an attribute that belongs to me; it alone cannot be separated from me. I am, I exist, that is certain. But how often? Just when I think; for it might possibly be the case if I ceased entirely to think, that I should likewise cease altogether to exist. I do not now admit anything which is not necessarily true: to speak accurately I am not more than a thing which thinks, that is to say a mind or a soul, or an understanding, or a reason, which are terms whose significance was formerly unknown to me. I am, however, a real thing and really exist; but what thing? I have answered: a thing which thinks.

And what more? I shall exercise my imagination [in order to see if I am not something more]. I am not a collection of members which we call the human body: I am not a subtle air distributed through these members, I am not a wind, a fire, a vapour, a breath, nor anything at all which I can imagine or conceive; because I have assumed that all these were nothing. Without changing that supposition I find that I only leave myself certain of the fact that I am somewhat. But perhaps it is true that these same things which I supposed were non-existent because they are unknown to me, are really not different from the self which I know. I am not sure about this, I shall not dispute about it now; I can only give judgment on things that are known to me. I know that I exist, and I inquire what I am, I whom I know to exist. But it is very certain that the knowledge of my existence taken in its precise significance does not depend on things whose existence is not yet known to me; consequently it does not depend on those which I can feign in imagination. And indeed the very term *feign* in imagination[2] proves to me my error, for I really do this if I image myself a something, since to imagine is nothing else than to contemplate the figure or image of a corporeal thing. But I already know for certain that I am, and that it may be that all these images, and, speaking generally, all things that relate to the nature of body are nothing but dreams [and chimeras]. For this reason I see clearly that I have as little reason to say, 'I shall stimulate my imagination in order to know more distinctly what I am,' than if I were to say, 'I am now awake, and I perceive somewhat that is real and true: but because I do not yet perceive it distinctly enough, I shall go to sleep of express purpose, so that my dreams may represent the perception with greatest truth and evidence.' And, thus, I know for certain that nothing of all that I can understand by means of my imag-

[2]Or 'form an image' (effingo).—trans.

ination belongs to this knowledge which I have of myself, and that it is
necessary to recall the mind from this mode of thought with the utmost
diligence in order that it may be able to know its own nature with perfect distinctness.

But what then am I? A thing which thinks. What is a thing which
thinks? It is a thing which doubts, understands, [conceives], affirms,
denies, wills, refuses, which also imagines and feels.

Certainly it is no small matter if all these things pertain to my nature.
But why should they not so pertain? Am I not that being who now doubts
nearly everything, who nevertheless understands certain things,
who affirms that one only is true, who denies all the others, who desires
to know more, is averse from being deceived, who imagines many
things, sometimes indeed despite his will, and who perceives many
likewise, as by the intervention of the bodily organs? Is there nothing
in all this which is as true as it is certain that I exist, even though I
should always sleep and though he who has given me being employed
all his ingenuity in deceiving me? Is there likewise any one of these
attributes which can be distinguished from my thought, or which might
be said to be separated from myself? For it is so evident of itself that
it is I who doubts, who understands, and who desires, that there is
no reason here to add anything to explain it. And I have certainly the
power of imagining likewise; for although it may happen (as I formerly
supposed) that none of the things which I imagine are true, nevertheless this power of imagining does not cease to be really in use, and it
forms part of my thought. Finally, I am the same who feels, that is
to say, who perceives certain things, as by the organs of sense, since
in truth I see light, I hear noise, I feel heat. But it will be said that these
phenomena are false and that I am dreaming. Let it be so; still it is
at least quite certain that it seems to me that I see light, that I hear
noise and that I feel heat. That cannot be false; properly speaking it
is what is in me called feeling; and used in this precise sense that is
no other thing than thinking.

From this time I begin to know what I am with a little more clearness
and distinction than before; but nevertheless it still seems to me, and
I cannot prevent myself from thinking, that corporeal things, whose
images are framed by thought, which are tested by the senses, are
much more distinctly known than that obscure part of me which does
not come under the imagination. Although really it is very strange to
say that I know and understand more distinctly these things whose
existence seems to me dubious, which are unknown to me, and which
do not belong to me, than others of the truth of which I am convinced,
which are known to me and which pertain to my real nature, in a word,

than myself. But I see clearly how the case stands: my mind loves to wander, and cannot yet suffer itself to be retained within the just limits of truth. Very good, let us once more give it the freest rein, so that, when afterwards we seize the proper occasion for pulling up, it may the more easily be regulated and controlled.

Let us begin by considering the commonest matters, those which we believe to be the most distinctly comprehended, to wit, the bodies which we touch and see; not indeed bodies in general, for these general ideas are usually a little more confused, but let us consider one body in particular. Let us take, for example, this piece of wax: it has been taken quite freshly from the hive, and it has not yet lost the sweetness of the honey which it contains; it still retains somewhat of the odour of the flowers from which it has been culled; its colour, its figure, its size are apparent; it is hard, cold, easily handled, and if you strike it with the finger, it will emit a sound. Finally all the things which are requisite to cause us distinctly to recognise a body, are met with in it. But notice that while I speak and approach the fire what remained of the taste is exhaled, the smell evaporates, the colour alters, the figure is destroyed, the size increases, it becomes liquid, it heats, scarcely can one handle it, and when one strikes it, no sound is emitted. Does the same wax remain after this change? We must confess that it remains; none would judge otherwise. What then did I know so distinctly in this piece of wax? It could certainly be nothing of all that the senses brought to my notice, since all these things which fall under taste, smell, sight, touch, and hearing, are found to be changed, and yet the same wax remains.

Perhaps it was what I now think, viz. that this wax was not that sweetness of honey, nor that agreeable scent of flowers, nor that particular whiteness, nor that figure, nor that sound, but simply a body which a little while before appeared to me as perceptible under these forms, and which is now perceptible under others. But what, precisely, is it that I imagine when I form such conceptions? Let us attentively consider this, and, abstracting from all that does not belong to the wax, let us see what remains. Certainly nothing remains excepting a certain extended thing which is flexible and movable. But what is the meaning of flexible and movable? Is it not that I imagine that this piece of wax being round is capable of becoming square and of passing from a square to a triangular figure? No, certainly it is not that, since I imagine it admits of an infinitude of similar changes, and I nevertheless do not know how to compass the infinitude by my imagination, and consequently this conception which I have of the wax is not brought about by the faculty of imagination. What now is this extension? Is it not also unknown? For it becomes greater when the wax is melted, greater when it is boiled, and greater still when the heat increases; and I should not conceive [clearly] according to truth what wax is, if I did not think that even this piece that we are considering is capable of receiving more variations in extension than I have ever imagined. We must then grant that I could not even understand through the imagination what this piece of wax is, and that it is my mind alone which perceives it. I say this piece of wax in particular, for as to wax in general it is yet clearer. But what is this piece of wax which cannot be understood excepting by the [understanding or] mind? It is certainly the same that I see, touch, imagine, and finally it is the same which I have always believed it to be from the beginning. But what must particularly be observed is that its perception is neither an act of vision, nor of touch, nor of imagination, and has never been such although it may have appeared formerly to be so, but only an intuition of the mind, which may be imperfect and confused as it was formerly, or clear and distinct as it is at present, according as my attention is more or less directed to the elements which are found in it, and of which it is composed.

Yet in the meantime I am greatly astonished when I consider [the great feebleness of mind] and its proneness to fall [insensibly] into error; for although without giving expression to my thoughts I consider all this in my own mind, words often impede me and I am almost deceived by the terms of ordinary language. For we say that we see the same wax, if it is present, and not that we simply judge that it is the same from its having the same colour and figure. From this I should conclude that I knew the wax by means of vision and not simply by the intuition of the mind; unless by chance I remember that, when looking from a window and saying I see men who pass in the street, I really do not see them, but infer that what I see is men, just as I say that I see wax. And yet what do I see from the window but hats and coats which may cover automatic machines? Yet I judge these to be men. And similarly solely by the faculty of judgment which rests in my mind, I comprehend that which I believed I saw with my eyes.

A man who makes it his aim to raise his knowledge above the common should be ashamed to derive the occasion for doubting from the forms of speech invented by the vulgar; I prefer to pass on and consider whether I had a more evident and perfect conception of what the wax was when I first perceived it, and when I believed I knew it by means of the external senses or at least by the common sense as it is called, that is to say by the imaginative faculty, or whether my present conception is clearer now that I have most carefully examined what it is, and in what way it can be known. It would certainly be absurd to doubt as to this. For what was there in this first perception which was distinct? What was there which might not as well have been perceived by any of the animals? But when I distinguish the wax from its external forms, and when, just as if I had taken from it its vestments, I consider it quite naked, it is certain that although some error may still be found in my judgment, I can nevertheless not perceive it thus without a human mind.

But finally what shall I say of this mind, that is, of myself, for up to this point I do not admit in myself anything but mind? What then, I who seem to perceive this piece of wax so distinctly, do I not know myself, not only with much more truth and certainty, but also with much more distinctness and clearness? For if I judge that the wax is or exists from the fact that I see it, it certainly follows much more clearly that I am or that I exist myself from the fact that I see it. For it may be that what I see is not really wax, it may also be that I do not possess eyes with which to see anything; but it cannot be that when I see, or (for I no longer take account of the distinction) when I think I see, that I myself who think am nought. So if I judge that the wax exists from the fact that I touch it, the same thing will follow, to wit, that I am; and if I judge that my imagination, or some other cause, whatever it is, persuades me that the wax exists, I shall still conclude the same. And what I have here remarked of wax may be applied to all other things which are external to me [and which are met with outside of me]. And further, if the [notion or] perception of wax has seemed to me clearer and more distinct, not only after the sight or the touch, but also after many other causes have rendered it quite manifest to me, with how much more [evidence] and distinctness must it be said that I now know myself, since all the reasons which contribute to the knowledge of wax, or any other body whatever, are yet better proofs of the nature of my mind! And there are so many other things in the mind itself which may contribute to the elucidation of its nature, that those which depend on body such as these just mentioned, hardly merit being taken into account.

But finally here I am, having insensibly reverted to the point I desired, for, since it is now manifest to me that even bodies are not properly speaking known by the senses or by the faculty of imagination, but by the understanding only, and since they are not known from the fact that they are seen or touched, but only because they are understood, I see clearly that there is nothing which is easier for me to know than my mind. But because it is difficult to rid oneself so promptly of an opinion to which one was accustomed for so long, it will be well that I should halt a little at this point, so that by the length of my meditation I may more deeply imprint on my memory this new knowledge.

Meditation VI.

Of the Existence of Material Things, and of the real distinction between the Soul and Body of Man.

Nothing further now remains but to inquire whether material things exist. And certainly I at least know that these may exist in so far as they are considered as the objects of pure mathematics, since in this aspect I perceive them clearly and distinctly. For there is no doubt that God possesses the power to produce everything that I am capable of perceiving with distinctness, and I have never deemed that anything was impossible for Him, unless I found a contradiction in attempting to conceive it clearly. Further, the faculty of imagination which I possess, and of which, experience tells me, I make use when I apply myself to the consideration of material things, is capable of persuading me of their existence; for when I attentively consider what imagination is, I find that it is nothing but a certain application of the faculty of knowledge to the body which is immediately present to it, and which therefore exists.

And to render this quite clear, I remark in the first place the difference that exists between the imagination and pure intellection [or conception]. For example, when I imagine a triangle, I do not conceive it only as a figure comprehended by three lines, but I also apprehend these three lines as present by the power and inward vision of my mind, and this is what I call imagining. But if I desire to think of a chiliagon, I certainly conceive truly that it is a figure composed of a thousand sides, just as easily as I conceive of a triangle that it is a figure of three sides only; but I cannot in any way imagine the thousand sides of a chiliagon [as I do the three sides of a triangle], nor do I, so to speak, regard them as present [with the eyes of my mind]. And although in accordance with the habit I have formed of always employing the aid of my imagination when I think of corporeal things, it may happen that in imagining a chiliagon I confusedly represent to myself some figure, yet it is very evident that this figure is not a chiliagon, since it in no way differs from that which I represent to myself when I think of a myriagon or any other many-sided figure; nor does it serve my purpose in discovering the properties which go to form the distinction between a chiliagon and other polygons. But if the question turns upon a pentagon, it is quite true that I can conceive its figure as well as that of a chiliagon without the help of my imagination; but I can also imagine it by applying the attention of my mind to each of its five sides, and at the same time to the space which they enclose. And thus I clearly recognise that I have need of a particular effort of mind in order to effect the act of imagination, such as I do not require in order to understand, and this particular effort of mind clearly manifests the difference which exists between imagination and pure intellection.

I remark besides that this power of imagination which is in one, inasmuch as it differs from the power of understanding, is in no wise a necessary element in my nature, or in [my essence, that is to say, in] the essence of my mind; for although I did not possess it I should doubtless ever remain the same as I now am, from which it appears that we might conclude that it depends on something which differs from me. And I easily conceive that if some body exists with which my mind is conjoined and united in such a way that it can apply itself to consider it when it pleases, it may be that by this means it can imagine corporeal objects; so that this mode of thinking differs from pure intellection only inasmuch as mind in its intellectual activity in some manner turns on itself, and considers some of the ideas which it possesses in itself; while in imagining it turns towards the body, and there beholds in it something conformable to the idea which it has either conceived of itself or perceived by the senses. I easily understand, I say, that the imagination could be thus constituted if it is true that body exists; and because I can discover no other convenient mode of explaining it, I conjecture with probability that body does exist; but this is only with probability, and although I examine all things with care, I nevertheless do not find that from this distinct idea of corporeal nature, which I have in my imagination, I can derive any argument from which there will necessarily be deduced the existence of body.

But I am in the habit of imagining many other things besides this corporeal nature which is the object of pure mathematics, to wit, the colours, sounds, scents, pain, and other such things, although less distinctly. And inasmuch as I perceive these things much better through the senses, by the medium of which, and by the memory, they seem to have reached my imagination, I believe that, in order to examine them more conveniently, it is right that I should at the same time investigate the nature of sense perception, and that I should see if from the ideas which I apprehend by this mode of thought, which I call feeling, I cannot derive some certain proof of the existence of corporeal objects.

And first of all I shall recall to my memory those matters which I hitherto held to be true, as having perceived them through the senses, and the foundations on which my belief has rested; in the next place I shall examine the reasons which have since obliged me to place them in doubt; in the last place I shall consider which of them I must now believe.

First of all, then, I perceived that I had a head, hands, feet, and all other members of which this body—which I considered as a part, or possibly even as the whole, of myself—is composed. Further I was sensible that this body was placed amidst many others, from which it was capable of being affected in many different ways, beneficial and hurtful, and I remarked that a certain feeling of pleasure accompanied those that were beneficial, and pain those which were harmful. And in addition to this pleasure and pain, I also experienced hunger, thirst, and other similar appetites, as also certain corporeal inclinations towards joy, sadness, anger, and other similar passions. And outside myself, in addition to extension, figure, and motions of bodies, I remarked in them hardness, heat, and all other tactile qualities, and, further, light and colour, and scents and sounds, the variety of which gave me the means of distinguishing the sky, the earth, the sea, and generally all the other bodies, one from the other. And certainly, considering the ideas of all these qualities which presented themselves to my mind, and which alone I perceived properly or immediately, it was not without reason that I believed myself to perceive objects quite different from my thought, to wit, bodies from which those ideas proceeded; for I found by experience that these ideas presented themselves to me without my consent being requisite, so that I could not perceive any object, however desirous I might be, unless it were present to the organs of sense; and it was not in my power not to perceive it, when it was present. And because the ideas which I received through the senses were much more lively, more clear, and even, in their own way, more distinct than any of those which I could of myself frame in meditation, or than those I found impressed on my memory, it appeared as though they could not have proceeded from my mind, so that they must necessarily have been produced in me by some other things. And having no knowledge of those objects excepting the knowledge which the ideas themselves gave me, nothing was more likely to occur to my mind than that the objects were similar to the ideas which were caused. And because I likewise remembered that I had formerly made use of my senses rather than my reason, and recognised that the ideas which I formed of myself were not so distinct as those which I perceived through the senses, and that they were most frequently even composed of portions of these last, I persuaded myself easily that I had no idea in my mind which had not formerly come to me through the senses. Nor was it without some reason that I believed that this body (which by a certain special right I call my own) belonged to me more properly and more strictly than any other; for in fact I could never be separated from it as from other bodies; I experienced in it and on account of it all my appetites and affections, and finally I was touched by the feeling of pain and the titillation of pleasure in its parts, and not in the parts of other bodies which were separated from it. But when I inquired, why, from some, I know not what, painful sensation, there follows sadness of mind, and from the pleasurable sensation there arises joy, or why this mysterious pinching of the stomach which I call hunger causes me to desire to eat, and dryness of throat causes a desire to drink, and so on, I could give no reason excepting that nature taught me so; for there is certainly no affinity (that I at least can understand) between the craving of the stomach and the desire to eat, any more than between the perception of whatever causes pain and the thought of sadness which arises from this perception. And in the same way it appeared to me that I had learned from nature all the other judgments which I formed regarding the objects of my senses, since I remarked that these judgments were formed in me before I had the leisure to weigh and consider any reasons which might oblige me to make them.

But afterwards many experiences little by little destroyed all the faith which I had rested in my senses; for I from time to time observed that those towers which from afar appeared to me to be round, more closely observed seemed square, and that colossal statues raised on the summit of these towers, appeared as quite tiny statues when viewed from the bottom; and so in an infinitude of other cases I found error in judgments founded on the external senses. And not only in those founded on the external senses, but even in those founded on the internal as well; for is there anything more intimate or more internal than pain? And yet I have learned from some persons whose arms or legs have been cut off, that they sometimes seemed to feel pain in the part which had been amputated, which made me think that I could not be quite certain that it was a certain member which pained me, even although I felt pain in it. And to those grounds of doubt I have lately added two others, which are very general; the first is that I never have believed myself to feel anything in waking moments which I cannot also sometimes believe myself to feel when I sleep, and as I do not think that these things which I seem to feel in sleep, proceed from objects outside of me, I do not see any reason why I should have this belief regarding objects which I seem to perceive while awake. The other was that being still ignorant, or rather supposing myself to be ignorant, of the author of my being, I saw nothing to prevent me from having been so constituted by nature that I might be deceived even in matters which seemed to me to be most certain. And as to the grounds on which I was formerly persuaded of the truth of sensible objects, I had not much trouble in replying to them. For since nature seemed to cause me to lean towards many things from which reason repelled me, I did not believe that I should trust much to the teachings of nature. And although the ideas which I receive by the senses do not depend on my will, I did not think that one should for that reason conclude that they proceeded from things different from myself, since possibly some faculty might be discovered in me—though hitherto unknown to me—which produced them.

But now that I begin to know myself better, and to discover more clearly the author of my being, I do not in truth think that I should rashly admit all the matters which the senses seem to teach us, but, on the other hand, I do not think that I should doubt them all universally.

And first of all, because I know that all things which I apprehend clearly and distinctly can be created by God as I apprehend them, it suffices that I am able to apprehend one thing apart from another clearly and distinctly in order to be certain that the one is different from the other, since they may be made to exist in separation at least by the omnipotence of God; and it does not signify by what power this separation is made in order to compel me to judge them to be different: and, therefore, just because I know certainly that I exist, and that meanwhile I do not remark that any other thing necessarily pertains to my nature or essence, excepting that I am a thinking thing, I rightly conclude that my essence consists solely in the fact that I am a thinking thing [or a substance whose whole essence or nature is to think]. And although possibly (or rather certainly, as I shall say in a moment) I possess a body with which I am very intimately conjoined, yet because. on the one side, I have a clear and distinct idea of myself inasmuch as I am only a thinking and unextended thing, and as, on the other, I possess a distinct idea of body, inasmuch as it is only an extended and unthinking thing, it is certain that this I [that is to say, my soul by which I am what I am], is entirely and absolutely distinct from my body, and can exist without it.

I further find in myself faculties employing modes of thinking peculiar to themselves, to wit, the faculties of imagination and feeling, without which I can easily conceive myself clearly and distinctly as a complete being; while, on the other hand, they cannot be so conceived apart from me, that is without an intelligent substance in which they reside, for [in the notion we have of these faculties, or, to use the language of the Schools] in their formal concept, some kind of intellection is comprised, from which I infer that they are distinct from me as its modes are from a thing. I observe also in me some other faculties such as that of change of position, the assumption of different figures and such like, which cannot be conceived, any more than can the preceding, apart from some substance to which they are attached, and consequently cannot exist without it; but it is very clear that these faculties, if it be true that they exist, must be attached to some corporeal or extended substance, and not to an intelligent substance, since in the clear and distinct conception of these is some sort of extension found to be present, but no intellection at all. There is certainly further in me a certain passive faculty of perception, that is, of receiving and recognising the ideas of sensible things, but this would be useless to me [and I could in no way avail myself of it], if there were not either in me or in some other thing another active faculty capable of forming and producing these ideas. But this active faculty cannot exist in me [inasmuch as I am a thing that thinks] seeing that it does not presuppose thought, and also that those ideas are often produced in me without my contributing in any way to the same, and often even against my will; it is thus necessarily the case that the faculty resides in some substance different from me in which all the reality which is objectively in the ideas that are produced by this faculty is formally or eminently contained, as I remarked before. And this substance is either a body, that is, a corporeal nature in which there is contained formally [and really] all that which is objectively [and by representation] in those ideas, or it is God Himself, or some other creature more noble than body in which that same is contained eminently. But, since God is no deceiver, it is very manifest that He does not communicate to me these ideas immediately and by Himself, nor yet by the intervention of some creature in which their reality is not formally, but only eminently, contained. For since He has given me no faculty to recognise that this is the case, but, on the other hand, a very great inclination to believe [that they are sent to me or] that they are conveyed to me by corporeal objects, I do not see how He could be defended from the accusation of deceit if these ideas were produced by causes other than corporeal objects. Hence we must allow that corporeal things exist. However, they are perhaps not exactly what we perceive by the senses, since this comprehension by the senses is in many instances very obscure and confused; but we must at least admit that all things which I conceive in them clearly and distinctly, that is to say, all things which, speaking generally, are comprehended in the object of pure mathematics, are truly to be recognised as external objects.

As to other things, however, which are either particular only, as, for example, that the sun is of such and such a figure, etc., or which are less clearly and distinctly conceived, such as light, sound, pain and the like, it is certain that although they are very dubious and uncertain, yet on the sole ground that God is not a deceiver, and that consequently He has not permitted any falsity to exist in my opinion which He has not likewise given me the faculty of correcting, I may assuredly hope to conclude that I have within me the means of arriving at the truth even here. And first of all there is no doubt that in all things which nature teaches me there is some truth contained; for by nature, considered in general, I now understand no other thing than either God Himself or else the order and disposition which God has established in created things; and by my nature in particular I understand no other thing than the complexus of all the things which God has given me.

But there is nothing which this nature teaches me more expressly [nor more sensibly] than that I have a body which is adversely affected when I feel pain, which has need of food or drink when I experience the feelings of hunger and thirst, and so on; nor can I doubt there being some truth in all this.

Nature also teaches me by these sensations of pain, hunger, thirst, etc., that I am not only lodged in my body as a pilot in a vessel, but that I am very closely united to it, and so to speak so intermingled with it that I seem to compose with it one whole. For if that were not the case, when my body is hurt, I, who am merely a thinking thing, should not feel pain, for I should perceive this wound by the understanding only, just as the sailor perceives by sight when something is damaged in his vessel; and when my body has need of drink or food, I should clearly understand the fact without being warned of it by confused feelings of hunger and thirst. For all these sensations of hunger, thirst, pain, etc. are in truth none other than certain confused modes of thought which are produced by the union and apparent intermingling of mind and body.

Moreover, nature teaches me that many other bodies exist around mine, of which some are to be avoided, and others sought after. And certainly from the fact that I am sensible of different sorts of colours, sounds, scents, tastes, heat, hardness, etc., I very easily conclude that there are in the bodies from which all these diverse sense-perceptions proceed certain variations which answer to them, although possibly these are not really at all similar to them. And also from the fact that amongst these different sense-perceptions some are very agreeable to me and others disagreeable, it is quite certain that my body (or rather myself in my entirety, inasmuch as I am formed of body and soul) may receive different impressions agreeable and disagreeable from the other bodies which surround it.

But there are many other things which nature seems to have taught me, but which at the same time I have never really received from her, but which have been brought about in my mind by a certain habit which I have of forming inconsiderate judgments on things; and thus it may easily happen that these judgments contain some error. Take, for example, the opinion which I hold that all space in which there is nothing that affects [or makes an impression on] my senses is void; that in a body which is warm there is something entirely similar to the idea of heat which is in me; that in a white or green body there is the same whiteness or greenness that I perceive; that in a bitter or sweet body there is the same taste, and so on in other instances; that the stars, the towers, and all other distant bodies are of the same figure and size as they appear from far off to our eyes, etc. But in order that in this there should be nothing which I do not conceive distinctly, I should define exactly what I really understand when I say that I am taught somewhat by nature. For here I take nature in a more limited signification than when I term it the sum of all the things given me by God, since in this sum many things are comprehended which only pertain to mind (and to these I do not refer in speaking of nature) such as the notion which I have of the fact that what has once been done cannot ever be undone and an infinitude of such things which I know by the light of nature [without the help of the body]; and seeing that it comprehends many other matters besides which only pertain to body, and are no longer here contained under the name of nature, such as the quality of weight which it possesses and the like, with which I also do not deal; for in talking of nature I only treat of those things given by God to me as a being composed of mind and body. But the nature here described truly teaches me to flee from things which cause the sensation of pain, and seek after the things which communicate to me the sentiment of pleasure and so forth; but I do not see that beyond this it teaches me that from those diverse sense-perceptions we should ever form any conclusion regarding things outside of us, without having [carefully and maturely] mentally examined them beforehand. For it seems to me that it is mind alone, and not mind and body in conjunction, that is requisite to a knowledge of the truth in regard to such things. Thus, although a star makes no larger an impression on my eye than the flame of a little candle there is yet in me no real or positive propensity impelling me to believe that it is not greater than that flame; but I have judged it to be so from my earliest years, without any rational foundation. And although in approaching fire I feel heat, and in approaching it a little too near I even feel pain, there is at the same time no reason in this which could persuade me that there is in the fire something resembling this heat any more than there is in it something resembling the pain; all that I have any reason to believe from this is, that there is something in it, whatever it may be, which excites in me these sensations of heat or of pain. So also, although there are spaces in which I find nothing which excites my senses, I must not from that conclude that these spaces contain no body; for I see in this, as in other similar things, that I have been in the habit of perverting the order of nature, because these perceptions of sense having been placed within me by nature merely for the purpose of signifying to my mind what things are beneficial or hurtful to the composite whole of which it forms a part, and being up to that point sufficiently clear and distinct, I yet avail myself of them as though they were absolute rules by which I might immediately determine the essence of the bodies which are outside me, as to which, in fact, they can teach me nothing but what is most obscure and confused.

But I have already sufficiently considered how, notwithstanding the supreme goodness of God, falsity enters into the judgments I make. Only here a new difficulty is presented—one respecting those things the pursuit or avoidance of which is taught me by nature, and also respecting the internal sensations which I possess, and in which I seem to have sometimes detected error [and thus to be directly deceived by my own nature]. To take an example, the agreeable taste of some food in which poison has been intermingled may induce me to partake of the poison, and thus deceive me. It is true, at the same time, that in this case nature may be excused, for it only induces me to desire food in which I find a pleasant taste, and not to desire the poison which is unknown to it; and thus I can infer nothing from this fact, except that my nature is not omniscient, at which there is certainly no reason to be astonished, since man, being finite in nature, can only have knowledge the perfectness of which is limited.

But we not unfrequently deceive ourselves even in those things to which we are directly impelled by nature, as happens with those who when they are sick desire to drink or eat things hurtful to them. It will perhaps be said here that the cause of their deceptiveness is that their nature is corrupt, but that does not remove the difficulty, because a sick man is none the less truly God's creature than he who is in health; and it is therefore as repugnant to God's goodness for the one to have a deceitful nature as it is for the other. And as a clock composed of wheels and counter-weights no less exactly observes the laws of nature when it is badly made, and does not show the time prop-

erly, than when it entirely satisfies the wishes of its maker, and as, if
I consider the body of a man as being a sort of machine so built up and
composed of nerves, muscles, veins, blood and skin, that though there
were no mind in it at all, it would not cease to have the same motions
as at present, exception being made of those movements which are due
to the direction of the will, and in consequence depend upon the mind
[as opposed to those which operate by the disposition of its organs],
I easily recognise that it would be as natural to this body, supposing it
to be, for example, dropsical, to suffer the parchedness of the throat
which usually signifies to the mind the feeling of thirst, and to be
disposed by this parched feeling to move the nerves and other parts
in the way requisite for drinking, and thus to augment its malady and
do harm to itself, as it is natural to it, when it has no indisposition,
to be impelled to drink for its good by a similar cause. And although,
considering the use to which the clock has been destined by its maker,
I may say that it deflects from the order of its nature when it does not
indicate the hours correctly; and as, in the same way, considering the
machine of the human body as having been formed by God in order to
have in itself all the movements usually manifested there, I have reason
for thinking that it does not follow the order of nature when, if the
throat is dry, drinking does harm to the conservation of health, nevertheless I recognise at the same time that this last mode of explaining
nature is very different from the other. For this is but a purely verbal
characterisation depending entirely on my thought, which compares
a sick man and a badly constructed clock with the idea which I have
of a healthy man and a well made clock, and it is hence extrinsic to
the things to which it is applied; but according to the other interpretation of the term nature I understand something which is truly
found in things and which is therefore not without some truth.

But certainly although in regard to the dropsical body it is only so
to speak to apply an extrinsic term when we say that its nature is cor-
rupted, inasmuch as apart from the need to drink, the throat is parched;
yet in regard to the composite whole, that is to say, to the mind or soul
united to this body, it is not a purely verbal predicate, but a real error
of nature, for it to have thirst when drinking would be hurtful to it.
And thus it still remains to inquire how the goodness of God does not
prevent the nature of man so regarded from being fallacious.

In order to begin this examination, then, I here say, in the first place,
that there is a great difference between mind and body, inasmuch as
body is by nature always divisible, and the mind is entirely indivisible.
For, as a matter of fact, when I consider the mind, that is to say, my-

self inasmuch as I am only a thinking thing, I cannot distinguish in myself any parts, but apprehend myself to be clearly one and entire; and although the whole mind seems to be united to the whole body, yet if a foot, or an arm, or some other part, is separated from my body, I am aware that nothing has been taken away from my mind. And the faculties of willing, feeling, conceiving, etc. cannot be properly speaking said to be its parts, for it is one and the same mind which employs itself in willing and in feeling and understanding. But it is quite otherwise with corporeal or extended objects, for there is not one of these imaginable by me which my mind cannot easily divide into parts, and which consequently I do not recognise as being divisible; this would be sufficient to teach me that the mind or soul of man is entirely different from the body, if I had not already learned it from other sources.

I further notice that the mind does not receive the impressions from all parts of the body immediately, but only from the brain, or perhaps even from one of its smallest parts, to wit, from that in which the common sense is said to reside, which, whenever it is disposed in the same particular way, conveys the same thing to the mind, although meanwhile the other portions of the body may be differently disposed, as is testified by innumerable experiments which it is unnecessary here to recount.

I notice, also, that the nature of body is such that none of its parts can be moved by another part a little way off which cannot also be moved in the same way by each one of the parts which are between the two, although this more remote part does not act at all. As, for example, in the cord *ABCD* [which is in tension] if we pull the last part *D*, the first part *A* will not be moved in any way differently from what would be the case if one of the intervening parts *B* or *C* were pulled, and the last part *D* were to remain unmoved. And in the same way, when I feel pain in my foot, my knowledge of physics teaches me that this sensation is communicated by means of nerves dispersed through the foot, which, being extended like cords from there to the brain, when they are contracted in the foot, at the same time contract the inmost portions of the brain which is their extremity and place of origin, and then excite a certain movement which nature has established in order to cause the mind to be affected by a sensation of pain represented as existing in the foot. But because these nerves must pass through the tibia, the thigh, the loins, the back and the neck, in order to reach from the leg to the brain, it may happen that although their extremities which are in the foot are not affected, but only certain ones of their intervening parts [which pass by the loins or the neck], this action will excite the same movement in the brain that might have been excited there by a hurt received in the foot, in consequence of which the mind will necessarily feel in the foot the same pain as if it had received a hurt. And the same holds good of all the other perceptions of our senses.

I notice finally that since each of the movements which are in the portion of the brain by which the mind is immediately affected brings about one particular sensation only, we cannot under the circumstances imagine anything more likely than that this movement, amongst all the sensations which it is capable of impressing on it, causes mind to be affected by that one which is best fitted and most generally useful for the conservation of the human body when it is in health. But experience makes us aware that all the feelings with which nature inspires us are such as I have just spoken of; and there is therefore nothing in them which does not give testimony to the power and goodness of the God [who has produced them]. Thus, for example, when the nerves which are in the feet are violently or more than usually moved, their movement, passing through the medulla of the spine to the inmost parts of the brain, gives a sign to the mind which makes it feel somewhat, to wit, pain, as though in the foot, by which the mind is excited to do its utmost to remove the cause of the evil as dangerous and hurtful to the foot. It is true that God could have constituted the nature of man in such a way that this same movement in the brain would have conveyed something quite different to the mind; for example, it might have produced consciousness of itself either in so far as it is in the brain, or as it is in the foot, or as it is in some other place between the foot and the brain, or it might finally have produced consciousness of anything else whatsoever; but none of all this would have contributed so well to the conservation of the body. Similarly, when we desire to drink, a certain dryness of the throat is produced which moves its nerves, and by their means the internal portions of the brain; and this movement causes in the mind the sensation of thirst, because in this case there is nothing more useful to us than to become aware that we have need to drink for the conservation of our health; and the same holds good in other instances.

From this it is quite clear that, notwithstanding the supreme goodness of God, the nature of man, inasmuch as it is composed of mind and body, cannot be otherwise than sometimes a source of deception. For if there is any cause which excites, not in the foot but in some part of the nerves which are extended between the foot and the brain, or even in the brain itself, the same movement which usually is produced when the foot is detrimentally affected, pain will be experienced as though it were in the foot, and the sense will thus naturally be deceived; for since the same movement in the brain is capable of causing but one sensation in the mind, and this sensation is much more frequently excited by a cause which hurts the foot than by another existing in some other quarter, it is reasonable that it should convey to the mind pain in the foot rather than in any other part of the body. And although the parchedness of the throat does not always proceed, as it usually does, from the fact that drinking is necessary for the health of the body, but sometimes comes from quite a different cause, as is the case with dropsical patients, it is yet much better that it should mislead on this occasion than if, on the other hand, it were always to deceive us when the body is in good health; and so on in similar cases.

And certainly this consideration is of great service to me, not only in enabling me to recognise all the errors to which my nature is subject, but also in enabling me to avoid them or to correct them more easily. For knowing that all my senses more frequently indicate to me truth than falsehood respecting the things which concern that which is beneficial to the body, and being able almost always to avail myself of many of them in order to examine one particular thing, and, besides that, being able to make use of my memory in order to connect the present with the past, and of my understanding which already has discovered all the causes of my errors, I ought no longer to fear that falsity may be found in matters every day presented to me by my senses. And I ought to set aside all the doubts of these past days as hyperbolical and ridiculous, particularly that very common uncertainty respecting sleep, which I could not distinguish from the waking state; for at present I find a very notable difference between the two, inasmuch as our memory can never connect our dreams one with the other, or with the whole course of our lives, as it unites events which happen to us while we are awake. And, as a matter of fact, if someone, while I was awake, quite suddenly appeared to me and disappeared as fast as do the images which I see in sleep, so that I could not know from whence the form came nor whither it went, it would not be without reason that I should deem it a spectre or a phantom formed by my brain [and similar to those which I form in sleep], rather than a real man. But when I perceive things as to which I know distinctly both the place from which they proceed, and that in which they are, and the time at which they appeared to me; and when, without any interruption, I can connect the perceptions which I have of them with the whole course of my life, I am perfectly assured that these perceptions occur while I am waking and not during sleep. And I ought in no wise to doubt the truth of such matters, if, after having called up all my senses, my memory, and my understanding, to examine them, nothing is brought to evidence by any one of them which is repugnant to what is set forth by the others. For because God is in no wise a deceiver, it follows that I am not deceived in this. But because the exigencies of action often oblige us to make up our minds before having leisure to examine matters carefully, we must confess that the life of man is very frequently subject to error in respect to individual objects, and we must in the end acknowledge the infirmity of our nature.

Gilbert Ryle

DESCARTES' MYTH[1]

1. The Official Doctrine.

There is a doctrine about the nature and place of minds which is so prevalent among theorists and even among laymen that it deserves to be described as the official theory. Most philosophers, psychologists and religious teachers subscribe, with minor reservations, to its main articles and, although they admit certain theoretical difficulties in it, they tend to assume that these can be overcome without serious modifications being made to the architecture of the theory. It will be argued here that the central principles of the doctrine are unsound and conflict with the whole body of what we know about minds when we are not speculating about them.

The official doctrine, which hails chiefly from Decartes, is something like this. With the doubtful exceptions of idiots and infants in arms every human being has both a body and a mind. Some would prefer to say that every human being is both a body and a mind. His body and his mind are ordinarily harnessed together, but after the death of the body his mind may continue to exist and function.

Human bodies are in space and are subject to the mechanical laws which govern all other bodies in space. Bodily processes and states can be inspected by external observers. So a man's bodily life is as

[1]Chapter I of *The Concept of Mind*, by Gilbert Ryle. (London: The Hutchinson Publishing Group; New York: Barnes & Noble, 1949). Reprinted by permission of the author and publishers.

much a public affair as are the lives of animals and reptiles and even as the careers of trees, crystals and planets.

But minds are not in space, nor are their operations subject to mechanical laws. The workings of one mind are not witnessable by other observers; its career is private. Only I can take direct cognizance of the states and processes of my own mind. A person therefore lives through two collateral histories, one consisting of what happens in and to his body, the other consisting of what happens in and to his mind. The first is public, the second private. The events in the first history are events in the physical world, those in the second are events in the mental world.

It has been disputed whether a person does or can directly monitor all or only some of the episodes of his own private history; but, according to the official doctrine, of at least some of these episodes he has direct and unchallengeable cognizance. In consciousness, self-consciousness and introspection he is directly and authentically apprised of the present states and operations of his mind. He may have great or small uncertainties about concurrent and adjacent episodes in the physical world, but he can have none about at least part of what is momentarily occupying his mind.

It is customary to express this bifurcation of his two lives and of his two worlds by saying that the things and events which belong to the physical world, including his own body, are external, while the workings of his own mind are internal. This antithesis of outer and inner is of course meant to be construed as a metaphor, since minds, not being in space, could not be described as being spatially inside anything else, or as having things going on spatially inside themselves. But relapses from this good intention are common and theorists are found speculating how stimuli, the physical sources of which are yards or miles outside a person's skin, can generate mental responses inside his skull, or how decisions framed inside his cranium can set going movements of his extremities.

Even when "inner" and "outer" are construed as metaphors, the problem how a person's mind and body influence one another is notoriously charged with theoretical difficulties. What the mind wills, the legs, arms and the tongue execute; what affects the ear and the eye has something to do with what the mind perceives; grimaces and smiles betray the mind's moods and bodily castigations lead, it is hoped, to moral improvement. But the actual transactions between the episodes of the private history and those of the public history remain mysterious, since by definition they can belong to neither series. They could not be reported among the happenings described in a person's autobiography of his inner life, but nor could they be reported among those described in some one else's biography of that person's overt career. They can be inspected neither by introspection nor by laboratory experiment. They are theoretical shuttlecocks which are forever being bandied from the physiologist back to the psychologist and from the psychologist back to the physiologist.

Underlying this partly metaphorical representation of the bifurcation of a person's two lives there is a seemingly more profound and philosophical assumption. It is assumed that there are two different kinds of existence or status. What exists or happens may have the status of physical existence, or it may have the status of mental existence. Somewhat as the faces of coins are either heads or tails, or somewhat as living creatures are either male or female, so, it is supposed, some existing is physical existing, other existing is mental existing. It is a necessary feature of what has physical existence that it is in space and time, it is a necessary feature of what has mental existence that it is in time but not in space. What has physical existence is composed of matter, or else is a function of matter; what has mental existence consists of consciousness, or else is a function of consciousness.

There is thus a polar opposition between mind and matter, an opposition which is often brought out as follows. Material objects are situated in a common field, known as "space," and what happens to one body in one part of space is mechanically connected with what happens to other bodies in other parts of space. But mental happenings occur in insulated fields, known as "minds," and there is, apart maybe from telepathy, no direct causal connection between what happens in one mind and what happens in another. Only through the medium of the public physical world can the mind of one person make a difference to the mind of another. The mind is its own place and in his inner life each of us lives the life of a ghostly Robinson Crusoe. People can see, hear and jolt one another's bodies, but they are irremediably blind and deaf to the workings of one another's minds and inoperative upon them.

What sort of knowledge can be secured of the workings of a mind? On the one side, according to the official theory, a person has direct knowledge of the best imaginable kind of the workings of his own mind. Mental states and processes are (or are normally) conscious states and processes, and the consciousness which irradiates them can engender no illusions and leaves the door open for no doubts. A person's present thinkings, feelings and willings, his perceivings, rememberings and imaginings are intrinsically "phosphorescent"; their existence and their nature are inevitably betrayed to their owner. The inner life is a stream of consciousness of such a sort that it would be absurd to suggest that the mind whose life is that stream might be unaware of what is passing down it.

True, the evidence adduced recently by Freud seems to show that there exist channels tributary to this stream, which run hidden from their owner. People are actuated by impulses the existence of which they vigorously disavow; some of their thoughts differ from the thoughts which they acknowledge; and some of the actions which they think they will to perform they do not really will. They are thoroughly gulled by some of their own hypocrisies and they successfully ignore facts about their mental lives which on the official theory ought to be patent to them. Holders of the official theory tend, however, to maintain that anyhow in normal circumstances a person must be directly and authentically seized of the present state and workings of his own mind.

Besides being currently supplied with these alleged immediate data of consciousness, a person is also generally supposed to be able to exercise from time to time a special kind of perception, namely inner perception, or introspection. He can take a (non-optical) "look" at what is passing in his mind. Not only can he view and scrutinize a flower through his sense of sight and listen to and discriminate the notes of a bell through his sense of hearing; he can also reflectively or introspectively watch, without any bodily organ of sense, the current episodes of his inner life. This self-observation is also commonly supposed to be immune from illusion, confusion or doubt. A mind's reports of its own affairs have a certainty superior to the best that is possessed by its reports of matters in the physical world. Sense-perceptions can, but consciousness and introspection cannot, be mistaken or confused.

On the other side, one person has no direct access of any sort to the events of the inner life of another. He cannot do better than make problematic inferences from the observed behavior of the other person's body to the states of mind which, by analogy from his own conduct, he supposes to be signalized by that behavior. Direct access to the workings of a mind is the privilege of that mind itself; in default of such privileged access, the workings of one mind are inevitably occult to everyone else. For the supposed arguments from bodily movements similar to their own to mental workings similar to their own would lack any possibility of observational corroboration. Not unnaturally, therefore, an adherent of the official theory finds it difficult to resist this consequence of his premises, that he has no good reason to believe that there do exist minds other than his own. Even if he prefers to believe that to other human bodies there are harnessed minds not unlike his own, he cannot claim to be able to discover their individual characteristics, or the particular things that they undergo and do. Absolute solitude is on this showing the ineluctable destiny of the soul. Only our bodies can meet.

As a necessary corollary of this general scheme there is implicitly prescribed a special way of construing our ordinary concepts of mental powers and operations. The verbs, nouns and adjectives, with which in ordinary life we describe the wits, characters and higher-grade performances of the people with whom we have do, are required to be construed as signifying special episodes in their secret histories, or else as signifying tendencies for such episodes to occur. When someone is described as knowing, believing or guessing something, as hoping, dreading, intending or shirking something, as designing this or being amused at that, these verbs are supposed to denote the occurrence of specific modifications in his (to us) occult stream of consciousness. Only his own privileged access to this stream in direct awareness and introspection could provide authentic testimony that these mental-conduct verbs were correctly or incorrectly applied. The onlooker, be he teacher, critic, biographer or friend, can never assure himself that his comments have any vestige of truth. Yet it was just because we do in fact all know how to make such comments, make them with general correctness and correct them when they turn out to be confused or mistaken, that philosophers found it necessary to construct their theories of the nature and place of minds. Finding mental-conduct concepts being regularly and effectively used, they properly sought to fix their logical geography. But the logical geography officially recommended would entail that there could be no regular or effective use of these mental-conduct concepts in our descriptions of, and prescriptions for, other people's minds.

2. The Absurdity of the Official Doctrine.

Such in outline is the official theory. I shall often speak of it, with deliberate abusiveness, as "the dogma of the Ghost in the Machine." I hope to prove that it is entirely false, and false not in detail but in principle. It is not merely an assemblage of particular mistakes. It is one big mistake and a mistake of a special kind. It is, namely, a category-mistake. It represents the facts of mental life as if they belonged to one logical type or category (or range of types or categories), when they actually belong to another. The dogma is therefore a philosopher's myth. In attempting to explode the myth I shall probably be taken to be denying well-known facts about the mental life of human beings, and my plea that I aim at doing nothing more than rectify the logic of mental-conduct concepts will probably be disallowed as mere subterfuge.

I must first indicate what is meant by the phrase "Category-mistake." This I do in a series of illustrations.

A foreigner visiting Oxford or Cambridge for the first time is shown a number of colleges, libraries, playing fields, museums, scientific departments and administrative offices. He then asks "But where is the University? I have seen where the members of the Colleges live, where the Registrar works, where the scientists experiment and the rest. But I have not yet seen the University in which reside and work the members of your University." It has then to be explained to him that the University is not another collateral institution, some ulterior counterpart to the colleges, laboratories and offices which he has seen. The University is just the way in which all that he has already seen is organized. When they are seen and when their coordination is understood, the University has been seen. His mistake lay in his innocent assumption that it was correct to speak of Christ Church, the Bodleian Library, the Ashmolean Museum *and* the University, to speak, that is, as if "the University" stood for an extra member of the class of which these other units are members. He was mistakenly allocating the University to the same category as that to which the other institutions belong.

The same mistake would be made by a child witnessing the march-past of a division, who, having had pointed out to him such and such battalions, batteries, squadrons, etc., asked when the division was going to appear. He would be supposing that a division was a counterpart to the units already seen, partly similar to them and partly unlike them. He would be shown his mistake by being told that in watching the battalions, batteries and squadrons marching past he had been watching the division marching past. The march-past was not a parade of battalions, batteries, squadrons *and* a division; it was a parade of the battalions, batteries and squadrons *of* a division.

One more illustration. A foreigner watching his first game of cricket learns what are the functions of the bowlers, the batsmen, the fielders, the umpires and the scorers. He then says "But there is no one left on the field to contribute the famous element of team-spirit. I see who does the bowling, the batting and the wicket-keeping; but I do not see whose role it is to exercise *esprit de corps.*" Once more, it would have to be explained that he was looking for the wrong type of thing. Team-spirit is not another cricketing-operation supplementary to all of the other special tasks. It is, roughly, the keenness with which each of the special tasks is performed, and performing a task keenly is not performing two tasks. Certainly exhibiting team-spirit is not the same thing as bowling or catching, but nor is it a third thing such that we can say that the bowler first bowls *and* then exhibits team-spirit or that a fielder is at a given moment *either* catching *or* displaying *esprit de corps*.

These illustrations of category-mistakes have a common feature which must be noticed. The mistakes were made by people who did not know how to wield the concepts *University, division* and *team-spirit*. Their puzzles arose from inability to use certain items in the English vocabulary.

The theoretically interesting category-mistakes are those made by people who are perfectly competent to apply concepts, at least in the situations with which they are familiar, but are still liable in their abstract thinking to allocate those concepts to logical types to which they do not belong. An instance of a mistake of this sort would be the following story. A student of politics has learned the main differences between the British, the French and the American Constitutions, and has learned also the differences and connections between the Cabinet, Parliament, the various Ministries, the Judicature and the Church of England. But he still becomes embarrassed when asked questions about the connections between the Church of England, the Home Office and the British Constitution. For while the Church and the Home Office are institutions, the British Constitution is not another institution in the same sense of that noun. So interinstitutional relations which can be asserted or denied to hold between the Church and the Home Office cannot be asserted or denied to hold between either of them and the British Constitution. "The British Constitution" is not a term of the same logical type as "the Home Office" and "the Church of England." In a partially similar way, John Doe may be a relative, a friend, an enemy or a stranger to Richard Roe; but he cannot be any of these things to the Average Taxpayer. He knows how to talk sense in certain sorts of discussions about the Average Taxpayer, but he is baffled to say why he could not come across him in the street as he can come across Richard Roe.

It is pertinent to our main subject to notice that, so long as the student of politics continues to think of the British Constitution as a counterpart to the other institutions, he will tend to describe it as a mysteriously occult institution; and so long as John Doe continues to think of the Average Taxpayer as a fellow-citizen, he will tend to think of him as an elusive insubstantial man, a ghost who is everywhere yet nowhere.

My destructive purpose is to show that a family of radical category-mistakes is the source of the double-life theory. The representation of a person as a ghost mysteriously ensconced in a machine derives from this argument. Because, as is true, a person's thinking, feeling and purposive doing cannot be described solely in the idioms of physics, chemistry and physiology, therefore they must be described in counterpart idioms. As the human body is a complex organized unit, so the human mind must be another complex organized unit, though one made of a different sort of stuff and with a different sort of structure. Or, again, as the human body, like any other parcel of matter, is a field of causes and effects, so the mind must be another field of causes and effects, though not (Heaven be praised) mechanical causes and effects.

3. The Origin of the Category-mistake.
One of the chief intellectual origins of what I have yet to prove to be the Cartesian category-mistake seems to be this. When Galileo showed that his methods of scientific discovery were competent to provide a mechanical theory which should cover every occupant of space, Descartes found in himself two conflicting motives. As a man of scientific genius he could not but endorse the claims of mechanics, yet as a religious and moral man he could not accept, as Hobbes accepted, the discouraging rider to those claims, namely that human nature differs only in degree of complexity from clockwork. The mental could not be just a variety of the mechanical.

He and subsequent philosophers naturally but erroneously availed themselves of the following escape-route. Since mental-conduct words are not to be construed as signifying the occurrence of mechanical processes, they must be construed as signifying the occurrence of non-mechanical processes; since mechanical laws explain movements in space as the effects of other movements in space, other laws must explain some of the non-spatial workings of minds as the effects of other non-spatial workings of minds. The difference between the human behaviors which we describe as intelligent and those which we describe as unintelligent must be a difference in their causation; so, while some movements of human tongues and limbs are the effects of mechanical causes, others must be the effects of non-mechanical causes, i.e. some issue from movements of particles of matter, others from workings of the mind.

The differences between the physical and the mental were thus represented as differences inside the common framework of the categories of "thing," "stuff," "attribute," "state," "process," "change," "cause," and "effect." Minds are things, but different sorts of things from bodies;

mental processes are causes and effects, but different sorts of causes and effects from bodily movements. And so on. Somewhat as the foreigner expected the University to be an extra edifice, rather like a college but also considerably different, so the repudiators of mechanism represented minds as extra centers of causal processes, rather like machines but also considerably different from them. Their theory was a para-mechanical hypothesis.

That this assumption was at the heart of the doctrine is shown by the fact that there was from the beginning felt to be a major theoretical difficulty in explaining how minds can influence and be influenced by bodies. How can a mental process, such as willing, cause spatial movements like the movements of the tongue? How can a physical change in the optic nerve have among its effects a mind's perception of a flash of light? This notorious crux by itself shows the logical mould into which Descartes pressed his theory of the mind. It was the self-same mould into which he and Galileo set their mechanics. Still unwittingly adhering to the grammar of mechanics, he tried to avert disaster by describing minds in what was merely an obverse vocabulary. The workings of minds had to be described by the mere negatives of the specific descriptions given to bodies; they are not in space, they are not motions, they are not modifications of matter, they are not accessible to public observation. Minds are not bits of clockwork, they are just bits of not-clockwork.

As thus represented, minds are not merely ghosts harnessed to machines, they are themselves just spectral machines. Though the human body is an engine, it is not quite an ordinary engine, since some of its workings are governed by another engine inside it—this interior governor-engine being one of a very special sort. It is invisible, inaudible and it has no size or weight. It cannot be taken to bits and the laws it obeys are not those known to ordinary engineers. Nothing is known of how it governs the bodily engine.

A second major crux points the same moral. Since, according to the doctrine, minds belong to the same category as bodies and since bodies are rigidly governed by mechanical laws, it seemed to many theorists to follow that minds must be similarly governed by rigid non-mechanical laws. The physical world is a deterministic system, so the mental world must be a deterministic system. Bodies cannot help the modifications that they undergo, so minds cannot help pursuing the careers fixed for them. *Responsibility, choice, merit* and *demerit* are therefore inapplicable concepts—unless the compromise solution is adopted of saying that the laws governing mental processes, unlike those governing physical processes, have the congenial attribute of being only rather rigid. The problem of the Freedom of the Will was the problem how to reconcile the hypothesis that minds are to be described in terms drawn from the categories of mechanics with the knowledge that higher-grade human conduct is not of a piece with the behavior of machines.

It is an historical curiosity that it was not noticed that the entire argument was broken-backed. Theorists correctly assumed that any sane man could already recognize the differences between, say, rational and non-rational utterances or between purposive and automatic behavior. Else there would have been nothing requiring to be salved from mechanism. Yet the explanation given presupposed that one person could in principle never recognize the difference between the rational and the irrational utterances issuing from other human bodies, since he could never get access to the postulated immaterial causes of some of their utterances. Save for the doubtful exception of himself, he could never tell the difference between a man and a robot. It would have to be conceded, for example, that, for all that we can tell, the inner lives of persons who are classed as idiots or lunatics are as rational as those of anyone else. Perhaps only their overt behavior is disappointing; that is to say, perhaps "idiots" are not really idiotic, or "lunatics" lunatic. Perhaps, too, some of those who are classed as sane are really idiots. According to the theory, external observers could never know how the overt behavior of others is correlated with their mental powers and processes and so they could never know or even plausibly conjecture whether their applications of mental-conduct concepts to these other people were correct or incorrect. It would then be hazardous or impossible for a man to claim sanity or logical consistency even for himself, since he would be debarred from comparing his own performances with those of others. In short, our characterizations of persons and their performances as intelligent, prudent and virtuous or as stupid, hypocritical and cowardly could never have been made, so the problem of providing a special causal hypothesis to serve as the basis of such diagnoses would never have arisen. The question, "How do persons differ from machines?" arose just because everyone already knew how to apply mental-conduct concepts before the new causal hypothesis was introduced. This causal hypothesis could not therefore be the source of the criteria used in those applications. Nor, of course, has the causal hypothesis in any degree improved our handling of those criteria. We still distinguish good from bad arithmetic, politic from impolitic conduct and fertile from infertile imaginations in the ways in which Descartes himself distinguished them before and after he speculated how the applicability of these criteria was compatible with the principle of mechanical causation.

He had mistaken the logic of his problem. Instead of asking by what criteria intelligent behavior is actually distinguished from non-intelligent behavior, he asked "Given that the principle of mechanical causation does not tell us the difference, what other causal principle will tell it us?" He realized that the problem was not one of mechanics and assumed that it must therefore be one of some counterpart to mechanics. Not unnaturally psychology is often cast for just this role.

When two terms belong to the same category, it is proper to construct conjunctive propositions embodying them. Thus a purchaser may say that he bought a left-hand glove and a right-hand glove, but not that he bought a left-hand glove, a right-hand glove and a pair of gloves. "She came home in a flood of tears and a sedan-chair" is a well-known joke based on the absurdity of conjoining terms of different types. It would have been equally ridiculous to construct the disjunction "She came home either in a flood of tears or else in a sedan-chair." Now the dogma of the Ghost in the Machine does just this. It maintains that there exist both bodies and minds; that there occur physical processes and mental processes; that there are mechanical causes of corporal movements and mental causes of corporal movements. I shall argue that these and other analogous conjunctions are absurd; but, it must be noticed, the argument will not show that either of the illegitimately conjoined propositions is absurd in itself. I am not, for example, denying that there occur mental processes. Doing long division is a mental process and so is making a joke. But I am saying that the phrase "there occur mental processes" does not mean the same sort of thing as "there occur physical processes," and, therefore, that it makes no sense to conjoin or disjoin the two.

If my argument is successful, there will follow some interesting consequences. First, the hallowed contrast between Mind and Matter will be dissipated, but dissipated not by either of the equally hallowed absorptions of Mind by Matter or of Matter by Mind, but in quite a different way. For the seeming contrast of the two will be shown to be as illegitimate as would be the contrast of "she came home in a flood of tears" and "she came home in a sedan-chair." The belief that there is a polar opposition between Mind and Matter is the belief that they are terms of the same logical type.

It will also follow that both Idealism and Materialism are answers to an improper question. The "reduction" of the material world to mental states and processes, as well as the "reduction" of mental states and processes to physical states and processes, presuppose the legitimacy of the disjunction "Either there exist minds or there exist bodies (but not both)." It would be like saying, "Either she bought a left-hand and a right-hand glove or she bought a pair of gloves (but not both)."

It is perfectly proper to say, in one logical tone of voice, that there exist minds and to say, in another logical tone of voice, that there exist bodies. But these expressions do not indicate two different species of existence, for "existence" is not a generic word like "colored" or "sexed." They indicate two different senses of "exist," somewhat as "rising" has different senses in "the tide is rising," "hopes are rising," and "the average age of death is rising." A man would be thought to be making a poor joke who said that three things are now rising, namely the tide, hopes and the average age of death. It would be just as good or bad a joke to say that there exist prime numbers and Wednesdays and public opinions and navies; or that there exist both minds and bodies. In the succeeding chapters I try to prove that the official theory does rest on a batch of category-mistakes by showing that logically absurd corollaries follow from it. The exhibition of these absurdities will have the constructive effect of bringing out part of the correct logic of mental-conduct concepts.

4. Historical Note.

It would not be true to say that the official theory derives solely from Descartes' theories, or even from a more widespread anxiety about the implications of seventeenth century mechanics. Scholastic and Reformation theology had schooled the intellects of the scientists as well as of the laymen, philosophers and clerics of that age. Stoic-Augustinian theories of the will were embedded in the Calvinist doctrines of sin and grace; Platonic and Aristotelian theories of the intellect shaped the orthodox doctrines of the immortality of the soul. Descartes was reformulating already prevalent theological doctrines of the soul in the new syntax of Galileo. The theologian's privacy of conscience became the philosopher's privacy of consciousness, and what had been the bogy of Predestination reappeared as the bogy of Determinism.

It would also not be true to say that the two-worlds myth did no theoretical good. Myths often do a lot of theoretical good, while they are still new. One benefit bestowed by the para-mechanical myth was that it partly superannuated the then prevalent para-political myth. Minds and their Faculties had previously been described by analogies with political superiors and political subordinates. The idioms used were those of ruling, obeying, collaborating and rebelling. They survived and still survive in many ethical and some epistemological discussions. As, in physics, the new myth of occult Forces was a scientific improvement on the old myth of Final Causes, so, in anthropological and psychological theory, the new myth of hidden operations, impulses and agencies was an improvement on the old myth of dictations, deferences and disobediences.

A. J. Ayer

"I THINK, THEREFORE I AM"[1]

The attempt to put knowledge on a foundation which would be impregnable to doubt is historically associated with the philosophy of Descartes. But Descartes, though he regarded mathematics as the paradigm of knowledge, was aware that its *a priori* truths are not indubitable, in the sense that he required. He allowed it to be possible that a malignant demon should deceive him even with respect to those matters of which he was the most certain.[2] The demon would so work upon his reason that he took false statements to be self-evidently true. The hypothesis of there being such an archdeceiver is indeed empty, since his operations could never be detected: but it may be regarded as a picturesque way of expressing the fact that intuitive conviction is not a logical guarantee of truth. The question which Descartes then raises is whether, of all the propositions which we think we know, there can be any that escape the demon's reach.

His answer is that there is one such proposition: the famous *cogito ergo sum:* I think, therefore I am.[3] The demon might perhaps have the

[1]Section iii of Chapter 2 of *The Problem of Knowledge* (London: Macmillan & Co. Ltd.; New York: St. Martin's Press Inc.; The Macmillan Company of Canada Ltd., 1956). Reprinted by permission of the author and publishers.
[2]René Descartes, *Meditations on the First Philosophy*, Meditation I [See Descartes selection above, pp. 2–6.—Ed.]
[3]*Vide Meditation* II [See Descartes selection above, pp. 6–14.—Ed.] and *Discourse on Method*, part IV.

power to make me doubt whether I was thinking, though it is difficult to see what this would come to; it is not clear what such a state of doubt would be. But even allowing that the expression "I am doubting whether I am thinking" describes a possible situation, the doubt must be unwarranted. However much he can shake my confidence, the demon cannot deceive me into believing that I am thinking when I am not. For if I believe that I am thinking, then I must believe truly, since my believing that I am thinking is itself a process of thought. Consequently, if I am thinking, it is indubitable that I am thinking, and if it is indubitable that I am thinking, then, Descartes argues, it is indubitable that I exist, at least during such times as I think.

Let us consider what this argument proves. In what sense is the proposition that I think, and consequently that I exist, shown to be indubitable? It is not a question for psychology. The suggestion is not that it is physically impossible to doubt that one is thinking, but rather that it somehow involves a logical impossibility. Yet while there may be some question about the meaning that one should attach to the statement that I doubt whether I am thinking, it has not been shown to be self-contradictory. Nor is the statement that I am thinking itself the expression of a necessary truth. If it seems to be necessary, it is because of the absurdity of denying it. To say "I am not thinking" is self-stultifying since if it is said intelligently it must be false: but it is not self-contradictory. The proof that it is not self-contradictory is that it might have been true. I am now thinking but I might easily not have been. And the same applies to the statement that I exist. It would be absurd for me to deny that I existed. If I say that I do not exist, it must be false. But it might not have been false. It is a fact that I exist, but not a necessary fact.

Thus neither "I think" nor "I exist" is a truth of logic: the logical truth is only that I exist if I think. And we have seen that even if they were truths of logic they would not for that reason be indubitable. What makes them indubitable is their satisfying a condition which Descartes himself does not make explicit, though his argument turns upon it. It is that their truth follows from their being doubted by the person who expresses them. The sense in which I cannot doubt the statement that I think is just that my doubting it entails its truth: and in the same sense I cannot doubt that I exist. There was therefore no need for Descartes to derive *"sum"* from *"cogito"*; for its certainty could be independently established by the same criterion.

But this certainty does not come to very much. If I start with the fact that I am doubting, I can validly draw the conclusion that I think and that I exist. That is to say, if there is such a person as myself, then there is such a person as myself, and if I think, I think. Neither does this apply only to me. It is obviously true of anyone at all that if he exists he exists and that if he thinks he thinks. What Descartes thought that he had shown was that the statements that he was conscious, and that he existed, were somehow privileged, that, for him at least, they were evidently true in a way which distinguished them from any other statements of fact. But this by no means follows from his argument. His argument does not prove that he, or anyone, knows anything. It simply makes the logical point that one sort of statement follows from another. It is of interest only as drawing attention to the fact that there are sentences which are used in such a way that if the person who employs them ever raises the question whether the statements which they express are true, the answer must be yes. But this does not show that these statements are in any way sacrosanct, considered in themselves.

Yet surely I can be certain that I am conscious, and that I exist. Surely my evidence for this could not be stronger than it is. But again it is not clear what is being claimed when it is said that these things are certain or that one can be certain of them. Perhaps only that I know that they are so, and of course I do. But these are not the only facts that I know, nor, as it sometimes appears to be suggested, is my knowing them a condition of my knowing anything else. It is conceivable that I should not have been self-conscious, which is to say that I should not know that I existed; but it would not follow that I could not know many other statements to be true. In theory, I could know any of the innumerable facts which are logically independent of the fact of my existing. I should indeed know them without knowing that I knew them, though not necessarily without knowing that they were known: my whole conception of knowledge would be impersonal. Perhaps this is a strange supposition, but it is not self-contradictory.

But while in the case of other facts which I may reasonably claim to know, it is at least conceivable that the evidence which I have for them should be even stronger than it is, surely the fact that I exist and the fact that I am conscious stand out for the reason that in their case the evidence is perfect. How could I possibly have better evidence than I do for believing that I am conscious, let alone for believing that I exist? This question is indeed hard to answer, but mainly because it seems improper in these cases to speak of evidence at all. If someone were to ask me How do you know that you are conscious? What evidence have you that you exist? I should not know how to answer him: I should not know what sort of answer was expected. The question would appear to be a joke, a parody of philosophical cautiousness. If it were seriously pressed, I might become indignant: What do you mean, how do I know that I exist? I am here, am I not, talking to you? If a "philosophical" answer were insisted on, it might be said that I proved that I existed and that I was conscious by appealing to my experience. But not then to any particular experience. Any feeling or perception that I cared to instance would do equally well. When Hume looked for an impression of his self, he failed to find one: he always stumbled instead upon some particular perception.[4] He allowed that others might be luckier, but in this he was ironical. For the point is not that to have an experience of one's self is to perform a remarkably difficult feat of introspection: it is that there is nothing that would count as having an experience of one's self, that the expression "having an experience of one's self" is one for which there is no use. This is not to say that people are not self-conscious, in the sense that they conceive of things as happening to themselves. It is that the consciousness of one's self is not one experience among others, not even, as some have thought, a special experience which accompanies all the others. And this is not a matter of psychology but of logic. It is a question of what self-consciousness is understood to mean.

If there is no distinctive experience of finding out that one is conscious, or that one exists, there is no experience at all of finding out that one is not conscious, or that one does not exist. And for this reason it is tempting to say that sentences like "I exist," "I am conscious," "I know that I exist," "I know that I am conscious" do not express genuine propositions. That Mr. A exists, or that Mr. A is conscious, is a genuine proposition; but it may be argued that it is not what is expressed by "I exist" or "I am conscious," even when I am Mr. A. For although it be true that I am Mr. A, it is not necessarily true. The word "I" is not synonymous with "Mr. A" even when it is used by Mr. A to refer to himself. That he is Mr. A, or that he is identifiable in any other manner, is an empirical statement which may be informative not only to others, but also in certain circumstances to Mr. A himself, for instance if he has lost his memory. It cannot therefore be reasoned that because one may succeed in expressing genuine propositions by replacing the "I" in such sentences as "I am conscious" or "I exist" by a noun, or descriptive phrase, which denotes the person concerned, these sentences still have a factual meaning when this replacement is not made.

All the same it is not difficult to imagine circumstances in which they

---

[4]David Hume, *A Treatise of Human Nature*, Book I, part IV, section vi. [See Hume selection below, pp. 46–57.—Ed.]

would have a use. "I am conscious" might be said informatively by someone recovering from a swoon. If I had been presumed to be dead there might be a point in my proclaiming that I still existed. On recovering consciousness after some accident or illness, I might make this remark even to myself, and make it with a sense of discovery. Just as there are moments between sleep and waking when one may seriously ask oneself if one is awake, so there are states of semiconsciousness in which saying "I exist" answers a genuine question. But what information does this answer give? If I have occasion to tell others that I exist, the information which they receive is that there exists a man answering to some description, whatever description it may be that they identify me by; it would not be the same in every case. But when I tell myself that I exist, I do not identify myself by any description: I do not identify myself at all. The information which I convey to myself is not that there exists a person of such and such a sort, information which might be false if I were mistaken about my own identity or character. Yet I am in fact a person of such and such a sort. There is nothing more to me than what can be discovered by listing the totality of the descriptions which I satisfy. This is merely an expression of the tautology that if a description is complete there is nothing left to be described. But can it not be asked what it is that one is describing? The answer is that this question makes sense only as a request for further description: it implies that the description so far given is incomplete, as in fact it always will be. But then if, in saying that I exist, I am not saying anything about a description's being satisfied, what can I be saying? Again it is tempting to answer that I am saying nothing.

Yet this would not be correct. Even when it is not doing duty for a description, nor coupled with one, the demonstrative "I" may have a use. In the case which we envisaged, the case of a return to consciousness, it signals the presence of some experience or other. It does not, however, characterize this experience in any way. It merely points to the existence of whatever it is, in the given circumstances, that makes its own use possible. And since it is a contingent fact that any such situation does exist, the assertion which simply serves to mark it may be held to be informative. The sentence "I exist," in this usage, may be allowed to express a statement which like other statements is capable of being either true or false. It differs, however, from most other statements in that if it is false it can not actually be made. Consequently, no one who uses these words intelligently and correctly can use them to make a statement which he knows to be false. If he succeeds in making the statement, it must be true.

It is, therefore, a peculiar statement; and not only peculiar but degenerate. It is degenerate in the way that the statements which are expressed by such sentences as "this exists" or "this is occurring now" are degenerate. In all these cases the verbs which must be added to the demonstratives to make a grammatical sentence are sleeping partners. The work is all done by the demonstrative: that the situation, to which it points, exists, or is occurring, is a condition of the demonstrative's use. It is for this reason that any statement of this sort which is actually expressed must be true. It is not necessarily true, since the situation to which the demonstrative points might not have existed; it is logically possible that the condition for this particular use of the demonstrative should not have obtained. It is, however, like an analytic statement in that, once we understand the use of the demonstrative, here functioning as subject, the addition of the predicate tells us nothing further. Divorced from its context the whole statement has no meaning. Taken in context it is informative just as drawing attention to whatever it may be that the demonstrative is used to indicate. It approximates, therefore, to a gesture or to an ejaculation. To say "I exist" or "this is occurring now" is like saying "look!" or pointing without words. The difference is that, in the formulation of the indicative sentence, the existential claim is made explicit; and it is because of this that the sentence may be said to express a statement, whereas the ejaculation or the gesture would not: one does not speak of ejaculations or gestures as being true or false. But there is no difference in the information conveyed.

Thus we see that the certainty of one's own existence is not, as some philosophers have supposed, the outcome of some primary intuition, an intuition which would have the distinctive property of guaranteeing the truth of the statement on which it was directed. It is indeed the case that if anyone claims to know that he exists, or that he is conscious, he is bound to be right. But this is not because he is then in some special state of mind which bestows this infallibility upon him. It is simply a consequence of the purely logical fact that if he is in any state whatever it follows that he exists; if he is in any conscious state whatever it follows that he is conscious. He might exist without knowing it; he might even be conscious without knowing it, as is presumably the case with certain animals: there is at any rate no contradiction in supposing them to be conscious without supposing them to be conscious of themselves. But, as we have seen, if anyone does claim to know that he exists or that he is conscious, his claim must be valid, simply because its being valid is a condition of its being made. This is not to say, however, that he, or anyone, knows any description of himself, or his state of consciousness, to be true. To know that one exists is not, in this sense, to know anything about oneself and more than knowing that *this* exists is knowing anything about *this*. Knowing that I exist, knowing that this is here, is having the answer to a question which is put in such a form that it answers itself. The answer is meaningful only in its context, and in its context the condition of its being meaningful is its being true. This is the ground for saying that statements like "I exist" are certain, but it is also the proof of their degeneracy: they have nothing to say beyond what is implied in the fact that they have a reference.

2 David Hume

OF PERSONAL IDENTITY[1]

There are some philosophers who imagine we are every moment intimately conscious of what we call our *self*; that we feel its existence and its continuance in existence; and are certain, beyond the evidence of a demonstration, both of its perfect identity and simplicity. The strongest sensation, the most violent passion, say they, instead of distracting us from this view, only fix it the more intensely, and make us consider their influence on *self* either by their pain or pleasure. To attempt a further proof of this were to weaken its evidence; since no proof can be derived from any fact of which we are so intimately conscious; nor is there anything of which we can be certain if we doubt of this.

Unluckily all these positive assertions are contrary to that very experience which is pleaded for them; nor have we any idea of *self*, after the manner it is here explained. For, from what impression could this idea be derived? This question it is impossible to answer without a manifest contradiction and absurdity; and yet it is a question which must necessarily be answered, if we would have the idea of self pass for clear and intelligible. It must be some one impression that gives rise to every real idea. But self or person is not any one impression, but that to which our several impressions and ideas are supposed to have a reference. If any impression gives rise to the idea of self, that impression must continue invariably the same, through the whole course of our lives; since self is supposed to exist after that manner. But there is no impression constant and invariable. Pain and pleasure, grief and joy, passions and sensations succeed each other, and never all exist at the same time. It cannot therefore be from any of these impressions, or from any other, that the idea of self is derived; and consequently there is no such idea.

But further, what must become of all our particular perceptions upon this hypothesis? All these are different, and distinguishable, and separable from each other, and may be separately considered, and may

[1]This selection consists of all but the last paragraph of section 6, Part IV, Book I, as well as part of the Appendix of Hume's *A Treatise of Human Nature*, a work first published in 1739 and 1740.

exist separately, and have no need of anything to support their existence. After what manner therefore do they belong to self, and how are they connected with it? For my part, when I enter most intimately into what I call *myself*, I always stumble on some particular perception or other, of heat or cold, light or shade, love or hatred, pain or pleasure. I never can catch *myself* at any time without a perception, and never can observe anything but the perception. When my perceptions are removed for any time, as by sound sleep, so long am I insensible of *myself*, and may truly be said not to exist. And were all my perceptions removed by death, and could I neither think, nor feel, nor see, nor love, nor hate, after the dissolution of my body, I should be entirely annihilated, nor do I conceive what is further requisite to make me a perfect nonentity. If any one, upon serious and unprejudiced reflection, thinks he has a different notion of *himself*, I must confess I can reason no longer with him. All I can allow him is, that he may be in the right as well as I, and that we are essentially different in this particular. He may, perhaps, perceive something simple and continued, which he calls *himself*; though I am certain there is no such principle in me.

But setting aside some metaphysicians of this kind, I may venture to affirm of the rest of mankind, that they are nothing but a bundle or collection of different perceptions, which succeed each other with an inconceivable rapidity, and are in a perpetual flux and movement. Our eyes cannot turn in their sockets without varying our perceptions. Our thought is still more variable than our sight; and all our other senses and faculties contribute to this change; nor is there any single power of soul, which remains unalterably the same, perhaps for one moment. The mind is a kind of theater, where several perceptions successively make their appearance; pass, repass, glide away, and mingle in an infinite variety of postures and situations. There is properly no *simplicity* in it at one time, nor *identity* in different, whatever natural propension we may have to imagine that simplicity and identity. The comparison of the theater must not mislead us. They are the successive perceptions only, that constitute the mind; nor have we the most distant notion of the place where these scenes are represented, or of the materials of which it is composed.

What then gives us so great a propension to ascribe an identity to these successive perceptions, and to suppose ourselves possessed of an invariable and uninterrupted existence through the whole course of our lives? In order to answer this question we must distinguish betwixt personal identity, as it regards our thought or imagination, and as it regards our passions or the concern we take in ourselves. The first is our present subject; and to explain it perfectly we must take the matter pretty deep, and account for that identity, which we attribute to plants and animals; there being a great analogy betwixt it and the identity of a self or person.

We have a distinct idea of an object that remains invariable and uninterrupted through a supposed variation of time; and this idea we call that of *identity* or *sameness*. We have also a distinct idea of several different objects existing in succession, and connected together by a close relation; and this to an accurate view affords as perfect a notion of *diversity* as if there was no manner of relation among the objects. But though these two ideas of identity, and a succession of related objects, be in themselves perfectly distinct, and even contrary, yet it is certain that, in our common way of thinking, they are generally confounded with each other. That action of the imagination, by which we consider the uninterrupted and invariable object, and that by which we reflect on the succession of related objects, are almost the same to the feeling, nor is there much more effort of thought required in the latter case than in the former. The relation facilitates the transition of the mind from one object to another, and renders its passage as smooth as if it contemplated one continued object. This resemblance is the cause of the confusion and mistake, and makes us substitute the notion of identity, instead of that of related objects. However at one instant we may consider the related succession as variable or interrupted, we are sure the next to ascribe to it a perfect identity, and regard it as invariable and uninterrupted. Our propensity to this mistake is so great from the resemblance above mentioned, that we fall into it before we are aware; and though we incessantly correct ourselves by reflection, and return to a more accurate method of thinking, yet we cannot long sustain our philosophy, or take off this bias from the imagination. Our last resource is to yield to it, and boldly assert that these different related objects are in effect the same, however interrupted and variable. In order to justify to ourselves this absurdity, we often feign some new and unintelligible principle, that connects the objects together, and prevents their interruption or variation. Thus we feign the continued existence of the perceptions of our senses, to remove the interruption; and run into the notion of a *soul*, and *self*, and *substance*, to disguise the variation. But, we may further observe, that where we do not give rise to such a fiction, our propension to confound identity with relation is so great, that we are apt to imagine something unknown and mysterious, connecting the parts, beside their relation; and this I take to be the case with regard to the identity we ascribe to plants and vegetables. And even when this does not take place, we still feel a propensity to confound these ideas, though we

are not able fully to satisfy ourselves in that particular, nor find anything invariable and uninterrupted to justify our notion of identity.

Thus the controversy concerning identity is not merely a dispute of
words. For when we attribute identity, in an improper sense, to variable or interrupted objects, our mistake is not confined to the expression, but is commonly attended with a fiction, either of something
invariable and uninterrupted, or of something mysterious and inexplicable, or at least with a propensity to such fictions. What will suffice
to prove this hypothesis to the satisfaction of every fair inquirer, is
to show, from daily experience and observation, that the objects which
are variable or interrupted, and yet are supposed to continue the same,
are such only as consist of a succession of parts, connected together
by resemblance, contiguity, or causation. For as such a succession
answers evidently to our notion of diversity, it can only be by mistake
we ascribe to it an identity; and as the relation of parts, which leads us
into this mistake, is really nothing but a quality, which produces an
association of ideas, and an easy transition of the imagination from one
to another, it can only be from the resemblance, which this act of the
mind bears to that by which we contemplate one continued object,
that the error arises. Our chief business, then, must be to prove, that
all objects, to which we ascribe identity, without observing their in-
variableness and uninterruptedness, are such as consist of a succession
of related objects.

In order to this, suppose any mass of matter, of which the parts are
contiguous and connected, to be placed before us; it is plain we must
attribute a perfect identity to this mass, provided all the parts continue
uninterruptedly and invariably the same, whatever motion or change of
place we may observe either in the whole or in any of the parts. But
supposing some very *small* or *inconsiderable* part to be added to the
mass, or subtracted from it; though this absolutely destroys the identity
of the whole, strictly speaking, yet as we seldom think so accurately,
we scruple not to pronounce a mass of matter the same, where we find
so trivial an alteration. The passage of the thought from the object
before the change to the object after it, is so smooth and easy, that we
scarce perceive the transition, and are apt to imagine, that it is nothing
but a continued survey of the same object.

There is a very remarkable circumstance that attends this experiment; which is, that though the change of any considerable part in a
mass of matter destroys the identity of the whole, yet we must measure
the greatness of the part, not absolutely, but by its *proportion* to the
whole. The addition or diminution of a mountain would not be sufficient
to produce a diversity in a planet; though the change of a very few

inches would be able to destroy the identity of some bodies. It will be impossible to account for this, but by reflecting that objects operate upon the mind, and break or interrupt the continuity of its actions, not according to their real greatness, but according to their proportion to each other; and therefore, since this interruption makes an object cease to appear the same, it must be the uninterrupted progress of the thought which constitutes the imperfect identity.

This may be confirmed by another phenomenon. A change in any considerable part of a body destroys its identity; but it is remarkable, that where the change is produced *gradually* and *insensibly*, we are less apt to ascribe to it the same effect. The reason can plainly be no other, than that the mind, in following the successive changes of the body, feels an easy passage from the surveying its condition in one moment, to the viewing of it in another, and in no particular time perceives any interruption in its actions. From which continued perception, it ascribes a continued existence and identity to the object.

But whatever precaution we may use in introducing the changes gradually, and making them proportionable to the whole, it is certain, that where the changes are at last observed to become considerable, we make a scruple of ascribing identity to such different objects. There is, however, another artifice, by which we may induce the imagination to advance a step further; and that is, by producing a reference of the parts to each other, and a combination to some *common end* or purpose. A ship, of which a considerable part has been changed by frequent reparations, is still considered as the same; nor does the difference of the materials hinder us from ascribing an identity to it. The common end, in which the parts conspire, is the same under all their variations, and affords an easy transition of the imagination from one situation of the body to another.

But this is still more remarkable, when we add a *sympathy* of parts to their *common end*, and suppose that they bear to each other the reciprocal relation of cause and effect in all their actions and operations. This is the case with all animals and vegetables; where not only the several parts have a reference to some general purpose, but also a mutual dependence on, and connection with, each other. The effect of so strong a relation is, that though every one must allow, that in a very few years both vegetables and animals endure a *total* change, yet we still attribute identity to them, while their form, size, and substance, are entirely altered. An oak that grows from a small plant to a large tree is still the same oak, though there be not one particle of matter or figure of its parts the same. An infant becomes a man, and is sometimes fat, sometimes lean, without any change in his identity.

We may also consider the two following phenomena, which are remarkable in their kind. The first is, that though we commonly be able to distinguish pretty exactly betwixt numerical and specific identity, yet it sometimes happens that we confound them, and in our thinking and reasoning employ the one for the other. Thus, a man who hears a noise that is frequently interrupted and renewed, says it is still the same noise, though it is evident the sounds have only a specific identity or resemblance, and there is nothing numerically the same but the cause which produced them. In like manner it may be said, without breach of the propriety of language, that such a church, which was formerly of brick, fell to ruin, and that the parish rebuilt the same church of freestone, and according to modern architecture. Here neither the form nor materials are the same, nor is there anything common to the two objects but their relation to the inhabitants of the parish; and yet this alone is sufficient to make us denominate them the same. But we must observe, that in these cases the first object is in a manner annihilated before the second comes into existence; by which means, we are never presented, in any one point of time, with the idea of difference and multiplicity; and for that reason are less scrupulous in calling them the same.

Secondly, we may remark, that though, in a succession of related objects, it be in a manner requisite that the change of parts be not sudden nor entire, in order to preserve the identity, yet where the objects are in their nature changeable and inconstant, we admit of a more sudden transition than would otherwise be consistent with that relation. Thus, as the nature of a river consists in the motion and change of parts, though in less than four-and-twenty hours these be totally altered, this hinders not the river from continuing the same during several ages. What is natural and essential to anything is, in a manner, expected; and what is expected makes less impression, and appears of less moment than what is unusual and extraordinary. A considerable change of the former kind seems really less to the imagination than the most trivial alteration of the latter; and by breaking less the continuity of the thought, has less influence in destroying the identity.

We now proceed to explain the nature of *personal identity*, which has become so great a question in philosophy, especially of late years, in England, where all the abstruser sciences are studied with a peculiar ardor and application. And here it is evident the same method of reasoning must be continued which has so successfully explained the identity of plants, and animals, and ships, and houses, and of all compounded and changeable productions either of art or nature. The identity which we ascribe to the mind of man is only a fictitious one, and of a like kind with that which we ascribe to vegetable and animal bodies. It cannot therefore have a different origin, but must proceed from a like operation of the imagination upon like objects.

But lest this argument should not convince the reader, though in my opinion perfectly decisive, let him weigh the following reasoning, which is still closer and more immediate. It is evident that the identity which we attribute to the human mind, however perfect we may imagine it to be, is not able to run the several different perceptions into one, and make them lose their characters of distinction and difference, which are essential to them. It is still true that every distinct perception which enters into the composition of the mind, is a distinct existence, and is different, and distinguishable, and separable from every other perception, either contemporary or successive. But as, notwithstanding this distinction and separability, we suppose the whole train of perceptions to be united by identity, a question naturally arises concerning this relation of identity, whether it be something that really binds our several perceptions together, or only associates their ideas in the imagination; that is, in other words, whether, in pronouncing concerning the identity of a person, we observe some real bond among his perceptions, or only feel one among the ideas we form of them. This question we might easily decide, if we would recollect what has been already proved at large, that the understanding never observes any real connection among objects, and that even the union of cause and effect, when strictly examined, resolves itself into a customary association of ideas. For from thence it evidently follows, that identity is nothing really belonging to these different perceptions, and uniting them altogether, but is merely a quality which we attribute to them, because of the union of their ideas in the imagination when we reflect upon them. Now, the only qualities which can give ideas a union in the imagination, are these three relations above mentioned. These are the uniting principles in the ideal world, and without them every distinct object is separable by the mind, and may be separately considered, and appears not to have any more connection with any other object than if disjoined by the greatest difference and remoteness. It is therefore on some of these three relations of resemblance, contiguity, and causation, that identity depends; and as the very essence of these relations consists in their producing an easy transition of ideas, it follows that our notions of personal identity proceed entirely from the smooth and uninterrupted progress of the thought along a train of connected ideas, according to the principles above explained.

The only question, therefore, which remains is, by what relations this uninterrupted progress of our thought is produced, when we consider existence of a mind or thinking person. And here it is evident we must confine ourselves to resemblance and causation, and must drop contiguity, which has little or no influence in the present case.

To begin with *resemblance;* suppose we could see clearly into the breast of another, and observe that succession of perceptions which constitutes his mind or thinking principle, and suppose that he always preserves the memory of a considerable part of past perceptions, it is evident that nothing could more contribute to the bestowing a relation on this succession amidst all its variations. For what is the memory but a faculty, by which we raise up the images of past perceptions? And as an image necessarily resembles its object, must not the frequent placing of these resembling perceptions in the chain of thought, convey the imagination more easily from one link to another, and make the whole seem like the continuance of one object? In this particular, then, the memory not only discovers the identity, but also contributes to its production, by producing the relation of resemblance among the perceptions. The case is the same, whether we consider ourselves or others.

As to *causation;* we may observe that the true idea of the human mind, is to consider it as a system of different perceptions or different existences, which are linked together by the relation of cause and effect, and mutually produce, destroy, influence, and modify each other. Our impressions give rise to their correspondent ideas; and these ideas, in their turn, produce other impressions. One thought chases another, and draws after it a third, by which it is expelled in its turn. In this respect, I cannot compare the soul more properly to anything than to a republic or commonwealth, in which the several members are united by the reciprocal ties of government and subordination, and give rise to other persons who propagate the same republic in the incessant changes of its parts. And as the same individual republic may not only change its members, but also its laws and constitutions; in like manner the same person may vary his character and disposition, as well as his impressions and ideas, without losing his identity. Whatever changes he endures, his several parts are still connected by the relation of causation. And in this view our identity with regard to the passions serves to corroborate that with regard to the imagination, by the making our distant perceptions influence each other, and by giving us a present concern for our past or future pains or pleasures.

As memory alone acquaints us with the continuance and extent of this succession of perceptions, it is to be considered, upon that account chiefly, as the source of personal identity. Had we no memory, we never should have any notion of causation, nor consequently of that chain of causes and effects, which constitute our self or person. But having once acquired this notion of causation from the memory, we can extend the same chain of causes, and consequently the identity of our persons beyond our memory, and can comprehend times, and circumstances, and actions, which we have entirely forgot, but suppose in general to have existed. For how few of our past actions are there, of which we have any memory? Who can tell me, for instance, what were his thoughts and actions on the first of January 1715, the eleventh of March 1719, and the third of August 1733? Or will he affirm, because he has entirely forgot the incidents of these days, that the present self is not the same person with the self of that time; and by that means overturn all the most established notions of personal identity? In this view, therefore, memory does not so much *produce* as *discover* personal identity, by showing us the relation of cause and effect among our different perceptions. It will be incumbent on those who affirm that memory produces entirely our personal identity, to give a reason why we can thus extend our identity beyond our memory.

The whole of this doctrine leads us to a conclusion, which is of great importance in the present affair, viz. that all the nice and subtile questions concerning personal identity can never possibly be decided, and are to be regarded rather as grammatical than as philosophical difficulties. Identity depends on the relations of ideas; and these relations produce identity, by means of that easy transition they occasion. But as the relations, and the easiness of the transition may diminish by insensible degrees, we have no just standard by which we can decide any dispute concerning the time when they acquire or lose a title to the name of identity. All the disputes concerning the identity of connected objects are merely verbal, except so far as the relation of parts gives rise to some fiction or imaginary principle of union, as we have already observed.

What I have said concerning the first origin and uncertainty of our notion of identity, as applied to the human mind, may be extended with little or no variation to that of *simplicity*. An object, whose different coexistent parts are bound together by a close relation, operates upon the imagination after much the same manner as one perfectly simple and indivisible, and requires not a much greater stretch of thought in order to its conception. From this similarity of operation we attribute a simplicity to it, and feign a principle of union as the support of this simplicity, and the center of all the different parts and qualities of the object.   .   .   .

Appendix

. . . Upon a more strict review of the section concerning *personal identity*, I find myself involved in such a labyrinth that, I must confess, I neither know how to correct my former opinions, nor how to render them consistent. If this be not a good *general* reason for scepticism, it is at least a sufficient one (if I were not already abundantly supplied) for me to entertain a diffidence and modesty in all my decisions. I shall propose the arguments on both sides, beginning with those that induced me to deny the strict and proper identity and simplicity of a self or thinking being.

When we talk of *self* or *substance*, we must have an idea annexed to these terms, otherwise they are altogether unintelligible. Every idea is derived from preceding impressions; and we have no impression of self or substance, as something simple and individual. We have, therefore, no idea of them in that sense.

Whatever is distinct is distinguishable, and whatever is distinguishable is separable by the thought or imagination. All perceptions are distinct. They are, therefore, distinguishable, and separable, and may be conceived as separately existent, and may exist separately, without any contradiction or absurdity.

When I view this table and that chimney, nothing is present to me but particular perceptions, which are of a like nature with all the other perceptions. This is the doctrine of philosophers. But this table, which is present to me, and that chimney, may, and do exist separately. This is the doctrine of the vulgar, and implies no contradiction. There is no contradiction, therefore, in extending the same doctrine to all the perceptions.

In general, the following reasoning seems satisfactory. All ideas are borrowed from preceding perceptions. Our ideas of objects, therefore, are derived from that source. Consequently no proposition can be intelligible or consistent with regard to objects, which is not so with regard to perceptions. But it is intelligible and consistent to say that objects exist distinct and independent, without any common *simple* substance or subject of inhesion. This proposition, therefore, can never be absurd with regard to perceptions.

When I turn my reflection on *myself*, I never can perceive this *self* without some one or more perceptions; nor can I ever perceive anything but the perceptions. It is the composition of these, therefore, which forms the self.

We can conceive a thinking being to have either many or few perceptions. Suppose the mind to be reduced even below the life of an oyster. Suppose it to have only one perception, as of thirst or hunger. Consider it in that situation. Do you conceive anything but merely that perception? Have you any notion of *self* or *substance?* If not, the addition of other perceptions can never give you that notion.

The annihilation which some people suppose to follow upon death, and which entirely destroys this self, is nothing but an extinction of all particular perceptions; love and hatred, pain and pleasure, thought and sensation. These, therefore, must be the same with self, since the one cannot survive the other.

Is *self* the same with *substance?* If it be, how can that question have place, concerning the substance of self, under a change of substance? If they be distinct, what is the difference betwixt them? For my part, I have a notion of neither, when conceived distinct from particular perceptions.

Philosophers begin to be reconciled to the principle, *that we have no idea of external substance, distinct from the ideas of particular qualities.* This must pave the way for a like principle with regard to the mind, *that we have no notion of it, distinct from the particular perception.*

So far I seem to be attended with sufficient evidence. But having thus loosened all our particular perceptions, when I proceed to explain the principle of connection, which binds them together, and makes us attribute to them a real simplicity and identity, I am sensible that my account is very defective, and that nothing but the seeming evidence of the precedent reasonings could have induced me to receive it. If perceptions are distinct existences, they form a whole only by being connected together. But no connections among distinct existences are ever discoverable by human understanding. We only *feel* a connection or determination of the thought to pass from one object to another. It follows, therefore, that the thought alone feels personal identity, when reflecting on the train of past perceptions that compose a mind, the ideas of them are felt to be connected together, and naturally introduce each other. However extraordinary this conclusion may seem, it need not surprise us. Most philosophers seem inclined to think, that personal identity *arises* from consciousness, and consciousness is nothing but a reflected thought or perception. The present philosophy, therefore, has so far a promising aspect. But all my hopes vanish when I come to explain the principles that unite our successive perceptions in our thought or consciousness. I cannot discover any theory which gives me satisfaction on this head.

In short, there are two principles which I cannot render consistent, nor is it in my power to renounce either of them, viz. *that all our dis-*

tinct perceptions are distinct existences, and *that the mind never perceives any real connection among distinct existences.* Did our perceptions either inhere in something simple and individual, or did the mind perceive some real connection among them, there would be no difficulty in the case. For my part, I must plead the privilege of a sceptic, and confess that this difficulty is too hard for my understanding. I pretend not, however, to pronounce it absolutely insuperable. Others, perhaps, or myself, upon more mature reflections, may discover some hypothesis that will reconcile those contradictions. . . .

Terence Penelhum

HUME ON PERSONAL IDENTITY[1]

I want in this paper to examine the arguments which Hume uses in the famous Sixth Section of Part IV of Book I of the *Treatise*,[2] not primarily as a work of scholarship, but in order to assess how good they are and to try to learn something from them when they are mistaken as well as when they are right. Hume's discussion of personal identity is the best there is; no one can feel the same about the problem after reading it as he did before; and, like so much that Hume says, it is incisive, penetrating, and most unsatisfying. It also has an additional, topical, interest: it gives us, I think, an excellent example of how complex and far-reaching the consequences of a mistake in linguistic or conceptual investigation can be.

[1]From *The Philosophical Review*, LXIV (1955), 571–589. Reprinted by permission of the author and *The Philosophical Review*.

 This paper is a revised version of one read to a meeting of the Pacific Division of the American Philosophical Association at the University of Washington, Seattle, on September 8, 1954.
[2]See Hume selection above, pp. 46–57.—Ed.

1

To consider first the general problem with which Hume deals: the problem of personal identity can be roughly described as that of trying to justify a practice which seems at first sight to be strange, and even paradoxical. This is the practice of talking about people as single beings in spite of the fact that they are constantly changing, and over a period of time may have changed completely. It almost seems a contradiction to say that John Smith at two and John Smith at fifty-two are the same person, because they are so different.

Of course the same problem could be raised in the case of other things—think of Heraclitus and the river. It might look as though the problem of personal identity were just one case of a general problem of the persistence of an object through change, and that any special interest we had in personal identity, rather than in fluminal, floral, or faunal identity, arose from the fact that the kind of thing in question is nearer home. But this last fact has had other effects as well: we are in a position to know that human beings have feelings and thoughts and images and pains, and that although these can be talked about by others, they cannot be *seen* or *had* by them, even though our bodily movements are open to public inspection. Now there has been a tendency among philosophers to do more than just recognize that people's lives *include* such private happenings—the tendency has been to regard them as forming a separate *thing* which has a purely contingent relationship to the body. This tendency to dualism has frequently restricted the way in which the problem of personal identity has been put. It has ceased to be "How are we to account for the unity we assume people to have throughout their lives?" and has become "How are we to account for the unity possessed by one *mind* throughout the changes in its (uniformly private) states?" A result of this restriction has been the invention of an entity called "the self," which Hume very properly derides. The purpose its invention serves is this: There is a certain type of solution to the problem of the identity of changing things which consists in saying that in spite of all appearances, which it is admitted are certainly to the contrary, there in fact *is* some item in the composition of changing objects, which does *not* change in any respect. A partiality to this type of solution in the case of persons might quite naturally lead to making the unchanging item a private one; but if this partiality is combined with the dualistic view of the nature of persons, then it is inevitable that the seat of personal identity should be thought to lie in the mind, and the unchanging item be mental.

This is, of course, "the self," which Hume begins by attacking. I shall now turn to his actual argument,[3] and expound it briefly.

2

He has already maintained in the previous Section that no one has rendered intelligible the relationship of "support" which is supposed to hold between "the self" and the other components of our mental histories. In Section VI he opens by disposing of the view that the existence of the self can be recognised empirically—he does this very simply by denying that anyone can find it, unless, of course, its defenders are differently constituted from himself. Assuming that this is not the case, then the whole of mankind are "nothing but a bundle or collection of different perceptions" in a constant state of change. There is none of the simplicity or identity that the self was supposed to provide. This means that it is a mistake to "suppose ourselves possessed of an invariable and uninterrupted existence through the whole course of our lives." Yet we all do suppose it (not merely, Hume implies, the philosophers who try to justify us). How does this mistake arise?

It is based, Hume says, on the confusion between two ideas: (a) that of an object which persists throughout a length of time without change or interruption—this is the idea of identity; (b) that of a succession of related objects—this, he says, is clearly a case of diversity.

We confuse these two because the succession is a succession of *related* objects, and contemplating or imagining such a succession feels much the same as contemplating or imagining an unchanging and uninterrupted object. Having been thus confused, we "substitute" the idea of identity for that of a related succession. And we cannot free ourselves from this confusion for long; the only result of reflecting on it is the bogus attempt to justify it by inventing "some new and unintelligible principle," like "substance" or "the self," which is somehow supposed to preserve the sequence unchanged.

To prove this thesis Hume thinks he has merely to show that those things we (mistakenly) call the same even though they are changing and interrupted consist of a succession of related parts. To show this he takes various kinds of changing things, claiming in each case

---

[3] All quotations in what follows are taken from the Selby-Bigge edition of Hume's *Treatise*, published at Oxford by the Clarendon Press. I have only given page references in the case of moderately lengthy quotations.

that the relation of the change to the whole which changes causes us to overlook its occurrence and continue to call the object the same. (The change, for example, is small in proportion to the whole, takes place only gradually, leaves the function of the whole unaffected, etc.) The same principles are at work in the case of persons; so in their case, as in all other cases, the identity we ascribe to them is "fictitious."

Hume ends by saying that his whole examination of this question reveals that most of the disputes about identity are "merely verbal." Since, as he puts it, "identity depends on the relations of ideas, and these relations produce identity by means of that easy transition they occasion," when these relations and the ease of transition grow less, the tendency to believe in identity grows less too. He gives no example here, but the kind of thing I take it he has in mind is this (I shall take a simple and nonpersonal instance): If a philosopher were to take a particular case like the history of a building from its initial construction to its final demolition, and were to ask at what point what was originally a mere pile of bricks became the house, and at what point what had been the house ceased to be this and gave place to a mere pile of bricks once more (should we date these events by the laying or crumbling of the foundations, or the tiling or stripping of the roof, or the installation or removal of the plumbing? etc., etc.), the answer to give him would be that the tendency to ascribe identity to the changing and complex object is in this case based on the relationship which all the parts have to a central function, viz., the usefulness of the building for sheltering people, but that when this relationship is equivocal (e.g., when the structure could hold people, but only uncomfortably) we simply have a stretch of time when the tendency to say that this is a house rather than a heap of bricks exists, but with less force. At such a time we can decide much as we please which to say it is, and it does not really matter. Our decision would only matter if we invented some philosophical fiction to bolster it up.

3

I wish first to comment briefly on Hume's statement that the whole of mankind are "nothing but a bundle or collection of different perceptions." What is meant by this? Part of what he means is, of course, that human beings are not composed of something called a "self" *plus* some other, less permanent, items, but only of these latter items themselves. So much would be a mere reiteration of what he has already said. But he is clearly committing himself besides to something much stronger and stranger than this, viz., to the view that these items of which, and of nothing-else-but, the whole of mankind are composed are "perceptions." Now this claim is clearly not of quite the same sort as the claim of some philosophers that material things are nothing but perceptions. For, (a) this latter claim is usually somewhat to the effect that statements made about any material thing can somehow be construed as being in fact statements about some of the things that happen to observers when they look at it; and if this were the sort of thing that Hume meant by saying that *people* were nothing but perceptions, it would follow that according to him each person is composed of *other people's* perceptions, that every statement about a given person ought to be construed as a statement about some *other* person or persons; I feel confident that he does not mean this. (b) I feel confident also that he is using the word "perception" in a much wider sense than the sense in which it is used by philosophers who claim that material things are nothing but perceptions, since they use it to mean events which might otherwise be called "sensations," whereas he seems to include in its meaning such events as dreams, feelings, images, etc.—all those events I mentioned earlier which are not open to public view in the way in which our bodily movements are.

What Hume's claim about human beings involves, then, is that they are nothing but the series of *their own* sensations, feelings, dreams, images, and the rest. Clearly, to reach this conclusion he must have been dealing not with the question "How are we justified in attributing identity to persons?" but the question "How are we justified in attributing identity to *minds?*" (where the word "mind" is understood as meaning the "theatre," to use Hume's own term, where these private events take place). It is far from trivial to notice that these two questions are not equivalent (obviously not, since the words "person" and "mind" are not); for answering the latter rather than the former restricts the discussion of personal identity considerably. It forces us to ignore, for example, that the most common way of settling practical problems of identification is by scrutinizing people's physical appearance; or that the gradualness of the changes in complex things which Hume claims to be one of the main contributing causes of our calling them identical is only a feature of human beings if one thinks of them partly in terms of their physical careers; or that the uninterruptedness which he thinks we erroneously attribute to them is in fact a feature of their physical lives.

Fortunately, however, this restriction does not affect the pertinence of his discussion as much as it might be expected to do. This is due to the fact that although he talks at various points as though the problem he is trying to answer is that of the unity of the *mind,* and refers to that of personal identity as though it were the same, the way in which he tries to illumine it is by putting forward a *general* thesis, which I have already outlined, concerning the *general* propensity to call complex and changing objects identical, a propensity of which the ascription of identity to persons is just one instance. It follows, therefore, that the objections I have just raised would apply rather to his view of what sort of thing a person *is* than to his *general* view of the *kinds* of factor at work when we ascribe identity to changing and complex things, whether they are persons or not. I am prepared to agree with him (a) that persons are changing and complex, and (b) that such features as the proportionate smallness of changes, or their gradualness, which he says consolidate our propensity, can be found in the case of persons (more easily, in fact, if we recognize that "person" means more than just "mind"), and this is all that it is necessary to agree to in order to admit that his thesis applies to the case of persons. My subsequent comments will be concerned with this central and general thesis, and are therefore independent of the foregoing criticisms of Hume's view that the life-histories of persons have merely mental components, just as the thesis itself could be stated independently of this view.

4

Hume's thesis turns on one central point, and stands or falls with it. This point is his contention that it is, "to a more accurate method of thinking," a confusion to call an object that changes the *same*. The "idea of identity or sameness" is the idea of an object that persists *without* changing. The fact that the parts of a changing thing may be related to one another does not, after all, alter the further fact that they do change; so in this case we do *not* have identity or sameness, and it must therefore be due to some ingrained tendency of the mind that we talk as though we do. From this point, which he brings in fairly unobtrusively, the remainder of his arguments follow naturally:

(1) The puzzle that remains is a psychological one, viz., what is it about us that makes this mistake possible?

(2) Any account of the relationships that hold between the parts of complex things will only be relevant to *this* question; they do not affect the question of whether we are *justified* in calling such objects the same, because we just aren't.

(3) Clearly, the borderline cases, where we are undecided whether to say that what is before us is the same object or another one, as it were, taking over where the first one left off, are merely verbal and

undecidable because *whatever* we decide will be groundless and mistaken. For the very fact that a change is taking place ought strictly to make us say it is not the same object, but the fact that other changes have preceded this one should have made us say that long before. There is no difference in *kind* between the borderline cases and the times of change during the previous history of the object. The only difference is in the degree of psychological compulsion acting on us—the propensity to misapply the notion of identity is beginning to falter when the borderline is reached, but has not done so before. The only possible *standard* is violated at *all* stages.

(4) The fictions of the self and substance have arisen because philosophers have sensed the nature of our common mistake, but have not been able to free themselves from it for long. The inevitable result of this conflict-state is that they have felt there *must*, really, underneath, out of sight, be an unchanging something-or-other which is the real object, so that our strange habit is justified after all.

All of these are natural consequences of what Hume says about the nature of identity in the early part of the Section. If it is true that we make a mistake in the first place by talking of identity through change at all, then all the rest follows. But I think it is not hard to show that *he* is making an elementary error here, not everyone else, and that the facts he brings to our notice are twisted and misapplied as a result.

It is important to keep in mind as one reads him that he does think he has uncovered a *mistake*, as his language does not always lay stress on this. For instance, when talking about persons, he says:

> *I cannot compare the soul more properly than to a republic or commonwealth . . . as the same individual republic may not only change its members, but also its laws and constitutions; in like manner the same person may vary his character and disposition, as well as his impressions and ideas, without losing his identity.*[4]

This does not, taken out of context, sound like the account of an alleged mistake at all, but it is quite clear from everything that has led up to it that it is, including in particular the fact that this passage is intended as a demonstration that the identity of the mind of a person is a "fictitious" one. The same applies too, of course, to the identity of a republic or commonwealth. Hume is not just saying that our common practice of attributing identity in such cases cannot be justified, or has no sound reason in its favor (as he says of our belief in the regu-

[4]*Treatise*, p. 261 [p. 53 above.—Ed.].

larity of nature): he is here making the less modest claim that our common practice is wrong, that the evidence points unequivocally to the opposite. We proceed not without, but in the face of, the evidence. But it would seem from the tone of the above passage, as well as from his well-known second thoughts in the Appendix, that even Hume found this odd and paradoxical sometimes.

For odd and paradoxical it certainly is. What he is actually claiming is that we are constantly making a mistake in referring to a person from day to day as the same person (in using the same proper name, for example), or in referring in this way to *anything* that has changed in the slightest. For, strictly speaking, a changed person would be literally *another* person. A little effort of imagination is enough to indicate just how much chaos would result from adopting Hume's diagnosis as the source of a prescription and using a different proper name whenever we noticed the slightest change, even in ourselves (or rather in the separate people that we would be from minute to minute). If we make a *mistake* in *not* doing this, it is a mistake we *all* make *all* the time, and a mistake of which the correction would require a complete overhaul of the concepts and syntax of our language. I suppose Hume would say this is one of the reasons why we continue to make the mistake—to avoid the desperate awkwardness of trying to live up to our moments of philosophical insight all the time. But I find it hard to believe that a mistake lies at the root of so much of our language, especially since Hume has claimed to reveal it by a piece of linguistic analysis. I want to show that his analysis is a bad one, that the "mistake" is not a mistake at all, and that its supposed revelation is not a piece of philosophical insight, but of short sight, or rather, astigmatism.

Once the basic point is located, it is not hard to see that Hume has gone wrong. Let us consider the essential three sentences:

> *We have a distinct idea of an object, that remains invariable and uninterrupted thro' a suppos'd variation of time; and this idea we call that of* identity *or* sameness. *We have also a distinct idea of several different objects existing in succession, and connected together by a close relation; and this to an accurate view affords as perfect a notion of* diversity, *as if there was no manner of relation among the objects. But tho' these two ideas of identity, and a succession of related objects be in themselves perfectly distinct, and even contrary, yet 'tis certain, that in our common way of thinking, they are generally confounded with each other.*[5]

[5]*Ibid.*, p. 253 [p. 48].

It is not hard to find his error here. What he is saying is that since we would call something the same for a given length of time when it continued without any alteration, and since we would say that a succession of objects was a collection or number or series of objects, it would obviously be a contradiction to say that in the latter case we would have *one* object. In a sense this is true, but not in the sense which Hume requires. He has not noticed what is wrong because he has chosen to talk in very general terms here, and to ignore the way in which we would actually talk on particular occasions. But a rebuttal can be produced even in general terms. Let us call the unchanging single object *X*. *X*, we would say, is the same throughout. Let us call our succession of distinct but related objects *A, B, C, D, E, F*, etc. Here, if we count, we obviously have several, not one. But we can quite easily produce a class-name for the series of them, say ψ, such that a ψ is, by definition, any group of things like *A, B, C, D, E, F*, etc. So there would be no contradition in saying there are six objects and one ψ; this is what a ψ *is*. Quite obviously, our ordinary language works this way. A succession of notes is one theme. A succession of words is one sentence. If the succession does not form a theme or sentence, it is still a *succession* or series. There is no contradiction in saying "There are six notes in this theme," or "There are six words in this sentence," though there would be in saying "There are six notes but only one," or "There are six words but only one." Naturally, *this* would be absurd, but no one ever says it (for that reason).

So, in spite of Hume, there is no contradiction in saying that certain kinds of things are composed of a succession of parts, and yet are each only one thing. Whether a thing can have many parts or not depends entirely on what sort of thing it is. Most things (including people) do.

There is another, closely related, mistake which Hume has made. This is the mistake of thinking that for anything to be entitled to be called "the same" it has to remain *unchanged* from one period to the next. This is a muddle of two things that he himself distinguishes at one point, viz., the two distinct senses of the word "identical" or "the same." These are the numerical and the specific senses, as he calls them. Two things can be the same as one another in the specific sense, i.e., exactly alike in some respect, yet they will still be two things; but if they are said to be the same in the numerical sense, they are being said to be not two things but one, after all. These two senses are distinct from one another. Now, to remain unchanged is to remain the same in the *specific* sense, i.e., to be now exactly as one was at an earlier time. But I can remain the same in the *numerical* sense without doing so in the specific sense—I can be numerically the same but changed. In fact, I cannot be said to have changed unless I *am* the same in the numerical sense. The only reason for saying that something is numerically different (something else, that is) when a change occurs, is if it is by definition an unchanging thing. When a note is played, for example, as soon as the tone is raised or lowered we have another note, not the same one at all. But in the case of most things, the words we use to talk about them are words the meanings of which allow us or require us to continue to use them throughout certain changes, though not, of course, *any* changes. What kind of changes can occur without our having to say that the thing has ceased to exist and given place to something else depends on what *kind* of thing we are talking about. To know what such changes are is part of what it is to know the meaning of the class-term for that sort of object. A house, or a person, is something which admits of many changes before we would say it had ceased to exist. To know what these changes are is to know, in part at least, what the words "house" and "person" mean.

The rejoinder to Hume, then, consists simply in saying that the pairs of expressions, (a) "numerically the same" and "containing many parts" and (b) "numerically the same" and "changed," are not pairs of contradictories. So we have not made a mistake in saying that a succession of related objects may form a unit of a certain kind, or that the same thing may undergo radical changes. Once this is admitted, the rest of what he says appears in quite a different light.

5

(1) His *examples* point quite a different moral from what he thinks:

(a) The paragraph I quoted can hardly be said to contain an example, but if we produce examples to fit it we get quite different results from those Hume intended. There is nothing about "an object that remains invariable and uninterrupted" *per se* which requires us to say it is the same thing throughout, and nothing about a succession of different but related ones *per se* which requires the opposite. It depends entirely on what concepts we are using when we talk about each. If we heard a continuous sound we would say it was one sound and not several; but it is not hard to imagine some situation in which we would be interested in counting the number of seconds of sound, in which case we would say there were, for example, ten of them. In the case of a succession of objects, the whole series might very well be said to form a unit: a succession of men may form a march-past. There is nothing revealing in choosing a single and uninterrupted sort of thing rather than a complex thing, and Hume has fallen into a conceptual muddle by doing so. He only makes it worse by talking of "an *object* that remains invariable" and "several *objects* existing in succession," because he is here using the same noun in each case, viz., "object"; and although this is the vaguest noun in the language, the mere fact that he uses the same one in each case suggests very easily that in the two phrases he is thinking of objects of the same kind, e.g., a single and uninterrupted note and a succession of distinct notes. This would point a contrast, though of dubious value to Hume;[6] but if we took the variable-word "object" at its face value and substituted different nouns in each phrase, the contrast would disappear: where is there a contrast between "an invariable and uninterrupted arithmetical progression" and "a succession of different but related numbers"? If it is thought that I have chosen a favorable example here, the reply is that I am quite entitled to do so. I am quite ready to admit that we could find a contrast here by making different substitutions, but this just bears out the essential point that whether we get one or not depends entirely on what nouns we choose to work with, and not on the concepts of identity and diversity. Put generally, whether the result is logically absurd, or logically possible, or logically necessary, if the two phrases "the same continuing *x*" and "several different *y*'s" are used of the same thing, depends entirely on what nouns we use to replace *x* and *y*. It does not depend on the words "same" and "different" in themselves.

(b) There are two specific examples which Hume does offer, but misunderstands. He offers both as instances of confusion between numerical and specific identity. The first is this:

A man, who hears a noise, that is frequently interrupted and renew'd, says it is still the same noise; tho' 'tis evident the sounds have only a specific identity or resemblance, and there is nothing numerically the same, but the cause, which produc'd them.[7]

I do not think the man in this case would be guilty of this confusion. When he says it is still the same noise, he may mean one of two things: (i) he might be using "same" in the specific sense, in which case he would be saying merely that the noise he hears now is exactly like the one he heard before; or (ii) he might be using the word "noise" as roughly equivalent to "an intermittent series of exactly similar sounds," in which case the constituent sounds of the noise, in this sense of "noise," can certainly come and go.

---

[6]It would be of dubious value to him because although if we replaced "object" by the same noun in each phrase we would get a contrast, we would quite clearly get a case where the confusion he has in mind would be altogether unlikely.

[7]*Treatise*, p. 258 [p. 51].

The second example is this:

In like manner it may be said, without breach of the propriety of language, that such a church, which was formerly of brick, fell to ruin, and that the parish rebuilt the same church of free-stone, and according to modern architecture. Here neither the form nor materials are the same, nor is there anything common to the two objects, but their relation to the inhabitants of the parish; and yet this alone is sufficient to make us denominate them the same.[8]

Here again the example does not bear out Hume's views at all. Of *course* the relationship of the building to the inhabitants is enough for us to call it the same, because the concept with which we are operating, say that of "the village church of Muddlehampton" is simply and solely the concept of *any* structure which has the unique purpose at any period of subserving the religious needs of the people of that parish. This is why we would use the same phrase whatever building was there, and would say, both before and after the rebuilding, that we had the same thing there; for, in the sense of the concept we would be using, we *would* have the same thing there. There is no mistake in this, as there would be in saying we had the same building, in the sense of the same pile of stones; but we would not say *that*. The village church of Muddlehampton can be pulled down and rebuilt again many times over with perfect logical propriety.

(2) But Hume's error of supposing that invariance is the standard of identity in all cases, when it is only the standard in a very few (those in which invariance is part of the concept of the thing), makes him not only misunderstand the import of his own examples, but miss the point of his otherwise very revealing account of *the relations between the parts of complex things.* Factors like the proportionate smallness of changes, or the conspiracy of the remaining parts to the same end, he claims to be factors which make us overlook the fact that changes have occurred at all. But we do not overlook this fact; we are perfectly aware of it. What Hume is actually describing here in general terms are the kinds of changes that are comprehended under the concepts of certain sorts of things. It is true that these are often small in proportion to the whole, that they take place slowly, and so on. But it is not true always; it is not true of the concept of a river, as Hume himself says. It depends on the concept. As he puts it himself, "What is

[8]*Ibid.*, p. 258 [p. 51].

natural and essential to any thing is, in a manner, expected"; that is to say, more changes are allowed in some things than others, depending on the kind. He should have added, "and it is embodied in the concept of the thing." This might have stopped him saying that these natural and essential changes merely make us misapply the concept of identity, and revealed instead that the standards for applying the concept of identity depend entirely on the substantives it is joined onto. The rules for using nouns (and it is the *modus operandi* of nouns to which his description is relevant) are evolved by generations of language-users, and we have to decide in terms of these at what point a noun applies to whatever we may be considering and when it ceases to.

(3) This decision is not always easy, since the rules we apply are at best very general ones, learned from experience, and not able to cover every eventuality. There are inevitable times when we do not know just what term applies. These are the *borderline cases*, the occasions when the "nice and subtile" questions about identity start coming up. In deciding whether the roofless structure in front of us is a house or a heap of stones, we may have reached a point where the conventions governing neither expression are sufficient to tell us, and we just have to decide for ourselves and, in so doing, make these conventions more precise. We can make mistakes here, like taking a decision which has unforeseen legal repercussions regarding the status of our property. But we do not make a mistake just because we are considering saying it is the same object when it has changed. Hume would have to say that in this case we are merely repeating an error which we have made many times already during the object's history, and just happen for strictly psychological reasons to be feeling uneasy about it this time. But we are uneasy because the rules for our words are not geared to meet every eventuality, not because they ought not to meet any at all. It is true that we lack a standard, but not because we have not been following one before.

(4) It is now time to consider *Hume's criticisms of other philosophers.* He pours scorn on theories of "the self" and "substance," whether they claim to be empirical or not. I do not want to dwell on his criticisms of these theories, since they seem to me to be sound ones. I am more interested in discussing his account of how such theories arise. He claims that they arise because philosophers, like the rest of us, are subject to those factors which produce the mistake of allowing numerical identity to complex and changing things, but are occasionally made aware, by the kind of argument he himself uses, that they *are* making this mistake. Being human, and unable therefore to shake off this

pernicious but convenient confusion, they have eventually tried to justify it by inventing fictions like "the self" to meet the requirement of invariance that they see could not be met otherwise. I have suggested that the factors he has enumerated do not contribute to a mistake or confusion, because there is none. But I agree that the self is a fiction. Such fictions have quite probably arisen in the way Hume describes. That is, the philosophers in question may have thought they found a contradiction between saying a thing has changed and saying it is still the same thing; and they may have tried to overcome this by saying that there is in fact some crucial respect in which the thing will *not* have changed, and inventing the self to fill the bill. But if I am right, they need not have bothered; since there is no contradiction there to be avoided, the fiction is unnecessary. What is of more interest is that Hume, in exposing the nature of their mistake, has conceded their main premise, viz., that there *is* a contradiction there, and has merely said that it is impossible to avoid it and recommended us by implication not to try to justify it. This is a sturdier course than theirs; but, as it proceeds from the same starting-point, it is not surprising that Hume's solution seems to him the sort of paradoxical scepticism for which the only cure is a change of subject or a game of backgammon. This is all the result, as far as I can see, of a linguistic error, of a misdescription of the way in which certain words in the language are in fact used.

I must now try to anticipate a criticism: it might seem that I have been too severe on Hume, too keen to stress the consequences of a position which is more austere than the one he actually holds. I might appear to have missed the point of the fact (noted above) that as his discussion proceeds he does not seem to be *objecting* to the practice of calling people, for all their complexity and changingness, the same throughout their lives; in the course of several pages devoted to the psychological influences on our linguistic conventions, Hume does not seem to be *criticizing*, but only to be *describing* the way in which we talk. He certainly says that our tendency to talk of changing things as identical is a mistake and a confusion, but he only says this at the beginning, in an attempt to discredit philosophical constructs like the self, which only occur when philosophers try to justify, or show rational ground for, a practice which is just a matter of habit and could not conceivably depend on anything *they* had to say. Hume is not trying to discredit our usage, but only to discredit misguided attempts to defend it.

This sort of view is held by Professor Kemp Smith,[9] who insists that Hume has no objection to our everyday use of the notion of identity, once this is understood to be based on custom and not on argument. It would follow from this (and Kemp Smith accepts this consequence) that when Hume refers to the identity of persons as "fictitious," he does not mean *fictitious*, but something less censorious, something more like "stretched": Kemp Smith suggests "Pickwickian." So, although he begins by maintaining that "to an accurate view" talk of the changing or complex as identical is paradoxical, Hume is not himself disposed to take the accurate view, nor to urge it on others — the fact that it is a universal custom *not* to take the accurate view makes it pointless to attempt to impose it in any case.

I have no particular wish either to welcome or to resist this interpretation of Hume's position, or to discuss how far Hume is consistent if this reading of his position is correct. For it is irrelevant to my main contentions:

(a) Whether he is saying that our habit of talking involves us in a paradox which we render tolerable by certain psychological mechanisms, or that the habit is only paradoxical when we take an overscrupulous view of it, but justifies itself pragmatically somehow and should therefore not distress us, he is in either case saying that it can be shown to involve a paradox on examination. However lightly he takes it, he believes it is there. I have denied it is there at all, whether we take an "accurate view" or not.

(b) Whether he thinks the use of the word "identical" with reference to complex things or changing things is a mistaken use or merely a stretched use, he certainly thinks the word is being at least mildly abused on these occasions. I have denied this.

(c) Whether his account of what makes us talk of identity in this mistaken or Pickwickian way is intended as a description of how we hide the paradox from ourselves, or merely of what enables us to talk with a (perfectly proper) lack of concern for it, it is in either case misdirected, since our apparent unconcern for the paradox is due to its nonexistence, and what he in fact describes are the factors governing the use of substantives, and not the *mis*use of the adjective "same."

In other words, however tolerant of our linguistic behavior Hume may be, there is nothing for him to be tolerant about.

[9]N. K. Smith, *The Philosophy of David Hume* (New York, 1941). See particularly pp. 96-98, 497-505.

6

Two points in conclusion: (1) I have not paid special attention to personal identity rather than any other kind. Here I am following Hume. While his chapter and my comments might well have been enriched by descriptions of the relationships between the various stages and facets of the life of persons, such descriptions would have been incidental to the issue which is the core of his argument, viz., the analysis of the concept of identity, and in particular its compatibility or incompatibility with the concepts of complexity and change. This question is the same whatever complex or changing objects we choose to take as examples. Admittedly, persons have a greater degree of complexity and a greater tendency to change than most other things, but to explore this complexity and these changes is to illuminate the concept of a person rather than that of identity.

But there is a positive danger also in laying special emphasis on persons, a danger to which Hume is very much alive: it makes one very susceptible to the suggestion that as we are persons ourselves we are in a better position in this one case to locate the unchanging particle which carries our identity with it, since we have access to human life from the inside as well as the outside. This makes it tempting to give a term like "the self" a quasi-empirical character, as though it referred to an object of introspection. It has been suggested that when this happens it is easy to believe that certain somatic sensations are revelations of the self. If this is true it might explain some of the (otherwise very extraordinary) empirical claims of the kind Hume mentions. It is one thing to claim the self must be there, but quite another to claim you have found it. But to follow the scent of this red herring is to be diverted from recognizing that the whole purpose for which the search was instigated is misconceived.

(2) Hume's language throughout makes it clear that he thinks the error he claims to detect is committed by everyone, that is, by every user of the language, not just by philosophers. If I am right, this is not the case and the ordinary language-user is quite innocent. He clearly holds that it is the philosophers who have invented the fictions of substances and selves. Here, he is right, of course. What emerges from this is that such philosophers, in inventing their fictions, are not defending the layman at all. For they concede, with Hume, that the only chance of showing there is no such paradoxical error in the layman's language is by finding the unchanging kernel within each changing thing. But the layman does not need this sort of defense, because there is no paradox there in the first place. So any claim that the doctrine of the self

is a defense of the layman or that it represents the "common sense position," if this means the same, would be bogus. This point is in no way altered by the fact (and it does seem to be one) that laymen beginning philosophy tend to prefer substance-type theories. For this would be the result of unclear theorizing *about* language (quite a different activity from the mere using of language, and demanding quite distinct aptitudes—rather as travel and cartography differ). Someone new to linguistic theorizing could quite well think he detected a paradox where others claimed to, and fail to notice that his own daily practice did not bear this out. Once this happened, the self might very well seem the only way of evading the paradox. But at this point we are not dealing with a layman any more, but with a philosophical novice. A view which the plain-man-newly-turned-philosopher prefers is not necessarily one he is committed to beforehand.

3 *Immanuel Kant*

THE PARALOGISMS OF PURE REASON[1]

A logical paralogism is a syllogism which is fallacious in form, be its content what it may. A transcendental paralogism is one in which there is a transcendental ground, constraining us to draw a formally invalid conclusion. Such a fallacy is therefore grounded in the nature of human reason, and gives rise to an illusion which cannot be avoided, although it may, indeed, be rendered harmless.

We now come to a concept which was not included in the general list of transcendental concepts but which must yet be counted as belonging to that list, without, however, in the least altering it or declaring it defective. This is the concept or, if the term be preferred, the judgment, "I think." As is easily seen, this is the vehicle of all concepts, and therefore also of transcendental concepts, and so is always included in the conceiving of these latter, and is itself transcendental. But it can have no special designation, because it serves only to introduce all our thought, as belonging to consciousness. Meanwhile, however free it be of empirical admixture (impressions of the senses), it yet enables us to distinguish, through the nature of our faculty of representation, two kinds of objects. "I," as thinking, am an object of inner sense, and am called "soul." That which is an object of the outer senses is called "body." Accordingly the expression "I," as a thinking being, signifies the object of that psychology which may be entitled the "rational doctrine of the soul," inasmuch as I am not here seeking to learn in regard to the soul anything more than can be inferred, independently of all experience (which determines me more specifically and *in concreto*), from this concept "I," so far as it is present in all thought.

The *rational* doctrine of the soul is really an undertaking of this kind; for if in this science the least empirical element of my thought, or any special perception of my inner state, were intermingled with the grounds of knowledge, it would no longer be a rational but an *empirical*

[1]From Immanuel Kant, *Critique of Pure Reason*, trans. Norman Kemp Smith, 1929. Reprinted by permission of Macmillan & Co. Ltd., The Macmillan Company of Canada Ltd., and St. Martin's Press, Inc. The first edition of this work was published in German in 1781, the second in 1787. Editor's footnotes below specify what is here included from the two editions.

doctrine of the soul. Thus we have here what professes to be a science built upon the single proposition "I *think*." Whether this claim be well or ill grounded, we may, very fittingly, in accordance with the nature of a transcendental philosophy, proceed to investigate. The reader must not object that this proposition, which expresses the perception of the self, contains an inner experience, and that the rational doctrine of the soul founded upon it is never pure and is therefore to that extent based upon an empirical principle. For this inner perception is nothing more than the mere apperception "*I think*," by which even transcendental concepts are made possible; what we assert in them is "I think substance, cause," etc. For inner experience in general and its possibility, or perception in general and its relation to other perception, in which no special distinction or empirical determination is given, is not to be regarded as empirical knowledge but as knowledge of the empirical in general, and has to be reckoned with the investigation of the possibility of any and every experience, which is certainly a transcendental enquiry. The least object of perception (for example, even pleasure or displeasure), if added to the universal representation of self-consciousness, would at once transform rational psychology into empirical psychology.

"*I think*" is, therefore, the sole text of rational psychology, and from it the whole of its teaching has to be developed. Obviously, if this thought is to be related to an object (myself), it can contain none but transcendental predicates of that object, since the least empirical predicate would destroy the rational purity of the science and its independence of all experience.

All that is here required is that we follow the guidance of the categories, with this difference only, that since our starting-point is a given thing, "I" as thinking being, we begin with the category of substance, whereby a thing in itself is represented, and so proceed backwards through the series, without, however, otherwise changing the order adopted in the table of the categories. The topic of the rational doctrine of the soul, from which everything else that it contains must be derived, is accordingly as follows:

1. The soul is **substance.**
2. As regards its quality it is **simple.**
3. As regards the different times in which it exists, it is nu-
   merically identical, that is, **unity** *(not plurality).*
4. It is in relation to **possible** *objects in space.*

All the concepts of pure psychology arise from these elements, simply by way of combination, without admission of any other principle. This substance, merely as object of inner sense, gives the concept of *im-materiality*; as simple substance, that of *incorruptibility*; its identity, as intellectual substance, *personality*; all these three together, *spiritual-ity*; while the relation to objects in space gives *commercium* with bodies, and so leads us to represent the thinking substance as the principle of life in matter, that is, as soul *(anima)*, and as the ground of *animality*. This last, in turn, as limited by spirituality, gives the concept of *im-mortality*.

In connection with these concepts we have four paralogisms of a transcendental psychology—which is wrongly regarded as a science of pure reason—concerning the nature of our thinking being. We can assign no other basis for this teaching than the simple, and in itself completely empty, representation "*I*"; and we cannot even say that this is a concept, but only that it is a bare consciousness which accom-panies all concepts. Through this I or he or it (the thing) which thinks, nothing further is represented than a transcendental subject of the thoughts = *X*. It is known only through the thoughts which are its predicates, and of it, apart from them, we cannot have any concept whatsoever, but can only revolve in a perpetual circle, since any judgment upon it has always already made use of its representation. And the reason why this inconvenience is inseparably bound up with it, is that consciousness in itself is not a representation distinguishing a particular object, but a form of representation in general, that is, of representation in so far as it is to be entitled knowledge; for it is only of knowledge that I can say that I am thereby thinking something.

It must, on first thoughts, seem strange that the condition under which alone I think, and which is therefore merely a property of myself as subject, should likewise be valid for everything that thinks, and that on a seemingly empirical proposition we can presume to base an apodeictic and universal judgment, namely, that that which thinks must, in all cases, be constituted as the voice of self-consciousness declares it to be constituted in my own self. The reason is this: we must assign to things, necessarily and *a priori*, all the properties that constitute the conditions under which alone we think them. Now I cannot have any representation whatsoever of a thinking being, through any outer ex-perience, but only through self-consciousness. Objects of this kind are, therefore, nothing more than the transference of this consciousness of mine to other things, which in this way alone can be represented as thinking beings. The proposition, "I think," is, however, here taken only problematically, not in so far as it may contain perception of an ex-istent (the Cartesian *cogito, ergo sum*), but in respect of its mere possibility, in order to see what properties applicable to its subject (be that subject actually existent or not) may follow from so simple a proposition.

If our knowledge of thinking beings in general, by means of pure reason, were based on more than the *cogito*, if we likewise made use of observations concerning the play of our thoughts and the natural laws of the thinking self to be derived from these thoughts, there would arise an empirical psychology, which would be a kind of *physiology* of inner sense, capable perhaps of explaining the appearances of inner sense, but never of revealing such properties as do not in any way belong to possible experience (e.g. the properties of the simple), nor of yielding any *apodeictic* knowledge regarding the nature of thinking beings in general. It would not, therefore, be a *rational* psychology.

Since the proposition "I think" (taken problematically) contains the form of each and every judgment of the understanding and accompanies all categories as their vehicle, it is evident that the inferences from it admit only of a transcendental employment of the understanding. And since this employment excludes any admixture of experience, we cannot, after what has been shown above, entertain any favorable anticipations in regard to its methods of procedure. We therefore propose to follow it, with a critical eye, through all the predicaments of pure psychology.

First Paralogism: of Substantiality

That, the representation of which is the *absolute subject* of our judgments and cannot therefore be employed as determination of another thing, is *substance*.

I, as a thinking being, am the *absolute subject* of all my possible judgments, and this representation of myself cannot be employed as predicate of any other thing.

Therefore I, as thinking being (soul), am *substance*.

Critique of the First Paralogism of Pure Psychology[2]

In all judgments I am the *determining* subject of that relation which constitutes the judgment. That the "I," the "I" that thinks, can be regarded always as *subject*, and as something which does not belong to thought as a mere predicate, must be granted. It is an apodeictic and indeed *identical* proposition; but it does not mean that I, as *object*, am for myself a *self-subsistent* being or *substance*. The latter statement goes very far beyond the former, and demands for its proof data which

[2]The first paragraph of this criticism is from the second edition; the remainder is from the first edition.—Ed.

are not to be met with in thought, and perhaps (in so far as I have regard to the thinking self merely as such) are more than I shall ever find in it.

* * *

It follows, therefore, that the first syllogism of transcendental psychology, when it puts forward the constant logical subject of thought as being knowledge of the real subject in which the thought inheres, is palming off upon us what is a mere pretence of new insight. We do not have, and cannot have, any knowledge whatsoever of any such subject. Consciousness is, indeed, that which alone makes all representations to be thoughts, and in it, therefore, as the transcendental subject, all our perceptions must be found; but beyond this logical meaning of the "I," we have no knowledge of the subject in itself, which as substratum underlies this "I," as it does all thoughts. The proposition, *"The soul is substance,"* may, however, quite well be allowed to stand, if only it be recognized that this concept [of the soul as substance] does not carry us a single step further, and so cannot yield us any of the usual deductions of the pseudo-rational doctrine of the soul as, for instance, the everlasting duration of the human soul in all changes and even in death—if, that is to say, we recognize that this concept signifies a substance only in idea, not in reality.

Second Paralogism: of Simplicity
That, the action of which can never be regarded as the concurrence of several things acting, is *simple.*

Now the soul, or the thinking "I," is such a being. Therefore, etc.

Critique of the Second Paralogism of Transcendental Psychology[3]
This is the Achilles of all dialectical inferences in the pure doctrine of the soul. It is no mere sophistical play, contrived by a dogmatist in order to impart to his assertions a superficial plausibility, but an inference which appears to withstand even the keenest scrutiny and the most scrupulously exact investigation. It is as follows.

Every *composite* substance is an aggregate of several substances, and the action of a composite, or whatever inheres in it as thus composite, is an aggregate of several actions or accidents, distributed among the plurality of the substances. Now an effect which arises from the concurrence of many acting substances is indeed possible, namely, when this effect is external only (as, for instance, the motion of a body

---

[3]This criticism, except for the penultimate paragraph, is from the first edition; the penultimate paragraph is from the second edition.—Ed.

is the combined motion of all its parts). But with thoughts, as internal accidents belonging to a thinking being, it is different. For suppose it be the composite that thinks: then every part of it would be a part of the thought, and only all of them taken together would contain the whole thought. But this cannot consistently be maintained. For representations (for instance, the single words of a verse), distributed among different beings, never make up a whole thought (a verse), and it is therefore impossible that a thought should inhere in what is essentially composite. It is therefore possible only in a *single* substance, which, not being an aggregate of many, is absolutely simple.[4]

The so-called *nervus probandi* of this argument lies in the proposition, that if a multiplicity of representations are to form a single representation, they must be contained in the absolute unity of the thinking subject. No one, however, can prove this proposition from *concepts*. For how should he set about the task of achieving this? The proposition, "A thought can only be the effect of the absolute unity of the thinking being," cannot be treated as analytic. For the unity of the thought, which consists of many representations, is collective, and as far as mere concepts can show, may relate just as well to the collective unity of different substances acting together (as the motion of a body is the composite motion of all its parts) as to the absolute unity of the subject. Consequently, the necessity of presupposing, in the case of a composite thought, a simple substance, cannot be demonstrated in accordance with the principle of identity. Nor will anyone venture to assert that the proposition allows of being known synthetically and completely *a priori* from mere concepts—not, at least, if he understands the ground of the possibility of *a priori* synthetic propositions, as above explained.

It is likewise impossible to derive this necessary unity of the subject, as a condition of the possibility of every thought, from experience. For experience yields us no knowledge of necessity, apart even from the fact that the concept of absolute unity is quite outside its province. Whence then are we to derive this proposition upon which the whole psychological syllogism depends?

It is obvious that, if I wish to represent to myself a thinking being, I must put myself in his place, and thus substitute, as it were, my own subject for the object I am seeking to consider (which does not occur in any other kind of investigation), and that we demand the absolute unity of the subject of a thought, only because otherwise we could not

---

[4]This proof can very easily be given the customary syllogistic correctness of form. But for my purpose it is sufficient to have made clear, though in popular fashion, the bare ground of proof.

say, "*I* think" (the manifold in one representation). For although the whole of the thought could be divided and distributed among many subjects, the subjective "*I*" can never be thus divided and distributed, and it is this "I" that we presuppose in all thinking.

Here again, as in the former paralogism, the formal proposition of apperception, "I think," remains the sole ground to which rational psychology can appeal when it thus ventures upon an extension of its knowledge. This proposition, however, is not itself an experience, but the form of apperception, which belongs to and precedes every experience; and as such it must always be taken only in relation to some possible knowledge, as a *merely subjective condition* of that knowledge. We have no right to transform it into a condition of the possibility of a knowledge of objects, that is, into a *concept* of thinking being in general. For we are not in a position to represent such being to ourselves save by putting ourselves, with the formula of our consciousness, in the place of every other intelligent being.

Nor is the simplicity of myself (as soul) really *inferred* from the proposition, "I think"; it is already involved in every thought. The proposition, "*I am simple*," must be regarded as an immediate expression of apperception, just as what is referred to as the Cartesian inference, *cogito, ergo sum*, is really a tautology, since the *cogito (sum cogitans)* asserts my existence immediately. "*I am simple*" means nothing more than that this representation, "I," does not contain in itself the least manifoldness and that it is absolute (although merely logical) unity.

Thus the renowned psychological proof is founded merely on the indivisible unity of a representation, which governs only the verb in its relation to a person. It is obvious that in attaching "I" to our thoughts we designate the subject of inherence only transcendentally, without noting in it any quality whatsoever—in fact, without knowing anything of it either by direct acquaintance or otherwise. It means a something in general (transcendental subject), the representation of which must, no doubt, be simple, if only for the reason that there is nothing determinate in it. Nothing, indeed, can be represented that is simpler than that which is represented through the concept of a mere something. But the simplicity of the representation of a subject is not *eo ipso* knowledge of the simplicity of the subject itself, for we abstract altogether from its properties when we designate it solely by the entirely empty expression "I," an expression which I can apply to every thinking subject.

This much, then, is certain, that through the "I," I always entertain the thought of an absolute, but logical, unity of the subject (simplicity). It does not, however, follow that I thereby know the actual simplicity of my subject. The proposition, "I am substance," signifies, as we have found, nothing but the pure category, of which I can make no use (empirically) *in concreto;* and I may therefore legitimately say: "I am a simple substance," that is, a substance the representation of which never contains a synthesis of the manifold. But this concept, as also the proposition, tells us nothing whatsoever in regard to my-self as an object of experience, since the concept of substance is itself used only as a function of synthesis, without any underlying intuition, and therefore without an object. It concerns only the condition of our knowledge; it does not apply to any assignable object. . . .

That the "I" of apperception, and therefore the "I" in every act of thought, is *one,* and cannot be resolved into a plurality of subjects, and consequently signifies a logically simple subject, is something al-ready contained in the very concept of thought, and is therefore an analytic proposition. But this does not mean that the thinking "I" is a simple *substance.* That proposition would be synthetic. The concept of substance always relates to intuitions which cannot in me be other than sensible, and which therefore lie entirely outside the field of the understanding and its thought. But it is of this thought that we are speaking when we say that the "I" in thought is simple. It would, in-deed, be surprising if what in other cases requires so much labor to determine—namely, what, of all that is presented in intuition, is sub-stance, and further, whether this substance can be simple (e.g. in the parts of matter)—should be thus given me directly, as if by revelation, in the poorest of all representations.

* * *

Thus the whole of rational psychology is involved in the collapse of its main support. Here as little as elsewhere can we hope to extend our knowledge through mere concepts—still less by means of the merely subjective form of all our concepts, consciousness—in the absence of any relation to possible experience. For [as we have thus found], even the fundamental concept of a *simple nature* is such that it can never be met with in any experience, and such, therefore, that there is no way of attaining to it, as an objectively valid concept.

Third Paralogism: of Personality
That which is conscious of the numerical identity of itself at different times is in so far a *person.*

Now the soul is conscious, etc.

Therefore it is a person.

Critique of the Third Paralogism of Transcendental Psychology[5]
The proposition, that in all the manifold of which I am conscious I am identical with myself, is likewise implied in the concepts themselves, and is therefore an analytic proposition. But this identity of the subject, of which I can be conscious in all my representations, does not concern any intuition of the subject, whereby it is given as object, and cannot therefore signify the identity of the person, if by that is understood the consciousness of the identity of one's own substance, as a thinking being, in all change of its states. No mere analysis of the proposition "I think" will suffice to prove such a proposition; for that we should require various synthetic judgments, based upon given intuition.

* * *

The identity of the consciousness of myself at different times is therefore only a formal condition of my thoughts and their coherence, and in no way proves the numerical identity of my subject. Despite the logical identity of the "I," such a change may have occurred in it as does not allow of the retention of its identity, and yet we may ascribe to it the same-sounding "I," which in every different state, even in one involving change of the [thinking] subject, might still retain the thought of the preceding subject and so hand it over to the subsequent subject.[6]

Although the dictum of certain ancient schools, that everything in the world is *in a flux* and nothing is *permanent* and abiding, cannot be reconciled with the admission of substances, it is not refuted by the unity of self-consciousness. For we are unable from our own consciousness to determine whether, as souls, we are permanent or not. Since we reckon as belonging to our identical self only that of which we are

---

[5]The first paragraph of this criticism is from the second edition; the remainder is from the first edition.—Ed.
[6]An elastic ball which impinges on another similar ball in a straight line communicates to the latter its whole motion, and therefore its whole state (that is, if we take account only of the positions in space). If, then, in analogy with such bodies, we postulate substances such that the one communicates to the other representations together with the consciousness of them, we can conceive a whole series of substances of which the first transmits its state together with its consciousness to the second, the second its own state with that of the preceding substance to the third, and this in turn the states of all the preceding substances together with its own consciousness and with their consciousness to another. The last substance would then be conscious of all the states of the previously changed substances, as being its own states, because they would have been transferred to it together with the consciousness of them. And yet it would not have been one and the same person in all these states.

conscious, we must necessarily judge that we are one and the same throughout the whole time of which we are conscious. We cannot, however, claim that this judgment would be valid from the standpoint of an outside observer. For since the only permanent appearance which we encounter in the soul is the representation "I" that accompanies and connects them all, we are unable to prove that this "I," a mere thought, may not be in the same state of flux as the other thoughts which, by means of it, are linked up with one another.

It is indeed strange that personality, and its presupposition, permanence, and therefore the substantiality of the soul, should have to be proved *at this stage and not earlier.* For could we have presupposed these latter [permanence and substantiality], there would follow, not indeed the continuance of consciousness, yet at least the possibility of a continuing consciousness in an abiding subject, and that is already sufficient for personality. For personality does not itself at once cease because its activity is for a time interrupted. This permanence, however, is in no way given prior to that numerical identity of our self which we infer from identical apperception, but on the contrary is inferred first from the numerical identity. (If the argument proceeded aright, the concept of substance, which is applicable only empirically, would first be brought in after such proof of numerical identity.) Now, since this identity of person [presupposing, as it does, numerical identity] in nowise follows from the identity of the "I" in the consciousness of all the time in which I know myself, we could not, earlier in the argument, have founded upon it the substantiality of the soul.

Meanwhile we may still retain the concept of personality—just as we have retained the concept of substance and of the simple—in so far as it is merely transcendental, that is, concerns the unity of the subject, otherwise unknown to us, in the determinations of which there is a thoroughgoing connection through apperception. Taken in this way, the concept is necessary for practical employment and is sufficient for such use; but we can never parade it as an extension of our self-knowledge through pure reason, and as exhibiting to us from the mere concept of the identical self an unbroken continuance of the subject. For this concept revolves perpetually in a circle, and does not help us in respect to any question which aims at synthetic knowledge. What matter may be as a thing in itself (transcendental object) is completely unknown to us, though, owing to its being represented as something external, its permanence as appearance can indeed be observed. But if I want to observe the mere "I" in the change of all representations, I have no other *correlatum* to use in my comparisons except again myself, with the universal conditions of my consciousness. Consequently, I can give none but tautological answers to all questions, in that I substitute my concept and its unity for the properties which belong to myself as object, and so take for granted that which the questioner has desired to know.

Fourth Paralogism: of Ideality (In Regard to Outer Relation)

That, the existence of which can only be inferred as a cause of given perceptions, has a merely doubtful existence.

Now all outer appearances are of such a nature that their existence is not immediately perceived, and that we can only infer them as the cause of given perceptions.

Therefore the existence of all objects of the outer senses is doubtful. This uncertainty I entitle the ideality of outer appearances, and the doctrine of this ideality is called *idealism*, as distinguished from the counter-assertion of a possible certainty in regard to objects of outer sense, which is called *dualism.*

Critique of the Fourth Paralogism of Transcendental Psychology[7]

That I distinguish my own existence as that of a thinking being, from other things outside me—among them my body—is likewise an analytic proposition; for *other* things are such as I think to be *distinct* from myself. But I do not thereby learn whether this consciousness of myself would be even possible apart from things outside me through which representations are given to me, and whether, therefore, I could exist merely as thinking being (i.e. without existing in human form).

The analysis, then, of the consciousness of myself in thought in general, yields nothing whatsoever towards the knowledge of myself as object. The logical exposition of thought in general has been mistaken for a metaphysical determination of the object.

Indeed, it would be a great stumbling-block, or rather would be the one unanswerable objection, to our whole critique, if there were a possibility of proving *a priori* that all thinking beings are in themselves simple substances, and that consequently (as follows from this same mode of proof) personality is inseparable from them, and that they are conscious of their existence as separate and distinct from all matter. For by such procedure we should have taken a step beyond the world of sense, and have entered into the field of noumena; and no one could

---

[7]This criticism is entirely from the second edition.—Ed.

then deny our right of advancing yet further in this domain, indeed of settling in it, and, should our star prove auspicious, of establishing claims to permanent possession. The proposition, "Every thinking being is, as such, a simple substance," is a synthetic *a priori* proposition; it is synthetic in that it goes beyond the concept from which it starts, and adds to the thought in general [i.e. to the concept of a thinking being] the mode of [its] existence: it is *a priori*, in that it adds to the concept a predicate (that of simplicity) which cannot be given in any experience. It would then follow that *a priori* synthetic propositions are possible and admissible, not only, as we have asserted, in relation to objects of possible experience, and indeed as principles of the possibility of this experience, but that they are applicable to things in general and to things in themselves—a result that would make an end of our whole critique, and would constrain us to acquiesce in the old-time procedure. Upon closer consideration we find, however, that there is no such serious danger.

The whole procedure of rational psychology is determined by a paralogism, which is exhibited in the following syllogism:

That which cannot be thought otherwise than as subject does not exist otherwise than as subject, and is therefore substance.

A thinking being, considered merely as such, cannot be thought otherwise than as subject.

Therefore it exists also only as subject, that is, as substance.

In the major premiss we speak of a being that can be thought in general, in every relation, and therefore also as it may be given in intuition. But in the minor premiss we speak of it only in so far as it regards itself, as subject, simply in relation to thought and the unity of consciousness, and not as likewise in relation to the intuition through which it is given as object to thought. Thus the conclusion is arrived at fallaciously, *per sophisma figurae dictionis.*[8]

That we are entirely right in resolving this famous argument into a paralogism will be clearly seen, if we call to mind what has been said

---

[8]"Thought" is taken in the two premisses in totally different senses: in the major premiss, as relating to an object in general and therefore to an object as it may be given in intuition; in the minor premiss, only as it consists in relation to self-consciousness. In this latter sense, no object whatsoever is being thought; all that is being represented is simply the relation to self as subject (as the form of thought). In the former premiss we are speaking of *things* which cannot be thought otherwise than as subjects; but in the latter premiss we speak not of *things* but of *thought* (abstraction being made from all objects) in which the "I" always serves as the subject of consciousness. The conclusion cannot, therefore, be, "I cannot exist otherwise than as subject," but merely, "In thinking my existence, I cannot employ myself, save as subject of the judgment [therein involved]." This is an identical proposition, and casts no light whatsoever upon the mode of my existence.

in the General Note to the Systematic Representation of the Principles and in the Section on Noumena. For it has there been proved that the concept of a thing which can exist by itself as subject and never as mere predicate, carries with it no objective reality; in other words, that we cannot know whether there is any object to which the concept is applicable—as to the possibility of such a mode of existence we have no means of deciding—and that the concept therefore yields no knowledge whatsoever. If by the term "substance" be meant an object which can be given, and if it is to yield knowledge, it must be made to rest on a permanent intuition, as being that through which alone the object of our concept can be given, and as being, therefore, the indispensable condition of the objective reality of the concept. Now in inner intuition there is nothing permanent, for the "I" is merely the consciousness of my thought. So long, therefore, as we do not go beyond mere thinking, we are without the necessary condition for applying the concept of substance, that is, of a self-subsistent subject, to the self as a thinking being. And with the objective reality of the concept of substance, the allied concept of simplicity likewise vanishes; it is transformed into a merely logical qualitative unity of self-consciousness in thought in general, which has to be present whether the subject be composite or not.

Refutation of Mendelssohn's[9] Proof of the Permanence of the Soul

This acute philosopher soon noticed that the usual argument by which it is sought to prove that the soul—if it be admitted to be a simple being—cannot cease to be through *dissolution,* is insufficient for its purpose, that of proving the necessary continuance of the soul, since it may be supposed to pass out of existence through simply *vanishing.* In his *Phaedo* he endeavored to prove that the soul cannot be subject to such a process of vanishing, which would be a true annihilation, by showing that a simple being cannot cease to exist. His argument is that since the soul cannot be diminished, and so gradually lose something of its existence, being by degrees changed into nothing (for since it has no parts, it has no multiplicity in itself), there would be no time between a moment in which it is and another in which it is not—which is impossible. He failed, however, to observe that even if we admit the simple nature of the soul, namely, that it contains no manifold of constituents external to one another, and therefore no extensive quantity, we yet cannot deny to it, any more than to any other existence, inten-

[9]Moses Mendelssohn, 1729–1786.—Ed.

sive quantity, that is, a degree of reality in respect of all its faculties, nay, in respect of all that constitutes its existence, and that this degree of reality may diminish through all the infinitely many smaller degrees. In this manner the supposed substance—the thing, the permanence of which has not yet been proved—may be changed into nothing, not indeed by dissolution, but by gradual loss *(remissio)* of its powers, and so, if I may be permitted the use of the term, by elanguescence. For consciousness itself has always a degree, which always allows of diminution, and the same must also hold of the faculty of being conscious of the self, and likewise of all the other faculties. Thus the permanence of the soul, regarded merely as object of inner sense, remains undemonstrated, and indeed indemonstrable. Its permanence during life is, of course, evident *per se,* since the thinking being (as man) is itself likewise an object of the outer senses. But this is very far from satisfying the rational psychologist who undertakes to prove from mere concepts its absolute permanence beyond this life.

* * *

Rational psychology exists not as *doctrine,* furnishing an addition to our knowledge of the self, but only as *discipline.* It sets impassable limits to speculative reason in this field, and thus keeps us, on the one hand, from throwing ourselves into the arms of a soulless materialism, or, on the other hand, from losing ourselves in a spiritualism which must be quite unfounded so long as we remain in this present life. But though it furnishes no positive doctrine, it reminds us that we should regard this refusal of reason to give satisfying response to our inquisitive probings into what is beyond the limits of this present life as reason's hint to divert our self-knowledge from fruitless and extravagant speculation to fruitful practical employment. Though in such practical employment it is directed always to objects of experience only, it derives its principles from a higher source, and determines us to regulate our actions as if our destiny reached infinitely far beyond experience, and therefore far beyond this present life.

From all this it is evident that rational psychology owes its origin simply to misunderstanding. The unity of consciousness, which underlies the categories, is here mistaken for an intuition of the subject as object, and the category of substance is then applied to it. But this unity is only unity in *thought,* by which alone no object is given, and to which, therefore, the category of substance, which always presupposes a given *intuition,* cannot be applied. Consequently, this subject cannot be known. The subject of the categories cannot by thinking the categories acquire a concept of itself as an object of the categories.

For in order to think them, its pure self-consciousness, which is what was to be explained, must itself be presupposed. Similarly, the subject, in which the representation of time has its original ground, cannot thereby determine its own existence in time. And if this latter is impossible, the former, as a determination of the self (as a thinking being in general) by means of the categories, is equally so.[10]

[10]The "I think" is, as already stated, an empirical proposition, and contains within itself the proposition "I exist." But I cannot say "Everything which thinks, exists." For in that case the property of thought would render all beings which possess it necessary beings. My existence cannot, therefore, be regarded as an inference from the proposition "I think," as Descartes sought to contend—for it would then have to be preceded by the major premiss "Everything which thinks, exists"—but is identical with it. The "I think" expresses an indeterminate empirical intuition, i.e., perception (and thus shows that sensation, which as such belongs to sensibility, lies at the basis of this existential proposition). But the "I think" precedes the experience which is required to determine the object of perception through the category in respect of time; and the existence here [referred to] is not a category. The category as such does not apply to an indeterminately given object but only to one of which we have a concept and about which we seek to know whether it does or does not exist outside the concept. An indeterminate perception here signifies only something real that is given, given indeed to thought in general, and so not as appearance, nor as thing in itself *(noumenon)*, but as something which actually exists, and which in the proposition, "I think," is denoted as such. For it must be observed, that when I have called the proposition, "I think," an empirical proposition, I do not mean to say thereby, that the "I" in this proposition is an empirical representation. On the contrary, it is purely intellectual, because belonging to thought in general. Without some empirical representation to supply the material for thought, the *actus,* "I think," would not, indeed, take place; but the empirical is only the condition of the application, or of the employment, of the pure intellectual faculty.

P. F. Strawson

SELF, MIND AND BODY[1]

One of the marks, though not a necessary mark, of a really great philosopher is to make a really great mistake: that is to say, to give a persuasive and lastingly influential form to one of those fundamental misconceptions to which the human intellect is prone when it concerns itself with the ultimate categories of thought. So today, more than three hundred years after the death of René Descartes, philosophers struggling with one of these fundamental misconceptions think of it under the name of Cartesian dualism. Not that they all think of the doctrine in question as a misconception. The doctrine has its defenders. Indeed if it did not represent a way of thinking about mind and body which has a powerful intellectual appeal, it would not be worth struggling against. There is little point in refuting errors which no one is inclined to make.

In this article I want to try to bring out the force of one way, which has received some attention in recent English philosophy, of demonstrating the, or a, central error in Cartesian dualism. First, we need a reasonably clear statement of the dualist position to work on.

It seems an obvious and uncontentious point that the sorts of things which we can truthfully say about ourselves and other human beings are very various, that they form a very mixed bag indeed. Thus we can and do ascribe to one and the same individual human being things as various as actions, intentions, sensations, thoughts, feelings, perceptions, memories, physical position, corporal characteristics, skills or abilities, traits of character and so on. A person or human being, as a subject of discourse, typically collects predicates of all these kinds. Now a Cartesian dualist is one who holds that this way of talking about people, though convenient and perhaps essential for practical purposes, tends to disguise rather than display the real nature of a human individual. We should first recognize, he thinks, that of these various predicates some refer directly to the states of consciousness of a person, some refer directly to his bodily condition and some refer in a more or less indirect and complicated way to both at once. But recognizing this is no more than a step in the right direction. It is not enough to acknowledge that a person has two sides to his nature and his history,

[1]From *Common Factor* (1966). Reprinted by permission of the author.

a mental or conscious side and a material or corporal side. For really the history of a human being is not the history of one two-sided thing, it is the history of two one-sided things. One of these things is a material object, a body; the other is an immaterial object, a soul or mind or spirit or individual consciousness. These are totally distinct kinds of thing, with totally distinct kinds of properties and states. None of the predicates which properly apply to bodies (like having a certain weight or size or coloring) properly apply to minds; and none of the predicates which properly apply to consciousnesses (like having a certain thought or experiencing a certain sensation) properly apply to bodies. During the lifetime of a human being, two of these things, one of each kind, are peculiarly intimately related; but the intimacy of their union does not count against or diminish the essential independence of their nature.

Now if the Cartesian were right in this, it seems that it should be possible in principle to lay down at least the general outlines of a new and more metaphysically revealing way of talking about people than that which we find practically convenient. This new way of talking would reflect, in a dualism of grammatical or linguistic subjects, the dualism of real or metaphysical subjects which the Cartesian finds conjoined in the human individual. If we assembled all the statements which in our ordinary way of talking have the name of one man as their grammatical subject, and reconstructed them in a Cartesian grammar, then for each statement there would be three possibilities of reconstruction: either the grammatical subject of the new statement would be the designation of a body or a part of a body or it would be the designation of a mind or consciousness or the original statement would be analysed into two separate statements, one of them about a mind and one of them about a body.

It might seem at first that the germs of an "improved" or Cartesian style of speech about people were already present in our ordinary style of speech about people. For included in our ordinary style of speech is a lot of perfectly intelligible talk in which we explicitly ascribe predicates to people's bodies (or parts of them) and also a lot of perfectly intelligible talk in which we explicitly ascribe predicates to people's minds or even consciousnesses. So it might look as if our ordinary habits of thought and speech already contained an implicit, though incomplete, acknowledgment of the truth of Cartesianism.

However, it is clearly not enough for the Cartesian to point to our habit of talking about people's minds and bodies as well as about people, as if this were conclusive evidence for his thesis. The difference between the Cartesian and his opponent is a difference of view about the *relation* between the concept of a person on the one hand and the concept of a person's mind on the other. The anti-Cartesian holds that the concept of a person's mind has a secondary or dependent status. The fundamental concept, for him, is that of a human being, a man, a type of thing to which predicates of *all* those various classes I distinguished earlier can be ascribed. To talk about the mind of a man is just a way of talking about a man, in respect of certain sorts of things that are true of him. Just so we can talk of the *surfaces* of tables as well as of tables, of the *score* in a football match as well as of a football match. But we recognize that the concept of a surface is dependent on the concept of a material object, that the concept of a score is dependent on the concept of a game. Similarly, the anti-Cartesian holds, the concept of a mind or consciousness is dependent on the concept of a living person.

But the Cartesian cannot admit this dependence. He must hold that the notion of an individual consciousness or mind is perfectly intelligible apart from the notion of a person whose mind or individual consciousness it is. He cannot admit that the idea of a mind presupposes that of a person; he must hold, on the contrary, that a dualistic *reduction* or *analysis* of the idea of a person is in principle possible or intelligible.

Let us consider more carefully what would be necessary in order for a Cartesian reduction to be successfully carried through. We begin with statements of which the subjects are the designations of people and the predicates are of the various kinds already mentioned. The Cartesian thesis requires that these be replaceable in principle with sentences of which the subjects are either the designations of minds (consciousnesses) or the designations of bodies. Hence it seems to require too that the predicates of our original sentences should either be already equivalent to consciousness-predicates or to body-predicates or be capable of being analysed into a body-predicate component and a consciousness-predicate component. Moreover the Cartesian reduction-sentences, it seems, must be genuinely, and not merely apparently, reductive. Consider, for example, the statement that John is writing a letter. 'Writing a letter' seems to be one of those predicates which must be split up into a mental component and a bodily component; but it would seem unsatisfactory to try to isolate the mental component by means of some such sentence as "His mind was going through the mental processes involved in writing a letter." For this leaves it open to the anti-Cartesian to say that the concept of such a mental process is dependent on the concept of writing a letter; and that writing a letter is essentially not something that a mind does or something that a body does, but something that a person does.

It seems, then, that there might be very considerable difficulties in effecting a genuine reduction of person-predicates to a mental component and a bodily component. And many of these difficulties are very clearly indicated in some work in recent British philosophy, notably in Professor Ryle's book, "The Concept of Mind," and in Wittgenstein's posthumous "Philosophical Investigations."[2] Yet I think that a convinced Cartesian might be comparatively unmoved by this kind of difficulty. He might agree that there were good reasons why our language was unequipped with, and perhaps was bound to remain unequipped with, the resources necessary for a genuine reduction of all such predicates as these to a mental component and a bodily component, and yet maintain that it was really quite obvious that all such activities as writing a letter really did involve both mental processes and bodily processes; and it would be hard to deny that on this point he was right in some sense, even if not in quite the sense he supposed.

What would move the Cartesian much more, I think, would be a clear demonstration that there was something wrong, not on the predicate side, but on the subject side, with the idea of a Cartesian reduction. We have already remarked that it is not sufficient for the Cartesian to appeal to the fact that we do intelligibly talk about people's minds and people's bodies. The anti-Cartesian thesis is not the thesis that there are no such things as minds, but that the concept of an individual mind or consciousness is only to be understood as logically derivative from the concept of an individual person. It is up to the Cartesian to show that this is not so, to show that we can make perfectly good sense of the idea of an individual mind without making that very idea dependent upon the idea of an individual person. Hence it is a *prima facie* awkwardness for the Cartesian that when we ordinarily talk about people's minds or consciousnesses, we do so by way of referring to the people whose minds or consciousnesses they are. Thus if we say "Mary's consciousness was entirely occupied by the thought of how becoming her dress was," the grammatical subject of our statement is certainly the designation of an individual mind or consciousness. But we succeed in designating the consciousness only by way of designating Mary; and Mary, happily, is not simply a consciousness; she is not only *thinking* about the dress, she is *wearing* it.

It is easy enough for the Cartesian to meet this difficulty in a formal way: that is, to give examples of expressions designating consciousnesses which don't formally depend on designating people. One general

[2]See Wittgenstein and Ryle selections in this anthology.—Ed.

form of substitute-designation might go something like this: "The consciousness which stands in a peculiarly intimate relation with the body in such-and-such a place." Another general form might run something like this: "The mind which is at such-and-such a time occupied by such-and-such thoughts and feelings." But we simply don't know whether, by the use of such forms, we achieve a reference to a mind which is genuinely independent of reference to a person, until we know the answer to a further and most important question: viz., what justifies us in using the little word "the"—implying reference to a single one—before "mind" or "consciousness."

It is here that we come—at last—to the central difficulty in Cartesianism. If we are to talk coherently about individual consciousnesses or minds, or about individual items of any kind whatever, there is one thing at least which we must know. We must know the difference between *one* such item and *two* such items. We must know, that is, on what principle such items are to be counted. And this means further— if they are supposed to be items capable of lasting through a period of time—that we must know how to identify the *same* item at different times. In general we have no idea what a *so-and-so* is unless we have some idea what *a* so-and-so is. If we have no idea of how the notions of numerical identity and difference apply to individual consciousnesses then we really have no clear concept at all of such items.

Now the anti-Cartesian is able to satisfy this requirement for having a coherent concept of an individual mind or consciousness. Since he regards this concept as secondary to, or derivative from, that of an individual person, he can advance the following simple rule: *one* person, *one* consciousness; *same* person, *same* consciousness. His recipe for counting individual minds is to count people; for him the identification of a mind presents no greater (and no less) a problem than the identification of a person. He does not have to pretend that the question as to what the criteria of personal identity are is an easy or straightforward question. But he can properly point out that we have, and know how to use, adequate criteria for ordinary cases; and that we can perfectly intelligibly discuss how our criteria should be interpreted or adapted for any extraordinary cases which we might encounter or imagine.

But how does the matter stand on the Cartesian philosopher's view? It is essential to his view that the application of the notions of identity and numerability to souls (consciousnesses) should *not* be determined by their application to persons. (The determining must be the other way about.) But then how *is* the application of these notions to souls or consciousnesses to be determined? Suppose I were

in debate with a Cartesian philosopher, say Professor X. If I were
to suggest that when *the man,* Professor X, speaks, there are a thousand
souls simultaneously thinking the thoughts his words express, having
qualitatively indistinguishable experiences such as he, the man, would
currently claim, how would he persuade me that there was only one
such soul? (How would each indignant soul, once the doubt has entered,
persuade itself of its uniqueness?) There is another, more familiar difficulty, about the identity of a soul from one time to another. If the
concept of the identity of a soul or consciousness over time is not derivative from, dependent upon, the concept of the identity of a person
over time, then how is it determined? What do we mean by "the same
consciousness" if not "the same person's consciousness"? Some
philosophers, like the British empiricist, Locke, used to suppose that
an adequate account of the identity of a consciousness through time
could be given in terms of memory alone; but the failure of such
accounts is a commonplace of philosophical criticism which I will
not repeat. Other philosophers refer, or used to refer, to a Pure Ego
or soul-substance, as if this exempted them from having any idea what
it *meant* to speak of *the same one* from one time to another. To them
one may reply, in a rough paraphrase of Kant: if you're allowed to invoke that hypothesis whenever you like, without being required to
elucidate the principle of its application, what is to prevent me from
introducing a rival hypothesis, also unelucidated: wherever you say
there's one continuing soul-substance, I say there's a whole series of
them, each of which transmits its states and the consciousness of them
to its successor, as motion might be transmitted from one to another
of a whole series of elastic balls.[3]

The dilemma is roughly, this. Either the concepts of identity and
difference of individual human consciousnesses are derivative from the
concepts of identity and difference of individual people (human beings,
men and women) or they are not. If they are, then our ordinary style
of talking about human beings is not even in principle reducible in
the way in which the Cartesian must hold that it is. If they are not, if
a Cartesian reduction is in principle possible, then it must also be
possible to make *independently* intelligible what is meant by identity
and difference of human consciousness. But there is not the slightest
reason for thinking that this can be done.

What, then, is the source of the Cartesian delusion? Well, no doubt
it has several sources. But I think a particularly important one is a
certain experience of intense looking within, or introspective concen-

---

[3] Cf. footnote 6, p. 82 above.—Ed.

tration, of which most of us are capable and which certainly seems to have been characteristic of Descartes' own meditations. One is tempted to say in such moments that one has direct experience of oneself as a conscious being. And this may be a harmless thing to say. But it may put us on the path of illusion. Let us see how it can do so.

The ordinary personal pronouns and possessives, including "I" and "my," are used in ordinary inter-personal communication for the purposes of personal reference. If the speaker says "I," his or her hearers know what man or woman is meant. But when we reflect philosophically on the type of introspective experience I have just described, we can quite easily get into a kind of daze about the meaning of "*I*" and "*my.*" We can say to ourselves things like "*I* am aware of *myself* now" or "This is how it is with *me* now" and say such things with the conviction of their expressing absolutely indubitable fact. And then perhaps we may begin to feel that we don't have to *explain* the notions of identity and difference as applied to the soul, for we have *direct experience* of the individuality and identity of the soul, experience which might be expressed in remarks like these. And no doubt an experience of some kind *is* expressed in such a remark. But, really, if we make this kind of *claim* about it (i.e., that it is direct experience of the individuality and identity of the human soul), then we are trying to have things both ways: we are trying to keep the immediacy and indubitability of the experience and at the same time to keep the ordinary referential force of "I," the word that the individual *man* uses to refer to himself. We are tricking ourselves by simultaneously withdrawing the pronoun from the ordinary game and yet preserving the illusion that we're still using it to play the ordinary game. And it should be easy to see this, since Kant exposed the illusion; yet, as Kant also remarked, the illusion is powerful. Perhaps a way to get at it is this. All the immediacy and indubitability of experience which seem to go with the use of "I" and "me" in such remarks as I've just quoted could be preserved while re-expressing the remarks in some such form as "*This* is a conscious experience" or "The soul having this experience is conscious of itself as having *this* experience." Then it would be apparent where the limits of immediacy and indubitability fall; it would be apparent that there is nothing in the experience itself to rule out the suggestion that there might be a thousand exactly similar experiences occurring in association with the same body—hence a thousand souls simultaneously associated with that body—and equally nothing to rule out the suggestion that the, or each, soul having such an experience is just one evanescent member of such a temporal series as Kant spoke of—hence, perhaps, a thousand souls the next moment. If this suggestion is to be ruled out, it must be on grounds extraneous to the experience itself. But the fact that this is so is masked by the use of "I" and "me"—expressions which, even while they seem in this context to shake off, yet surreptitiously invoke, the ordinary criteria of distinctness and identity of persons. For when *a man says* "I," then there speaks *one* identifiable man: he can be *distinguished* as *one* by ordinary criteria and *identified* by ordinary criteria as, perhaps, Professor X, the Cartesian.

The fact is that a Cartesian and an anti-Cartesian alike, and anyone else who wants to be taken seriously on the subject of the soul, wants his doctrine to have the consequence that a perfectly ordinary man, in the course of a perfectly ordinary life, has just one soul or consciousness which lasts him throughout. There is only one way of guaranteeing this consequence; and that is to allow that the notions of singularity and identity of souls or consciousnesses are conceptually dependent on those of singularity and identity of men or people. But if we allow this, we must reject a Cartesian conception of the soul.

The arguments I have used to bring out a central incoherence in the doctrine of Cartesian dualism are arguments of a partly logical, and partly epistemological, character. They turn essentially on the notions of the identity, and of the identification, of particular things. The importance of these notions, both in the present connection and in others, has recently received a fair measure of acknowledgment in English philosophy. But, as my references to Kant have shown, these arguments are not essentially novelties, any more than is the recognition of the importance of these notions. The progress of philosophy, at least, is dialectical: we return to old insights in new and, we hope, improved forms.

P. F. Strawson

SOUL[1]

Kant's exposure of the illusions of rational psychology is both brilliant and profound. It is philosophical criticism of the highest order. Yet it must be confessed that the development of the thought in the text is often dark and involved; and much of its obscurity is due to a certain incompleteness in the exposure, an inadequate consideration of a matter of central importance. I begin by noting, crudely and briefly, (1) the nature of the doctrine to be attacked, (2) the main line of Kant's attack upon it, and (3) the diagnosis which Kant offers of the sources of the illusion. Then I proceed to explain and elaborate and, where necessary, to criticize and to supplement, Kant's doctrine.

The doctrine to be attacked is the doctrine that each of us, by the mere fact of conscious experience, knows that he exists as a Cartesian thinking substance, i.e., as an immaterial, persisting, non-composite, individual subject of thoughts and experiences, capable of existence in total independence of body or matter.

The main line of attack is in accordance with the principle of significance. In order to claim knowledge of the existence of an object falling under a certain concept, we must have, and must have occasion to make use of, empirical criteria for the application of that concept. Sensible intuition, in Kant's terminology, must offer us an object which satisfies those criteria. A crucial concept in the present case is that of numerical identity through time, the persistence of an identical thing;[2] but there neither is, nor could be, any intuition (empirical awareness) of a persisting immaterial subject of experiences.

The diagnosis of the sources of the illusion is that the rational psychologist, the Cartesian philosopher of the soul, confuses the unity of experiences with the experience of unity. It is indeed a necessary condition of the possibility of representations constituting *experience*

---

[1]Part 3, Section II of *The Bounds of Sense: An Essay on Kant's Critique of Pure Reason* (London: Methuen & Co., 1966). Reprinted by permission of the author and publisher.
  As is standard, Strawson's page references to the first edition of Kant's *Critique of Pure Reason* are prefaced by an "A," and to the second edition by a "B." The page references in brackets are to the selections from the *Critique* which appear in the present volume.
[2]A 365 [See Kant selection above, p. 83.—Ed.].

that there should be such unity and connection between the members of a temporally extended series of experiences as to provide the basis of the possibility of that ascription of experiences to oneself in which we express our empirical self-consciousness. This does not mean that there is any such thing as awareness of an immaterial object which is the unitary subject of all those experiences; though only such awareness would justify the Cartesian conception of the soul. Yet by a natural and powerful illusion we mistake the necessary unity of consciousness for just such an awareness of a unitary subject.

Set out as above, the diagnosis may well puzzle us. Why should unity of consciousness, a certain connectedness of experiences, be misunderstood in just this way? There seems, at least, to be a step missing. There are, in fact, several steps missing. We must try to fill them in; and since the matter is not uncomplicated, the exposition shall proceed, in the next section, by numbered paragraphs.

1. The Exposure of the Illusion: A Reconstruction

1. The transcendental unity of apperception. It will be helpful first to remind ourselves of the significance of the idea of the necessary unity of consciousness, or the unity of apperception, as this emerged from the discussion of the Transcendental Deduction. What was the transcendental unity of consciousness required for, and what did it require? It required that a temporally extended series of experiences should have a certain character of connectedness and unity, secured to it by concepts of the objective, and it required this as a fundamental condition of the possibility of empirical self-consciousness. That experience should be experience of a unified objective world at least makes room for the idea of *one* subjective or experiential route through the world, traced out by *one* series of experiences which together yield *one* unified experience of the world—a potential autobiography. We have here, as it were, the basic ground for the possibility of an empirical use for the concept of the subject of such an autobiography, the concept of the self.

2. The empirical concept of a subject of experience: a person. This necessary unity, however, supplies only the basic ground, not the full conditions, for the use of such a concept. It is quite clearly implicit in Kant's position that any use of the concept of a numerically identical subject of experiences persisting through time requires empirically applicable criteria of identity, and that none such are supplied merely by the kind of connectedness of inner experiences provided for by the necessary unity of apperception. On the second point we shall have more to say later. On the first point we must remark now that it is one of the weaknesses of Kant's exposition that he barely alludes to the fact that our ordinary concept of *personal* identity does carry with it empirically applicable criteria for the numerical identity through time of a subject of experiences (a man or human being) and that these criteria, though not the same as those for bodily identity, involve an essential reference to the human body.[3] Kant does not pass the point over entirely in silence. He alludes to it, though obscurely, in the sentence: "Its [the soul's] permanence during life is of course evident, since the thinking being (as man) is itself likewise an object of the outer senses."[4]

The point to which Kant thus alludes in passing is surely of the first importance. It means that we have, after all, a concept, which satisfies the most stringent critical requirements, of a persisting subject of experiences (a man). This concept supplies an absolutely firm basis for a genuinely object-referring use of personal names, and of personal pronouns, in sentences in which states of consciousness, inner experiences, are ascribed to the objects referred to by the names or pronouns. A man is something perceptibly (if only relatively) permanent, a persistent and identifiable object of intuition, a possible subject of a biography or autobiography. Instead of talking, dubiously, of an experiential route through the world, of one series of experiences constituting such a route, we may talk, confidently, of an undeniably persistent object, a man, who perceptibly traces a physical, spatio-temporal route through the world and to whom a series of experiences may be ascribed with no fear that there is nothing persistent to which they are being ascribed.

3. *No criteria of personal identity invoked in immediate self-ascription of current or recalled experiences.* And now we come to the fact that lies at the root of the Cartesian illusion. It may be put as follows. When a man (a subject of experience) ascribes a current or directly remembered state of consciousness to himself, no use whatever of any criteria of personal identity is required to justify his use of the pronoun "I" to refer to the subject of that experience. It would make no sense to think or say: *This* inner experience is occurring, but is it occurring to *me*? (This feeling is anger; but is it I who am feeling it?) Again, it would make no sense to think or say: I distinctly remember *that* inner experience occurring, but did it occur to me? (I remember that terrible feeling of loss; but was it I who felt it?) There is nothing

---

[3]The topic of personal identity has been well discussed in recent philosophy. I shall take the matter as understood.
[4]B 415 [p. 87].

that one can thus encounter or recall in the field of inner experience
such that there can be any question of one's applying criteria of subject-
identity to determine whether the encountered or recalled experience
belongs to oneself—or to someone else. (I think it could be said, without
serious exaggeration, that it is because Kant recognized this truth that
his treatment of the subject is so greatly superior to Hume's.)

*4. Reference to the empirically identifiable subject not in practice
lost in criterionless self-ascription.*   When "I" is thus used, without any
need or any possibility of its use being justified by empirical criteria
of subject-identity, it does not, however, lose its role of referring to a
subject. "I" can be used without criteria of subject-identity and yet refer
to a subject. It can do so because—perhaps—it issues publicly from
the mouth of a man who is recognizable and identifiable as the person
he is by the application of empirical criteria of personal identity; or,
even if used in soliloquy, is used by a person who would acknowledge
the applicability of those criteria in settling questions as to whether he,
the very man who now ascribes to himself this experience, was or was
not the person who, say, performed such-and-such an action in the past.
"I" can be used without criteria of subject-identity and yet refer to
a subject because, even in such a use, the links with those criteria
are not in practice severed.

*5. The illusion of a purely inner reference for "I" (of an independent
immaterial individual; of soul as substance).*   The links between
criterionless self-ascription and empirical criteria of subject-identity
are not *in practice* severed. But in philosophical reflection they may be.
It is easy to become intensely aware of the immediate character, of the
purely inner basis, of such self-ascription while both retaining the sense
of ascription to a subject and forgetting that immediate reports of experience have this character of ascriptions to a subject only because of
the links I have mentioned with ordinary criteria of personal identity.
Thus there arises a certain illusion: the illusion of a purely inner and
yet subject-referring use for "I." If we try to abstract this use, to shake
off the connection with ordinary criteria of personal identity, to arrive at a kind of subject-reference which is wholly and adequately based
on nothing but inner experience, what we really do is simply to deprive
our use of "I" of any referential force whatever. It will simply express,
as Kant would say, "consciousness in general." If we nevertheless
continue to think of the "I" as having referential force, as referring to
a subject, then, just because we have really nothing left but the bare
form of reference, it will appear that the object of this reference must be
an object of singular purity and simplicity—a pure, individual, immaterial substance.

Kant sees clearly how the key fact, that immediate self-ascription of thoughts and experiences involves no application of criteria of subject-identity, simultaneously explains three things: it explains the temptation to permit ourselves the use of the notion of the subject of experience ("I") while thinking exclusively in terms of the inner contents of consciousness (the contents of "inner sense"); it explains why that notion, so used, is really quite empty of content; and it explains why it *seems*, therefore, to be the notion of an absolutely simple, identical, immaterial individual.

6. Kant's short cut. Kant's insight was unparalleled, but his exposition is obscure. One of the reasons for its obscurity is that he takes a short cut. As I have remarked, he makes only a minimal reference to the empirical criteria of subject-identity, to the empirical concept of a subject of experience. He does not explicitly say that the delusive use of "I" which has just been discussed results from abstracting it from its ordinary setting, from ignoring its connection with the empirical concept of a subject. Instead he connects that use with the philosophical employment which he has already made of the first personal pronoun in expounding the doctrine of the necessary unity of consciousness, the transcendental unity of apperception. He says that the delusive use of "I" merely *expresses* that unity which makes experience possible.

Is this a flaw in his exposition? I think the omission is a flaw. That bits of the diagnosis have to be supplied means that it is, so far, incomplete. But the doctrine that the delusive, non-referential use of "I" (or: the delusive, non-referential thought of the subject) "expresses" the necessary unity of consciousness might, I think, be defended. For any empirical (i.e., legitimate) use to be made of the concept of a subject of experiences it is required, certainly, that there should be such empirically applicable criteria of subject-identity as are supplied by our ordinary concept of a person as something which, *inter alia*, is an object of outer sense. This rule is general. As we have seen, not even the use of the concept of a subject which is made in ascription of immediate experiences to oneself (in consciousness of *oneself* as being in such-and-such a state) would be possible unless this requirement were satisfied. Nevertheless, in the theory of the transcendental unity of apperception, Kant has shown that there are certain necessary conditions of the possibility of self-consciousness which can be described coherently without describing the *full* conditions of this possibility and in particular without referring to our conception of a subject of experiences as himself being an object of outer sense. It is not unreasonable to hold that when we abstract from this last feature of our conception of such a subject, as we certainly do when we entertain the delusive, non-referential thought of a pure subject of experience, we retain in this thought (though no doubt confusedly enough) the idea of that connectedness of experiences which has been shown to be a fundamental necessary condition of the possibility of empirical self-consciousness, a minimal condition of the occurrence of anything that can properly be called experience. Whether we realize it or not, our delusive thought is at least the thought of experiences so connected, so unified. The satisfaction of the conditions required by the transcendental unity of apperception is a necessary condition of our illusion, as it is of the empirical concept of a subject of experience. It is not a sufficient condition of either, not even of the illusion; for in fact we arrive at the illusion by abstraction from the empirical concept. But when we thus abstract from the empirical concept to generate the illusion, we do not also abstract from the conditions required by the transcendental unity of apperception. So it can, after all, be said that it is, in effect, just this unity of consciousness which, when in the grip of the illusion, we are led to mistake for the consciousness of a unitary subject.

7. *The coup de grâce to Cartesianism.* Kant is not content merely to expose the illusion in rational psychology. He underlines its emptiness by pointing out that, if we succumb to the illusion, we are powerless to defend our conclusions against alternative and equally empty theories. The rational psychologist maintains that every man has immediate assurance of the existence of his own soul as immaterial substance, identical throughout the succession of its states. To this we can reply that whatever assurance he expresses by this claim is equally compatible with the hypothesis of a whole series of soul-substances, each of which transmits its states and the consciousness of them to the next in the series, along with all that it has acquired by earlier transmissions of the same kind from earlier members of the series— as motion might be transmitted from one to another of a series of elastic balls.[5] This suggestion is no more, and no less, futile than the original claim.

This line of attack could be pressed farther than Kant presses it. Thus when the man (a rational psychologist?) speaks, we could suggest that there are, perhaps, a thousand souls simultaneously thinking the thoughts his words express, having qualitatively indistinguishable experiences such as he, the man, would currently claim. How could the man persuade us that there was only one such soul associated with his body? (How could the—or each—soul persuade itself of its uniqueness?)

---

[5] A 363-4, footnote [p. 82].

The generalized point of such attacks is this. We *have* criteria of singularity and identity for subjects of experience (people, men). If we are to talk of individual souls or consciousnesses as well, we *need* criteria of singularity and identity for them. The only way to guarantee a consequence which must surely rate as an adequacy condition for an admissible concept of an individual soul or consciousness—viz., that a normal man, in the course of a normal life, has at any time just one soul or consciousness which lasts him throughout—is to allow that the notions of singularity and identity of souls or consciousnesses are conceptually dependent on, conceptually derivative from, the notions of singularity and identity of men or people. The rule for deriving the criteria we need from the criteria we have is very simple. It is: *one* person, *one* consciousness; *same* person, *same* consciousness. Acceptance of this rule of derivation, however, is the suicide of rational psychology.

Kant's failure to press this point home is but an aspect of his neglect of the empirical concept of a subject of experience.

2. *Hume and Kant on the Self*

Between Kant's treatment of the topic of the self and Hume's there are points of resemblance. There are also profound differences. Kant's repeated point, that there is no inner intuition of the subject itself, that "in inner intuition there is nothing permanent"[6], recalls Hume's famous sentence: "When I enter most intimately into what I call myself, I always stumble on some particular perception or other . . . I never catch myself at any time without a perception, and can never observe anything but the perception."[7] Again, the scantiness of allusion, in Kant, is paralleled by the total absence of allusion, in Hume, to the man as "object of the outer sense", to the role played by bodily identity in the empirical concept of a subject of experience.

Here the resemblance ends. Hume is obliged to give some account of the idea of "what he calls himself". He attempts to do so by finding between the members of the class of his "perceptions" such relations (of resemblance and causation) as will account for the "feigning" of an identical subject to which they all belong. He attempts to reproduce in this field the very same kind of analysis or explanation of the notion of identity as has served him in the discussion of our belief in the continued identity of material objects through discontinuous observation. Distinct perceptions are counted as perceptions of the

---

[6]B 413 [p. 86], cf. also B 420, A 381, etc.
[7]*Treatise of Human Nature*, Book I, Part IV, Chapter 6 [See Hume above.—Ed.].

same body because certain relations obtain between them. Just so, he suggests, distinct perceptions are counted as belonging to the same self because certain relations obtain between *them*. It does not matter much here how we read this "because": whether as introducing a reference to criteria of identity or, in Hume's own anti-rationalist spirit, as introducing a reference to factors which *cause* our fictions. Either way we must be struck by the fatal lack of analogy between the two types of case. In so far as such an explanation (or analysis) seems satisfactory for the case of taking distinct perceptions to be perceptions of the same body, it does so because we are able to think of the psychological mechanisms (or criteria) involved as having a field of perceptions to work on, upon which they can operate *selectively*, producing a feigning (a judgment) of identity here, inhibiting one there. Even a fictitious identity needs a contrast. Nothing could induce the thought: Here's (an appearance of) the same *x* as before, unless something could induce the thought: Here's (an appearance of) a different *x*. But in the case of self-identity nothing which belongs to the field in which the mechanisms are supposed to operate can possibly be excluded by those mechanisms from ascription to the one self. The mechanisms are idle; or, rather, it is they that are the fictions. The search for them has the same futility as the search for criteria of subject-identity to be applied in the field of inner experience to determine whether a current experience is or is not one's own.

From the incoherence into which Hume's theory of the self thus lapses, and of which he himself was not unaware, Kant's exposure of the illusion of rational psychology is altogether free. His analysis indeed needs supplementation, as I have tried to show, by a far more explicit acknowledgment than any he makes of the role of empirically applicable criteria of subject-identity. The point is, however, that nothing in Kant's account excludes, and everything in it invites, such supplementation. Hume, on the other hand, does not simply offer to dispel a philosophers' (rational psychologists') illusion. His attempt is to give an adequate explanation of the vulgar conception of the self as subject of experience; but the terms in which he conceives of such an explanation make it impossible for the attempt to succeed.

3. The Complications of Transcendental Idealism
So far, in this discussion of the Paralogisms, I have completely ignored Kant's commitment to the doctrines of transcendental idealism; and it is an important point that the force of Kant's exposure of the illusions of rational psychology can be conveyed without any reference to those doctrines. To Kant himself, however, the commitment to trans-

cendental idealism seemed to make the exposure of the illusion a matter of particular urgency.

It would be a great stumbling-block, or rather would be the one unanswerable objection, to our whole critique if there were a possibility of knowing a priori *that all thinking beings are in themselves simple substances . . . and that they are conscious of their existence as separate and distinct from all matter. For by such procedure we should have taken a step beyond the world of sense and have entered into the field of noumena.*[8]

I shall reserve until later a general discussion of the complications of transcendental idealism; and not till then shall I consider fully the first edition version of the fourth paralogism, in which this doctrine figures so largely. But something must be said now to show how Kant views the connection between that doctrine and the issues I have just been discussing.

Let us begin by noting how it might be possible to read even the cry of alarm I have just quoted in a way consistent with the weakest possible interpretation of transcendental idealism. What is at risk, it might be said, if the doctrine of rational psychology is upheld, is simply the principle that any significant claim to nonanalytic knowledge of objects depends on the use of empirical criteria for the application of the concepts in terms of which the claim is expressed. To "enter the field of noumena" would simply be to make good a knowledge-claim of such a kind as to show that this principle could, in at least one case, be violated with impunity. The general methodological importance of dispelling, by careful diagnosis of its sources, the illusion of rational psychology consists in precisely this, that success in dispelling the illusion enables us to reaffirm the principle in the face of the most seductive of all apparent counter-examples to it.

It would be unplausible to hold that this is all Kant means. The doctrine that things in space and time are appearances only, that things are not *in themselves* extended, that I do not, as I am *in myself*, first feel sick, then sorry, is more plausibly held to mean at least that successive feelings and perceptions and their apparent objects are (in an unknown way) dependent for their existence on something of a character completely different (and completely unknown). The "field of noumena" is the field of that upon which these dependent existences are thus dependent.

[8]B 409 [p. 84].

Among the multitude of naïve questions which spontaneously suggest themselves let us approach the one which it is most relevant to ask now by way of another which seems to present less immediate diffi-culty. Why, if the character of the noumenal is completely unknown, does Kant speak, on the one hand, of outer objects as *they* are in them-selves and, on the other, of ourselves as *we* are in ourselves? Is it at least known that the field of the noumenal contains two distinct types of existence? An at least partially Kantian answer to this question might go as follows. Nothing of the kind is known. It is just that within ex-perience (the field of appearances) a distinction is drawn, without which experience would be impossible, between perceived objects of outer sense (bodies in space) and the successive experiences which human beings count as states of themselves. (On one interpretation of transcen-dental idealism, indeed, this distinction is not ultimate. For the moment we may disregard this. The fact is that the distinction is drawn, and must be drawn if experience is to be possible at all.) Now the general depen-dence of both bodies in space and inner states of ourselves on the noumenal unknown is expressed by describing both of the former, in relation to the latter, as "appearances" of "things as they are in them-selves." Hence it becomes natural to speak, on the one hand, of outer objects as *they* are in themselves and, on the other, of ourselves as *we* are in ourselves. But this way of speaking reflects nothing more than the distinction which is drawn, and must be drawn, in experience, between outer objects and states of consciousness. It implies no knowl-edge of any distinction between types of noumenal existence. For all we know the noumenal may be quite homogeneous.[9]

This answer takes account of only some of the features of trans-cendental idealism. Now let us ask the harder question. Granted that, in the way just indicated, transcendental idealism is much more than a methodological principle of significance, why is Kant so sure that if the pretensions of rational psychology could be made out, we should have entered the field of noumena? Why should the rational psycholo-gist, if successful, have done more than show that a certain principle of significance in knowledge-claims is, at least in one peculiar instance, untenable? Why should it not still be possible to maintain that the nou-menal, that upon which all the content of experience, inner and outer, depends, is completely unknown and in principle unknowable? The answer we must give to this question shows how inadequate is the an-swer we ventured to the previous one. When all is said and done, Kant's theory of the self is *not* exhausted by deploying, and supplementing,

[9]A 359–360.

those features of it which are called upon in dispelling the illusions of rational psychology; nor is the thesis of transcendental idealism exhausted by that short statement of it in terms of dependence of existence which I have just given. The reason in both cases is the same. What Kant intends to express by the "I think" of apperception is not simply that connectedness of experiences, ensured by means of concepts of the objective, which is the fundamental condition of the possibility of empirical self-consciousness. For him the "I think" of apperception represents also the tangential point of contact between the field of noumena and the world of appearances. "In the consciousness of myself in mere thought I am the *being itself*, although nothing in myself is thereby given for thought."[10]

Of course transcendental idealism would scarcely merit its name unless some such point of contact were made. The title of "idealism" might indeed be justified by the recurrent suggestion that outer objects are reducible to "representations." The title of "transcendentalism" might indeed be justified by the doctrine that all that we know in experience, including our own states of mind, is dependent upon some unknown ground inaccessible to experience. But if that were all, there would be nothing particularly transcendental about the idealism and nothing particularly idealist about the transcendentalism. What makes the name "transcendental idealism" more than a mere conjunction is the language of extreme subjectivism in which the source of *all* the structural features of the world is declared to be in *our* subject, "the subject in which the representation of time has its original ground."[11] But what could we make of this language unless the "subject" of these slogans were *somehow* connected with what we ordinarily understand by ourselves?

The concept of a thinking being "in general" is supposed to supply the point of connection. Each human being, though he can never be conscious of an object, himself, as merely a thinking being, but only as a being who thinks, feels or perceives, successively, now this, now that, yet *is* a thinking being, a seat of the categories, and to that extent a source, and not merely an outcome, of the conditions of experience. Kant goes much further, of course, in accordance with the demands of the disastrous model whose sources we have not yet fully explored. It is not merely *our* understanding which is the source of the categories, it is *our* sensibility to which the forms of space and time are due; and it is because the former must affect the latter in the generation of empiri-

[10]B 429.
[11]B 422 [p. 88].

cal self-knowledge that *we* appear to *ourselves* otherwise than *we* are in *ourselves*. The confident use of first personal pronouns is bewildering enough; but it is more than bewildering. It shows the model shaking itself to pieces. After all, it seems, a good deal can be known about the noumenal self, though not quite what the rational psychologist hoped. In a quite extraordinary clause Kant writes: "The being that thinks in us is under the impression that it knows itself through pure categories and precisely through those categories which (in each type of category) express absolute unity."[12] To that extent the "being that thinks in us" appears to be deluded. But if the being that thinks in us is under the impression that its understanding affects its sensibility in the production of a temporal succession of connected perceptions, feelings and thoughts (including this one), then, apparently, the being that thinks in us is not deluded at all, but absolutely right! I do not deny that all this, too, might be construed as a mere manner of speaking about the structural characteristics of phenomenal fact. So to construe it would be to treat the model *as* a model, an expository framework to be discarded when its purposes are served. But it seems, to say the least, unlikely that this is how Kant viewed the matter.[13]

[12]B 402.
[13]See further Part IV, especially Section 4 [of *The Bounds of Sense*—Ed.].

4
Franz Brentano

THE DISTINCTION BETWEEN MENTAL AND PHYSICAL PHENOMENA[1]

1

The data of our consciousness make up a world† which, taken in its entirety, falls into two great classes, the class of *physical* and the class of *mental* phenomena. We spoke of this distinction much earlier, in the course of defining the concept of psychology, and we returned to it again in our investigation of method. But what was said is still insufficient; what was then only suggested in passing we must now delineate more firmly and rigorously.

The fact that neither unity nor complete clarity has yet been achieved regarding the line of demarcation between the two areas seems to make this all the more necessary. We have already had occasion to see how physical phenomena which appear in the imagination have been taken to be mental. But there are many other cases of confusion as well. Even psychologists of considerable importance may find it difficult to vindicate themselves against the charge of self-contradiction.[2] We occasionally encounter such assertions as that sensation and imagination are differentiated by the fact that one occurs as the result of

[1]From Franz Brentano, *Psychology from the Empirical Standpoint*, trans. D. B. Terrell (London: Routledge & Kegan Paul, Ltd; New York: Humanities Press, forthcoming publication), Vol. 1, Book II, Chap. 1. Reprinted by permission of the publishers. First published in German in 1874.

†[TRANSLATOR'S NOTE: The original, which reads, "Die gesamte Welt unserer Erscheinungen," would be too misleading in literal translation as "the entire world of our phenomena," or "of our appearances." Brentano rejected the Kantian interpretation of "phenomenon" in the first chapter of the *Psychologie vom empirischen Standpunkt*, and for him the word *Erscheinung* functions very much as did "idea" for Locke and "perception" for Hume, i.e., as a general term for any datum of consciousness. The entire sentence is very probably an echo of the beginning of Bain's *Mental Science*: "Human Knowledge, Experience, or Consciousness, falls under two great departments. . . ." D.B.T.]

[2]Thus I, at least, am unable successfully to bring into harmony the various definitions which A. Bain has given in one of his latest psychological works, *Mental Science* (London, 3d ed., 1872). On page 120, No. 59, he says that mental science (Science of Mind, which he also calls Subject Science) is based on self-consciousness or introspective attention;

a physical phenomenon, while the other is evoked, according to the laws of association, by means of a mental phenomenon. But along with this the same psychologists admit that what appears in sensation does not correspond to its efficient cause. Accordingly, it turns out that what they call physical phenomena never appear to us in actual fact, and that we have no presentation of them whatsoever; surely this is a strange way in which to misuse the term "phenomenon"! When affairs are in such a state, we can not refrain from taking a somewhat closer look at the problem.

2

We do not aim to clear up the matter by a definition according to the traditional rules of logicians. These rules have lately been subjected to impartial criticism of various kinds, and there is still much more that might be added to what has been said against them. Our object is the elucidation of the two terms: physical phenomenon—mental phenomenon. We wish to exclude misunderstanding and confusion in connection with them. And for this we needn't be concerned about the means used, if only they really serve to produce clarity.

Giving more general, superordinate definitions is not the only useful means that can be employed for such an end. Just as induction is contrasted with deduction in the sphere of demonstration, here definition by way of the specific, i.e., by way of an example, is contrasted with definition by means of the more general. And the former method will be more appropriate as long as the particular term is more intelligible than the general. Hence, it may be a more effective procedure to define the term "color" by saying that it designates the general class for red, blue, green, and yellow, than to choose to give an account of

the eye, the ear, the organs of touch, are means of observing the physical world, the "object world," as he expresses himself. On the other hand, on page 198, No. 4 he says that: "The perception of matter or the Object consciousness is connected with the putting forth of Muscular Energy, as opposed to Passive Feeling." And in his explanation he adds: "In purely *passive* feeling, as in those of our sensations that do not call forth our muscular energies, we are not perceiving matter, we are in a state of subject consciousness." He explains this in terms of the sensation of warmth when one takes a warm bath, and in terms of those cases of gentle contact in which no muscular activity occurs, and explains that under the same conditions, sound, even possibly light and color as well, can be purely subject-experiences. Thus for examples of subject-consciousness, he draws on those very sensations by way of eye, ear, and organs of touch which in the other passage he had indicated to be the mediators of object-consciousness in contrast to subject-consciousness. [All quotations from sources originally written in English are given in the original version, rather than having been retranslated from Brentano's German version.]

red—following the opposite procedure—as a particular species of color. Definition by way of particular cases will perform still more useful service in connection with terms, such as those involved in our case, which are not at all common in ordinary life, while the names of the particular phenomena comprehended under them are familiar enough. So let us start with an attempt to make our concepts clear by way of examples.

Every presentation *(Vorstellung)* of sensation or imagination offers an example of the mental phenomenon; and here I understand by presentation not that which is presented, but the act of presentation. Thus, hearing a sound, seeing a colored object, sensing warm or cold, and the comparable states of imagination as well, are examples of what I mean; but thinking of a general concept, provided such a thing does actually occur, is equally so. Furthermore, every judgment, every recollection, every expectation, every inference, every conviction or opinion, every doubt, is a mental phenomenon. And again, every emotion, joy, sorrow, fear, hope, pride, despair, anger, love, hate, desire, choice, intention, astonishment, wonder, contempt, etc., is such a phenomenon.

Examples of physical phenomena, on the other hand, are a color, a shape, a landscape, which I see; a musical chord, which I hear; heat, cold, odor, which I sense; as well as comparable images, which appear to me in my imagination.

These examples may suffice as concrete illustrations of the distinction between the two classes.

3

Nevertheless, we will attempt to give a definition of the mental phenomenon in another, more unified way. For this, there is available a definition we have used before, when we said that by the term, mental phenomena, we designate presentations and, likewise, all those phenomena which are based on presentations. It scarcely requires notice that, once again, by presentation we understand here not what is presented but the presenting of it. This presentation forms the basis not merely of judgments, but also of desires, as well as of every other mental act. We cannot judge of anything, cannot desire anything, cannot hope for anything, or fear anything, if it is not presented. Hence, the definition which we gave embraces all of the examples just introduced and, in general, all of the phenomena belonging to this domain.

It is a sign of the immature state in which psychology finds itself that one can scarcely utter a single sentence about mental phenomena which would not be disputed by many. Still, the great majority agree with what we just said; presentations are the basis for the other mental phenomena. Thus, Herbart is quite correct in saying: "In every case of emotion, something, no matter how diversified and complicated, must be in consciousness as something presented; so that this particular presentation is included in this particular feeling. And every time we have a desire . . . [we] also have in our thoughts that which we desire."[3]

Herbart then goes farther, however. He sees nothing but certain states of presentation, which are derivable from presentations, in all other phenomena; a viewpoint which has already been attacked repeatedly, especially by Lotze, on decisive grounds. Among others, J. B. Meyer recently set forth a lengthy criticism of it in his exposition of Kant's psychology. But he is not satisfied with denying that feelings and desires can be derived from presentations; he maintains that phenomena of this sort can exist even without any presentation.[4] Indeed, Meyer believes that the lowest animals have only feelings and desires, but no presentations, and that the life even of the higher animals and of human beings begins with mere feeling and desire, while presentation first emerges as development progresses.[5] In this way he, too, seems to come into conflict with our contention.

Nevertheless, if I am not mistaken, the contradiction is more apparent than real. From several of his expressions it seems to me to follow that Meyer understands the concept of presentation more narrowly than we have understood it, while he broadens the concept of feeling to an equal extent. "Presentation," he says, "first enters in when the sensed change in one's own state can be understood as the result of an outer stimulus, even if this expresses itself, at first, only in the unconscious looking or feeling around for an external object which results from it." If Meyer were to understand the same thing under presentation as we do, then it would be impossible for him to speak in this way. He would see that a state like the one which he describes as the origin of presentation would already include an abundant number of presentations: for example, presentations of temporal proximity, of spatial proximity, and of cause and effect. If all of this must already be present in the soul in order that a presentation in J. B. Meyer's sense might be formed, it is surely clear that such a thing cannot be the basis of every other mental phenomenon. On the contrary, the very state of being present *(Gegenwartig-sein)* which belongs to each of the things named is precisely a state of being presented *(Vorgestelltsein)* in our sense. And

---

[3]*Psych. als Wissensch*, Part II, Sec. l, chap. i, § 103. Cf. also Drobisch, *Empir. Psychol.*, pp. 38 and 348, and others of Herbart's school.
[4]*Kant's Psychologie* (Berlin, 1870), pp. 92 ff.
[5]*Ibid.*, p. 94.

such is the case generally, wherever something appears in consciousness: whether it be hated or loved or regarded indifferently; whether it be affirmed or rejected, or, in the case of complete withholding of judgment—I cannot express myself better than by saying—presented. As we use the word "to present," "to be presented" comes to the same thing as "to appear."

Even J. B. Meyer recognizes that a presentation in this sense is presupposed by every feeling, even the most lowly feelings of pleasure and displeasure; but deviating from us in his terminology he calls *it* a feeling and not a presentation. This seems to me to follow from these words: "Between non-sensation and sensation there is no intermediate state . . . Now the simplest form of sensation does not need to be more than the mere *sensing* of the *change* in one's own body or a part of it which results from some stimulus. A creature endowed with sensation of this sort would then have only a *feeling of its own states.* A sensibility of the soul for the changes which are advantageous or harmful to it could very well be immediately connected *with this vital feeling* for the events beneath one's own skin, even if this *new sensitivity* were not simply derivable from that feeling; such a soul could have *feelings* of pleasure and displeasure *along with the sensation* . . . A soul so endowed would still possess no presentation . . ."[6] We see clearly that what is, in our opinion, the only thing to deserve the name "feeling," also arises, in J. B. Meyer's opinion, as a successor [to something else. Its predecessor] falls under the concept of presentation, as we understand it, and forms the indispensable presupposition of the other. Hence it appears that if Meyer's viewpoint is translated into our language, the contradiction disappears of its own accord.

Perhaps the same is also true of others who express themselves similarly to Meyer. Still, we may surely find that, as regards some kinds of sensual feelings of pleasure and displeasure, someone does actually hold the opinion that there is no presentation, even in our sense, on which they are based. We cannot deny a certain temptation in that direction, at least. This holds, for example, in regard to feelings which are caused by a cut or a burn. If someone is cut, then for the most part he

---

[6]Kant's *Psychol.*, p. 92. J. B. Meyer appears to understand sensation just as Ueberweg does in his *Logik*, I, 36 (2d ed., p. 64): "Perception is distinguished from mere sensation . . . by the fact that consciousness in the latter is attached only to the subjective state, but in perception it is directed to an element which is perceived and accordingly . . . stands over against the act of perception as a distinct and objective thing." If this opinion of Ueberweg concerning sensation as distinct from perception were correct, sensation would none the less include a presentation in our sense. Why we hold it not to be correct will be shown later.

has no further perception of touch; if he is burned, no further perception of heat; but pain alone seems to be present in the one case and the other.

Nonetheless, there is no doubt that even here the feeling is based on a presentation. In such cases we always have the presentation of a definite spatial location, which we ordinarily specify in relation to one or the other of the visible and palpable parts of our body. We say that our foot hurts, or our hand hurts, this or the other place on our body is in pain. In the first place, then, those who look on such a spatial presentation as something originally given by means of the neural stimulation itself will therefore be unable to deny that a presentation is the basis of this feeling. But others, too, cannot avoid making the same assumption. For we have within us not merely the presentation of a definite spatial location, but also that of a particular sensory quality, analogous to color, sound, and other so-called sensory qualities, a quality which belongs among the physical phenomena and which is definitely to be distinguished from the accompanying feeling. If we hear a pleasant, mild sound or a shrill one, a harmonious chord or a discord, it will occur to no one to identify the sound with the accompanying feeling of pleasure or pain. But, likewise, when a cut, a burn, or a tickle arouses a feeling of pain or pleasure in us, we must maintain in a similar manner the distinction between a physical phenomenon, which enters in as the object of outer perception, and a mental phenomenon of feeling, which accompanies its appearance, even though the superficial observer is rather inclined to confusion here.

The principal basis of the illusion is probably the following. It is well known that our sensations are mediated by the so-called afferent *(sensibeln)* nerves. It was believed earlier that specialized nerves served exclusively as conductors for each class of sensory qualities, color, sound, and so on. Recently, physiology has inclined more and more to the opposite point of view.[7] Particularly, it teaches almost universally that the nerves for tactile sensations, when stimulated in one way, produce in us the sensations of heat and cold, and when stimulated in another way, produce the so-called sensations of pain and pleasure. In fact, however, something similar holds for all nerves, insofar as a sensory phenomenon of the kind just mentioned can be aroused in us by way of every nerve. If they are very strongly stimulated, all nerves arouse painful phenomena, which are not distinguished in kind one from another.[8] If a nerve serves as the medium of diverse classes of sensations, it often happens that it serves as the medium of

[7] Cf. especially Wundt, *Physiol. Psychol.*, pp. 345 ff.
[8] Cf. below, Book II, chap. iii, § 6.

several at the same time, as, for example, looking at an electric light results simultaneously in a "beautiful" sensation of color, i.e., one that is pleasant to us, and a painful phenomenon of another class. The nerves of the tactile sense frequently communicate at the same time a so-called sensation of touch, a sensation of heat or cold, and a so-called sensation of pain or pleasure. Now it is manifest that when several sensory phenomena appear together, it is not seldom the case that they are regarded as being *one*. This has been demonstrated in a striking way in connection with the sensations of taste and smell. It is established that almost all of the differences which we are accustomed to look upon as differences of taste are, in fact, only differences in simultaneously occurring phenomena of smell. It is a similar matter when we eat a food cold or warm: we often believe ourselves to have differences in taste which are in fact only differences in phenomena of temperature. It is not to be wondered at, then, if we do not always maintain a strict distinction between what is a phenomenon of temperature and what is a tactile phenomenon. Indeed, we would perhaps not distinguish them at all if they did not ordinarily appear independently of each other. But if now we consider the sensations of feeling *(Gefühlsempfindungen)* we find that for the most part they are bound up with sensations of another class and that when the excitation is very strong these other sensations sink into insignificance beside them. It is very easy, then, to account for the fact that we should be deceived about the occurrence of a particular class of sensory qualities and believe ourselves to have a single sensation instead of two. Since the supervening presentation was accompanied by a relatively very strong feeling, incomparably stronger than the one which followed upon the first kind of quality, this mental phenomenon was regarded as the only one which had newly been experienced. And if the first kind of quality disappeared entirely, then we would believe that we possessed nothing besides a feeling, without any presentation on which it was based.

A further basis of the illusion is that the quality on which the feeling ensues, and the feeling itself, do not bear two distinct names. We call the physical phenomenon, which occurs along with the feeling of pain, itself pain in this case. We do not say that this or that phenomenon in the foot is experienced with pain so much as we say that pain is experienced in the foot. To be sure, this is an equivocation such as we find elsewhere, whenever things stand in a close relationship to each other. We call the body healthy, and in connection with it, the air, food, facial color, and so on, but plainly in different senses. In our case, a physical phenomenon itself is called pleasure or pain, after the feeling of pleasure or pain which accompanies its appearance, and here too the sense is modified. It is as if we should say of a harmonious sound that it is a pleasure to us, because we experience a feeling of pleasure on its occurrence; or that the loss of a friend is a great sorrow to us. Experience shows that equivocation is one of the foremost hindrances to our knowledge of distinctions. It must necessarily be very much so here, where a danger of being deluded exists in and of itself, and the transference of the term was perhaps itself the result of a confusion. Hence, many psychologists were deceived, and further errors were tied up with this one. Many arrived at the false conclusion that the experiencing subject must be present at the place of the injured limb in which a painful phenomenon is localized in perception. For, insofar as they identified the phenomenon with the accompanying feeling of pain, they regarded it as a mental, not as a physical, phenomenon. And for just that reason, they believed its perception in the limb to be an inner, and consequently, an evident and infallible perception.[9] But their opinion is contradicted by the fact that the same phenomena often appear in the same way after the limb has been amputated. Others accordingly argued rather to the opposite effect, skeptically opposing the self-evidence *(Evidenz)* of inner perception. This is all resolved, if one has learned to distinguish between the pain in the sense in which the term designates the apparent property of a part of our body and the feeling of pain which is tied up with sensing it. But if one has done this, then one is no longer inclined to hold that the feeling of sensory pain which one experiences on being injured is not based on any presentation.

We may, accordingly, regard it as an indubitably correct definition of mental phenomena that they are either presentations or (in the sense which has been explained) rest on presentations as their basis. In this we would thus have a second definition of the concept [of mental phenomena] which breaks down into fewer terms. Yet it is not entirely unified, since it presents mental phenomena as divided into two groups.

4

The attempt has been made to give a perfectly unified definition which distinguishes all of the mental phenomena, as contrasted with the physical, by means of negation. All physical phenomena, it is said, manifest extension and definite spatial location, whether they are appearances to sight or another sense, or products of the imagination, which presents

[9]This is the opinion of the Jesuit, Tongiorgi, in his very widely circulated philosophy textbook.

similar objects to us. The opposite, however, is true of mental phenomena; thinking, willing, and so on appear as unextended and without a situation in space.

According to this view, we would be in a position to characterize the physical phenomena easily and rigorously in contrast to the mental, if we were to say that they are those which appear extended and spatial. And, with the same exactitude, the mental phenomena would then be definable, as contrasted with the physical, as those which exhibit no extension or definite spatial location. One could call on Descartes and Spinoza in support of such a differentiation, but particularly on Kant, who declares space to be the form of intuition of outer sensation.

A. Bain has recently given the same definition: "The department of the Object, or Object-World," he says, "is exactly circumscribed by one property, Extension. The world of Subject-experience is devoid of this property.

"A tree or a river is said to possess extended magnitude. A pleasure has no length, breadth, or thickness; it is in no respect an extended thing. A thought or idea may refer to extended magnitudes, but it cannot be said to have extension in itself. Neither can we say that an act of the will, a desire, a belief, occupy dimensions in space. Hence all that comes within the sphere of the Subject is spoken of as the Unextended.

"Thus, if Mind, as commonly happens, is put for the sum total of Subject-experiences, we may define it negatively by a single fact—the absence of Extension."[10]

So it appears that we have found, negatively at least, a unified definition for the sum-total of mental phenomena.

But here, too, unanimity does not prevail among the psychologists, and for diverse reasons we often hear it denied that extension and the absence of extension are differentiating characteristics distinguishing physical and mental phenomena.

Many believe that the definition is false because not only mental, but also many physical phenomena, appear without extension. Thus, a large number of not unimportant psychologists teach that the phenomena of certain senses, or even of the senses in general, originally manifest themselves free of all extension and definite spatial character. This is very generally believed [to be true] of sounds and of the phenomena of smell. According to Berkeley, the same holds true of colors, and according to Platner, of the phenomena of the sense of touch. According to Herbart and Lotze, as well as Hartley, Brown, the two

[10]*Mental Science*, Intro., chap. i.

Mills, H. Spencer, and others, [it is true] of the phenomena of all the external senses. To be sure, it appears to us as if the phenomena which the external senses, particularly vision and the sense of touch, manifest to us were all spatially extended. But the reason for this, it is said, is the fact that on the basis of prior experience we connect with them our gradually developed presentation of *space;* originally without definite spatial location, they are later localized by us. If this should really be the only way in which physical phenomena attain definite spatial location, then we could plainly no longer distinguish the two realms by reference to this property. [The possibility of such a distinction] is decreased still more by the fact that mental phenomena are also localized by us in such a way, as, for example, when we mistakenly place a phenomenon of anger in the irritable lion, and our own thoughts in the space that is filled by us.

So that would be one way, from the point of view of a large number of important psychologists, in which the stated definition must be contested. When all is said, even Bain, who seems to advance it, is to be counted among these thinkers; for he follows Hartley's line of thought completely. He is able to speak as he has spoken only because (even though without complete consistency) he has not included the phenomena of the external senses, in and for themselves, among the physical phenomena.[11]

Others, as I have said, will reject the definition for contrary reasons. It is not so much the claim that all physical phenomena appear extended that arouses their opposition. It is the claim, rather, that all mental phenomena lack extension; according to them, certain mental phenomena also manifest themselves as extended. Aristotle appears to have been of this opinion when, in the first chapter of his treatise on sensation and the object of sense, he regards it as evident, immediately and without previous proof, that sense perception is the act of a physical organ.[12] Modern psychologists and physiologists express themselves similarly at times in connection with certain affects. They speak of feelings of pleasure and pain which appear in the external organs, sometimes, indeed, even after the amputation of the member; and surely, feeling, like perception, is a mental phenomenon. Many also say of sensual desires that they appear localized; and the fact that poets speak, perhaps not of thought, but of bliss and yearning which suffuse the heart and all the parts of the body, is in accord with that view.

[11]See note 2.

[12]*De sens. et sens* 1. p. 436, b, 7. See also what he says in *De anim.* I. 1. p. 403, a, 16 about the affects, especially those of fear.

So we see that the stated distinction is assailed with regard to both physical and mental phenomena. Perhaps both points raised against it are equally unfounded.[13] Nevertheless, a further definition common to mental phenomena is still desirable in any case. For conflict over the question whether certain mental and physical phenomena appear extended or not shows at once that the alleged attribute does not suffice for a distinct differentiation; furthermore, for the mental phenomena it is negative only.

5

What positive attribute will we now be able to advance? Or is there, perhaps, no positive definition at all which holds true of all mental phenomena generally?

A. Bain says that in fact there is none.[14] Nonetheless, psychologists of an earlier period have already directed attention to a particular affinity and analogy which exists among all mental phenomena, while the physical do not share in it. Every mental phenomenon is characterized by what the scholastics of the Middle Ages called the intentional (and also mental)[15] inexistence *(Inexistenz)* of an object *(Gegenstand)*, and what we could call, although in not entirely unambiguous terms, the reference to a content, a direction upon an object (by which we are not to understand a reality in this case), or an immanent objectivity. Each one includes something as object within itself, although not always in the same way. In presentation something is presented, in judgment something is affirmed or denied, in love [something is] loved, in hate [something] hated, in desire [something] desired, etc.[16]

This intentional inexistence is exclusively characteristic of mental phenomena. No physical phenomenon manifests anything similar.

[13]The claim that even mental phenomena appear extended rests plainly on a confusion between physical and mental phenomena similar to the one we became convinced of above, when we established that even sensory feelings are necessarily based on a presentation.

[14]*The Senses and the Intellect,* Intro.

[15]They also use the expression "to be in something objectively," which, if we should wish to make use of it now, could possibly be taken in just the opposite sense, as the designation of a real existence outside of the mind. Nevertheless, it reminds one of the expression "to be immanently objective," which we sometimes use in a similar sense, and in which the "immanently" is intended to exclude the misunderstanding that was to be feared.

[16]Aristotle has already spoken of this mental inherence. In his books on the soul, he says that what is experienced, insofar as it is experienced, is in the one experiencing it, that sense contains what is experienced without its matter, that what is thought is in the thinking intellect. In Philo we likewise find the doctrine of mental existence and inexistence.

Consequently, we can define mental phenomena by saying that they are such phenomena as include an object intentionally within themselves.

But here, too, we come up against conflict and contradiction. And it is Hamilton in particular who denies the alleged property of a whole broad class of mental phenomena, namely, of all those which he designates as feelings, of pleasure and pain in their most diverse shades and varieties. He is in agreement with us concerning the phenomena of thinking and desire. Obviously, there would be no thinking without an object which is thought, no desire without an object which is desired. "In the phenomena of Feeling—the phenomena of Pleasure and Pain —on the contrary, consciousness does not place the mental modification or state before itself; it does not contemplate it apart—as separate from itself—but is, as it were, fused into one. The peculiarity of Feeling, therefore, is that there is nothing but what is subjectively subjective; there is no object different from self—no objectification of any mode of self."[17] In the first case, there would be something there which, according to Hamilton's way of expression, is "objective"; in the second, something which is "objectively subjective," as in self-knowledge, whose object Hamilton therefore calls subject-object; Hamilton, in denying both with regard to feeling, most definitely denies any intentional inexistence to it.

However, what Hamilton says is surely not entirely correct. Certain feelings are unmistakably referred to objects, and language itself indicates these through the expressions it uses. We say that a person rejoices in or about something, that a person sorrows or grieves about something. And once again: that delights me, that pains me, that hurts me, and so on. Joy and sorrow, like affirmation and denial, love and hate, desire and aversion, distinctly ensue upon a presentation and are referred to what is presented in it.

In confusing this, however, with existence in the strict sense, he arrives at his doctrine of the Logos and Ideas, with its wealth of contradictions. The like holds true of the Neo-Platonists. Augustine touches on the same fact in his theory of the *Verbum mentis* and its internal origin. Anselm does so in his well-known ontological argument; and many have alleged the basis of his fallacy to be the fact that he regarded mental existence as if it were actual existence (see Ueberweg, *History of Philosophy*, Vol. II). Thomas Aquinas teaches that what is thought is intentionally in the one thinking, the object of love in the person loving, what is desired in the person desiring, and uses this for theological purposes. When the scripture speaks of an indwelling of the Holy Ghost, he explains this as an intentional indwelling by way of love. And he also seeks to find in intentional inexistence, in the cases of thinking and loving, a certain analogy for the mystery of the Trinity and the procession of the Word and Spirit.

[17]*Lect. on Metaph.*, I, 432.

At the utmost, one could be inclined to agree with Hamilton in *those* cases in which one succumbs most easily, as we saw before, to the illusion that feeling is not based on any presentation: the case of the pain which is aroused by a cut or burn, for example. But its basis is none other than the very temptation toward this hypothesis, which, as we saw, is erroneous. Moreover, even Hamilton recognizes with us the fact that, without exception, presentations form the basis of feelings, and consequently [do so] in these cases as well. Therefore, his denial that feelings have an object seems so much the more striking.

To be sure, one thing is to be granted. The object to which a feeling refers is not always an external object. Even when I hear a harmonious chord, the pleasure which I feel is not really a pleasure in the sound, but a pleasure in the hearing [of it]. Indeed, one might not be mistaken in saying that it even refers to itself in a certain way and, therefore, that what Hamilton asserts, namely, that the feeling is "fused into one" with its object, *does* occur more or less. But this is nothing which does not likewise hold true of many phenomena of presentation and knowledge, as we shall see in our study of inner consciousness. Nevertheless, in them there is still a mental inexistence, a subject-object, to speak Hamilton's language; and the same will therefore hold true of these feelings as well. Hamilton is mistaken when he says that, in them, everything is "subjectively subjective," an expression which is indeed really self-contradictory; for where we can no longer speak of an object, we can no longer speak of a subject either. Even when Hamilton spoke of a fusion-into-one of the feeling with the mental modification, he gave witness against himself if we consider the matter exactly. Every fusion is a unification of several things; and consequently the pictorial expression, which is intended to make us concretely aware of the distinctive character of feeling, still indicates a certain duality in the unity.

We may thus take it to be valid that the intentional inexistence of an object is a general distinguishing characteristic of mental phenomena, which differentiates this class of phenomena from the class of physical phenomena.

6

It is a further general characteristic of all mental phenomena that they are perceived only in inner consciousness, while only outer perception is possible for the physical. Hamilton advances this distinguishing attribute.[18]

---

[18]*Ibid.*

One could believe that such a definition says little, since it would seem more natural to take the opposite course, defining the act by reference to its object, and so defining inner perception, in contrast to all others, as perception of mental phenomena. But inner perception has still another characteristic, apart from the special nature of its object, which distinguishes it: namely, that immediate, infallible self-evidence, which pertains to it alone among all the cases in which we know objects of experience. Thus, if we say that mental phenomena are those which are grasped by means of inner perception, we have accordingly said that their perception is immediately evident.

Still more! Inner perception is not merely unique as immediately evident perception; it is really unique as perception *(Wahrmehmung)* in the strict sense of the word. We have seen that the phenomena of so-called outer perception can in no way be demonstrated to be true and real, even by means of indirect reasoning. Indeed, we have seen that anyone who placed confidence in them and took them to be what they presented themselves as being is misled by the way the phenomena hang together. Strictly speaking, so-called outer perception is thus not perception; and mental phenomena can accordingly be designated as the only ones of which perception in the strict sense of the word is possible.

Mental phenomena are also adequately characterized by means of this definition. It is not as if all mental phenomena are introspectively perceivable for everyone, and therefore that everything which a person cannot perceive he is to count among the physical phenomena. On the contrary, it is obvious, and was already expressly remarked by us earlier, that no mental phenomenon is perceived by more than a single individual; but on that occasion we also saw that every type of mental phenomenon is represented in the psychical life of every fully developed human being. For this reason, reference to the phenomena which constitute the realm of inner perception serves our purpose satisfactorily.

7

We said that mental phenomena are the only ones of which a perception in the strict sense is possible. We could just as well say that they are the only phenomena to which actual, as well as intentional, existence pertains. Knowledge, joy, desire, exist actually; color, sound, heat, only phenomenally and intentionally.

There are philosophers who go so far as to say that it is self-evident that no actuality *could* correspond to a phenomenon such as we call a physical one. They maintain that anyone who assumes this and ascribes to physical phenomena any existence other than mental holds a view which is self-contradictory in itself. Bain, for example, says that some people have attempted to explain the phenomena of outer perception by the hypothesis of a material world, "in the first instance, detached from perception, and, afterwards, coming into perception, by operating upon the mind." "This view," he says, "involves a contradiction. The prevailing doctrine is that a tree is something in itself apart from all perception; that, by its luminous emanations, it impresses our mind and is then perceived; the perception being an effect, and the unperceived tree [i.e., the one which exists outside of perception] the cause. But the tree is known only through perception; what it may be anterior to, or independent of, perception, we cannot tell; we can think of it as perceived but not as unperceived. There is a manifest contradiction in the supposition; we are required at the same moment to perceive the thing and not to perceive it. We know the touch of iron, but we cannot know the touch apart from the touch."[19]

I must confess that I am not in a position to be convinced of the correctness of this argument. As certain as it is that a color only appears to us when it is an object of our presentation [*wenn wir sie vorstellen*], it is nevertheless not to be inferred from this that a color could not exist without being presented. Only if being presented were included as one factor in the color, just as a certain quality and intensity is included in it, would a color which is not presented signify a contradiction, since a whole without one of its parts is truly a contradiction. This, however, is obviously not the case. Otherwise it would be strictly inconceivable how the belief in the actual existence of the physical phenomenon outside of our presentation of it could have, not to say originated, but achieved the most general dissemination, been maintained with the utmost tenacity, and, indeed, even long been shared by thinkers of the first rank. If what Bain says were correct: "We can think of [a tree] as perceived, but not as unperceived. There is manifest contradiction in the supposition," then his further conclusion would surely no longer be subject to objection. But it is precisely this which is not to be granted. Bain explains his dictum by saying: "We are required at the same moment to perceive the thing and not to perceive it." But it is not true that this is required: For, in the first place, not every case of thinking is a perception; and further, even if this were the case, it would only follow that a person could only think of trees perceived by him, but not that he could only think of trees *as perceived by him*. To taste a white piece of sugar does not mean to taste a piece

[19]*Mental Science*, 3d ed., p. 198.

of sugar *as white*. The fallacy reveals itself quite distinctly when it is applied to mental phenomena. If one should say: "I cannot think of a mental phenomenon without thinking of it; and so I can only think of mental phenomena as thought by me; hence no mental phenomena exists outside of my thinking," this mode of inference would be exactly like the one Bain uses. Nonetheless, Bain himself will not deny that his individual mental life is not the only thing to which actual existence belongs. When Bain adds, "We know the touch of iron, but it is not possible that we should know the touch apart from the touch," he uses the word "touch," in the first place, obviously, in the sense of what is felt, and then in the sense of the feeling of it. These are different concepts even if they have the same name. Accordingly, only someone who permits himself to be deceived by the equivocation could make the concession of immediate evidence required by Bain.

It is not true, then, that the hypothesis that a physical phenomenon like those which exist intentionally in us exists outside of the mind in actuality includes a contradiction. It is only that, when we compare one with the other, conflicts are revealed, which show clearly that there is no actual existence corresponding to the intentional existence in this case. And even though this holds true in the first instance only as far as our experience extends, we will, nevertheless, make no mistake if we quite generally deny to physical phenomena any existence other than intentional existence.

8

Still another circumstance has been taken as a distinguishing characteristic for physical and mental phenomena. It has been said that mental phenomena occur only one after the other, while many physical phenomena, on the other hand, occur at the same time. This has not always been asserted in one and the same sense; and not every sense which has been attached to the contention appears to be in accord with the truth.

H. Spencer expressed his opinion on this subject recently: "The two great classes of vital actions called Physiology and Psychology are broadly distinguished in this, that while the one includes both simultaneous and successive changes the other includes successive changes only. The phenomena forming the subject-matter of Physiology present themselves as an immense number of different series bound up together. Those forming the subject-matter of Psychology present themselves as but a single series. A glance at the many continuous actions constituting the life of the body at large, shows that they are synchronous—that digestion, circulation, respiration, excretion, secretion, etc., in all their many sub-divisions, are going on at one time in mutual dependence. And the briefest introspection makes it clear that the actions constituting thought occur, not together, but one after another."[20] Thus, in making his comparison, Spencer has particularly in view the physiological and physical phenomena within one and the same organism to which a consciousness is attached. If he had not done this, he would have had to grant that several series of mental phenomena can also run concurrently, since there is, surely, more than one living thing in the world endowed with consciousness. But even within the limits he gives, the contention he advances is still not entirely true. And Spencer himself is so far from failing to recognize this fact that he immediately calls attention to those kinds of lower animals, e.g., the *Radiata*, in which a manifold psychological life spins itself out within *one* body. Here, he says—something which others, however, will not readily admit—that there is little difference between mental and physical existence. And he makes still further concessions, according to which the alleged difference between physiological and mental phenomena is weakened to a matter of a mere more or less. Still more! If we ask ourselves what Spencer understands by physiological phenomena, alterations in which are supposed to occur simultaneously, in contrast to mental phenomena, it appears that he does not really mean physical phenomena by this term, but their causes, which are in themselves unknown; for with respect to the physical phenomena which present themselves in sensation, it may be undeniable that they could not vary simultaneously unless the sensations also admitted of simultaneous variations. Hence we could not arrive at a distinguishing characteristic for the two classes in this way.

Others have chosen to see a peculiarity of mental life in the fact that only *one* object can ever be grasped in consciousness, and never several at the same time. They point to the noteworthy case of error in time-determination which regularly occurs in astronomical observations, in that the simultaneous swing of the pendulum does not enter into consciousness simultaneously with, but earlier or later than, the moment when the observed star touches the hairline in the telescope.[21] Thus, mental phenomena always merely follow one another in a simple series. But certainly a person would be mistaken to generalize on the basis of what such a case (involving the utmost concen-

---

[20]*Principles of Psychol.*, 2d ed., Vol. I, § 177, p. 395.
[21]Cf. Bessel, *Astron. Beobachtungen* (Konigsberg, 1823), Intro., Part. VIII; Struve, *Expedition Chronometrique*, etc. (Petersburg, 1844), p. 29.

tration of attention) shows, without any further evidence. Spencer, at least, says: "I find that there may sometimes be detected as many as five simultaneous series of nervous changes, which in various degrees rise into consciousness so far that we cannot call any of them absolutely unconscious. When walking, there is the locomotive series; there may be, under certain circumstances, a tactual series; there is very often (in myself at least) an auditory series, constituting some melody or fragment of a melody which haunts me; and there is the visual series: all of which, subordinate to the dominant consciousness formed by some train of reflection, are continually crossing it and weaving themselves into it."[22] Hamilton, Cardaillac, and other psychologists make similar reports on the basis of their experiences. But if it were assumed to be correct that all cases of perception are like the astronomer's, would we not always have to grant at least that we often have a presentation of something and simultaneously make a judgment about it or desire it? So there would still be several simultaneous mental phenomena. Indeed, one could more correctly advance the opposite contention, that, often enough, several mental phenomena are present but never more than one physical phenomenon.

What is the only sense, then, in which we might say that invariably only one mental phenomenon is apparent but, on the other hand, that many physical phenomena appear simultaneously? We can say this insofar as the entire multiplicity of mental phenomena which appear to someone in inner perception always manifests itself to him as a unity, while this does not hold true of the physical phenomena which he simultaneously grasps by means of so-called outer perception. As is commonly the case elsewhere, many persons have confused unity with simplicity here and therefore maintain that they perceive themselves in inner consciousness as something simple. Others, in contradicting the simplicity of the phenomenon, at the same time denied its unity. But just as the former group could not maintain a consistent position, since, as soon as they described what was within them, a great number of different factors came to be mentioned, so the latter could also not prevent themselves from testifying involuntarily to the unity of the mental phenomenon. They speak, as do others, of an "I" and not a "we," and sometimes call this entity a "bundle" of perceptions, sometimes by other names which describe a state of hanging-together in an internal unity. When we perceive simultaneously color, sound, heat, smell, nothing hinders us from ascribing each to a partic-

---

[22]*Ibid.*, p. 398. Likewise, Drobisch says, it is "a fact, that several series of presentations can go through the mind simultaneously, but at different levels, as it were" (*Empir. Psych.*, p. 140).

ular thing. On the other hand, we are obliged to take the diverse set of corresponding acts of sensation, seeing, hearing, sensing heat, and smelling, and with them the willing and feeling and considering going on at the same time, and the inner perception by which we are aware of all of them as well, to be partial phenomena of a unified phenomenon which includes them, and to take them to be a single, unified thing. We shall thoroughly discuss the reason we are obliged to do so somewhat later and shall present in greater detail and more fully at that time more that is pertinent to the question. For what we touched on here is nothing other than the so-called unity of consciousness, a fact of psychology which is one of the richest in its consequences and which is, nevertheless, still disputed.

9

In conclusion, let us summarize the results of our comments on the distinction between physical and mental phenomena. First of all, we made ourselves concretely aware of the distinctive nature of the two classes by means of *examples*. We then defined mental phenomena as *presentations* and such phenomena which are *based upon presentations;* all the rest belong to the physical. We next spoke of the attribute of *extension*, which was taken by psychologists to be a distinctive characteristic of all physical phenomena; all mental phenomena were supposed to lack it. The contention had not remained uncontested, however, and only later investigations could decide the issue; that in fact mental phenomena do invariably appear unextended was all that could be confirmed now. We next found *intentional inexistence*, the reference to something as an object, to be a distinguishing feature of all mental phenomena; no physical phenomenon manifests anything similar. We further defined mental phenomena as the exclusive *object of inner perception;* they alone are therefore perceived with immediate evidence; indeed, they alone are perceived in the strict sense of the word. And with this there was bound up the further definition, that they alone are phenomena which possess *actual* existence besides their intentional existence. Finally, we advanced it as a distinguishing [feature] that the mental phenomena which someone perceives *always* appear *as a unity* despite their variety, while the physical phenomena which he may perceive simultaneously are not all presented in the same way as partial phenomena within a single phenomenon.

There can be no doubt but that the characteristic which is more distinctive of mental phenomena than any of the others is intentional inexistence. We may now regard them as distinctly defined, over against the physical phenomena, by this, as well as by the other properties which were introduced.

The definitions of mental and physical phenomena which have been given cannot fail to throw a brighter light on our earlier definitions of mental science and physical science *(psychischer und Naturwissenschaft)*: indeed, we said of the latter that it is the science of physical phenomena and of the former that it is the science of mental phenomena. It is now easy to see that both definitions implicitly include certain limitations.

This holds true principally of the definition of physical science. For it is not concerned with all physical phenomena; not with those of imagination, but only with those which appear in sensation. And it determines laws for these only insofar as they depend upon physical stimulation of the sense organs. We could express the scientific task of physical science precisely by saying that physical science is the science which attempts to explain the succession of physical phenomena which are normal and pure (not influenced by any particular psychological states and events) on the basis of the hypothesis [that they are the effect] of the stimulation of our sense organs by a world which is quasi-spatially *(raumähnlich)* extended in three dimensions and which proceeds quasi-temporally *(zeitähnlich)* in *one* direction.[23] Without giving any particulars concerning the absolute nature of this world, [physical science] is satisfied to ascribe to it powers which evoke the sensations and mutually influence each other in their working, and to determine the laws of coexistence and succession for these powers. In those laws, it then indirectly gives the laws governing the succession of the physical phenomena of sensation when, by means of scientific abstraction from concomitant psychological conditions, these are regarded as pure and as occuring in relation to a constant sensory capacity. Hence, "science of physical phenomena" must be interpreted in this somewhat complicated way, if it is made synonymous with physical science.[24]

[23]On this point see Ueberweg *(System der Logik)*, in whose analysis, to be sure, not everything is deserving of approval. He is mistaken particularly when he considers the external causes to be spatial instead of quasi-spatial, temporal instead of quasi-temporal.

[24]The interpretation would not be quite as Kant would have it; nevertheless, it approximates his interpretations as far as is feasible. In a certain sense, it comes closer to the viewpoint of Mill in his book against Hamilton (chap. xi), but still without agreeing with him in all the essential respects. What Mill calls permanent possibilities of sensations has a close relationship with what we call powers. The relationship to, as well as the most important departure from, Ueberweg's view was already touched upon in the preceding note.

We have seen, along the way, how the expression "physical phenomenon" is sometimes misused by being applied to the above-men-
tioned powers themselves. And, since the object of a science is naturally
designated as the one for which it determines laws directly and explicitly, I believe I make no mistake in also assuming with respect to
the definition of physical science as the science of physical phenomena
that there is ordinarily bound up with this term the concept of powers
belonging to a world which is quasi-spatially extended and which proceeds quasi-temporally, powers which evoke sensations by their effect
on the sense organs and which reciprocally influence one another, and
for which physical science investigates the laws of coexistence and
succession. If one regards these powers as the object [of physical
science], this also has the convenient feature that something which
truly and actually exists appears as object of the science. This last
would be just as attainable if we defined physical science as the science
of sensations, implicitly adding the same limitation of which we just
spoke. What made the expression "physical phenomenon" seem pref-
erable was, probably, primarily the fact that the external causes of
sensation were thought of as corresponding to the physical phenomena
appearing in it, (whether this be in every respect, as was originally
the case, or whether it be, as now, in respect at least to extension in
three dimensions). From this, there also arose the otherwise inappropriate term, "outer perception." It is pertinent, however, that the
act of sensation manifests, along with the intentional inexistence of
the physical phenomenon, still other properties with which the physical
scientist *(Naturforscher)* is not at all concerned, since sensation does
not give through them similar information about the distinctive relationships of the external world.

With respect to the definition of psychology, it may be apparent
in the first place that the concept of mental phenomena is to be broad-
ened rather than narrowed. For the physical phenomena of imagination,
at least, fall completely within its scope just as much as do mental
phenomena, in the sense defined earlier; and those which appear in
sensation can also not remain unconsidered in the theory of sensation.
But it is obvious that they come into consideration only as the content
of mental phenomena, when the characteristics of those phenomena
are being described. And the same holds true of all mental phenomena
which possess exclusively phenomenal existence. It is only mental
phenomena in the sense of actual states which we shall have to regard
as the true object of psychology. And it is exclusively with reference
to them that we say psychology is the science of mental phenomena.

Roderick M. Chisholm

BRENTANO ON DESCRIPTIVE PSYCHOLOGY AND THE INTENTIONAL[1]

1. According to Edmund Husserl, Brentano's "conversion of the scholastic concept of intentionality into a descriptive root-concept of psychology constitutes a great discovery, apart from which phenomenology could not have come into being at all."[2] It is fitting, therefore, to begin a course of lectures on phenomenology and existentialism with a discussion of what Brentano had to say about descriptive psychology and the intentional. We should remind ourselves, however, that the primary significance of Brentano's philosophy does not lie in the philosophical movements to which it happens to have given rise. This may be said with all due respect to the work of Husserl, Meinong, Twardowski, Marty, and the countless other philosophers who have been influenced by his work. Franz Brentano, as Husserl suggested to Kraus, was a philosopher of the ages and his greatness should not be measured by reference merely to the philosophical movements of our own time.[3]

2. Brentano's doctrine of the intentional, as well as much of the rest of what we would now call his philosophy, was a part of what he called "descriptive psychology." Brentano's "descriptive psychology" and Husserl's "phenomenology" are closely related. Husserl had studied with Brentano in Vienna from 1884 to 1886.[4] Brentano had used "beschreibende Phänomenologie" as an alternative name for descriptive

---

[1]*Phenomenology and Existentialism*, eds. Edward N. Lee and Maurice Mandelbaum (Baltimore: The Johns Hopkins Press, 1967), Essay One. Reprinted by permission of the author and publisher.

[2]See the "Author's Preface to the English Edition" of *Ideas: General Introduction to Pure Phenomenology* (London: 1931), p. 23.

[3]"Brentano ist eine historische Grösse—was keinesfalls heisst ein fur allemal erledigt—eine gewisse Überzeitlichkeit sollte in der Edition walten." Husserl was speaking of the edition of Brentano's writings which was being prepared by Oskar Kraus and Alfred Kastil. The quotation appears in the Introduction to Brentano's *Vom sinnlichen und noetischen Bewusstsein*, also referred to as *Psychologie, Band Drei*, ed. Oskar Kraus (Leipzig: 1928), p. xlviii.

[4]See Husserl's "*Erinnerungen an Franz Brentano*," in Oskar Kraus, *Franz Brentano: Zur Kenntnis seines Lebens und seine Lehre* (Munich: 1919).

psychology but evidently did not use "Phänomenologie" in this way after 1889.

The relation that descriptive psychology bears to genetic or explanatory psychology, Brentano said, is analogous to the relation that anatomy bears to physiology and to the relation that "geognosy" bears to geology (hence "psychognosy" was still another term that Brentano used for descriptive psychology).[5] Genetic or explanatory psychology is concerned with the causal status of psychological phenomena and hence with the relations that such phenomena bear to physical and chemical processes. It is not an exact science but, like meteorology, must qualify its generalizations with such terms as "on the average" and "for the most part." But descriptive psychology, Brentano thought, was an exact science.

The descriptive psychologist is concerned with "the totality of ultimate psychological elements":

All other psychological phenomena are derived from the combinations of these ultimate psychological elements, as the totality of words may be derived from the totality of letters. Completion of this task would provide the basis for a Characteristica universalis *of the sort that had been conceived by Leibniz, and before him, by Descartes. Genetic psychology, on the other hand, is concerned with the laws in accordance with which psychological phenomena come into being and pass away. Since these phenomena are undoubtedly dependent upon processes in the nervous system, the conditions of their coming and going are largely physiological; hence the investigation of genetic psychology must be entwined with that of physiology.*[6]

The task of descriptive psychology to which this passage refers has been described as being, in part, a matter of taking a "psychological inventory."[7] But it is also possible for descriptive psychology to formulate laws or theorems, and these laws or theorems, like those of mathematics and logic and unlike those of genetic psychology, are exact and apodictic. They hold universally and not merely "for the most part." Examples of such laws are the following, from the theory of evidence (which Brentano regarded as a part of descriptive psychology): Every judgment is either correct or incorrect; if one person makes a

[5]See Franz Brentano, *Grundzüge der Ästhetik*, ed. F. Mayer-Hillebrand, pp. 36 ff., and *Meine letzten Wünsche für Oesterreich* (Stuttgart: 1895).
[6]*Meine letzten Wünsche für Oesterreich*, pp. 34–35.
[7]Oskar Kraus, *Franz Brentano*, p. 21.

correct judgment about a certain object, then no other person can make
a similar judgment about the same object without also judging correctly.[8]

But we cannot properly understand Brentano's descriptive psychology unless we have a more detailed example. I shall attempt to summarize, therefore, what Brentano says about the nature of an act of
will *(das Wollen)*. I choose this particular example partly because of
its intrinsic merit, partly because it provides an introduction to Brentano's doctrine of the intentional, and partly because it may be useful as
a means of contrasting Brentano's psychological descriptions with those
of subsequent phenomenology.

I refer to the account of willing that is set forth in Brentano's posthumous *Grundlegung und Aufbau der Ethik* (Bern, 1952), constructed
by F. Mayer-Hillebrand from the notebooks that Brentano had used
in lecturing on ethics at the University of Vienna from 1876 to 1894.
Brentano here describes the way in which an act of will is constituted
out of elementary psychological phenomena.

Within the sphere of the intellect, according to Brentano, the elementary phenomena are accepting and rejecting; within the sphere of
the emotions they are loving, hating, and preferring. The terms "love"
and "hate" should here be construed broadly: We love an object or
state of affairs if we take a pro attitude toward that object or state
of affairs; and we hate an object or state of affairs if we take an anti
attitude toward that object or state of affairs. These phenomena—
accepting, rejecting, loving, hating, and preferring—all presuppose
and involve still another elementary phenomenon—that of having an
idea of a thing *(das Vorstellen)*. But although they do thus involve this
further phenomenon, they may still be called elementary, for they are
not themselves constituted by combining this further phenomenon
with still *other* elementary phenomena. Being "red," similarly, involves
or presupposes being "colored"; but red is not a combination of color
and something else. How, then, is an act of will to be constituted out
of such phenomena as these?

An act of will is, in part, a wish or want that involves a decision.

[8]Brentano is frequently charged with "psychologism." But if by psychologism we mean
the doctrine according to which the laws of logic, evidence, and morality are merely
contingent generalizations about the way in which people happen to think or feel, then
the charge is not just. Brentano had criticized psychologistic theories of the evident in
the first edition (1889) of the *Ursprung sittlicher Erkenntnis* (3rd ed.; Leipzig: 1934).
Part of this critique is reprinted in *The True and the Evident*, ed. Oskar Kraus (English
edition, ed. Roderick M. Chisholm [London: 1966], pp. 52–59; see also pp. 110–111, and
Kraus's Introduction, pp. xx–xxii).

And a wish or want that involves a decision is, in part, an act of love that involves a preference. What, then, is the difference between an act of love *simpliciter* and an act of love that involves a preference? Of two situations, each of which is an object of my love or favorable inclination, I may yet *prefer* one to the other. For example, my friend's receiving a sudden stroke of good fortune might be something that I prefer as such, taken in itself and as if alone, to a similar stroke of good fortune on the part of a certain man who happens to be a total stranger. Here, then, we have love that involves a preference: I think of an object; I take a pro attitude toward it; and I prefer it to another object.

The good fortune of my friend is something that I prefer as such, taken in itself and as if alone, to the good fortune of the stranger. I may yet decide, however, that the latter rather than the former is the one I want to see realized. I thus arrive at a wish or want that involves a decision when (a) I have considered these two situations in the contexts of what I take to be their total consequences and then (b) arrive at a preference with respect to these two sets of total consequences. Hence Brentano says that a wish that involves a decision is related to a love or preference that does not involve a decision in the way in which, according to the traditional theological doctrine, the "consequent will" of God is related to his "antecedent will."[9]

We have, then, the concept of a wish that involves a decision, but we have not yet arrived at the concept of an act of will. Although, as our example may suggest, "coming to a decision does not always involve an act of will, an act of will always involves coming to a decision."[10] What further differentiates an act of will is the fact that its object is "always something that we ourselves have to bring about. We can will only those things that fall within our power, or, at any rate, those things which are such that we earnestly believe that they fall within our power."[11]

And now Brentano is prepared to give us his definition of an act of will. "Thus we can define an act of will as a wish or want having these characteristics: it is such that it involves a decision and it has as its object something that we are to bring about ourselves and that we con-

---

[9]Compare Franz Brentano, *Vom Ursprung sittlicher Erkenntnis* (3rd ed. Leipzig: 1934), pp. 112–115, 156–158. The first edition of this work was translated into English by Cecil Hague as *The Origin of our Knowledge of Right and Wrong* (London: 1902). The third edition contains much more important material, including the passages cited, which did not appear in the first edition. The third edition is now being translated into English by Roderick M. Chisholm and Elizabeth Schneewind.
[10]*Grundlegung und Aufbau der Ethik*, p. 219.
[11]*Ibid.*

fidently expect will result from the desires that we have. Hence one might say that an act of will is a want or a wish such that we have arrived at it by coming to a decision and such that we believe it can be realized by our own endeavors."[12]

This complex concept of an act of will, then, contains a multiplicity of elements: love, conviction, preference, and causation. The first three of these are psychological and the fourth—that of causation—occurs only as part of the intentional object of the second.

Here, then, we have what seems to me to be a paradigm case of descriptive psychology, as Brentano conceived it.

3. Now we may turn to Brentano's conception of the intentional, beginning with the doctrine of intentional inexistence which he propounded in 1874 and was subsequently to abandon.

In his *Psychologie vom empirischen Standpunkt*, first published in 1874, Brentano proposed the doctrine of intentional inexistence as a means of distinguishing the mental or psychical from the physical. The familiar passage follows:

Every mental phenomenon is characterized by what the scholastics of the middle ages called the intentional (and also mental) inexistence of an object, and what we would call, although not in entirely unambiguous terms, the reference to a content, a direction upon an object (by which we are not to understand a reality), or an immanent objectivity. Each one includes something as an object within itself, although not always in the same way. In presentation something is presented, in judgment something is affirmed or denied, in love something is loved, in hate something is hated, in desire something is desired, etc. This intentional inexistence is exclusively characteristic of mental phenomena. No physical phenomenon manifests anything similar. Consequently, we can define mental phenomena by saying that they are such phenomena as include an object intentionally within themselves.[13]

---

[12]"Wir können das Wollen also definieren als ein entscheidendes Wunschen, das etwas von uns selbst zu Verwirklichendes zum Gegenstand hat und von uns als Wirkung unseres Begehrens überzeugt erwartet wird. Es ist m. a. W. ein Wunsch, für den wir uns entschieden haben und an dessen Realisierbarkeit durch unser Eingreifen wir glauben." *Ibid.*

[13]The passage may be found on pp. 124–125 of Volume I of the Second Edition of the *Psychologie vom empirischen Standpunkt* (Leipzig: 1924). The present version is from D. B. Terrell's translation of the chapter in which it appeared ("The Distinction between Mental and Physical Phenomena"), in *Realism and the Background of Phenomenology*, ed. Roderick M. Chisholm (Glencoe, Illinois: 1960); the passage appears on pp. 50-51. [See Brentano selection above, pp. 119–120.—Ed.]

We have here an ontological thesis concerning "intentional inexistence," which Brentano was later to abandon, and a psychological thesis, implying that reference to an object is what distinguishes the mental from the physical. Each of these theses seems to me to be important. The ontological thesis seems to me to be problematic and not, as Brentano subsequently thought, to be obviously false. And the psychological thesis seems to me to be true. Let us consider them in order.

We are readily led to the ontological doctrine of intentional inexistence, though not, of course, to the particular terminology that Brentano used, if we ask ourselves what is involved in having thoughts, beliefs, desires, purposes, and other intentional attitudes that are directed upon objects that do not exist. There is a distinction between a man who is thinking about a horse and a man who is thinking about a unicorn. The distinction lies in the *objects* of their respective thoughts. It does *not* lie in the fact that where the first man has an object the second man does not, for this is not a fact. There is a distinction between a man who is thinking about a unicorn and a man who is thinking about nothing at all; *this* distinction lies in the fact that where one man has an object of thought the other man does not.[14] What, then, is the ontological status of the object that the man is intentionally related to when he is thinking about a unicorn?

One is tempted to say that although the man's thought quite obviously has an object, this object—also quite obviously—cannot be a unicorn. For one might reason as follows: If the man's thought is directed upon *something* and if there are no unicorns, then his thought must be directed upon something other than a unicorn. But what could this something possibly be? Moreover, if the man is thinking about something that is *not* a unicorn, how, then, can we say that he is thinking about a unicorn?

The doctrine of intentional inexistence may seem, at first consid-

---

[14]Compare Plato's *Theaetetus* 189a–b:
Soc. And does not he who thinks, think some one thing?
Theaet. Certainly.
Soc. And does not he who thinks some one thing, think something which is?
Theaet. I agree.
Soc. Then he who thinks of that which is not, thinks of nothing?
Theaet. Clearly.
Soc. And he who thinks of nothing, does not think at all?
Theaet. Obviously.
Soc. Then no one can think that which is not, either as a self-existent substance or as a predicate of something else?
Theaet. Clearly not.

eration, to provide us with answers to our questions. It seems to tell
us three different things. It tells us, first, that the object of the man's
thought *is* a unicorn. It tells us, secondly, that this unicorn is not an
actual unicorn (for there are no actual unicorns). And it tells us, thirdly,
that this unicorn has a certain mode of being other than actuality.
Whatever has this mode of being—called "intentional inexistence"
or "immanent objectivity"—is an entity that is mind-dependent and
therefore appropriately called an *ens rationis,* in the traditional sense
of this term. The intentionally inexistent unicorn is an entity that
is *produced* by the mind or intellect; it comes into being as soon as
the man starts to think about a unicorn and it ceases to be as soon as
he stops.[15]

Are there, then, certain objects such as intentionally inexistent
unicorns which are produced by the mind? In *The True and the Evident,*
we find this interesting passage, which was written sometime prior to
1903. Brentano asks us to consider a person whose thought is directed
upon a certain object A and, in this case, an A that happens also to
be actual:

> *The concept of this object A, like that of the person who is thinking,*
> *is the concept of a thing. We may also say of this thing A that it is an*
> *object which is thought about. It is just as true that this A is a con-*
> *templated A [ein gedachtes A] as it is that this A is an actual A, ex-*
> *isting in reality. A can cease to be actual and yet continue to be thought*
> *about—so long as the thinking person does in fact think about it. And*
> *conversely it can cease to be thought about—if the person stops thinking*
> *about it—and yet continue to be actual.*
>
> *In contrasting the A which is contemplated or thought about with the*
> *A which is actual, are we saying that* the contemplated A *is itself nothing*

---

[15]This doctrine is at the basis of St. Anselm's ontological argument; for St. Anselm
takes it to be self-evident that if God is thought about then God does "exist in the understanding." William of Ockham contrasted the "intentional existence" (he did not use
"inexistence") of the object of thought with the "subjective existence" of the thinking
itself. "Objective existence" (meaning existence as an object of thought) came to be a
synonym for "intentional (in)existence." Thus Descartes contrasted the *formale esse*
of actual objects with the *objective in intellectu esse* of objects that are merely thought
about. In the present century, the late Professor A. O. Lovejoy of Johns Hopkins appealed
to those entities that are objects merely of thought (unicorns, as well as many of the
objects of dreams and hallucinations) in order to defend what he called "psychophysical
dualism"—the view that there is, in addition to the world of physical things, a world of
nonphysical, mental things, "a second world to which could be allocated all experienced
objects which do not appear to satisfy the rules of membership in the physical system."
See A. O. Lovejoy, *The Revolt against Dualism* (New York: 1930), pp. 28-29.

actual or true? By no means! The contemplated A *can be something actual and true without being an actual A. It is an actual contemplated A and therefore—since this comes to the same thing—it is an actual* contemplated A [*ein wirkliches gedachtes A*] *which may be contrasted with what is a mere* contemplated contemplated A [*ein gedachtes gedachtes A*]. *(One may* think *that someone is thinking about an A.)*

There cannot be anyone who contemplates an A unless there is a contemplated A; and conversely. But we must not infer from this fact that the one who is thinking about the A is identical with the A which he is thinking about. The two concepts are not identical but they are correlative. Neither can correspond to anything in reality unless the other does as well. But only one of these is the concept of a thing— the concept of something which can act and be acted upon. The second is the concept of a being which is only a sort of accompaniment to the first; when the first thing comes into being, and when it ceases to be, then so does the second.[16]

Brentano took these considerations to show that there *are* certain entities that are not concrete individual things. For, he says, the situation that he has described involves an actual thinker and an *actual contemplated A* (just as the situation he refers to parenthetically involves an actual, contemplated contemplated A). The contemplated A and the contemplated contemplated A are *entia rationis* that are *produced* by the mind.

According to Brentano's earlier doctrine, then, as soon as a man starts to think about a unicorn there comes into being an actual contemplated unicorn. This actual contemplated unicorn is an *ens rationis* that depends upon the thinker for its existence and that ceases to be as soon as the man ceases to think about a unicorn.

In the fourteenth century, Walter Burleigh had appealed to a slightly different aspect of the phenomenon of intentionality in order to make out a case for still another type of entity—an entity that, like the merely contemplated A, is not a concrete individual thing, but that, unlike the merely contemplated A, exists "outside the mind." It will be useful at this point to recall Burleigh's argument, for, as we shall see, it will throw light upon Brentano's thought and upon the subsequent fate of the doctrine of intentionality. Burleigh argued in this way:

---

[16]*The True and the Evident*, p. 27; the passage appears on page 31 of *Wahrheit und Evidenz*. Compare also *The True and the Evident*, p. 64: "There is nothing universal in the things; the so-called universal, as such, is only in the one who is thinking." *(Wahrheit und Evidenz*, p. 74.)

Something about which real promises and contracts are made, such as buying and selling, donations, pledges, etc., exists outside the soul. But contracts are not always made about individual things. Therefore something exists outside the soul that is other than an individual nature. The major is obvious. The proof of the minor is that in the statement "I promise you an ox," something outside the soul is being promised to you, and yet no individual thing is being promised to you because you cannot lay claim to this or that particular ox on the strength of this promise.

Therefore something outside the soul that is other than an individual thing is being promised to you.[17] Since the entities with which Burleigh is here concerned are not produced by the mind and are not in any way dependent upon the mind, they are not properly called *"entia rationis."* Hence we need a more general term to cover non-things in general, non-things that may or may not be *entia rationis.* Brentano proposed the expressions *"entia non realia," "entia irrealia,"* or simply *"irrealia."*[18]

For the present, let us restrict ourselves to those *irrealia* that are also *entia rationis* and consider some of the difficulties involved in the concept of intentional inexistence.

4. The doctrine of intentional inexistence may seem at least to have this advantage: It provides us with a literal interpretation for the traditional dictum, "Veritas est adaequatio intellectus rei." One could say that an affirmative judgment is true provided only that the properties of the intentional object are the same as those of the actual object.

But the very statement of this advantage betrays the fact that what the true affirmative judgment is directed upon is the actual object and not the intentional object.

To be sure, our intentional attitudes *may* be directed upon objects that do not exist. But they may also be directed upon objects that *do* exist: I may think of a golden mountain, but I may also think about Mt. Monadnock. Diogenes looked for an honest man and perhaps there

---

[17]Walter Burleigh, "On the Existence of Universals," in *Philosophy in the West: Readings in Ancient and Medieval Philosophy*, ed. Joseph Katz and R. H. Weingartner (New York: 1965), pp. 563–569. The passage appears on p. 564. For an account of Jean Buridan's treatment of the same problem, see Peter Geach, "A Medieval Discussion of Intentionality," *Proceedings of the 1964 International Congress for Logic, Methodology and Philosophy of Science*, Jerusalem, August 26-September 2, 1964 (Amsterdam: 1965), pp. 425–433.

[18]Compare *The True and the Evident*, pp. 80f.

was none; but there *are* many dishonest men who are also objects of quests, as the police files will indicate. And these objects are not things having mere intentional inexistence.

And even in those cases where the objects of our intentional attitudes do *not* exist, our attitudes are not normally directed upon an immanent, intentionally inexisting object. Whether or not there are honest men, Diogenes in his quest was looking for an *actual* honest man, not for an intentionally inexisting honest man. If the doctrine of intentional inexistence is true, the very fact that Diogenes was looking for an honest man implies that he already had the immanent object; hence *it* could not be the object of his quest. Thus Brentano was later to say that "what we think about is *the object* or *thing* and not the 'object of thought [*vorgestelltes Objekt*].'"[19]

The ontological use of the word "intentional," therefore, seems to undermine its psychological use. Intentionally inexistent objects were posited in the attempt to understand intentional reference, but the attempt did not succeed—precisely because the objects so posited *were* intentionally inexistent. Thus Husserl said, with the later Brentano, that the objects of our "intentional experiences" are never objects that exist merely in the understanding; they are always something "transcendent."[20]

There are still other difficulties in the ontological doctrine of intentionally inexisting objects, actual intentionally inexisting objects, as Brentano was later to emphasize. "If there are such objects, in the strict and proper sense of the term *are*, then, whenever anyone thinks

---

[19]*The True and the Evident*, p. 77. In this passage, Brentano also seems to deny ever having held the doctrine of intentional inexistence, as I have formulated it. Kraus believes, however, that by the time Brentano wrote the passage (March 17, 1905), the older doctrine (which, Kraus believes, Brentano had in fact held) "had become so foreign to him that he questioned whether he had ever enunciated it" *(op. cit.*, p. 154). One might try to reconcile this passage with what seems to have been Brentano's earlier doctrine by taking the earlier doctrine to be this: (1) an actual intentionally inexistent unicorn is *produced* when one thinks about a unicorn; (2) one's thought, however, is *not* directed upon this actual intentionally inexistent unicorn; and yet (3) it is *in virtue of* the existence of the intentionally inexistent unicorn that one's thought may be said to be directed upon a unicorn. But in this case, what point would there be in supposing that there *is* the inexistent unicorn? Compare Brentano's further remarks, *op. cit.*, pp. 77–79, and the notes by Oskar Kraus, *ibid.*, pp. 165–170. Compare also Jan Srzednicki, *Franz Brentano's Analysis of Truth* (The Hague: 1965), Chapter II.

[20]E. Husserl, *Logische Untersuchungen* (4th ed.; Halle: 1928), Vol. II, Part I, p. 425; compare pp. 373–374.

of anything that is contradictory, there comes into being an object that *is* contradictory."[21]

Almost all intentionally inexisting objects, moreover, violate the law of excluded middle. Consider, for example, the promised ox that was the object of *our* thought a while back. It may have been brown and presumably it had four legs, a head, and a tail. Presumably also it was heavy. But was it such that it weighed 817 pounds, or was it such that it did not weigh 817 pounds? Evidently we must answer both of these questions in the negative. In this case, the actual intentionally inexisting ox was what Meinong called an "incomplete object."[22] Whatever the status of such objects in Meinong's realm of *Aussersein*, Brentano was certain, in his later thoughts, that there are *no* such objects, whether "in" or "outside" the mind. (This incompleteness of the immanent object would seem to insure disaster for the attempt to construe truth as a relation of correspondence or adequacy holding between the immanent object and the actual object. For, since all actual objects are complete and no immanent objects are complete, no immanent object can be adequate to any actual object.)

And what, finally, of Walter Burleigh's *ens irreale*—the promised ox that is not identical with any individual ox? Brentano, in a letter to Kraus, had considered a slightly different example. You might promise to marry and yet not promise with respect to any particular person, to marry *that* particular person. But what happens if you keep the promise? "It would be paradoxical to the highest degree," Brentano said, "to suppose that you could promise to marry an *ens rationis* and then to keep the promise by marrying an actual, concrete particular."[23]

But it is much easier to ridicule the doctrine of *entia non realia* than it is to find a way of getting along without them. Let us consider, then, how Brentano himself made out in his subsequent attempts to get along without the ontology of intentionally inexistent objects.

5. Brentano's later thought was what Kotarbinski has called "reistic." The only things that can be said to *be*, in the strict and proper sense of the expression "to be," are particular, individual things. (But Brentano's reism, unlike that of Kotarbinski, is not also a "somatism." For Brentano held that there are concrete individual things that are not

[21]Franz Brentano, *Kategorienlehre*, ed. Alfred Kastil (Leipzig: 1933).

[22]See A. Meinong, *Über Möglichkeit und Wahrscheinlichkeit* (Leipzig: 1915), pp. 168–181.

[23]Quoted by Oskar Kraus in his Introduction to *Psychologie vom empirischen Standpunkt* (2nd ed.; Leipzig: 1924), p. xlix. Presumably Brentano should have written *"ens irreale"* instead of *"ens rationis."*

material things—for example, human souls and God.) Brentano thus repudiated all *entia rationis* and *entia irrealia*.

Our language contains a multiplicity of terms, purporting to refer to non-things, or *entia irrealia*. Brentano says that such terms are convenient fictions, comparable to such expressions as "negative quantities," "irrational numbers," "imaginary numbers," and the like.[24] When we find a true sentence, ostensibly referring to a non-thing, then, according to Brentano, we can "form an equivalent in which the subject and predicate are replaced by expressions referring only to things."[25] For example, the sentence "There is a dearth of bread in the larder" may seem to affirm the existence of a *privativum*—that non-thing which is the absence of bread. But actually, according to Brentano, it is concerned with the denial or rejection of a *thing:* namely bread in the larder. Again, "There is redness" and "Red is a color" may seem to pertain to *abstracta* and thus, once again, to non-things. But "There is redness," Brentano says, is just another way of saying "There are red things"; and what "Red is a color" tells us is simply that red things, *as such*, are colored.[26]

In a similar way, Brentano attempts to translate away all ostensible reference to propositional objects. Thus, in the second edition of the *Psychologie* and in *The True and the Evident*, he defends a non-propositional theory of judgment. Language suggests that judgment involves a relation between a man and a proposition (or content, state of affairs, or objective). We say, "He believes that there are horses," thus seeming to describe a relation between the believer and that non-thing named by the propositional clause "that there are horses." But actually, Brentano says, what "He believes that there are horses" tells us is simply that the believer accepts or affirms *(anerkennt)* horses. And if we say, "He believes that there are no unicorns," we are simply saying that he rejects or denies *(leugnet)* unicorns. "He believes that some horses are red" tells us that he accepts red horses, and "He believes that no horses are green" tells us that he rejects green horses. Brentano's theory becomes complex, after this point.[27] But what it is that he is attempting to do is clear throughout: he wishes to translate those true sentences that seem to refer to non-things into sentences that refer

---

[24]*The True and the Evident*, p. 83.

[25]*Psychologie vom empirischen Standpunkt*, 2nd ed., II, 163.

[26]Brentano's reism is set forth in detail in *Kategorienlehre* and *The True and the Evident*. Compare the exposition in Srzednicki, *op. cit.*, pp. 42-49.

[27]See *Psychologie*, II, 158–172; part of this passage is translated by D. B. Terrell in *Realism and the Background of Phenomenology*, ed. by Roderick M. Chisholm, pp. 62–70.

only to things. In this way, he thinks, he will eliminate one of the most
fundamental sources of error and confusion in philosophy. Philosophers
go wrong and fall into confusion "when they take some word to be a
name when in fact the word is not a name at all, and then look for the
concept which this ostensible name designated."[28] Brentano's reism
thus led him to revise his original doctrine of the intentional in two
ways. First, he gave up the doctrine that our intentional attitudes are
sometimes directed upon non-things or *entia irrealia*. Whatever language we may use for the description of our intentional attitudes—
whether we use words ostensibly referring to *abstracta, privativa,
negativa*, whether we use clauses ostensibly referring to propositions or
what Meinong called *"Objektive"*—our attitudes are in fact always
directed upon *things*. Second, Brentano gave up the doctrine that our
intentional attitudes, whatever they may be directed upon, do somehow
involve actual intentionally inexistent objects.

What, then, is the reistic replacement for the actual intentionally
inexistent object?

6. The following passage, dictated in 1914, may be found in the *Kategorienlehre* (p. 8):

> *Instead of saying that a person is thinking about a thing, one may
> also say that there is something which is the object of his thought.
> But this is not the strict or proper sense of* is. *For the thinker may in
> fact deny that there is any such object as the object he is thinking about.
> Moreover, one can think about what is contradictory, but nothing that
> is contradictory can possibly be said to be. We said above that round-
> ness cannot be said to* be, *in the strict and proper sense of the term;
> that which is round, but not roundness, may be said to be. And so too,
> in the present case. What there is in the strict and proper sense is not
> the round thing that is thought about; what there* is *is the person who
> is thinking about it. The thing "as object of thought" is a fiction which,
> in many contexts, is perfectly harmless. But if we do not see that it is
> a fiction, then we will be led to the most blatant of absurdities. We are
> not dealing here with a type of being, in the strict sense of the term.
> What we say can be expressed in such a way that we do refer to a being
> in the strict sense of the term—namely, the thinker who has the thought.
> And what holds generally for that which is thought about also holds
> more particularly, for that which is accepted, that which is rejected,
> that which is loved, that which is hated, that which is hoped for, that
> which is feared, that which is willed, and so on.*

[28]Franz Brentano, *Die Lehre vom richtigen Urteil*, ed. F. Mayer-Hillebrand (Bern: 1956),
pp. 45-46.

Saying that there *is* an immanent object, then, is just another way of saying that there *is* an actual person who is thinking about that object. *"Es gibt ein Gedachtes"* says no more nor less than *"Es gibt ein Denkendes."*[29] Hence if we continue to say, as Brentano had said earlier, that there is an *actual* intentionally inexistent unicorn when an actual man is thinking about a unicorn, we are using the first "actual" in its loose and improper sense and the second "actual" in its strict and proper sense. And where Brentano had said earlier that our thought *produces* an entity, he now denies that our thought thus produces any entity at all.

There are four possible views here that are easily confused with each other. There is what I have taken to be Brentano's original view; there is the later reistic view; and then there seem to be two different ways of combining the first two views. Let us consider these possibilities more explicitly.

i. According to what I have taken to be Brentano's view of 1874, when a man thinks about a unicorn there is *produced* an immanent or intentionally inexistent unicorn. This immanent or intentionally inexistent unicorn is an actual immanent or intentionally inexistent unicorn. And therefore it is an entity *in addition to* the man who is thinking.

ii. According to Brentano's later, reistic view, when a man thinks about a unicorn no intentionally inexistent unicorn is produced and therefore the situation involves no actual entity other than the man who is thinking.

iii. Suarez, in his *Metaphysicae Disputationes*, seems to combine these two views in the following way. He seems to suggest that when a man thinks about a unicorn, the act of thought *produces* an immanent or intentionally inexistent unicorn; hence we have an element of Brentano's first view. But Suarez adds that the unicorn that is thus *produced* is *not* an *actual* immanent or intentionally inexistent unicorn and therefore it is not an entity in addition to the thinker himself; hence we have an element of Brentano's second view.[30] Now if this immanent or intentionally inexistent unicorn is produced, or (to use the terms that Suarez used) if this *ens rationis* that has only "objective being in the mind" had an efficient cause, then, one would

---

[29]*Wahrheit und Evidenz*, p. 79; compare *The True and the Evident*, p. 68.
[30]See disputation LIV (*"De Ente Rationis"*), Section 1. It is quite obvious that Brentano was influenced by this discussion in Suarez; compare the *Psychologie*, II, 272. I am indebted to the late Professor Ralph M. Blake for calling my attention to the importance of this and other discussions in the *Metaphysicae Disputationes*.

think, the entity must be actual. If there *is* production or causation, then there must *be* that which is caused or produced.[31]

iv. There is, finally, still another way of combining the first and second views of Brentano; this final view is suggested by one passage in G. E. Moore. We could say (a) that when a man thinks about a unicorn, there is involved an *actual* intentionally inexistent unicorn; hence we have an element of Brentano's first view. And then we could add (b) that to say that there is such an actual intentionally inexistent unicorn is to say no more nor less than that the man is thinking about a unicorn.[32]

Do we have, then, a clear alternative to the original doctrine of intentional inexistence?

7. It seems to me that these alternatives to the doctrine of intentional inexistence involve a serious difficulty, and I am not at all sure that I know how it ought to be treated. The difficulty may be seen if we try to give a positive answer to the question "How are we using the word 'unicorn' when we say, 'John is thinking about a unicorn'?"

Brentano in his later view gives the question a negative answer. That is to say, he tells us how we are *not* using the word "unicorn" when we say, "John is thinking about a unicorn." But he formulates this negative answer affirmatively—in very much the way in which, according to him, "There is a dearth of bread in the larder" expresses a negative belief affirmatively. He tells us that in the sentence "John is thinking about a unicorn," the word "unicorn" is being used syncategorematically or synsemantically.[33] And this may be said to be a negative answer

---

[31]It should be noted that Suarez is fully aware of the difficulty (which he attributes to one Bernardinus Mirandulus) and that he attempts to resolve it. We *could* so interpret the view of Suarez that it becomes identical with Brentano's second view above. Where Brentano had distinguished a strict and proper sense and a loose and improper sense of "is," we might read into Suarez a distinction between a strict and proper sense and a loose and improper sense of "produce" or "cause." He could then be interpreted as saying that it is only in the latter sense of "cause" that an *ens rationis* may be said to have an efficient cause.

[32]". . . if it should happen that at the present moment two different people are having an hallucination of a different tame tiger, it will follow there are at the present moment two different imaginary tigers. . . . The sentence 'There are some tame tigers which do not exist' is, therefore, certainly significant, if it means only that there are some imaginary tigers. . . . But what it means is that either some real people have written stories about imaginary tigers, or are having or have recently had hallucinations of tame tigers, or, perhaps, are dreaming or have dreamed of particular tame tigers. If nothing of this sort has happened or is happening to anybody, then there are no imaginary tame tigers." G. E. Moore, *Philosophical Papers* (London: 1959), p. 120.

[33]See *The True and the Evident*, p. 68.

to our question, for to say that a word is being used syncategorematically or synsemantically is to say, negatively, that the word is *not* being used referentially—that the word is *not* being used to designate or to refer to an object. Thus our question now becomes, more positively: If the word is not being used to designate or refer to an object, how *is* it being used?

We may say, as Brentano suggests, that in "John is thinking about a unicorn" the word "unicorn" is being used to contribute to the description of John. But *how* does it contribute to the description of John? We are *not* saying, obviously, that John is a unicorn. We are saying that John is *thinking* about a unicorn, and so one might be tempted to say the word "unicorn" is being used to describe John's thought. But *how* does the word "unicorn" contribute to the description of John's thought? We are not saying, obviously, that John's *thought* is a unicorn. We are saying—again, obviously—that the *object* of John's thought is a unicorn. But, Brentano tells us, statements ostensibly about the object of John's thought are actually statements about John. And so we have completed a kind of circle. For now we can ask, once again: what does this use of "unicorn" tell us about John?

One may be tempted to say that the use of "unicorn" in such sentences as "John is thinking about a unicorn" and "John believes that there are unicorns" has no connection at all with what would be its designative or referential use. What we have here, one is tempted to continue, are simply two different predicates of John—predicates that might be written as "thinking-about-a-unicorn" and "believing-that-there-are-unicorns." Better still, the hyphens could be removed, thereby making it clear that the predicates have no more to do with unicorns than they have to do with, say, ink, or with hats, or with corn, or with her, or with any of the other objects whose names happen to be imbedded in our intentional predicates.

That this suggestion will not do, however, is indicated by the fact that "John believes that there are unicorns" (or "John believesthat-thereareunicorns") and "All of John's beliefs are true" together imply "There are unicorns"—a mode of inference that would not be valid if "unicorn" functioned here as an equivocal middle term.[34]

[34] "One may have the feeling that in the sentence 'I expect he is coming' one is using the words 'he is coming' in a different sense from the one they have in the assertion 'He is coming.' But if it were so how could I say that my expectation had been fulfilled? If I wanted to explain the words 'he' and 'is coming,' say by means of ostensive definitions, the same definitions of these words would go for both sentences." Ludwig Wittgenstein, *Philosophical Investigations* (Oxford: 1953), p. 130e. The following passage occurs on this same page: "'The report was not so loud as I had expected.'—'Then there was a louder bang in your expectation?'"

Alonzo Church has suggested that the English sentence "Schliemann sought the site of Troy" tells us that a certain relation obtains between Schliemann and the *concept* of the site of Troy, suggesting therefore that seeking is a relation between a person and an *abstractum*. But *what* relation is asserted to obtain between Schliemann and the concept of the site of Troy? He was not *seeking* the concept, since he already had it when he set out on his quest. Church says, negatively, that the relation that Schliemann bore to the concept of the site of Troy is "not quite like that of having sought," but he does not tell us more positively what it is.[35]

Rudolf Carnap once suggested that *words* or other linguistic entities are the objects of our intentional attitudes. "Charles thinks (asserts, believes, wonders about) A," he said, might be translated as "Charles thinks 'A.'"[36] But when we say that Charles wonders whether there are unicorns, we do not mean to say that Charles wonders whether there is the word "unicorn." And when we make the semantic statement, "The word 'unicorn' in English designates unicorn," we cannot replace the last word in our statement with the expression "the word 'unicorn.'"[37]

One way out, if we are to avoid *entia irrealia* and at the same time do justice to the phenomenon of intentionality, is to follow Meinong's suggestion: There are certain truths which hold of objects that do not exist. There are no unicorns; yet there are certain truths that hold of unicorns; hence unicorns have certain properties, among them that of being the object, on occasion, of our intentional attitudes. But this suggestion was anathema to Brentano. as it is to most contemporary logicians.[38]

8. Brentano's doctrine of intentional inexistence was proposed as a way of distinguishing mental or psychical phenomena from physical phenomena: mental phenomena are distinguished by the fact that they contain objects immanently within themselves. If we give up the doctrine of intentional inexistence, how are we to make the distinction between the mental and the physical?

---

[35]Alonzo Church, *Introduction to Mathematical Logic* (Princeton: 1955), p. 8n.

[36]Rudolf Carnap, *The Logical Syntax of Language* (New York: 1937), p. 248.

[37]Israel Scheffler's "inscriptionalism" might be interpreted as saying that linguistic entities constitute the objects of our intentional attitudes. But if we do interpret it in this way, it becomes very difficult to ascertain just what relation is being asserted to hold between a man and an inscription when we say of him that he is thinking, wondering, desiring, loving, and the like. See Israel Scheffler, *The Anatomy of Inquiry* (New York: 1963), pp. 57ff.

[38]See A. Meinong, "The Theory of Objects," in *Realism and the Background of Phenomenology*, ed. Roderick M. Chisholm. I have attempted to defend Meinong in *"Jenseits vom Sein und Nichtsein,"* in *Dichtung und Deutung*, ed. Karl S. Guthke (Bern and Munich: 1961).

In the *Klassification der psychischen Phänomene*, published in 1911 and included in the second edition of the *Psychologie vom empirischen Standpunkt*, Brentano said that, since every psychical phenomenon involves a relation to something as object, psychical activity may be described as being essentially relational. But psychical relations, he said, are distinguished from other relations in the following way:

> *In the case of other relations, the Fundament as well as the Terminus must be an actual thing. . . . If one house is larger than another house, then the second house as well as the first house must exist and have a certain size. . . . But this is not at all the case with psychical relations. If a person thinks about something, the thinker must exist but the objects of his thought need not exist at all. Indeed, if the thinker is denying or rejecting something, and if he is right in so doing, then the object of his thinking must not exist. Hence the thinker is the only thing that needs to exist if a psychical relation is to obtain. The Terminus of this so-called relation need not exist in reality. One may well ask, therefore, whether we are dealing with what is really a relation at all. One could say instead that we are dealing with something which is in a certain respect similar to a relation, and which, therefore, we might describe as being something that is "relation-like" [etwas "relativliches"].*[39]

This passage suggests the possibility of a logical distinction between the mental and the physical. We might say that the language we use in characterizing the mental has certain logical properties that are not shared by the language we use in characterizing the physical. We could say, for example, that in characterizing the mental we must use "intentional terms" and that we do not need to use such terms when we characterize the physical; and we might then attempt to characterize intentional terms logically. The following definition of "intentional sentence," which is suggested by the passage from Brentano above, may be found in *Webster's Third New International Dictionary*: A simple categorical statement (for example, "Parsifal sought the Holy Grail") is intentional if it uses a substantial expression (in this instance "the Holy Grail") without implying either that there is or that there isn't anything to which the expression truly applies.

But this characterization of "intentional sentence," as it stands, is too broad. The following sentences, none of them concerned with what is mental, satisfy the conditions of the criterion: "The site of Troy is not New Zealand"; "That lady has a profile like the profile of Satan"; "It is possible that the Loch Ness monster exists."

[39]*Psychologie vom empirischen Standpunkt*, II, 133–134.

We will be more faithful to Brentano's intention if we look for a peculiar characteristic of the expressions we use to designate "intentional relations." And possibly we will find one if we remind ourselves of the type of situation involved in Walter Burleigh's promise: The man promised to deliver an ox, but there was no particular ox that he promised to deliver. Expressions for intentional relations may exhibit a unique type of behavior when they are found in contexts of quantification.[40] An example involving believing will illustrate the point; similar examples may be constructed which will hold of knowing, desiring, doubting, being pleased, being displeased, hoping, fearing, and still other intentional attitudes.

Consider the two formulae

(1)   (Ex)   (Ey)   (y = a & xRa)
(2)   (Ex)   (Ey)   (y = a & xRy).

Let us here restrict the values of variables to concrete entities. An expression which may occupy the place of "R" in such formulae could be said to be intentional if there is an individual term that may occupy the place of "a" with the results that (1) does not imply (2); (2) does not imply (1); and no well-formed sentence that is part of (1) is noncontingent.

We find an example of such an intentional expression if we replace "a" by "the next President" and "R" by "believes that the Mayor of New York is." Let us now suppose that Senator Robert Kennedy is the next President and that one of Mayor Lindsay's supporters believes that he, the Mayor of New York, is the next President. In this case (1) will be true. But (1) is consistent with the negation of (2). That is to say, affirming (1) is consistent with denying that there is anyone who mistakes Kennedy for the Mayor, i.e., with denying that there is anyone who supposes with respect to Kennedy that the Mayor of New York is he. But let us assume that there is, in fact, a man who mistakes Kennedy for the Mayor (expecting the Mayor on a certain occasion and then seeing the Senator in a conspicuous position, he takes it for granted that the man he sees, *viz.*, the Senator, is the Mayor). In this case (2) will be true. But (2) is consistent with the negation of (1). That is to say, affirming (2) is consistent with denying that there is anyone who believes that the Mayor of New York is the next President.

We might say, then, that a well-formed sentence is intentional if it contains an intentional expression (e.g., "believes that the Mayor

---

[40]In "Notes on the Logic of Believing," *Philosophy and Phenomenological Research*, XXIV (1963), 195-201, I described one such possibility, somewhat different from the one referred to here.

of New York is") and in addition to that only individual terms or quantifiers and variables. We could also say that a well-formed sentence is intentional if it is consistent and implies a sentence that is intentional. The psychological thesis of intentionality could then be put by saying, "All intentional sentences pertain to what is psychological."

If I am not mistaken, no expressions designating nonpsychological phenomena have the logical properties that the expression "R" has just been described as having. And if this is so, then we may say with Brentano that what distinguishes the psychological from the physical is *"etwas 'relativliches.' "*[41]

---

[41]Since the writing of this essay, the following work has appeared: Franz Brentano, *Die Abkehr vom Nichtrealen*, ed. Franziska Mayer-Hillebrand (Bern: 1966). This book is composed of selections, taken from Brentano's correspondence and hitherto unpublished manuscripts, concerning the repudiation of *entia irrealia*. It also contains a useful discussion of Brentano's reism by Professor Mayer-Hillebrand.

PART II

Contemporary Philosophers of Mind

5

WITTGENSTEIN'S NOTES FOR LECTURES ON "PRIVATE EXPERIENCE" AND "SENSE DATA"[1]

1. Note on the Text by Rush Rhees

Wittgenstein wrote these notes in pencil in three paper-covered notebooks. They are not dated, but the first of them seems to have been written in the latter part of 1934 or the beginning of 1935 and the last of them in March, 1936.

When he was making notes for his own writing, Wittgenstein almost always wrote in German. But he wrote these notes in English, changing to German occasionally for a single remark or perhaps two or three together. The reason, I think, is that he wrote the first of the notebooks while he was still working on the material of his dictations to Francis Skinner and Alice Ambrose (which became *The Brown Book)* and the rest in thinking of lectures he was giving in Cambridge. There is a similar notebook written before these three and running over into the first of them, with more than half of it in English notes for *The Brown Book.* A still earlier notebook contains English drafts for passages toward the end of *The Blue Book.* I say "drafts"; but Wittgenstein revised and changed them when he dictated, both in *The Blue Book* and in *The Brown Book.* Some sentences stand as in the notebooks; but more often they are changed, and the arrangement is generally very different. Some of the suggestions in the notes are discarded, and the dictated versions have things not in the notes at all. (He wrote his last German version of *The Brown Book* in August, 1936. This is unfinished, but it contains important changes and it will be published.)

The first notes printed here come after discussions developed in *The Brown Book:* the impressions one gets from words in reading; the sense in which the color pattern of a pansy "says something"; understanding a facial expression; whether a feeling of pastness distinguishes memory images from others. "Take as example the feeling of 'long, long ago,' because this is a strong and clearly circumscribed experience. And yet in a sense it seems just as elusive as any

[1]From *The Philosophical Review* (1968). Reprinted by permission of Rush Rhees, G.E.M. Anscombe, and G. H. von Wright; and the editor. These notes and the Malcolm selection should be read together.

other feeling of memory. ('Far away look in his eyes.')" (This is from the notebook. Compare *The Brown Book*, p. 184.)

While he was still making notes for *The Brown Book* (though he never called it that) Wittgenstein began writing notes for the criticism of [Bertrand] Russell's theory of numbers which he developed in lectures on the foundations of mathematics during the Lent and summer terms (from January to early June) of 1935. But the main body of notes for those lectures comes in the same notebook with remarks printed here: between "'I know what I mean by "toothache" . . .'" and "When one says 'I talk to myself' . . . ," given here on page 157. I call them "notes for those lectures" because there are parallels between what he has written in them and what he said, and especially because so many of the diagrams drawn in the notes were used in the lectures. On the other hand, the notes do not contain or even suggest all that he talked about. And when he did make the same point as he had written, his statement was probably no nearer to the notebook than the dictated *Brown Book* is to the notes for that.

The notes which come after those on the foundations of mathematics are related to what he was saying in lectures during 1935-1936. But in these lectures he also spoke of many things that are not mentioned in the notebooks, and what he wrote here was not always something he was going to say. What is printed here from page 161 onward is generally connected with his lectures from January to early June, 1936. Some notes are clearly drafts or versions of what he said, and they are often phrased as though he were addressing a class. But we cannot say, "These are the lectures he gave." Only in the final passage printed here—from page 190 to the end—does he seem to be writing a lecture. The first part of this is pretty much what he did say, I think; and if he did not give the rest (which is not complete) he gave something close to it. But he did not lecture from notes, and what he said was both a revision and a discussion of what he had thought and written in preparing.

Between the remark on page 186 which ends "Isn't this due to a misunderstanding?" and the remark "I wish to say . . ." which I have placed just after it, he had begun what looks like the draft of another lecture on the philosophy of mathematics: this time about existence proofs—"Are there an infinite number of primes or not?," "Are there 777 in the development of π?"—and what a question is in mathematics. He did lecture on questions which he treats here, in four or five lectures at the end of January and the beginning of February, 1936, but none of them was just the lecture he has written in the notebook.

For special reasons, I have not included the sections on mathematics. In the longest of them the diagrams are so inseparable from what he says that a reproduction of the notes would have to be a photograph. Anyway, it would have made the whole selection too long. Yet without them the selection is misleading: it leaves out something of the way Wittgenstein thought about questions of "personal experience." Of course he never thought that personal experience provided a foundation for mathematics. But again and again we find the same sort of difficulties here, in our thinking about private experience and in our thinking about mathematics. (This may be important in considering what he means in speaking of "a deep seated disease of language or of thought.")

For example, Russell once expressed his axiom of infinity as: "If n be any inductive cardinal number, there is at least one class of individuals having n terms"; and he added that "without this axiom we should be left with the possibility that n and $n + 1$ might both be the null-class. . . . Suppose there were exactly nine individuals in the world. . . . Then the inductive cardinals from 0 up to 9 would be such as we expect, but 10 (defined as $9 + 1$) would be the null-class. . . . Thus 10 and all subsequent cardinals will all be identical, since they will all be the null-class" (*Int.* [roduction to] *Math.* [ematical] *Phil.* [osophy], pp. 131, 132). In explaining his notation for identity in the *Tractatus*, Wittgenstein said that "what the axiom of infinity is intended to say would express itself in language through the existence of infinitely many names with different meanings" (5.535). In such "expressing" there would be nothing like "there is a class of individuals having n terms," which would be meaningless. Russell needs this phrase because he gives an analysis of the cardinal number 10 in terms of a function satisfied by exactly ten different arguments; and he thinks we can ask whether there *is* any such function. Now we might show that 10 and 11 were signs with different meanings by constructing each of them in a formal series of cardinal numbers. But although this "expresses itself in our symbolism," we still cannot say that our symbolism shows the existence of a function satisfied by ten individuals as arguments. Or suppose I did write $(\exists\varphi.): (E10x).\varphi x;$ I could not add: "If I *say* there is such a function—if I write this down—then there must *be* such a function, for I have written it as a paradigm in my expression." The paradigm shows what I am saying. But here I seem to be treating it both as a paradigm and as something *for which* it is a paradigm. It is like saying that the presence of the standard meter rod in Paris shows that there *is* something which is exactly one meter long. It is the same with confusions about the grammar of ostensive definition when we speak of private experiences and sense data. Here we confuse *giving* a sample (to explain what color "indigo" is) and *using* a sample (to show what color my neighbor's curtain is). If I tell myself, "I now have a visual impression of *this* color" (concentrating on it), I am trying to use the impression to show me what color it is.

In both cases Wittgenstein would say: "Nothing has been said so far to show us how this paradigm is *used*—in what sense it is a paradigm." This is one of many parallels which anyone can find.

All that is printed here is a collection of rough notes or memoranda which Wittgenstein made for his own use. He would never have published them—he would not even have had them typed—without revising and rearranging them. Certainly he would have revised the language. I have left the Germanisms even when I felt sure he would have corrected them, as one reminder that these are rough notes. The notes are in the order in which they come in the manuscript, except for two passages given as footnotes to other remarks. I have left out certain remarks, particularly in the first part. These are: *(a)* earlier versions of what is much better said later on in these notes; *(b)* jottings which are too sketchy to be intelligible; and *(c)* some remarks which do not seem closely connected with the main discussions. Wittgenstein kept returning to questions he had treated earlier. This was not a fault, and repetition of this sort can stand.

2. Notes for Lectures on "Private Experience" and "Sense Data" by Ludwig Wittgenstein

The experience of fright appears to us (when we philosophize) to be an amorphous experience behind the experience of starting.

All I want to say is that it is misleading to say that the word "fright" signifies something which goes along with the experience of expressing fright.

The "far away" look, the dreamy voice seem to be only means for conveying the real inner feeling.

The philosophical problem is: "What is it that puzzles me in this matter?"

Es läßt sich über die bestimmte Erfahrung einiges sagen und außerdem scheint es etwas, und zwar das Wesentlichste, zu geben was sich nicht beschreiben läßt.[2]

---

[2]Some things can be said about the particular experience and besides this there seems to be something, the most essential part of it, which cannot be described.

Man sagt hier, daß ein bestimmter Eindruck benannt wird. Und darin liegt etwas seltsames und problematisches. Denn es ist als wäre der Eindruck etwas zu ätherisches um ihn zu benennen. (Den Reichtum einer Frau heiraten). [3]

Du sagst, Du hast einen ungreifbaren Eindruck. Ich bezweifle nicht, was Du sagst. Aber ich frage ob Du damit etwas gesagt hast. D.h., wozu hast Du diese Worte geäußert, in welchem Spiel? [4]

It is as though, although you can't tell me exactly what happens inside you, you can nevertheless tell me something general about it. By saying e.g. that you are having an impression which can't be described.

As it were: There is something further about it, only you *can't say* it; you can only make the general statement.

It is this idea which plays hell with us.

"There is not only the gesture but a particular feeling which I can't describe": instead of that you ought to have said: "I am trying to point out a feeling to you"—this would be a grammatical remark showing how my information is meant to be used. This is almost similar as though I said: "This I call 'A' and I am pointing out a *color* to you and not a shape."

How can we point to the color and not to the shape? Or to the feeling of toothache and not to the tooth, etc.?

What does one call "describing a feeling to someone"?

"I'm giving the feeling which I'm having now a name."—I don't quite know what you are doing.

"This pain I call 'toothache' and I can never make him understand what it means."

But we are under the impression that we can point to the pain, as it were unseen by the other person, and name it.

For what does it mean that this feeling is the meaning of this name?

---

[3]We say here that a name is given to a particular impression. And this is strange and puzzling. For it seems as though the impression were too ethereal to be named. (Marrying a woman's wealth.)

[4]You say you have an intangible impression. I am not doubting what you say. But I question whether you have said anything by it. I.e., what was the point of uttering these words, in what game?

Or, that the pain is the bearer of the name?

"I know what I mean by 'toothache' but the other person can't *know* it."

When one says "I talk to myself" one generally means just that one speaks and is the only person listening.

If I look at something red and say to myself, this is red, am I giving myself information? Am I communicating a personal experience to myself? Some people philosophizing might be inclined to say that this is the only real case of communication of personal experience because only I know what I really mean by "red."

Remember in which special cases only it has sense to inform another person that the color which he sees now is red.

The difficulty is that we feel we have said something about the nature of pain when we say that one person can't have another person's pain. Perhaps we shouldn't be inclined to say that we had said anything physiological or even psychological, but something metapsychological, metaphysical. Something about the essence, nature, of pain as opposed to its causal connections with other phenomena.

Es scheint etwa als wäre es zwar nicht falsch sondern unsinnig zu sagen "ich fühle seine Schmerzen," aber als wäre dies so infolge der Natur des Schmerzes, der Person etc. Als wäre also jene Aussage letzten Endes doch eine Aussage über die Natur der Dinge.

Wir sprechen also etwa von einer Asymmetrie unserer Ausdrucksweise und fassen diese auf als ein Spiegelbild des Wesens der Dinge.[5]

Kann man sagen: "In das was ich über die Erfahrung des Andern sage, spielt solche Erfahrung selbst nicht hinein. In das was ich über meine Erfahrung sage, spielt diese Erfahrung selbst hinein?"

"Ich spreche über meine Erfahrung, sozusagen, in ihrer Anwesenheit."[6]

[5]It seems as though it would be not false but meaningless to say "I feel his pains," and as though this were because of the nature of pain, of the person etc. So that the assertion would after all be an assertion about the nature of things.

So we speak perhaps of an asymmetry in our mode of expression and we look on this as a mirror image of the nature of the things.

[6]Can one say: "In what I say of someone else's experience, the experience itself does not play any part. But in what I say of my experience the experience itself does play a part?"

"I speak about my experience, so to say, in its presence."

Aber die Erfahrung, die ich habe, scheint eine Beschreibung dieser Erfahrung, in gewissem Sinne, zu ersetzen. "Sie ist ihre eigene Beschreibung."[7]

(I can't know whether he sees anything at all or only behaves as I do when I see something.) There seems to be an undoubted asymmetry in the use of the word "to see" (and all words relating to personal experience). One is inclined to state this in the way that "I know when I see something by just seeing it, without hearing what I say or observing the rest of my behavior, whereas I know *that* he sees and *what* he sees only by observing his behavior, i.e., indirectly."

(a) There is a mistake in this, viz.: "I know what I see because I see it." What does it mean to know that?

(b) It is true to say that my reason for saying that I see is not the observation of my behavior. But this is a grammatical proposition.

(c) It seems to be an imperfection that I can only know — — — — [indirectly that he sees]. But this is just the way we use the word — — — — ["see"]. Could we then — — — — [say I know directly that he sees] if we would? Certainly.[8]

Should we say that the person who has not learned the language knows that he sees red but can't express it?—Or should we say: "He knows what he sees but can't express it"?—So, besides seeing it, he also knows what he sees?

Now suppose I asked: "How do I know that I see, and that I see red? I.e., how do I know that I do what you call seeing and seeing red?" For we use the words 'seeing' and 'red' in a game we play with one another.

Use of: "He knows what color he sees," "I know what color I saw," etc.

How do we know what color a person sees? By the sample he points to? And how do we know what relation the sample is meant to have to the original? Now are we to say "We never know . . ."? Or had we better cut these "We never know" out of our language and consider how as a matter of fact we are wont to use the word "to know"?

What if someone asked: "How do I know that what I call seeing red isn't an *entirely* different experience every time? and that I am not deluded into thinking that it is the same or nearly the same?" Here

---

[7]But the experience which I have seems, in a certain sense, to take the place of a description of this experience. "It is its own description."
[8]The manuscript contains only the dashes, not the words suggested in brackets.

again the answer "I can't know" and the subsequent removal of the question.

"He's in a better position to say what he sees than we are." That depends.

If we say "he'll tell us what he saw," it is as though he would make use of language which we had never taught him.

It is as if now we have got an *insight* into something which before we had only seen from the outside.

Inside and outside!

"Our teaching connects the word 'red' (or is meant to connect it) with a particular impression of his (a private impression, an impression in him). He then communicates this impression—indirectly, of course—through the medium of speech."

As long as you use the picture direct-indirect you can't trust yourself about the grammatical situation otherwise [in other ways].

Is telling what one sees something like turning one's inside out? And learning to say what one sees learning to let others see inside us?

"We teach him to make us see what he sees." He seems in an indirect way to show us *the object* which he sees, the object which is before his mind's eye. "We can't look at it, it is in him."

The idea of the private *object* of vision. Appearance, sense datum.

Whence the idea of the privacy of sense data?

"But do you really wish to say that they are not private? That one person can see the picture before the other person's eye?"

Surely you wouldn't think that *telling* someone what one sees could be a more direct way of communicating than by pointing to a sample!

If I say what it is I see, how do I compare what I say with what I see in order to know whether I say the truth?

Lying about what I see, you might say, is knowing what I see and saying something else. Supposing I said it just consists of saying to myself 'this is red' and aloud 'this is green.'[9]

Compare lying and telling the truth in the case of telling what color you see, with the case of describing a picture which you saw, or telling the right number of things you had to count.

[9]See below, page 171 72.

Collating what you say and what you see.
Is there always a collating?

Or could one call it giving a picture of the color I see if I say the word red? Unless it be a picture by its connections with a sample.

• But isn't it giving a picture if I point to a sample?

"What I show *reveals* what I see"—in what sense does it do that? The idea is that now you can so to speak look inside me. Whereas I only reveal to you what I see in a game of revealing and hiding which is entirely played with signs of one category. "Direct-indirect."

We are thinking of a game in which there is an inside in the normal sense.

We must get clear about how the metaphor of revealing (outside and inside) is actually applied by us; otherwise we shall be tempted to look for an inside behind that which in our metaphor is the inside.

"If he had learned to show me (or tell me) what he sees, he could now show me." Certainly—but what is it like to show me what he sees? It is pointing to something under particular circumstances. Or is it something else (don't be misled by the idea of indirectness)?
You compare it with such a statement as: "If he had learned to open up, I could now see what's inside." I say yes, but remember what opening up in this case is like.

But what about the criterion whether there is anything inside or not? Here we say "I know there's something inside in *my* case. This is how I know about an inside and am led to suppose it in the other person too."

Further, we are not inclined to say that only hitherto we have not known the inside of another person, but that the idea of this knowledge is bound up with the idea of myself.

"So if I say 'he has toothache' I am supposing that he has what I have when I have toothache." Suppose I said: "If I say 'I *suppose* he has toothache' I am supposing that he has what I have if I have toothache"—this would be like saying "If I say 'this cushion is red' I mean that it has the same color which the sofa has if it is red." But this isn't what I intended to say with the first sentence. I wished to say that talking about his toothache at all was based upon a supposition, a supposition which by its very essence could not be verified.

But if you look closer you will see that this is an entire misrepresentation of the use of the word 'toothache.'

Can two people have the same afterimage?

Language game: 'Description of the picture before one's mind's eye.'

Can two persons have the same picture before their mind's eye?

In which case would we say that they had two images exactly alike but not identical?

It seems as though I wished to say that to me L.W. something applied which does not apply to other people. That is, there seems to be an asymmetry.

I *express* things asymmetrically and could express them symmetrically; only then one would see what facts prompt us to the asymmetrical expression.

I do this by spreading the use of the word "I" over all human bodies as opposed to L.W. alone.

I want to describe a situation in which I should not be tempted to say that I assumed or believed that the other had what I have. Or, in other words, a situation in which we would not speak of *my consciousness* and *his consciousness*. And in which the idea would not occur to us that we could only be conscious of our own consciousness.

The idea of the ego inhabiting a body to be abolished.

If whatever consciousness (there is) spreads over all human bodies, then there won't be any temptation to use the word 'ego.'

If it is absurd to say that I only know that *I* see but not that the others do—isn't this at any rate less absurd than to say the opposite?

Ist eine Philosophie undenkbar, die das diametrale Gegenteil des Solipsismus ist?[10]

The idea of the constituent of a fact: "Is my person (or a person) a constituent of the fact that I see or not?" This expresses a question concerning the symbolism just as if it were a question about nature.

Language game: I paint, for myself, what I see. The picture doesn't contain *me*.

[10]Is it impossible to imagine a philosophy that would be the diametrical opposite of solipsism?

What if the other person always correctly described what I saw and imagined, would I not say he knows what I see?—"But what if he describes it wrongly on some occasion? Mustn't I say he was mistaken?" Why should I say this and not, rather, he has forgotten the meanings of his words?

"But after all, only I can finally decide whether what he said is right. We can't assume that *he* knows what I see and *I don't!*" We can also do this!

Can a man doubt whether what he sees is red or green? (Elaborate this.)

"Surely if he knows anything he must know what he sees!"—It is true that the game of "showing or telling what one sees" is one of the most fundamental language games; which means that what we in ordinary life call using language mostly presupposes this game.

I can for what I see use the impersonal form of description, and the fact that I say "for what I see" doesn't say at all that after all this is only a disguised personal description! For I just expressed myself in *our* ordinary form of expression, in English.

Does the solipsist also say that only he can play chess?

But he will say that behind the sentence 'I see . . .' when he says it and it's true, there stands something which does not stand behind "he sees" or "I see" when the other man says it.

"Surely," I want to say, "if I'm to be quite frank I must say that I have something which nobody has."—But who's I?—Hell! I don't express myself properly, but there's *something!* You can't deny that there is my personal experience and that this in a most important sense *has no neighbor.*—But you don't mean that it *happens* to be alone but that its grammatical position is that of having no neighbor.

"But somehow our language doesn't bring it out that there is something unique, namely real present experience, and do you just wish me to resign myself to that?"

(Funny that in ordinary life we never feel that we have to resign ourselves to something by using ordinary language.)

The normal use of the expression "he sees red where . . ." is this: We take it as the criterion for meaning the same by 'red' as we do, that as a rule he agrees with us in giving the same names to the colors of objects as we do. If then in a particular instance he says something is red where we should say it's green, we say he sees it different from us.

Notice how in such cases we would behave. We should look for a cause of his different judgment, and if we had found one we should certainly be inclined to say that he saw red where we saw green. It is further clear that even before ever finding such a cause we might under circumstances be inclined to say this. But also that we can't give a strict rule for. . . .

Consider this case: someone says "I can't understand it, I see everything red blue today and vice versa." We answer "it must look queer!" He says it does and, e.g., goes on to say how cold the glowing coal looks and how warm the clear (blue) sky. I think we should under these or similar circumstances be inclined to say that he saw red what we saw blue. And again we should say that we know that he means by the words 'blue' and 'red' what we do as he has always used them as we do.

On the other hand: Someone tells us today that yesterday he always saw everything red blue, and so on. We say: But you called the glowing coal red, you know, and the sky blue. He answers: That was because I had also changed the names. We say: But didn't it feel very queer? and he says: No, it seemed all perfectly natural. Would we in this case too say: . . . . ?

The case of contradictory memory images: tomorrow he remembers this, the day after tomorrow something else.

The whole trend, to show that the expression "letting one look into his soul," is often misleading.

Now I ask what are our criteria for there being or having been a personal experience besides the expression? And the answer seems to be that for the other man the criteria are indeed mere outside expressions, but that I myself know whether I have an experience or not; in particular, whether I see red or not.

But let me ask: what is knowing that I see red like? I mean: look at something red, 'know that it is red,' and ask yourself what you are doing. Don't you mean seeing red and impressing it on your mind that you are doing so? But there are, I suppose, several things that you are doing: You probably *say* to yourself the word 'red' or 'this is red' or something of the sort, or perhaps glance from the red object to another red one which you're taking to be the paradigm of red, and suchlike. On the other hand you just silently stare at the red thing.

In part of their uses the expression "visual image" and "picture" run parallel; but where they don't, the analogy which does exist tends to delude us.

(Tautology.)[11]
The grammar of 'seeing red' is connected to the expression of seeing red closer than one thinks.

We may say a blind man doesn't see anything. But not only do we say so but he too says that he does not see. I don't mean "he agrees with us that he does not see—he doesn't dispute it," but rather: he too describes the facts in this way, having learned the same language as we have. Now whom shall we call blind? What is our criterion for blindness? A certain kind of behavior. And if the person behaves in that particular way, we not only call him blind but teach him to call himself blind. And in *this* sense his behavior also determines the meaning of blindness for *him*. But now you will say: "Surely blindness isn't a behavior; it's clear that a man can behave like a blind man and not be blind. Therefore 'blindness' means something different; his behavior only helps him to understand what we mean by 'blindness.' The outward circumstances are what both he and we know. Whenever he behaves in a certain way, we say that he sees nothing; but he notices that a certain private experience of his coincides with all these cases and so concludes that we mean this experience of his by saying that he sees nothing."

The idea is that we teach a person the meaning of expressions relating to personal experiences *indirectly.* Such an indirect mode of teaching we could imagine as follows. I teach a child the names of colors and a game, say, of bringing objects of a certain color when 'the name of the color' is called out. I don't however teach him the color names by pointing to a sample which I and he see and saying, e.g., the word red. Instead I have various spectacles each of which, when I look through it, makes me see the white paper in a different color. These spectacles are also distinguished by their outside appearance: the one that makes me see red has circular lenses, another one elliptical ones, etc. I now teach the child in this way: that when I see him putting the circular ones on his nose I say the word 'red,' when the elliptical ones 'green,' and so forth. This one might call teaching the child the meanings of the color names in an indirect way, because one could in this case say that I led the child to correlate the word 'red' with something that I didn't see but hoped the child would see if he

---

[11]A few pages later in the same manuscript:
  "But it seems to me that I either see red or don't see red. Whether I express it or not.
  "Picture we use here.
  "This picture is not questioned, but its application.
  "Other cases of tautologies."

looked through the circular glasses. And this way is indirect as opposed to the direct way of pointing to a red object etc.

(Mind-reading)

From this it should follow that we sometimes rightly, sometimes wrongly, teach a man to say that he is blind: for what if he saw all the time but nevertheless behaved exactly like a blind man?—Or should we say: "Nature wouldn't play such a trick on us!"

We can see here that we don't quite understand the real use of the expression "to see something" or "to see nothing."

And what is so misleading to us when we consider this use is the following. We say, "Surely we can see something without ever saying or showing that we do, and on the other hand we can say that we see so-and-so without ever seeing it; therefore seeing is *one* process and expressing what we see another, and all that they have to do with one another is that they sometimes coincide—they have the same connections as being red and being sweet. Sometimes what is red is sweet —etc." Now this is obviously not quite true and not quite false. It seems somehow that we look at the use of these words with some prejudice. It is clear that we in our language use the words 'seeing red' in such a way that we can say "*A* sees red but doesn't show it"; on the other hand it is easy to see that we should have no use for these words if their application was severed from the criteria of behavior. That is to say: to the language game which we play with these words it is both essential that the people who play it behave in the particular way we call expressing (saying, showing) what they see, and also that sometimes they more or less entirely conceal what they see.

Balance.[12] The point of the game depends on what *usually* happens.

[12]Weighing. Later in the notebook: Sometimes these bodies change their weight, and then we look for the cause of the change and find, say, that something's come off the body. Sometimes however the weight of the body changes and we can't account for the change at all. But we nevertheless don't say that weighing it had lost its point "because now the body really doesn't have any weight." Rather we say that the body had changed somehow —that this was the cause of the change of weight—but that so far we have not found this cause. That is, we shall go on playing the game of weighing, and we try to find an explanation for the exceptional behavior.

We use the form of expression "the weight of this body" to designate something inherent in the body, something which could only be diminished by destroying part of the body. The same body—the same weight.

Grocer.

Supposing what in fact is the rule became the exception. Under certain peculiar circumstances indeed a body kept on weighing the same; say, iron in the presence of mercury. A piece of cheese, on the other hand, though keeping its size, calories, etc., weighed different weights at different times unaccountably. Would we still. . . .

But doesn't the word "seeing red" mean to me a particular experience, a *fact* in the realm of primary experience—which surely is utterly different from saying certain words?

The words "'seeing red' means a particular experience" are useless unless we can follow them up by: "namely this—(pointing)." Or else they may say experience as opposed to physical object; but then this is grammar.

How does he know that he sees red (or has the visual image), i.e., how does he connect the word 'red' with 'a particular color'? In fact what does the expression 'a particular color' here mean? What is the criterion for his connecting the word always to the same experience? Is it not often just that he calls it red?

In fact, if he is to play a language game, the possibility of this will depend upon his own and other people's reactions. The game depends upon the agreement of these reactions; i.e., they must *call* the same things 'red.'

"But if he speaks to himself, surely this is different. For then he needn't consult other people's reactions and he just gives the name 'red' now to *the same color* to which he gave it on a previous occasion." But how does he know that it is *the same color?* Does he also recognize the sameness of color as what he used to call sameness of color, and so on ad infinitum?

"Surely seeing is one thing, and showing that I see is another thing." —This certainly is like saying "skipping is one thing and jumping another." But there is a supplement to this statement—"skipping is this (showing it) and jumping is this (showing it)." Now how about this supplement in the first case? "Seeing red is this (showing it) and showing that we see red is this (showing it)." The point is that there just isn't a 'showing that I see' except showing that I see. "But can't I say 'seeing red is what I'm doing now' (looking at something red)? And although in a sense the other man can't directly see what I'm talking about (be aware of the activity), I certainly know what it is that I'm talking about. That is, although for him I can't point directly to my seeing red, for myself I can point to it; and in this sense I can give an ostensive definition of the expression to myself." But an ostensive definition is not a magic act.

So what does giving myself the ostensive definition of red consist in?—Now how am I to describe it? shall I say: seeing red and saying to myself 'I see red,'—or is it "seeing a certain color sensation and saying 'I see red'"? The first version I don't like. It assumes that the other knows the very same private impression which I am having. So I would rather leave it open what color I am concentrating my attention on. But then how can I call it a color? Isn't it just as uncertain that I mean by 'color' what they mean as that I mean by 'red' what they mean? And the same applies of course to 'seeing' (for what here I mean by this word is not an activity of the inner eye).

"But it's a blatant error to mix up 'seeing red' with showing that you see red! I know what seeing red is and I know what showing . . . is." Couldn't we say that knowing what showing . . . is is seeing showing? Now what is knowing what seeing is?

In knowing what seeing red is you seem to say to yourself 'seeing red is this'—you seem to give yourself a sample but you don't because the usual criteria for the sameness of the sample don't apply. I can say I call 'red' always the same color, or whenever I explain 'red' I point to a sample of the same color.

Consider the proposition: He makes sure what it means *to him* by. . . . Would you say the word had meaning to him if it meant something else every time? And what is the criterion of the same color coming twice?

If we describe a game which he plays with himself, is it relevant that he should use the word 'red' for the same color in our sense, or would we also call it a language game if he used it anyhow? Then what is the criterion for using it in the same way? Not merely the connection between "same," "color," and "red."

"Let me see if I still know which of these colors is red?—(Looking about.) Yes I know." (Here I could have said "is called red.")

Making sure that you know what 'seeing red' means, is good only if you can make use of this knowledge in a further case. Now what if I see a color again, can I say I made sure I knew what 'red' was so now I shall know that I recognize it correctly? In what sense is having said the words 'this is red' before a guarantee that I now see the same color when I say again I see red?

The grammar of 'private sense data.'

"'Toothache' is a word which I use in a game which I play with other people, but it has a private meaning to me."

In the use of the word 'meaning' it is essential that the same meaning is kept throughout a game.

"Are you sure that you call 'toothache' always the same private experience?"

What's the use here of being sure, if it doesn't follow that it is so and if your being sure is the only criterion there is for its being so?

This means: This isn't at all a case of being sure, of conviction.

"So-and-so has excellent health, he never had to go to the dentist, never complained about toothache; but as toothache is a private experience, we can't know whether he hasn't had terrible toothache all his life."

How does one assume such and such to be the case? What is an assumption that, e.g., '*A* has toothache'? Is it saying the words "*A* has toothache"? Or doesn't it consist in doing something with these words?

"A game of assumption."—

Assuming: a state of mind. Assuming: a gesture.

Certain behavior under certain circumstances we call showing our toothache, and other behavior hiding our toothache. Now would we talk about this behavior in this way if people didn't ordinarily behave in the way they do? Suppose I and they described my behavior without such a word as pain, would the description be incomplete? The question is: do *I* consider it incomplete? If so, I will distinguish between two cases of my behavior, and the others will say that I use two words alternately for my behavior and thereby they will acknowledge that I have toothache.

"But can't he have toothache without in any way showing it? And this shows that the word 'toothache' has a meaning entirely independent of a behavior connected with toothache."

The game we play with the word 'toothache' entirely depends upon there being a behavior which we call the expression of toothache.

"We use 'toothache' as the name of a personal experience."—Well, let's see how we *use* the word!

"But you know the sensation of toothache! So you can give it a name, say, '*t*.'"

But what is it like to give a sensation a name? Say it is pronouncing the name while one has the sensation and possibly concentrating on the sensation,—but what of it? Does this name thereby get magic powers? And why on earth do I call these sounds the 'name' of the sensation? I know what I do with the name of a man or of a number, but have I by this act of "definition" given the name a use?

"To give a sensation a name" means nothing unless I know already in what sort of a game this name is to be used.

We describe a certain behavior by "it is obvious that he was hiding his pain," or: "I think he was hiding his pain," or: "I don't know at all whether he was hiding pain."

But can't I just assume with some degree of certainty that he has pain although I have no reason whatever for it? I can say "I assume . . . ," but if I sent them all to the doctor although they showed no sign of pain (illness), I should just be called mad.

In our private language game we had, it seemed, given a name to an impression—in order, of course, to use the name for this impression in the future. The definition, that is, should have determined on future occasions for what impression to use the name and for which not to use it. Now we said that on certain occasions after having given the definition we did use the word and on others we didn't; but we described these occasions only by saying that we had 'a certain impression'—that is, we didn't describe them at all. The only thing that characterized them was that we used such and such words. What seemed to be a definition didn't play the rôle of a definition at all. It did not justify one subsequent use of the word; and all that remains of our private language game is therefore that I sometimes without any particular reason write the word 'red' in my diary.

"But surely I feel justified when normally I use the word 'red' although I don't think of a definition while doing so." Do you mean that whenever normally you use the word 'red' you have a particular feeling which you call a feeling of justification? I wonder if that is true. But anyhow by 'justification' I didn't mean a feeling. But I think I know what makes you say that on saying, e.g., 'this book is red' you have a feeling of being justified in using the word. For you might ask: isn't there an obvious difference between the case in which I use a word in its well known meaning—as when I say to someone "the sky is blue today"—and the case in which I say any arbitrary word on such an occasion, e.g., "the sky is moo." In this case, you will say, I either know that I am just *giving* a meaning to the word 'moo,' or else I shall feel that there is no justification whatever for using the word. The word

is just *any* word and not the appropriate word. I quite agree that there
is a difference between the cases of 'using the name of the color,'
'giving a new name to the color,' and 'using some arbitrary word in
place of the name of the color.' But that doesn't mean that it is correct
to say that I have a feeling of appropriateness in the first case which is
absent in the third. "But 'red' somehow seems to us to fit this color."
We certainly may be inclined to say this sentence on certain occasions,
but it would be wrong to say that therefore we had a feeling of fitting
when ordinarily we said that something was red.

"But do you mean that one man couldn't play a game of chess with
himself and without anyone else knowing that he did?"—What would
you say he should do to be playing a private game of chess? Just anything?

I suppose you would say, e.g., that he imagines a chessboard with
chessmen on it, that he imagines certain moves, etc. And if you were
asked what it means to imagine a *chessboard,* you would explain it by
pointing to a real chessboard, or say to a picture of one, and analogously
if you were asked what does it mean to imagine the king of chess, a
pawn, a knight's move etc. Or should you have said: he must go through
certain . . . ? But what private experiences are there? and would any
of them do in this case? For instance, feeling hot? "No! The private
experience I am talking of must have the multiplicity of the game of
chess." But again, does he recognize two private experiences to be
different by a further private experience and this to be the same in
different cases? (Private experience in fiction.) Mustn't we say in this
case that we can't say anything whatever about private experiences
and are in fact not entitled to use the word 'experiences' at all? What
makes us believe that we are is that we really think of the cases in
which we can describe his private experiences, describing different
ways of playing chess in one's imagination.

What is it that happens when in the one case I say "I see red/have
toothache/" and mean it, and am not lying, and on the other hand I say
the words but know that they are not true; or say them not knowing
what they mean, etc.?

The criteria for it being the truth are laid down in *language,* in
rules, charts, etc. "But how am I to know how in the particular case
to apply them? For in so far as they are laid down in common language,
they join the rest of the rules of common language; i.e., they do not
help me in my particular case. Is there such a thing as justifying what
I do in the particular case, merely by what then is the case and not by

a rule? Can I say I am now justified in using the sentence . . . just by what is now the case?" No!

Nor does it help me to say "I am justified—when I *feel* justified." For about feeling justified the same thing can be said as about feeling toothache.

But showing toothache can never be lying.
I must assume an expression which is *not* lying.

When I say that moaning is the expression of toothache, then under certain circumstances the possibility of its being the expression without the feeling behind it mustn't enter my game.

Es ist Unsinn zu sagen: der Ausdruck kann immer lügen.[13]

The language games with expressions of feelings are based on games with expressions of which we don't say that they may lie.

"But was I when a baby taught that 'toothache' meant my expression of toothache?"—I was taught that a certain behavior was called expression of toothache.

"But surely there's a case in which I'm justified in saying 'I see red,' where I'm not lying, and one where I'm not justified in saying so!" Of course I can be justified by the ostensive definition or by asking the others "now isn't this red?" and they answer that it is. But you didn't mean this by justification, but one which justifies me privately, whatever the others may say.

If I say "I see red" without reason, how can I distinguish between saying it with truth and saying it as a lie?

It is important here that I exclude the case of saying the untruth by mistake.

Wir haben hier keinen Vergleich des Satzes mit der Wirklichkeit! (Kollationieren.)[14]

Imagine a Robinson Crusoe lying to himself.—Why is this difficult to imagine?

But one might call it lying to oneself if one, e.g., turns one's watch forward to make oneself get up earlier.

Falsifying an account. I add up numbers, arrive at 273 shillings, then rub out 3 and put a 5 instead.

---

[13]It is senseless to say: the expression may always lie.
[14]Here there is no comparing of proposition and reality. (Collating.)

When in this discussion we talk of lying, it ought always to mean *subjectively* lying, and subjectively lying to the other person and not to oneself.

One could imagine someone constantly lying *subjectively* but not objectively.

He always lies calling red 'green' and green 'red,' but as a matter of fact what he says agrees with the usage of other people and so his lying is never taken notice of.

"Der lügt, der sagt 'ich sehe rot' und sieht die Farbe, die er selbst mit dem Worte 'grün' bezeichnen würde." *Aber das heißt doch,* wahrheitsgemäß *so bezeichnen würde. Oder können wir sagen,* "für sich *so bezeichnen würde"?*

Daher ist die Idee, daß man lügen kann indem man laut das eine und leise das andere sagt—und was man laut sagt ist hier die lüge.[15]

Was soll es dann heißen: einen Farbeneindruck wahrheitsgemäß mit "rot" bezeichnen? Paßt das Wort denn einem Eindruck besser als dem andern?[16]

Man könnte hier auch sagen: man solle gar nicht von subjektiver Wahrheit des Satzes sprechen. Die Wahrheit des Satzes "ich habe Zahnschmerz" habe nur objektiv beurteilt zu werden.[17]

The word 'lying' was taught us in a particular way in which it was fastened to a certain behavior, to the use of certain expressions under certain circumstances. Then we use it, saying that we have been lying, when our behavior was not like the one which first constituted the meaning.

'Expressions can always be lying.' How can we say this of the expressions to which we fasten our words?

Suppose a child learned the word 'toothache' as an equivalent for its moaning, and noticed that whenever it said the word or moaned the grown-ups treated it particularly well. The child then uses moaning or

---

[15]"He is lying if he says 'I see red' when he sees the color that he himself *would call* 'green.'" But this means: he would call it that if he were speaking *truthfully.* Or can we say, "would call it that *to himself"?*

Hence the idea that one may lie by saying one thing softly and something else out loud —and what one says out loud is the lie.

[16]What could be meant by: truthfully calling a color impression "red"? Does the word fit one impression better than another?

[17]We might even say here: one ought not to talk of the subjective truth of the sentence. The truth of the sentence "I have a toothache" can be judged only objectively.

the word 'toothache' as a means to bring about the desired effect: is the child lying?

You say: "Surely I can moan with toothache and I can moan without toothache; so why shouldn't it be so with the child? Of course I only see and hear the child's behavior but from my own experience I know what toothache is (I know toothache apart from behavior) and I am led to believe that the others sometimes have the pains I have."—The first sentence already is misleading. It isn't the question whether I *can* moan with or without toothache, the point is that I distinguish 'moaning with toothache' and 'moaning without toothache' and now we can't go on to say that of course in the child we make the same distinction. In fact we don't. We teach the child to use the words "I have toothache" to replace its moans, and this was how I too was taught the expression. How do I know that I've learned the word 'toothache' to mean what they wanted me to express? I ought to say I *believe* I have!

Now one can moan because one has pain, or, e.g., one can moan on the stage. How do I know that the child, small as it is, doesn't already act, and in this case I teach it to mean by 'toothache' something I don't intend it to mean.

I have taught the child to use the expression 'I have toothache' under certain circumstances. And now it uses the words under these circumstances.—But what are these circumstances? Shall I say "the circumstances under which it moaned," and what are these?

But now I also teach the child to moan on the stage! That is to say, I *teach* it to use this expression in a different game. I also teach it to read out the sentence 'I have toothache' from a book, when it hasn't toothache. In fact I could teach it to lie, as a separate language game. (In fact we often play this kind of game with children.)

"But doesn't what you say come to this: that it doesn't matter what the persons feel as long as only they behave in a particular way?"

"Do you mean that you can define pain in terms of behavior?" But is this what we do if we teach the child to use the expression 'I have toothache'? Did I define: "Toothache is such and such a behavior"? This obviously contradicts entirely the normal use of the word! "But can't you, on the other hand, at least for yourself give an *ostensive* definition of 'toothache'? Pointing to the place of your pain and saying 'this is . . .'?" Can't I give a name to the pain I've got? Queer idea to give one's pain a name! What's it to do with a name? Or what do I do with it? What do I do with the name of a person whom I *call* by the name? What connection is the name to have with the pain? The only connection so far is that you had toothache, pointed to your cheek, and pronounced the word 'moo.' "So what?" Remember what we said about private ostensive definition.

"But aren't you neglecting something—the experience or whatever you might call it—? Almost *the world* behind the mere words?"

But here solipsism teaches us a lesson: It is that thought which is *on the way* to destroy this error. For if the *world* is idea it isn't any person's idea. (Solipsism stops short of saying this and says that it is my idea.) But then how could I say what the world is if the realm of ideas has no neighbor? What I do comes to defining the word 'world.'

'I neglect that which goes without saying.'

"What is seen *I* see" (pointing to my body). I point at my geometrical eye, saying this. Or I point with closed eyes and touch my breast and feel it. In no case do I make a connection between what is seen and a person.

Back to 'neglecting'! It seems that I neglect life. But not life physiologically understood but life as consciousness. And consciousness not physiologically understood, or understood from the outside, but consciousness as the very essence of experience, the appearance of the world, the world.

Couldn't I say: If I had to add the world to my language it would have to be one sign for the whole of language, which sign could therefore be left out.

How am I to describe the way the child learns the word 'toothache'— like this? The child sometimes has toothache, it moans and holds its cheek, the grown-ups say ". . . ," etc. Or: The child sometimes moans and holds its cheek, the grown-ups . . . ? Does the first description say something superfluous or false, or does the second leave out something essential? Both descriptions are correct.

"But it seems as if you were neglecting something." But what more can I do than *distinguish* the case of saying 'I have toothache' when I really have toothache, and the case of saying the words without having toothache. I am also (further) ready to talk of any *x* behind my words so long as it keeps its identity.

Isn't what you reproach me of as though you said: "In your language you're only *speaking!*"

But why shouldn't I say "*I* have toothache in his tooth"? I would insist on his tooth being extracted. Who is supposed to cry out if it is? What does it mean: distributing primary experience over all subjects?[18] Imagine that they all have *real* toothache in their teeth. The one which you only have. I now describe certain facts. (Not metaphysical ones, but facts about the coincidence of certain experiences.)

He gets a blow and cries—I think: "no wonder for it really hurts." But wouldn't I say to myself: Queer that *he* cries, for *I* feel the pain all right—but he?!

It seems there is a phenomenon which in general I refer to as 'my toothache,' which, experience teaches me, is always connected with one particular person (not 'I' but) L.W. I now imagine facts other than they are and connect up this phenomenon to all sorts of persons so as to make it not at all tempting to call this phenomenon "my toothache."

"I see so-and-so" does not mean "the person so-and-so, e.g., L.W., sees so-and-so."

A language game in which everybody calls out what he sees but without saying "I see . . . ." Could anybody say that what I call out is incomplete because I have left out to mention the person?!

A language game in which everybody (and I too) calls out what *I* see without mentioning *me*.

They always know what I see. If they don't seem to, I misunderstand what they say.[19]

I am tempted to say: "It seems at least a fact of experience that at the source of *the visual field* there is mostly a small man with grey flannel trousers, in fact L.W."—Someone might answer to this: It is true you almost always wear grey flannel trousers and often look at them.

"*Ich bin* doch *bevorzugt. Ich bin der Mittelpunkt der Welt.*" *Denken wir uns ich sähe mich in einem Spiegel das sagen und auf mich zeigen! Wäre es noch richtig?*[20]

When I say I play a unique role I really mean the geometrical eye.

[18]Cf. above, p. 160–161.
[19]Cf. above, p. 161–162.
[20]"But I *am* in a favored position. I am the center of the world." Suppose I saw myself in the mirror saying this and pointing to myself. Would it still be all right?

On the other hand, if I describe the visual appearance of my body around the geometrical eye, this is on the same level as saying that in the middle of the visual field there is in general a brown table and at the edges a white wall (as I generally sit in my room).

Now suppose I described this in the form: The visual world in general is like this: (follows the description). Would this be wrong?—Why should it be wrong?! But the question is, what game I intend to be played with this sentence; e.g., who is allowed to say it and in what way are those to whom it is said to react to it? I should like to say that it's I who say it—not L.W., but the person at the source of the visual field. But this I seem not to be able to explain to anyone. (Queer state of affairs.) The game played might be the one which is in general played with "I see so-and-so."

What if I see before me a picture of the room as I am seeing the room? Is this a language game?

Can't I say something to nobody, neither to anybody else *nor* to myself? What is the criterion of saying it to myself?

I want to say: "the visual world is like this . . ."—but why *say* anything?

But the point is that I don't establish a relation between a person and what is seen. All I do is that alternately I point in front of me and to myself.

But what I now see, this view of my room, plays a unique rôle, it is the visual world!

(Der Solipsist flattert und flattert in der Fliegenglocke, stößt sich an den Wänden, flattert weiter. Wie ist er zur Ruhe zu bringen?)[21]

But the real question for me here is: How am *I* defined? Who is it that is favored? *I*. But may I lift up my hand to indicate who it is?— Supposing I constantly change and my surrounding does: is there still some continuity, namely, by it being *me* and *my surrounding* that change?

(Isn't this similar to thinking that when things in space have changed entirely there's still one thing that remains the same, namely space.) (Space confused with room.)

---

[21](The solipsist flutters and flutters in the flyglass, strikes against the walls, flutters further. How can he be brought to rest?)

Suppose someone asked me, "What does it mean to play a private game of chess with oneself?" and I answered: "Anything, because if I said I was playing a game of chess I would to be so sure that I was that I would stick to what I said, whatever anyone else might say."

Suppose someone painted pictures of the landscape which surrounds him. He sometimes paints the leaves of trees orange, sometimes blue, sometimes the clear sky red, etc. Under what circumstances would we agree with him that he was portraying the landscape?

Under what circumstances would we say that he did what we call portraying, and under what circumstances that he called something portraying which we didn't call that? Suppose here we said: "Well I can never know what he does inwardly"—would this be anything more than resignation?

We call something a calculation if, for instance, it leads to a house being built.

We call something a language game if it plays a particular rôle in our human life.

"But can't he play a game with color names, against whatever anybody else says?" But why call it a game with color names? "But if *I* played it I would stick to saying that I was playing a game with color names." But is that all I can say about it; is all that I can say for its being this kind of game that I stick to calling it so?

Under what circumstances do I say that I'm entitled to say that I'm seeing red? The answer is showing a sample, i.e., giving the rule. But if now I came into constant contradiction with what anybody else said, should I not say that I am applying the rule in a way which prevents me from playing the game? That is: is all that is necessary that the rule I give should be the rule they give, or isn't besides this an agreement in the application necessary?

If "having the same pain" *means* the same as "saying that one has the same pain," then "I have the same pain" means the same as "I say that I have the same pain" and the exclamation "Oh!" means "I say 'Oh!'"

Roughly speaking: The expression 'I have toothache' stands for a moan[22] but it does not mean 'I moan.'

---

[22]In lectures W. said "is a substitute for moaning" and "replaces moaning": "Of course 'toothache' is not *only* a substitute for moaning—but it is *also* a substitute for moaning:

If I say we must assume an expression which can't lie, this can't be explained by saying that pain really corresponds to this expression.

We aren't lying, we are speaking the truth, if a fact corresponds to the sentence. This is no explanation at all but a mere repetition unless we can supplement it by 'namely this → ' and a demonstration; and the whole explanation lies just in this demonstration. The whole problem here only arose through the fact that the demonstration of 'I see red,' 'I have toothache,' seems indirect.

"But aren't you saying that all that happens is that he moans, and that there is nothing behind it?" I am saying that there is nothing *behind* the moaning.

"So you really don't have pain, you just moan?!"—There seems to be a *description* of my behavior, and also, in the same sense, a description of my pain! The one, so to speak, the description of an external, the other of an internal fact. This corresponds to the idea that in the sense in which I can give a part of my body a name, I can give a name to a private experience (only indirectly).

And I am drawing your attention to this: that the language games are very much more different than you think.

You couldn't call moaning a description! But this shows you how far the proposition 'I have toothache' is from a description, and how far teaching the word 'toothache' is from teaching the word 'tooth.'

One could from the beginning teach the child the expression "I think he has toothache" instead of "he has toothache," with the corresponding uncertain tone of voice. This mode of expression could be described by saying that we can only believe that the other has toothache.

But why not in the child's own case? Because there the tone of voice is simply *determined* by nature.

In "I have toothache" the expression of pain is brought to the same form as a description "I have 5 shillings."

We teach the child to say "I have been lying" when it has behaved in a certain way. (Imagine here a typical case of a lie.) Also this ex-

and to say this shows how utterly different it is from a word like 'Watson.'"—And again: "Suppose you were asked 'What were the phenomena which were pointed out when you learned the word "pain"'? There were certain noises in others, and then one's own. Then one is taught to replace the moan by 'I have pain.' . . . You might ask 'What does the moan stand for?' Nothing at all. 'But you don't just wish to say that you moan?' No; but the moan is not the statement 'I moan.'" Cf. above, pp. 172–173.

pression goes along with a particular situation, facial expressions, say of shame, tones of reproach, etc.

"But doesn't the child know that it is lying before ever I teach him the word?" Is this meant to be a metaphysical question or a question about facts? The child doesn't know it in words. And why should it know it at all?—"But do you assume that it has only the facial expression of shame, e.g., without the feeling of shame? Mustn't you describe the inside situation as well as the outside one?"—But what if I said that by facial expression of shame I meant what you mean by 'the facial expression + the feeling,' unless I explicitly distinguish between genuine and simulated facial expressions? It is, I think, misleading to describe the genuine expression as a *sum* of the expression and something else, though it is just as misleading—we get the function of our expressions wrong—if we say that the genuine expression is a particular behavior and nothing besides.

We teach the child the use of the word "to speak."—Later it uses the expression "I spoke to myself."—We then say "We never know whether and what a person speaks to himself."

Surely the description of the facial expression can be meant as a description of feelings and can be meant otherwise. We constantly use such expressions as "when he heard that, he pulled a long face" and don't add that the expression was genuine. In other cases we describe the acting[23] of a person in the same words, or again we wish to leave it open whether the expression was genuine or not. To say that we describe the feeling indirectly by the description of expressions is wrong!

Imagine a language in which toothache is called "moaning" and the difference between just moaning and moaning with pain is expressed by the moaning or dry tone in which the word is pronounced. People would not say in this language that it became clear later on that *A* didn't really have pain, but they would perhaps in an angry tone say that at first he moaned and then he suddenly laughed.

Suppose he says to himself "I lie," what is to show that he means it? But we would any day describe this lying by saying: "He said . . . , and told himself at the same time that he was lying." Is this too an indirect description of lying?

But couldn't one say that if I speak of a man's angry voice, meaning that he was angry, and again of his angry voice, not meaning that he

---

[23]On the stage.

was angry, in the first case the meaning of the description of his voice was much further reaching than in the second case? I will admit that our description in the first case doesn't *omit* anything and is as complete as though we had said that he really was angry—but somehow the meaning of the expression then reaches below the surface.

But how does it do that? The answer to this would be an explanation of the two uses of the expression. But how could this explanation reach *under the surface?* It is an explanation about symbols and it states in which cases these symbols are used. But how does it characterize these cases? Can it in the end do more than distinguish two expressions? i.e., describe a game with two expressions?

"Then is there nothing under the surface?!" But I said that I was going to distinguish two expressions, one for the 'surface' and one for 'what is below the surface'—only remember that these expressions themselves correspond just to a *picture*, not to its usage. It is just as misleading to say that there is just the surface and nothing underneath it, as that there is something below the surface and that there isn't just the surface. Because we naturally use this picture to express the distinction between 'on the surface' and 'below the surface.' Because once we make use of the picture of the 'surface' it is most natural to express with it the distinction as on and below the surface. But we misapply the picture if we ask whether both cases are or aren't on the surface.

Now in order that with its normal meaning we should teach a child the expression "I have lied" the child must behave in the normal way. E.g., it must under certain circumstances 'admit' that it lied, it must do so with a certain facial expression etc., etc., etc. We may not always find out whether he lied or not, but if we never found out, the word would have a different meaning. "But once he has learned the word he can't be in doubt whether he is lying or not!"

This of course is like saying that he can't be in doubt whether he has toothache or whether he sees red, etc. On the one hand: doubting whether I have the experience E is not like doubting whether someone else has it. On the other hand, one can't say "surely I must know what it is I see" unless 'to know what I see' is to mean 'to see whatever I see.' The question is what we are to call "knowing what it is I see," "not being in doubt about what it is I see." Under what circumstances are we to say that a person is in no doubt (or is in doubt) about this? (Such cases as being in no doubt about whether this looks red to the normal eye, and analogous ones, of course don't interest us here.) I suppose that the knowledge of what it is I see must be the knowledge that it is so-and-so I see; 'so-and-so' standing for some expressions, verbal or otherwise. (But remember that I don't give myself information by pointing to something I see with my finger and saying to myself I see this.) 'So-and-so' in fact stands for a word of a language game. And doubting what it is I see is doubting, e.g., what to call what I see. Doubting, for instance, whether to say 'I see red' or 'I see green.' "But this is a simple doubt about the appellation of a color, and it can be settled by asking someone what this color (pointing) is called." But are all such doubts removable by this question (or which comes to the same, by giving a definition: "I shall call this color so-and-so")?

"What color do you see?"—"I don't know, is it red or isn't it red; I don't know what color it is I see."—"What do you mean? Is the color constantly changing, or do you see it so very faintly, practically black?" Could I say here: "don't you see what you see?"? This obviously would make no sense.

It seems as though, however the outward circumstances change, once the word is fastened to a particular personal experience it now retains its meaning; and that therefore I can now use it with sense whatever may happen.

To say that I can't doubt whether I see red is in a sense absurd, as the game I play with the expression 'I see red' doesn't contain a doubt in this form.

It seems, whatever the circumstances I always know whether to apply the word or not. It seems, at first it was a move in a special game but then it becomes independent of this game.

(This reminds one of the way the idea of length seems to become emancipated from any particular method of measuring it.)[24]

We are tempted to say: "damn it all, a rod has a particular length however I express it." And one could go on to say that if I see a rod I always see (know) how long it is, although I can't say how many feet, meters, etc.—But suppose I just say: I always know whether it looks tiny or big!

But can't the old game lose its point when the circumstances change, so that the expression ceases to have a meaning, although of course I can still pronounce it.

He sticks to saying that he has been lying although none of the usual

[24]Wittgenstein marked this whole passage as unsatisfactory and wrote "vague" in the margin.

consequences follow. What is there left of the language game except that he says the expression?

We learn the word 'red' under particular circumstances. Certain objects are usually red, and keep their colors; most people agree with us in our color judgments. Suppose all this changes: I see blood, unaccountably sometimes one sometimes another color, and the people around me make different statements. But couldn't I in all this chaos retain my meaning of 'red,' 'blue,' etc., although I couldn't now make myself understood to anyone? Samples, e.g., would all constantly change their color—'or does it only seem so to me?' "Now am I mad or did I really call this 'red' yesterday?"

The situations in which we are inclined to say "I must have gone mad!"

"But we could always call a color-impression 'red' and stick to this appellation!"

Die Atmosphäre, die dieses Problem umgibt, ist schrecklich. Dichte Nebel der Sprache sind um den problematischen Punkt gelagert. Es ist beinahe unmöglich, zu ihm vorzudringen.[25]

Do I by painting what I see tell myself what I see?

"This picture is unique, for it represents what is really seen."
What is my *justification* for saying this?

I see two spots on this wall and lift two fingers. Do I tell myself that I see two spots? But on the other hand couldn't this be the sign for my seeing two spots?

Ist das Bild ausgezeichnet oder zeichne ich es aus?[26]

"Today he points at *me;* and yesterday he pointed at *me* also."

The meaning of: "He points at me."

"I see that he points at *A.*"
"I see that he points at me."

Imagine a game: One person tells the other what he (the other) sees; if he has guessed it rightly he is rewarded. If *A* hasn't guessed correctly what *B* sees, *B* corrects him and says what it is he sees. This

---

[25]The atmosphere surrounding this problem is terrible. Dense mists of (our) language are situated about the crucial point. It is almost impossible to get through to it.
[26]Is it a special picture or do I give it special attention?

game is more instructive if we imagine the persons not to say what is seen but to paint or make models of it. Now let me imagine that I am one of the players.

Wouldn't I be tempted to say: "The game is asymmetrical, for only what I say I see corresponds to a visual image."

The problem lies thus: This ↗ is what's seen; and this is also what I see.

Frage Dich: Kann das ↗ nur ich sehen, oder kann es auch ein Andrer sehen? Warum nur ich?[27]

Für mich existiert kein Unterschied zwischen ich und das ↗; und das Wort "ich" ist für mich kein Signal, das einen Ort oder eine Person hervorhebt.[28]

Ich versuche das ganze Problem auf das nicht-Verstehen der Funktion des Wortes "Ich" (und "das ↗ ") zu reduzieren.[29]

When I stare at a colored object and say "this is red," I seem to know exactly to what I give the name red. As it were, to that which I am drinking in.

It is as though there was a magic power in the words *"this is. . . ."*

I can bring myself to say: There is no toothache there ↗ (in the man's cheek who says he has toothache). And what would be the expression for this in ordinary language? Wouldn't it be *my* saying that *I* have no toothache there?

"But who says this?"—"I!" And who says *this?*—"I!"—

Suppose I give this rule: "Whenever I said 'I have toothache' I shall from now on say 'there is toothache.'"

I tell the waiter: Bring me always clear soup, and thick soup to all the others. He tries to remember my face.

Suppose I change my face (body) every day entirely, how is he to know which is me? But it's a question of the *existence* of the game. "If all chessmen were alike, how should one know which is the king?"

Now it seems that, although *he* couldn't know which is me, *I* would still know it.

Suppose now I said: "it wasn't so-and-so, it was I who asked for

---

[27]Ask yourself: Can only *I* see this ↗ , or can someone else see it too? Why only I?
[28]There is no difference, for me, between *I* and *this ↗* ; and for me the word "I" is not a signal calling attention to a place or a person.
[29]I am trying to bring the whole problem down to our not understanding the function of the word "I" (and "this ↗ ").

clear soup"—couldn't I be wrong? Certainly. I.e., I may think that
I *asked* him, but didn't. Now are there *two* mistakes I can make: one,
thinking that I *asked* him, the other, thinking that *I* asked him? I say:
"I remember having asked you yesterday," he replies: "You weren't
there at all yesterday." Now I could say either: "well then I suppose
I remember wrongly," or: "I was here only I looked like him yesterday."

It seems that I can *trace* my identity, quite independent of the identity
of my body. And the idea is suggested that I trace the identity of something dwelling in a body, the identity of my mind.

"If anybody asks me to describe *what I see*, I describe *what's seen*."

What we call a description of my sense datum, of what's seen,
independent of what is the case in the physical world, is still a description for the other person.

If I speak of a description of *my* sense datum, I don't *mean* to give
a particular person as its possessor.

(No more do I want to speak about a particular person when I moan
with pain.)

It must be a serious and deep-seated disease of language (one might
also say 'of thought') which makes me say: "Of course this ↗ is what's
really seen."

I can tell you the fact *p* because I know that *p* is the case. It has sense
to say "it rained and I knew it," but not "I had toothache and knew
that I had." "I know that I have toothache" means nothing, or the same
as "I have toothache."

This, however, is a remark about the use of the word "I," whoever
uses it.

Examine the sentence: "There is something there," referring to the
visual sensation I'm now having.

Aren't we inclined to think that this is a statement making sense
and being true? And on the other hand, isn't it a pseudo-statement?

But what (what entity) do you refer to when you say that sentence?
—Aren't we here up against the old difficulty, that it seems to us that
meaning something was a special state or activity of mind? For it is
true that in saying these words I am in a special state of mind, I stare
at something—but this just doesn't constitute meaning.

Compare with this such a statement as: "Of course I know what I am
referring to by the word 'toothache.'"

Think of the frame of mind in which you say to yourself that $p \cdot \sim p$

does make sense and by repeating a statement of this form you are, as it were by introspection, trying to find out what it means.

The phenomenon of *staring* is closely bound up with the whole puzzle of solipsism.

"If I am asked 'what do you see?,' I describe the visual world." —Couldn't I say instead of this "... I am describing what is there ↗ " (pointing before me)?

But now consider the case of someone having a picture before him of the part of his room he is seeing, and he says: "This in the picture is like *this* (a part of his visual field as he is looking at his room)."

Supposing I said "there is something there"; and being asked "What do you mean?," I painted a picture of what I see. Would this justify making that statement?—Wouldn't this picture have to be understood 'in a system'? And mustn't *I* understand it as an expression within a system?

[Reference to a geometrical diagram of two perpendiculars drawn to a given point on a line:] 'Look at the geometrical proposition as a member of the whole system of geometrical propositions, then you will see whether you really want to accept this proposition!'

"It's no use saying that the other person knows what he sees and not what I see and that therefore all is symmetrical, because there is just nothing else corresponding to my visual image, my visual image is unique!"[30]

"But I can persuade myself that nobody else has pains even if they say they have, but not that I haven't."
It makes no sense to say "I persuade myself that I have no pain," whoever says this. I don't say anything about myself when I say that I can't persuade myself that I haven't pain, etc.

If I say "*I* see this ↗ " I am likely to tap my chest to show which person I am. Now suppose I had no head and pointing to my geometrical eye I would point to an empty place above my neck: wouldn't I still feel that I pointed to the person who sees, tapping my chest? Now I might ask "how do you know in this case who sees this?" But what is *this?* It's no use just pointing ahead of me, and if, instead, I point to a description and tap both my chest and the description and say '*I* see *this*'—it has no sense to ask "How do you know it's *you* who

[30]In the margin: "*sehr wichtig, wenn auch schlecht gesagt.*" (Very important, although badly expressed.)

sees it?," for I don't *know* that it's this person and not another one which sees before I point.—This is what I meant by saying that I don't choose the mouth which says "I have toothache."

Isn't it queer that if I look in front of me and point in front of me and say "this!," I should know what it is I mean. "I mean just these shades of color and shapes, the *appearance.*"

If I say "I mean the appearance," it seems I am telling you what it is I am pointing to or looking at, e.g., the chair as opposed to the bed, etc. It is as though by the word "appearance" I had actually *directed your attention* to something else than, e.g., the physical objects you are looking at. And indeed there corresponds a particular stare to this 'taking in the appearance.' Remember here what philosophers of a certain school used to say so often: "*I believe* I mean something, if I say '....'"

It seems that the visual image which I'm having is something which I can point to and talk about; that I can say of it, it is unique. That I am pointing to the physical objects in my field of vision, but not meaning them by the *appearance.* This object I am talking about, if not to others then to myself. (It is almost like something painted on a screen which surrounds me.)

This object is inadequately described as "that which I see," "my visual image," since it has nothing to do with any particular human being. Rather I should like to call it "what's seen." And so far it's all right, only now I've got to say what can be said about this object, in what sort of language game "what's seen" is to be used. For at first sight I should feel inclined to use this expression as one uses a word designating a physical object, and only on second thought I see that I can't do that.—When I said that here there seems to be an object I can point to and talk about, it was just that I was comparing it to a physical object. For only on second thought it appears that the idea of "talking about" isn't applicable here. (I could have compared the 'object' to a theater decoration.)

Now when could I be said to speak about this object? When would I say I did speak about it?—*Obviously* when I describe—as we should say—my visual image. And perhaps only if *I* describe it, and only if I describe it to myself.

But what is the point, in this case, of saying that when I describe to myself what I see, I describe an object called "what's seen"? Why talk of a particular object here? Isn't this due to a misunderstanding?

I wish to say that we can't adduce the 'private experience' as a justification for expressing it.

We can't say "he is justified in moaning because he has pains" if we call pain *the* justification for moaning.—We can't say "he is justified in expressing pain, because he has pain" unless we wish to distinguish this case of being justified in expressing pain from another way of justification, e.g., that he is on the stage and has to act as a sick man.

If I am tempted to say "my justification for moaning is having pain," it seems I point—at least for myself—to something to which I give expression by moaning.

The idea is here that there is an 'expression' for everything, that we know what it means 'to express something,' 'to describe something.' Here is a feeling, an experience, and now I could say to someone "express it!" But what is to be the relation of the expression to what it expresses? In what way is this expression the expression of this feeling rather than another?! One is inclined to say "we *mean* this feeling by its expression," but what is meaning a feeling by a word like? Is this quite clear if, e.g., I have explained what "meaning this person by the name '*N*'" is like?

"We have two expressions, one for moaning without pain, and one for moaning with pain." To what states of affairs am I pointing as explanations of these two expressions?

"But these 'expressions' can't be mere words, noises, which you make; they get their importance only from what's *behind* them (the state you're in when you use them)!"—But how can this state give importance to noises which I produce?

Suppose I said: The expressions get their importance from the fact that they are not used coolly but that we can't help using them. This is as though I said: laughter gets its importance only through being a *natural* expression, a natural phenomenon, not an artificial code.

Now what makes a 'natural form of expression' natural? Should we say "An experience which stands behind it"?

If I use the expression "I have toothache" I may think of it as 'being used naturally' or otherwise, but it would be wrong to say that I had a *reason* for thinking either.—It is very queer that *all* the importance of our expressions seems to come from that *X, Y, Z*, the private experiences, which forever remain in the *background* and can't be drawn into the foreground.

But is a cry when it is a cry of pain not a mere cry?

Why should I say the 'expression' derives its meaning from the feeling behind it—and not from the circumstances of the language game in which it is used? For imagine a person crying out with pain alone in the desert: is he using a language? Should we say that this cry had *meaning?*

We labor under the queer temptation to describe our language and its use, introducing into our descriptions an element of which we ourselves say that it is not part of the language. It is a peculiar phenomenon of iridescence which seems to fool us.

"But can't you imagine people behaving just as we do, showing pain etc., etc., and then if you imagine that *they don't feel pain* all their behavior is, as it were, dead. You can imagine all this behavior *with* or *without* pain.—"

The pain seems to be the atmosphere in which the expression exists. (The pain seems to be a *circumstance.*)

Suppose we say that the image I use in the one case is different from the image I use in the other. But I can't point to the two images. So what does it come to, to say this, except just to saying it, using *this* expression.

We are, as I have said, tempted to describe our language by saying that we use certain elements, images, which however in the last moment we again withdraw.

Isn't the expression *in its use* an image—why do I refer back to an image which I can't show?

"But don't you talk as though (the) pain weren't something terribly real?"—Am I to understand this as a proposition about pain? I suppose it is a proposition about the use of the word 'pain,' and it is one more utterance, and essential part of the surrounding in which we use the word 'pain.'

Feeling justified in having expressed pain.
I may *concentrate on the memory of pain.*

Now what's the difference between using my expressions as I do but yet not using "toothache" to mean real pain, and the proper use of the word?—

The private experience is to serve as a paradigm, and at the same time admittedly it can't be a paradigm.

The 'private experience' is a degenerate construction of our grammar (comparable in a sense to tautology and contradiction). And this grammatical monster now fools us; when we wish to do away with it, it seems as though we denied the existence of an experience, say, toothache.

What would it mean to deny the existence of pain?!

"But when we say we have toothache we don't just talk of expressing toothache in this or that way!"—Certainly not—we express toothache! "But you admit that the same behavior may be the expression of pain or may not be that."—If you imagine a man cheating—cheating is done secretly but this secrecy is not that of the 'private experience.' Why shouldn't it be considered wrong in him to use language in this way?

We say "only he knows whether he says the truth or lies." "Only you can know if what you say is true."

Now compare secrecy with the 'privateness' of personal experience! In what sense is a thought of mine secret? If I think aloud it can be heard.—"I have said this to myself a thousand times but not to anyone else."

"Only you can know what color you see." But if it is true that only you can know, you can't even impart this knowledge nor can you express it.

Why shouldn't we say that I know better than you what color you see if you say the wrong word and I can make you agree to my word, or if you point to the wrong sample, etc.?

"I didn't know that I was lying."—"You *must* have known!"

Examine: "If you don't know that you're having a toothache, you aren't having a toothache."

"I don't just *say* 'I've got toothache,' but *toothache makes me say this*." (I deliberately didn't write 'the feeling of toothache,' or 'a certain feeling.')

This sentence distinguishes between, say, saying it as an example of a sentence, or on the stage, etc., and saying it as an assertion. But it is no explanation of the expression "I have toothache," of the use of the word "toothache."

"I know what the word 'toothache' means, it makes me concentrate my attention on one particular thing." But on what? You're now inclined to give criteria of behavior. Ask yourself: "what does the word 'feeling,' or still better 'experience,' make you concentrate on?" What is it like to concentrate on experience? If *I* try to do this I, e.g., open my eyes particularly wide and stare.

"I know what the word 'toothache' means, it produces one particular image in my mind." But *what* image? "That can't be explained."—But if it can't be explained what was the meaning of saying that it produced one particular image? You could say the same about the words "image in your mind." And all that it comes to is that you are using certain words without an explanation. "But can't I explain them to myself? or understand them myself without giving an explanation? Can't I give a private explanation?" But is this anything you can call an explanation? Is staring a private explanation?

But how does this queer delusion come about?!

Here is language—and now I try to embody something in language as an explanation, which is no explanation.

. . . .

Privacy of sense data. I must bore you with a repetition of what I said last time. We said that one reason for introducing the idea of the sense datum was that people, as we say, sometimes see different things, colors, e.g., looking at the same object. Cases in which we say "he sees dark red whereas I see light red." We are inclined to talk about an object other than the physical object which the person sees who is said to see the physical object. It is further clear that we only gather from the other person's behavior (e.g., what he tells us) what that object looks like, and so it lies near to say that he has this object before his mind's eye and that we don't see it. Though we can also say that we might have it before our mind's eye as well, without however knowing that he has it before his mind's eye. The 'sense datum' here—the way the physical object appears to him. In other cases no physical object enters.

Now I want to draw your attention to one particular difficulty about the use of the 'sense datum.' We said that there were cases in which we should say that the person sees green what I see red. Now the question suggests itself: if this can be so at all, why should it not be always the case? It seems, if once we have admitted that it can happen under peculiar circumstances, that it may always happen. But then it is clear that the very idea of seeing red loses its use if we can never know if the other does not see something utterly different. So what are we to do: Are we to say that this can only happen in a limited number of cases? This is a very serious situation.—We introduced the expression that *A* sees something else than *B* and we mustn't forget that this had use only under the circumstances under which we introduced it. Consider the proposition: "Of course we never know whether new circumstances wouldn't show that after all he saw what we see." Remember that this whole notion need not have been introduced. "But can't I *imagine* all blind men to see as well as I do and only behaving differently; and on the other hand imagine them really blind? For if I can imagine these possibilities, then the question, even if never answerable makes sense." Imagine a man, say W., now blind, now seeing, and observe what you do? How do these images give sense to the question? They don't, and you see that the expression stands and falls with its usefulness.

The idea that the other person sees something else than I, is only introduced to account for certain expressions: whereas it seems that this idea can exist without any reference to expressions. "Surely what I have he too can have."

"And remember that we admit that the other may have pain without showing it! So if this is conceivable, why not that he never shows pain; and why not that everybody has pain constantly without showing it; or that even things have pain?!" What strikes us is that there seem to be a few useful applications of the idea of the other person's having pain without showing it, and a vast number of useless applications, applications which look as though they were no applications at all. And these latter applications seem to have their justification in this, that we can imagine the other person to have what we have and in this way the proposition that he has toothache seems to make sense apart from any expression at all. "Surely," we say, "I can imagine him to have pain or to see, etc." Or, "As I can see myself, so I can imagine him to do the same." In other words I can imagine him to play the same role in the act of seeing which I play. But does saying this determine what I mean by "he sees"?

We arrive at the conclusion that imagining him to have pain (etc.) does not fix the sense of the sentence "he has pain."

"He may all along mean something different by 'green' than I mean." Evidence (verification). But there is this consideration: "Surely I mean something particular, a particular impression, and therefore he may have another impression; surely I know what that would be like!" "Surely I know what it is like to have the impression I call 'green'!" But what is it like? You are inclined to look at a green object and to say "it's like *this!*" And these words, though they don't explain anything to anybody else, seem to be at any rate an explanation you give yourself. But are they?! Will this explanation justify your future use of the word 'green'? In fact seeing green doesn't allow you to make the substitutions of someone else for you and of red for green.

"The sense datum is private" is a rule of grammar, it forbids [rules out] the use of such expressions as "they saw the same sense datum"; it may (or may not) allow such sentences as "he guessed that the other had a sense datum of this . . . kind." It may only allow expressions of the form: "The other looked round, had a sense datum and said. . . ." You see that this word in such a case has no use at all. But if you like to use it, do!—

"But surely I distinguish between having toothache and expressing it, and merely expressing it; and I distinguish between these two in myself." "Surely this is not merely a matter of using different expressions, but there are two distinct experiences!" "You talk as though the case of having pain and that of not having pain were only distinguished by the way in which I expressed myself!"

But do we always distinguish between 'mere behavior' and 'experience + behavior'? If we see someone falling into flames and crying out, do we say to ourselves: "there are of course two cases: . . ."? Or if I see you here before me do I distinguish? Do you? You can't! That we do in certain cases, doesn't show that we do in all cases. This to some of you must sound silly and superficial; but it isn't. When you see me do you see one thing and conjecture another? (Don't talk of conjecturing subconsciously!) But supposing you expressed yourself in the form of such a supposition, wouldn't this come to adopting a *'façon de parler'*?

Can we say that 'saying that I lie is justified by a particular experience of lying'? Shall we say '. . . by a particular private experience'? or '. . . by a particular private experience of lying'? or 'by a particular private experience characterized in such and such ways'?

"But what, in your opinion, *is* the difference between the mere expression and the expression + the experience?"

"Do you know what it means that W. behaves as he does but sees nothing; and on the other hand that he sees?"

If you ask yourself this and answer 'yes' you conjure up some sort of image. This image is, it seems, derived from the fact of your seeing or not seeing (if you close your eyes), and by this derivation, it seems, it must be the picture we interpret to correspond to our sentence "he sees," "he doesn't see."—As when I substitute for my body, his body, and for holding a match, holding a pen.—But substituting his body for my body might mean that my body has changed so as to be now like his, and perhaps vice versa. It seems a direct and simple thing to understand "thinking that he has what I have," but it isn't at all. The case is simple only if we speak, e.g., of physiological processes. "I know only indirectly what he sees, but directly what I see" embodies an absolutely misleading picture. I can't be said to know that I have toothache if

I can't be said not to know that I have toothache. I can't be said to know indirectly what the other has if I can't be said to know it directly. The misleading picture is this: I see my own matchbox but I know only from hearsay what his looks like. We can't say: "I say he has toothache because I observe his behavior, but I say that I have because I *feel* it." (This might lead one to say that 'toothache' has two meanings, one for me and one for the other person.)

"I say 'I have toothache' because I *feel* it" contrasts this case with, say, the case of acting on the stage, but can't explain what 'having toothache' means because having toothache = feeling toothache, and the explanation would come to: "I say I have it because I have it" = I say I have it because it is true = I say I have it because I don't lie. One wishes to say: In order to be able to say that I have toothache I don't observe my behavior, say in the mirror. *And this is correct*, but it doesn't follow that you describe an observation of any other kind. Moaning is not the description of an observation. That is, you can't be said to *derive* your expression from what you observe. Just as you can't be said to derive the word *'green'* from your *visual impression* but only from a sample.—Now against this one is inclined to say: "Surely if I call a color green I don't just say that word, but the word comes in a particular way," or "if I say 'I have toothache' I don't just use this phrase but it must come in a particular way!" Now this means nothing, for, if you like, it always comes in a particular way. "But surely seeing and saying something *can't be all!*" Here we make the confusion that there is still an object we haven't mentioned. You imagine that there is a *pure* seeing and saying, and one + something else. Therefore you imagine all distinctions to be made as between *a*, *a* + *b*, *a* + *c*, etc. The idea of this addition is mostly derived from consideration of our bodily organs. All that ought to interest you is whether I make all the distinctions that you make: whether, e.g., I distinguish between cheating and telling the truth.—"There is something else!" —"There is nothing else!"—"But what else is there?"—"Well, this ↗!"

"But surely I know that I am not a mere automaton!"—What would it be like if I were?—"How is it that I can't imagine myself not experiencing seeing, hearing etc.?"—We constantly confuse and change about the commonsense use and the metaphysical use.

"I know that I see."—

"I see."—you seem to read this off some fact; as though you said: "There is a chair in this corner."

"But if in an experiment, e.g., I say 'I see,' why do I say so? surely because I see!"

It is as though our expressions of personal experience needn't even spring from regularly recurrent inner experiences but just from *something.*

Confusion of description and samples.

The idea of the *'realm of consciousness.'*

6
Jean-Paul Sartre

CONSCIOUSNESS AND THE SELF[1]

A. The Theory of the Formal Presence of the I

If we reject all the more or less forced interpretations of the *I Think*
offered by the post-Kantians, and nevertheless wish to solve the problem of the existence *in fact* of the *I* in consciousness,[2] we meet on our
path the phenomenology of Husserl. Phenomenology is a scientific,
not a critical, study of consciousness. Its essential way of proceeding
is by intuition.[3] Intuition, according to Husserl, puts us in the presence
of *the thing*. We must recognize, therefore, that phenomenology is a

[1]Reprinted from *The Transcendence of the Ego* by Jean-Paul Sartre, tr. Forrest Williams
and Robert Kirkpatrick, pp. 35–54, by permission of Farrar, Straus & Giroux, Inc.
Copyright © 1957 by the Noonday Press, Inc. First published in French in 1937.
[2]I shall use here the term "consciousness" ["*conscience*"] to translate the German word
Bewusstsein, which signifies both the whole of consciousness—the monad—and each
moment of this consciousness. The expression "state of consciousness" seems to me
inaccurate owing to the passivity which it introduces into consciousness. [AUTHOR.]
[3]No single term is more central to phenomenology and more alien to current trends in
British and American philosophy than the term "intuition." Its exposition would merit
an essay longer than this translation. The interested reader is referred to the classic
discussions by Edmund Husserl in *Ideen zu einer reinen Phänomenologie und phänomenologischen Philosophie*—Volume I, published in *Jahrbuch für Philosophie und phänomenologische Forschung*, I (1922), pp. 1-323 (henceforth abbreviated *Ideen I*). An English
translation to which the reader may refer by Section numbers is published under the
title *Ideas* (New York: Macmillan, 1931). The most relevant passages are in Secs. 1-4,
7, and 18-24.
 Perhaps the essential point to be retained in connection with this phenomenologically
oriented essay by Sartre is that for the phenomenologist the primary mode of evidence is
intuitive. An intuition (summarily explained) is an act of consciousness by which the
object under investigation is *confronted*, rather than merely indicated *in absentia*. Thus,
it is one thing merely to indicate the Eiffel Tower (merely "to have it in mind," as we say),
and another thing to confront the indicated object by an act of imagination or perception.
The indicative act is "empty"; the intuitive act of imagination or perception is "filled
out." Once this distinction has been made, it would seem difficult to disagree with the
phenomenologist that every cognitive inquiry must ultimately base its claims upon acts
of intuition, even if supplementary modes of evidence (e.g., inductive reasoning regarding
the external world which is confronted by perceptual intuition) must be invoked to develop
the inquiry. For an object must be present, confronted, to be investigated, however far
from such original confrontation the investigation may wander as it proceeds. In the
physical sciences, the reliance in the last analysis upon perceptual evidence is patent.
In phenomenology, the subject matter under investigation is consciousness. The method

science of *fact*, and that the problems it poses are problems *of fact*,[4] which can be seen, moreover, from Husserl's designation of phenomenology as a *descriptive* science. Problems concerning the relations of the *I* to consciousness are therefore existential problems. Husserl, too, discovers the transcendental consciousness of Kant, and grasps it by the ἐποχή.[5] But this consciousness is no longer a set of logical

is intuitive, then, in the sense that consciousness must regard itself to determine just what consciousness is, what consciousness does and does not include. In the present essay, of course, the issue is whether consciousness is or is not inhabited by an "I" or ego operating within or behind consciousness. When Sartre writes in the present passage, therefore, that phenomenology is a "scientific" rather than a "critical" study of consciousness because phenomenology proceeds by "intuition," he means that as in any descriptive science the first requirement is to *look at* the subject matter, in contrast to Kantian philosophy, which might be said to begin with the nature of science and to construct subsequently an account of consciousness by inference.

Owing to the impracticality of a detailed account in this place of the phenomenological concept of intuition, it may be helpful to note briefly some familiar senses of "intuition" which would be quite out of place. First, intuitive knowledge has no traffic with mystical insight. The "filling out" of a previously empty consciousness of an object represents a logically distinct kind of consciousness, not some flow of feeling. Second, intuitive knowledge is not an identification with the object in the Bergsonian sense. Third, intuitive knowledge is not limited to the familiar type of intuition of the external world which we call "sense-perception." Intuition may be directed to consciousness itself (i.e., introspectively). Intuition may be directed to a highly complex object, i.e., a "state of affairs," previously set forth for consciousness by a process of judgment. For example, I may confront by an act of intuition the state of affairs "that this knife is to the right of the plate." Fourth, as may be evident from the last example, intuition is possible at any level of abstraction (e.g., I may confront in intuition the genus Red). Fifth, almost invariably to intuit an object or state of affairs is not to know its existence (e.g., to imagine the Eiffel Tower and to perceive the Eiffel Tower are both intuitive confrontations of the object). The exception concerns reflective intuition of the specious present. Sixth, to intuit an object is not necessarily to know everything about it, viz., the inadequacy of sense-perception, which is always an apprehension of the object "in profile." (Cf. below, n. 18, on the alleged inadequacy of intuition of the ego.) Thus, the notion of intuition in phenomenology does not necessarily imply the notion of certain knowledge. Yet the primary mode of evidence in any cognitive inquiry must be intuitive, according to the phenomenologist, for to learn, one must at the very least confront some of the objects in question, e.g., physical things, psychological states, number, principles of logic. [TRS.]

[4]Husserl would say, "a science of essences." But, for the point of view we adopt, it amounts to the same. [AUTHOR.] In a study of consciousness by consciousness, *what* present consciousness is (its essence) and *that* it is (the fact that it exists) obviously make up only one question. Consequently, Sartre speaks indifferently of an "essential" and a "factual" inquiry. This would not appear to be orthodox Husserlian phenomenology (viz., *Ideen I*, Introduction). [TRS.]

[5]The *epochē* (ἐποχή) is an act of withdrawal from the usual assertiveness of consciousness regarding what does and does not exist in the world. The effect of this withdrawal is to reveal the world as a correlate of consciousness. The term "reduction" employed in the same paragraph has the same meaning. (Cf. *Ideen I*, Secs. 31-34.) [TRS.]

conditions. It is a fact which is absolute. Nor is this transcendental consciousness a hypostatization of validity, an unconscious which floats between the real and the ideal. It is a real consciousness accessible to each of us as soon as the "reduction" is performed. And it is indeed this transcendental consciousness which constitutes our empirical consciousness, our consciousness "in the world," our consciousness with its psychic and psycho-physical *me*. For our part, we readily acknowledge the existence of a constituting consciousness. We find admirable all of Husserl's descriptions in which he shows transcendental consciousness constituting the world by imprisoning itself in empirical consciousness. Like Husserl, we are persuaded that our psychic and psycho-physical *me* is a transcendent object which must fall before the ἐποχή. But we raise the following question: is not this psychic and psycho-physical *me* enough? Need one double it with a transcendental *I*, a structure of absolute consciousness?

The consequences of a reply are obvious. If the reply is negative, the consequences are:

First, the transcendental field becomes impersonal; or, if you like, "pre-personal," *without an I*.

Second, the *I* appears only at the level of humanity and is only one aspect of the *me*, the active aspect.

Third, the *I Think* can accompany our representations because it appears on a foundation of unity which it did not help to create; rather, this prior unity makes the *I Think* possible.

Fourth, one may well ask if personality (even the abstract personality of an *I*) is a necessary accompaniment of a consciousness, and if one cannot conceive of absolutely impersonal consciousnesses.

To this question, Husserl has given his reply. After having determined (in *Logische Untersuchungen*[6]) that the *me* is a synthetic and transcendent production of consciousness, he reverted in *Ideen zu einer reinen Phänomenologie und phänomenologischen Philosophie*[7] to the classic position of a transcendental *I*. This *I* would be, so to speak, behind each consciousness, a necessary structure of consciousnesses whose rays *(Ichstrahlen)* would light upon each phenomenon presenting itself in the field of attention. Thus transcendental consciousness becomes thoroughly personal. Was this notion necessary? Is it compatible with the definition of consciousness given by Husserl?[8]

---

[6]Halle, 1900-1901 (5th Investigation, Sec. 4). See also, Marvin Farber, *The Foundation of Phenomenology* (Cambridge, 1943), pp. 337–338. [TRS.]

[7]Cf. *Ideen I*, Sec. 57. [TRS.]

[8]Two paragraphs below Sartre asserts that "consciousness is defined by intentionality."

It is ordinarily thought that the existence of a transcendental *I* may be justified by the need that consciousness has for unity and individuality. It is because all my perceptions and all my thoughts refer themselves back to this permanent seat that my consciousness is unified. It is because I can say *my* consciousness, and because Peter and Paul can also speak of *their* consciousnesses, that these consciousnesses distinguish themselves from each other. The *I* is the producer of inwardness.

Now, it is certain that phenomenology does not need to appeal to any such unifying and individualizing *I*. Indeed, consciousness is defined by intentionality. By intentionality consciousness transcends itself. It unifies itself by escaping from itself. The unity of a thousand active consciousnesses by which I have added, do add, and shall add two and two to make four, is the transcendent object "two and two make four." Without the permanence of this eternal truth a real unity would be impossible to conceive, and there would be irreducible operations as often as there were operative consciousnesses. It is possible that those believing "two and two make four" to be the *content* of my representation may be obliged to appeal to a transcendental and subjective principle of unification, which will then be the *I*. But it is precisely Husserl who has no need of such a principle. The object is transcendent to the consciousnesses which grasp it, and it is in the object that the unity of the consciousnesses is found.

It will be said that a principle of unity *within duration* is nonetheless needed if the continual flux of consciousness is to be capable of positing transcendent objects outside the flux. Consciousnesses must be perpetual syntheses of past consciousnesses and present consciousness. This is correct. But it is characteristic that Husserl, who studied this subjective unification of consciousnesses in *Vorlesungen zur Phänomenologie des inneren Zeitbewusstseins*,[9] never had recourse to a synthetic power of the *I*. It is consciousness which unifies itself, concretely, by a play of "transversal" intentionalities which are concrete and real retentions of past consciousnesses. Thus consciousness refers perpetually to itself. Whoever says "a consciousness" says "the whole of consciousness," and this singular property belongs to consciousness itself, aside from whatever relations it may have to the *I*. In *Cartesia-*

Five paragraphs after that assertion, reference is made once more to "the fruitful definition cited earlier." Strictly speaking, Husserl never concerned himself with a final definition, but certainly he regarded intentionality as essential to consciousness, i.e., consciousness is necessarily consciousness *of something*. (Cf. *Ideen I*, Sec. 84.) [TRS.]

[9] Published in *Jahrbuch für Philosophie und phänomenologische Forschung*, IX (1928), pp. 367–498. [TRS.]

nische Meditationen,[10] Husserl seems to have preserved intact this conception of consciousness unifying itself in time.

Furthermore, the individuality of consciousness evidently stems from the nature of consciousness. Consciousness (like Spinoza's substance) can be limited only by itself. Thus, it constitutes a synthetic and individual totality entirely isolated from other totalities of the same type, and the *I* can evidently be only an *expression* (rather than a condition) of this incommunicability and inwardness of consciousnesses. Consequently we may rely without hesitation: the phenomenological conception of consciousness renders the unifying and individualizing role of the *I* totally useless. It is consciousness, on the contrary, which makes possible the unity and the personality of my *I*. The transcendental *I*, therefore, has no *raison d'être*.

But, in addition, this superfluous *I* would be a hindrance. If it existed it would tear consciousness from itself; it would divide consciousness; it would slide into every consciousness like an opaque blade. The transcendental *I* is the death of consciousness. Indeed, the existence of consciousness is an absolute because consciousness is consciousness of itself. This is to say that the type of existence of consciousness is to be consciousness of itself. And consciousness is aware of itself *in so far as it is consciousness of a transcendent object.* All is therefore clear and lucid in consciousness; the object with its characteristic opacity is before consciousness, but consciousness is purely and simply consciousness of being consciousness of that object. This is the law of its existence.

We should add that this consciousness of consciousness—except in the case of reflective consciousness which we shall dwell on later— is not *positional,* which is to say that consciousness is not for itself its own object. Its object is by nature outside of it, and that is why consciousness *posits* and *grasps* the object in the same act. Consciousness knows itself only as absolute inwardness. We shall call such a consciousness: consciousness in the first degree, or *unreflected* consciousness.

Now we ask: is there room for an *I* in such a consciousness? The reply is clear: evidently not. Indeed, such an *I* is not the object (since by hypothesis the *I* is inner); nor is it an *I of consciousness,* since it is something for consciousness. It is not a translucent quality of consciousness, but would be in some way an inhabitant. In fact, however

[10]Published in *Husserliana,* I (1950), pp. 1–183. A French translation by G. Peiffer and E. Levinas is published under the title *Méditations Cartésiennes* (Paris, J. Vrin, 1947). For the discussion of temporal unifications, see esp. Secs. 18 & 37. [TRS.]

formal, however abstract one may suppose it to be, the *I*, with its personality, would be a sort of center of opacity. It would be to the concrete and psycho-physical *me* what a point is to three dimensions: it would be an infinitely contracted *me*. Thus, if one introduces this opacity into consciousness, one thereby destroys the fruitful definition cited earlier. One congeals consciousness, one darkens it. Consciousness is then no longer a spontaneity; it bears within itself the germ of opaqueness. But in addition we would be forced to abandon that original and profound view which makes of consciousness a *nonsubstantial* absolute. A pure consciousness is an absolute quite simply because it is consciousness of itself. It remains therefore a "phenomenon" in the very special sense in which "to be" and "to appear" are one. It is all lightness, all translucence. This it is which differentiates the *Cogito* of Husserl from the Cartesian *Cogito*. But if the *I* were a necessary structure of consciousness, this opaque *I* would at once be raised to the rank of an absolute. We would then be in the presence of a monad. And this, indeed, is unfortunately the orientation of the new thought of Husserl (see *Cartesianische Meditationen*[11]). Consciousness is loaded down; consciousness has lost that character which rendered it the absolute existent *by virtue of non-existence*. It is heavy and *ponderable*. All the results of phenomenology begin to crumble if the *I* is not, by the same title as the world, a relative existent: that is to say, an object *for* consciousness.

B. The Cogito as Reflective Consciousness
The Kantian *I Think* is a condition of possibility. The *Cogito* of Descartes and of Husserl is an apprehension of fact. We have heard of the "factual necessity"[12] of the *Cogito*, and this phrase seems to me most apt. Also, it is undeniable that the *Cogito* is personal. In the *I Think* there is an *I* who thinks. We attain here the *I* in its purity, and it is indeed from the *Cogito* that an "Egology" must take its point of departure. The fact that can serve for a start is, then, this one: each time we apprehend our thought, whether by an immediate intuition or by an intuition based on memory, we apprehend an *I* which is the *I* of the apprehended thought, and which is given, in addition, as transcending this thought and all other possible thoughts. If, for example, I want to remember a certain landscape perceived yesterday from the train, it is possible for me to bring back the memory of that landscape as such.

[11]Cf. *op. cit.*, "Meditation V." [TRS.]
[12]The phrase is quoted from *Ideen I*, Sec. 46. In the *Cogito*, the fact that the *Cogito* is taking place is necessarily so. [TRS.]

But I can also recollect that *I* was seeing that landscape. This is what Husserl calls, in *Vorlesungen zur Phänomenologie des inneren Zeit-bewusstseins,*[13] the possibility of *reflecting in memory.* In other words, I can always perform any recollection whatsoever in the personal mode, and at once the *I* appears. Such is the *factual* guarantee of the Kantian claim *concerning validity.* Thus it seems that there is not one of my consciousnesses which I do not apprehend as provided with an *I.*

But it must be remembered that all the writers who have described the *Cogito* have dealt with it as a reflective operation, that is to say, as an operation of the second degree. Such a *Cogito* is performed by a consciousness *directed upon consciousness,* a consciousness which takes consciousness as an object. Let us agree: the certitude of the *Cogito* is absolute, for, as Husserl said, there is an indissoluble unity of the re-flecting consciousness and the reflected consciousness (to the point that the reflecting consciousness could not exist without the reflected consciousness). But the fact remains that we are in the presence of a synthesis of two consciousnesses, one of which is consciousness *of* the other. Thus the essential principle of phenomenology, "all con-sciousness is consciousness *of* something,"[14] is preserved. Now, my reflecting consciousness does not take itself for an object when I effect the *Cogito.* What it affirms concerns the reflected consciousness. In-sofar as my reflecting consciousness is consciousness of itself, it is *non-positional* consciousness. It becomes positional only by directing itself upon the reflected consciousness which itself was not a positional consciousness of itself before being reflected. Thus the consciousness which says *I Think* is precisely not the consciousness which thinks. Or rather it is not *its own* thought which it posits by this thetic act. We are then justified in asking ourselves if the *I* which thinks is common to the two superimposed consciousnesses, or if it is not rather the *I* of the reflected consciousness. All reflecting consciousness is, indeed, in itself unreflected, and a new act of the third degree is necessary in order to posit it. Moreover, there is no infinite regress here, since a consciousness has no need at all of a reflecting consciousness in order to be conscious of itself. It simply does not posit itself as an object.

But is it not precisely the reflective act which gives birth to the *me* in the reflected consciousness? Thus would be explained how every thought apprehended by intuition possesses an *I,* without falling into the difficulties noted in the preceding section. Husserl would be the first to acknowledge that an unreflected thought undergoes a radical modi-

[13]Cf. *op. cit.* [TRS.]
[14]Cf. *Ideen I,* Sec. 84. [TRS.]

fication in becoming reflected. But need one confine this modification to a loss of "naïveté"? Would not the appearance of the *I* be what is essential in this change?

One must evidently revert to a concrete experience, which may seem impossible, since by definition such an experience is reflective, that is to say, supplied with an *I*. But every unreflected consciousness, being non-thetic consciousness of itself, leaves a non-thetic memory that one can consult. To do so it suffices to try to reconstitute the complete moment in which this unreflected consciousness appeared (which by definition is always possible). For example, I was absorbed just now in my reading. I am going to try to remember the circumstances of my reading, my attitude, the lines that I was reading. I am thus going to revive not only these external details but a certain depth of unreflected consciousness, since the objects could only have been perceived *by* that consciousness and since they remain relative to it. That consciousness must not be posited as object of a reflection. On the contrary, I must direct my attention to the revived objects, but *without losing sight of the unreflected consciousness*, by joining in a sort of conspiracy with it and by drawing up an inventory of its content in a non-positional manner. There is no doubt about the result: while I was reading, there was consciousness *of* the book, *of* the heroes of the novel, but the *I* was not inhabiting this consciousness. It was only consciousness of the object and non-positional consciousness of itself. I can now make these a-thetically apprehended results the object of a thesis and declare: there was no *I* in the unreflected consciousness. It should not be thought that this operation is artificial or conceived for the needs of the case. Thanks to this operation, evidently, Titchener could say in his *Textbook of Psychology*[15] that the *me* was very often absent from his consciousness. He went no further, however, and did not attempt to classify the states of consciousness lacking a *me*.

It is undoubtedly tempting to object that this operation, this non-reflective apprehension of one consciousness by another consciousness, can evidently take place only by memory, and that therefore it does not profit from the absolute certitude inherent in a reflective act. We would then find ourselves, *on the one hand*, with an absolutely certain act which permits the presence of the *I* in the reflected consciousness to be affirmed, and, *on the other hand*, with a questionable memory which would purport to show the absence of the *I* from the unreflected consciousness. It would seem that we have no right to oppose the latter

---

[15]Cf. E. B. Titchener, *Textbook of Psychology* (New York: Macmillan, 1919), pp. 544-545. [TRS.]

to the former. But I must point out that the memory of the unreflected consciousness is not opposed to the data of the reflective consciousness. No one would deny for a moment that the *I* appears in a reflected consciousness. It is simply a question of opposing a reflective memory of my reading ("I was reading"), which is itself of a questionable nature, to a non-reflective memory. The validity of a present reflection, in fact, does not reach beyond the consciousness presently apprehended. And reflective memory, to which we are obliged to have recourse in order to reinstate elapsed consciousnesses, besides its questionable character owing to its nature as memory, remains suspect since, in the opinion of Husserl himself, reflection *modifies* the spontaneous consciousness. Since, in consequence, all the non-reflective memories of unreflected consciousness show me a consciousness *without a me*, and since, on the other hand, theoretical considerations concerning consciousness which are based on intuition of essence have constrained us to recognize[16] that the *I* cannot be a part of the internal structure of *Erlebnisse*, we must therefore conclude: there is no *I* on the unreflected level. When I run after a streetcar, when I look at the time, when I am absorbed in comtemplating a portrait, there is no *I*. There is consciousness *of the streetcar-having-to-be-overtaken*, etc., and non-positional consciousness of consciousness. In fact, I am then plunged into the world of objects; it is they which constitute the unity of my consciousnesses; it is they which present themselves with values, with attractive and repellent qualities—but *me*, I have disappeared; I have annihilated myself. There is no place for *me* on this level. And this is not a matter of chance, due to a momentary lapse of attention, but happens because of the very structure of consciousness.

This is what a description of the *Cogito* will make even more obvious to us. Can one say, indeed, that the reflective act apprehends the *I* and the thinking consciousness to the same degree and in the same way? Husserl insists on the fact that the certitude of the reflective act comes from apprehending consciousness without facets, without profiles, completely (without *Abschattungen*). This is evidently so. On the contrary, the spatio-temporal object always manifests itself through an infinity of aspects and is, at bottom, only the ideal unity of this infinity. As for meanings, or eternal truths, they affirm their transcendence in that the moment they appear they are given as independent of time, whereas the consciousness which apprehends them is, on the contrary, individuated through and through in duration. Now we ask: when a reflective consciousness apprehends the *I Think*, does it apprehend a

[16]Cf. above, Part I, Sec. A. [Trs.] [pp. 195–200 above.—Ed.].

full and concrete consciousness gathered into a real moment of concrete duration? The reply is clear: the *I* is not given as a concrete moment, a perishable structure of my actual consciousness. On the contrary, it affirms its permanence beyond this consciousness and all consciousnesses, and—although it scarcely resembles a mathematical truth—its type of existence comes much nearer to that of eternal truths than to that of consciousness.

Indeed, it is obvious that Descartes passed from the *Cogito* to the idea of thinking substance because he believed that *I* and *think* are on the same level. We have just seen that Husserl, although less obviously, is ultimately subject to the same reproach. I quite recognize that Husserl grants to the *I* a special transcendence which is not the transcendence of the object, and which one could call a transcendence "from above." But by what right? And how account for this privileged treatment of the *I* if not by metaphysical and critical preoccupations which have nothing to do with phenomenology? Let us be more radical and assert without fear that *all transcendence* must fall under the ἐποχή; thus, perhaps, we shall avoid writing such awkward chapters as Section Sixty-one of *Ideen zu einer reinen phänomenologischen Philosophie.*[17] If the *I* in *I Think* affirms itself as transcendent, this is because the *I* is not of the same nature as transcendental consciousness.

Let us also note that the *I Think* does not appear to reflection as the reflected consciousness: it is given *through* reflected consciousness. To be sure, it is apprehended by intuition and is an object grasped with evidence. But we know what a service Husserl has rendered to philosophy by distinguishing diverse kinds of evidence. Well, it is only too certain that the *I* of the *I Think* is an object grasped with neither apodictic nor adequate evidence.[18] The evidence is not apodictic, since by saying *I* we affirm far more than we know. It is not adequate, for the *I* is presented as an opaque reality whose content would have to be unfolded. To be sure, the *I* manifests itself as the source of consciousness. But that alone should make us pause. Indeed, for this very reason the

---

[17]The awkwardness alluded to is presumably the attempt made by Husserl in Section 61 of *Ideen I* to distinguish essences into two types, "transcendent" and "immanent." A consciousness not inhabited by an ego would doubtless have no "immanent essences," thus obviating the necessity for such a distinction. [TRS.]

[18]The "I" is grasped "with evidence" in reflection in the sense that the "I" is intuitively apprehended (cf. above, n. 3). Evidence is "adequate" when the object in question is grasped in its entirety (e.g., perceptual intuition is always inadequate evidence). Evidence is "apodictic" when the object or state of affairs in question is apprehended as being necessarily thus-and-so (e.g., that color is extended may be known apodictically). Sartre points out that the "I" with which reflective intuition is confronted is grasped neither adequately nor apodictically. [TRS.]

I appears veiled, indistinct through consciousness, like a pebble at the bottom of the water. For this very reason the *I* is deceptive from the start, since we know that nothing but consciousness can be the source of consciousness.

In addition, if the *I* is a part of consciousness, there would then be *two I*'s: the *I* of the reflective consciousness and the *I* of the reflected consciousness. Fink, the disciple of Husserl, is even acquainted with a third *I*, disengaged by the ἐποχή, the *I* of transcendental consciousness. Hence the problem of the three *I*'s, whose difficulties Fink agreeably mentions.[19] For us, this problem is quite simply insoluble. For it is inadmissible that any communication could be established between the reflective *I* and the reflected *I* if they are real elements of consciousness; above all, it is inadmissible that they may finally achieve identity in one unique *I*.

By way of conclusion to this analysis, it seems to me that one can make the following statements:

First, the *I* is an *existent*. It has a concrete type of existence, undoubtedly different from the existence of mathematical truths, of meanings, or of spatio-temporal beings, but no less real. The *I* gives itself as transcendent.

Second, the *I* proffers itself to an intuition of a special kind[20] which apprehends it, always inadequately, behind the reflected consciousness.

Third, the *I* never appears except on the occasion of a reflective act. In this case, the complex structure of consciousness is as follows: there is an unreflected act of reflection, without an *I*, which is directed on a reflected consciousness. The latter becomes the object of the reflecting consciousness without ceasing to affirm its own object (a chair, a mathematical truth, etc.). At the same time, a new object appears which is the occasion for an affirmation by reflective consciousness, and which is consequently not on the same level as the unreflected consciousness (because the latter consciousness is an absolute which has no need of reflective consciousness in order to exist), nor on the same level as the object of the reflected consciousness (chair, etc.). This transcendent object of the reflective act is the *I*.

---

[19]Cf. Eugen Fink, "Die phänomenologische Philosophie Edmund Husserls in der gegenwartigen Kritik. Mit einem Vorwort von Edmund Husserl," *Kantstudien*, XXXVIII (1933), pp. 356 ff., 381 ff. [TRS.]

[20]It will be recalled (see above, n. 3 and n. 18) that there are no mystical or magical connotations to this "special kind" of "intuition." In reflection, consciousness can intuit the "I" in a "special" manner in the sense that confronting this transcendent object is not the same as, say, confronting a physical thing by an act of perceptual intuition. [TRS.]

Fourth, the transcendent *I* must fall before the stroke of phenomenological reduction. The *Cogito* affirms too much. The certain content of the pseudo- "Cogito" is not *"I have* consciousness of this chair," but "There is consciousness of this chair." This content is sufficient to constitute an infinite and absolute field of investigation for phenomenology.

7

Gilbert Ryle

SELF-KNOWLEDGE[1]

1. Foreword.

A natural counterpart to the theory that minds constitute a world other than "the physical world" is the theory that there exist ways of discovering the contents of this other world which are counterparts to our ways of discovering the contents of the physical world. In sense perception we ascertain what exists and happens in space; so what exists or happens in the mind must also be ascertained in perception, but perception of a different and refined sort, one not requiring the functioning of gross bodily organs.

More than this, it has been thought necessary to show that minds possess powers of apprehending their own states and operations superior to those they possess of apprehending facts of the external world. If I am to know, believe, guess or even wonder anything about the things and happenings that are outside me, I must, it has been supposed, enjoy constant and mistake-proof apprehension of these selfsame cognitive operations of mine.

It is often held therefore (1) that a mind cannot help being constantly aware of all the supposed occupants of its private stage, and (2) that it can also deliberately scrutinize by a species of nonsensuous perception at least some of its own states and operations. Moreover both this constant awareness (generally called "consciousness"), and this nonsensuous inner perception (generally called "introspection") have been supposed to be exempt from error. A mind has a twofold Privileged Access to its own doings, which makes its self-knowledge superior in quality, as well as prior in genesis, to its grasp of other things. I may doubt the evidence of my senses but not the deliverances of consciousness or introspection.

One limitation has always been conceded to the mind's power of finding mental states and operations, namely that while I can have direct knowledge of my own states and operations, I cannot have it of yours. I am conscious of all my own feelings, volitions, emotions and thinkings, and I introspectively scrutinize some of them. But I cannot intro-

[1]Chapter VI of *The Concept of Mind* (London: The Hutchinson Publishing Group; New York: Barnes & Noble, 1949). Reprinted by permission of the author and publishers.

spectively observe, or be conscious of, the workings of your mind. I can satisfy myself that you have a mind at all only by complex and frail inferences from what your body does.

This theory of the twofold Privileged Access has won so strong a hold on the thoughts of philosophers, psychologists and many laymen that it is now often thought to be enough to say, on behalf of the dogma of the mind as a second theatre, that its consciousness and introspection discover the scenes enacted in it. On the view for which I am arguing consciousness and introspection cannot be what they are officially described as being, since their supposed objects are myths; but champions of the dogma of the ghost in the machine[2] tend to argue that the imputed objects of consciousness and introspection cannot be myths, since we are conscious of them and can introspectively observe them. The reality of these objects is guaranteed by the venerable credentials of these supposed ways of finding them.

In this chapter, then, I try to show that the official theories of consciousness and introspection are logical muddles. But I am not, of course, trying to establish that we do not or cannot know what there is to know about ourselves. On the contrary, I shall try to show how we attain such knowledge, but only after I have proved that this knowledge is not attained by consciousness or introspection, as these supposed Privileged Accesses are normally described. Lest any reader feels despondency at the thought of being deprived of his twofold Privileged Access to his supposed inner self, I may add the consolatory undertaking that on the account of self-knowledge that I shall give, knowledge of what there is to be known about other people is restored to approximate parity with self-knowledge. The sorts of things that I can find out about myself are the same as the sorts of things that I can find out about other people, and the methods of finding them out are much the same. A residual difference in the supplies of the requisite data makes some differences in degree between what I can know about myself and what I can know about you, but these differences are not all in favor of self-knowledge. In certain quite important respects it is easier for me to find out what I want to know about you than it is for me to find out the same sorts of things about myself. In certain other important respects it is harder. But in principle, as distinct from practice, John Doe's ways of finding out about John Doe are the same as John Doe's ways of finding out about Richard Roe. To drop the hope of Privileged Access is also to drop the fear of epistemological isolationism; we lose the bitters with the sweets of Solipsism.

---

[2]See Ryle above.—Ed.

2. Consciousness.

Before starting to discuss the philosophers' concept or concepts of consciousness, it is advisable to consider some ways in which the words "conscious" and "consciousness" are used, when uncommitted to special theories, in ordinary life.

(*a*) People often speak in this way; they say, "I was conscious that the furniture had been rearranged," or, "I was conscious that he was less friendly than usual." In such contexts the word "conscious" is used instead of words like "found out," "realized" and "discovered" to indicate a certain noteworthy nebulousness and consequent inarticulateness of the apprehension. The furniture looked different somehow, but the observer could not say what the differences were; or the man's attitude was unaccommodating in a number of ways, but the speaker could not enumerate or specify them. Though there are philosophically interesting problems about vagueness as well as about the inexpressibility of the very nebulous, this use of "conscious" does not entail the existence of any special faculties, methods, or channels of apprehension. What we are conscious of, in this sense, may be a physical fact, or a fact about someone else's state of mind.

(*b*) People often use "conscious" and "self-conscious" in describing the embarrassment exhibited by persons, especially youthful persons, who are anxious about the opinions held by others of their qualities of character or intellect. Shyness and affectation are ways in which self-consciousness, in this sense, is commonly exhibited.

(*c*) "Self-conscious" is sometimes used in a more general sense to indicate that someone has reached the stage of paying heed to his own qualities of character or intellect, irrespective of whether or not he is embarrassed about other people's estimations of them. When a boy begins to notice that he is fonder of arithmetic, or less homesick, than are most of his acquaintances he is beginning to be self-conscious, in this enlarged sense.

Self-consciousness, in this enlarged sense is, of course, of primary importance for the conduct of life, and the concept of it is therefore of importance for Ethics; but its ingenuous use entails no special doctrines about how a person makes and checks his estimates of his own qualities of character and intellect, or how he compares them with those of his acquaintances.

The Freudian idioms of the "Unconscious" and the "Subconscious" are closely connected with this use of "conscious"; for at least part of what is meant by describing jealousy, phobias or erotic impulses as "unconscious" is that the victim of them not only does not recognize their strength, or even existence, in himself, but in a certain way *will* not recognize them. He shirks a part of the task of appreciating what sort of a person he is, or else he systematically biases his appreciations. The epistemological question how a person makes his estimates or mis-estimates of his own dispositions is not, or need not be, begged by the Freudian account of the aetiology, diagnosis, prognosis and cure of the tendencies to shirk and bias such estimates.

(d) Quite different from the foregoing uses of "conscious," "self-conscious" and "unconscious," is the use in which a numbed or anaesthetized person is said to have lost consciousness from his feet up to his knees. In this use "conscious" means "sensitive" or "sentient" and "unconscious" means anaesthetized or insensitive. We say that a person has lost consciousness when he has ceased to be sensitive to any slaps, noises, pricks or smells.

(e) Different from, though closely connected with this last use, there is the sense in which a person can be said to be unconscious of a sensation, when he pays no heed to it. A walker engaged in a heated dispute may be unconscious, in this sense, of the sensations in his blistered heel, and the reader of these words was, when he began this sentence, probably unconscious of the muscular and skin sensations in the back of his neck, or in his left knee. A person may also be unconscious or unaware that he is frowning, beating time to the music, or muttering.

"Conscious" in this sense means "heeding"; and it makes sense to say that a sensation is hardly noticed even when the sensation is moderately acute, namely when the victim's attention is fixed very strongly on something else. Conversely, a person may pay sharp heed to very faint sensations; when, for instance, he is scared of appendicitis, he will be acutely conscious, in this sense, of stomachic twinges which are not at all acute. In this sense, too, a person may be keenly conscious, hardly conscious, or quite unconscious, of feelings like twinges of anxiety, or qualms of doubt.

The fact that a person takes heed of his organic sensations and feelings does not entail that he is exempt from error about them. He can make mistakes about their causes and he can make mistakes about their locations. Furthermore, he can make mistakes about whether they are real or fancied, as hypochondriacs do. "Heeding" does not denote a peculiar conduit of cognitive certainties.

Philosophers, chiefly since Descartes, have in their theories of knowledge and conduct operated with a concept of consciousness which has relatively little affinity with any of the concepts described above. Working with the notion of the mind as a second theatre, the episodes enacted in which enjoy the supposed status of "the mental" and correspondingly lack the supposed status of "the physical," thinkers of many sorts have laid it down as the cardinal positive property of these episodes that, when they occur, they occur consciously. The states and operations of a mind are states and operations of which it is necessarily aware, in some sense of "aware," and this awareness is incapable of being delusive. The things that a mind does or experiences are self-intimating, and this is supposed to be a feature which characterises these acts and feelings not just sometimes but always. It is part of the definition of their being mental that their occurrence entails that they are self-intimating. If I think, hope, remember, will, regret, hear a noise, or feel a pain, I must, *ipso facto*, know that I do so. Even if I dream that I see a dragon, I must be apprised of my dragon-seeing, though, it is often conceded, I may not know that I am dreaming.

It is naturally difficult, if one denies the existence of the second theatre, to elucidate what is meant by describing the episodes which are supposed to take place in it as self-intimating. But some points are clear enough. It is not supposed that when I am wondering, say, what is the answer to a puzzle and am *ipso facto* consciously doing so, that I am synchronously performing two acts of attention, one to the puzzle and the other to my wondering about it. Nor, to generalize this point, is it supposed that my act of wondering and its self-intimation to me are two distinct acts or processes indissolubly welded together. Rather, to relapse perforce into simile, it is supposed that mental processes are phosphorescent, like tropical sea-water, which makes itself visible by the light which it itself emits. Or, to use another simile, mental processes are "overheard" by the mind whose processes they are, somewhat as a speaker overhears the words he is himself uttering.

When the epistemologists' concept of consciousness first became popular, it seems to have been in part a transformed application of the Protestant notion of conscience. The Protestants had to hold that a man could know the moral state of his soul and the wishes of God without the aid of confessors and scholars; they spoke therefore of the God-given "light" of private conscience. When Galileo's and Descartes' representations of the mechanical world seemed to require that minds should be salved from mechanism by being represented as constituting a duplicate world, the need was felt to explain how the contents of this ghostly world could be ascertained, again without the help of schooling, but also without the help of sense perception. The metaphor of "light" seemed peculiarly appropriate, since Galilean science dealt so largely with the optically discovered world. "Consciousness" was imported to play in the mental world the part played by light in the mechanical world. In this metaphorical sense, the contents of the mental world were thought of as being self-luminous or refulgent.

This model was employed again by Locke when he described the deliberate observational scrutiny which a mind can from time to time turn upon its current states and processes. He called this supposed inner perception "reflexion" (our "introspection"), borrowing the word "reflexion" from the familiar optical phenomenon of the reflections of faces in mirrors. The mind can "see" or "look at" its own operations in the "light" given off by themselves. The myth of consciousness is a piece of para-optics.

These similes of "over-hearing," "phosphorescence" or "self-luminousness" suggest another distinction which needs to be made. It is certainly true that when I do, feel or witness something, I usually could and frequently do pay swift retrospective heed to what I have just done, felt or witnessed. I keep, much of the time, some sort of log or score of what occupies me, in such a way that, if asked what I had just been hearing or picturing or saying, I could usually give a correct answer. Of course, I cannot always be actually harking back to the immediate past; or else, within a few seconds of being called in the morning, I should be recalling that I had just been recalling that I had just been recalling . . . hearing the knock on the door; one event would generate an endless series of recollections of recollections . . . of it, leaving no room for me to pay heed to any subsequent happening. There is, however, a proper sense in which I can be said generally to know what has just been engaging my notice or half-notice, namely that I generally could give a memory report of it, if there was occasion to do so. This does not exclude the possibility that I might sometimes give a misreport, for even short-term reminiscence is not exempt from carelessness or bias.

The point of mentioning this fact that we generally could, if required, report what had just been engaging our notice is that consciousness, as the prevalent view describes it, differs from this log-keeping in one or two important respects. First, according to the theory, mental processes are conscious, not in the sense that we do or could report on them *post mortem*, but in the sense that their intimations of their own occurrences are properties of those occurrences and so are not posterior to them. The supposed deliverances of consciousness, if verbally expressible at all, would be expressed in the present, not in the past tense. Next, it is supposed that in being conscious of my present mental states and acts I know what I am experiencing and doing in a non-dispositional sense of "know"; that is to say, it is not merely the case that I could, if occasion demanded, tell myself or you what I am experiencing and doing, but that I am actively cognizant of it. Though a double act of attention does not occur, yet when I discover that my watch has stopped, I am synchronously discovering that I am discovering that my watch has stopped; a truth about myself is flashed or shone upon me at the same moment as a truth about my watch is ascertained by me.

I shall argue that consciousness, as so described, is a myth and shall probably therefore by construed as arguing that mental processes are, in some mortifying sense, unconscious, perhaps in the sort of way in which I often cannot tell of my own habitual and reflex movements. To safeguard against this misinterpretation I say quite summarily first, that we do usually know what we are about, but that no phosphorescence-story is required to explain how we are apprised of it; second, that knowing what we are about does not entail an incessant actual monitoring or scrutiny of our doings and feelings, but only the propensity *inter alia* to avow them, when we are in the mood to do so; and, third, that the fact that we generally know what we are about does not entail our coming across any happenings of ghostly status.

The radical objection to the theory that minds must know what they are about, because mental happenings are by definition conscious, or metaphorically self-luminous, is that there are no such happenings; there are no occurrences taking place in a second-status world, since there is no such status and no such world and consequently no need for special modes of acquainting ourselves with the denizens of such a world. But there are also other objections which do not depend for their acceptance upon the rejection of the dogma of the ghost in the machine.

First, and this is not intended to be more than a persuasive argument, no one who is uncommitted to a philosophical theory ever tries to vindicate any of his assertions of fact by saying that he found it out "from consciousness," or "as a direct deliverance of consciousness," or "from immediate awareness." He will back up some of his assertions of fact by saying that he himself sees, hears, feels, smells or tastes so and so; he will back up other such statements, somewhat more tentatively, by saying that he remembers seeing, hearing, feeling, smelling or tasting it. But if asked whether he really knows, believes, infers, fears, remembers or smells something, he never replies "Oh yes, certainly I do, for I am conscious and even vividly conscious of doing so." Yet just such a reply should, according to the doctrine, be his final appeal.

Next, it is supposed that my being conscious of my mental states and operations either is my knowing them, or is the necessary and sufficient ground for my doing so. But to say this is to abuse the logic and even the grammar of the verb "to know." It is nonsense to speak of knowing, or not knowing, this clap of thunder or that twinge of pain, this colored surface or that act of drawing a conclusion or seeing a joke; these are accusatives of the wrong types to follow the verb "to know." To know and to be ignorant are to know and not to know that something is the case, for example that that rumble is a clap of thunder or that that colored surface is a cheese-rind. And this is just the point where the metaphor of light is unhelpful. Good illumination helps us to see cheese-rinds, but we could not say "the light was too bad for me to know the cheese-rind," since knowing is not the same sort of thing as looking at, and what is known is not the same sort of thing as what is illuminated. True, we can say "owing to the darkness I could not recognize what I saw for a cheese-rind," but again recognizing what I see is not another optical performance. We do not ask for one torch to help us to see and another to help us to recognize what we see. So even if there were some analogy between a thing's being illuminated and a mental process's being conscious, it would not follow that the owner of the process would recognize that process for what it was. It might conceivably explain how mental processes were discernible but it could not possibly explain how we ascertain truths and avoid or correct mistakes about them.

Next, there is no contradiction in asserting that someone might fail to recognize his frame of mind for what it is; indeed, it is notorious that people constantly do so. They mistakenly suppose themselves to know things which are actually false; they deceive themselves about their own motives; they are surprised to notice the clock stopping ticking, without their having, as they think, been aware that it had been ticking; they do not know that they are dreaming, when they are dreaming, and sometimes they are not sure that they are not dreaming, when they are awake; and they deny, in good faith, that they are irritated or excited, when they are flustered in one or other of those ways. If consciousness was what it is described as being, it would be logically impossible for such failures and mistakes in recognition to take place.

Finally, even though the self-intimation supposed to be inherent in any mental state or process is not described as requiring a separate act of attention, or as constituting a separate cognitive operation, still what I am conscious of in a process of inferring, say, is different from what the inferring is an apprehension of. My consciousness is of a process of inferring, but my inferring is, perhaps, of a geometrical conclusion from geometrical premises. The verbal expression of my inference might be, "because this is an equilateral triangle, therefore each angle is 60 degrees," but the verbal expression of what I am conscious of might be "Here I am deducing such and such from so and so." But, if so, then it would seem to make sense to ask whether, according to the doctrine, I am not also conscious of being conscious of inferring, that is, in a position to say "Here I am spotting the fact that here I am deducing such and such from so and so." And then there would be no stopping-place; there would have to be an infinite number of onion-skins of consciousness embedding any mental state or process whatsoever. If this conclusion is rejected, then it will have to be allowed that some elements in mental processes are not themselves things we can be conscious of, namely those elements which constitute the supposed outermost self-intimations of mental processes; and then "conscious" could no longer be retained as part of the definition of "mental."

The argument, then, that mental events are authentic, because the deliverances of consciousness are direct and unimpeachable testimony to their existence, must be rejected. So must the partly parallel argument from the findings of introspection.

3. Introspection.

"Introspection" is a term of art and one for which little use is found in the self-descriptions of untheoretical people. More use is found for the adjective "introspective," which is ordinarily used in an innocuous sense to signify that someone pays more heed than usual to theoretical and practical problems about his own character, abilities, deficiencies and oddities; there is often the extra suggestion that the person is abnormally anxious about these matters.

The technical term "introspection" has been used to denote a supposed species of perception. It was supposed that much as a person may at a particular moment be listening to a flute, savoring a wine, or regarding a waterfall, so he may be "regarding," in a non-optical sense, some current mental state or process of his own. The state or process is being deliberately and attentively scrutinized and so can be listed among the objects of his observation. On the other hand, introspection is described as being unlike sense observation in important respects. Things looked at, or listened to, are public objects, in principle observable by any suitably placed observer, whereas only the owner of a mental state or process is supposed to be able introspectively to scrutinize it. Sense perception, again, involves the functioning of bodily organs, such as the eyes, the ears, or the tongue, whereas introspection involves the functioning of no bodily organ. Lastly, sense perception is never exempt from the possibility of dullness or even of illusion, whereas, anyhow according to the bolder theories, a person's power of observing his mental processes is always perfect; he may not have learned how to exploit his power, or how to arrange or discriminate its findings, but he is immune from any counterparts to deafness, astigmatism, color-blindness, dazzle or *muscae volitantes*. Inner perception, on these theories, sets a standard of veridical perception, which sense perception can never emulate.

The findings of introspection are reputed to differ in one way at least from the supposed deliverances of consciousness; introspection is an attentive operation and one which is only occasionally performed, whereas consciousness is supposed to be a constant element of all mental processes and one of which the revelations do not require to be receipted in special acts of attention. Moreover we introspect with the intention of finding the answers to particular problems, whereas we are conscious, whether we wish it or not; everyone is constantly conscious, while awake, but only those people introspect who are from time to time interested in what is going on in their minds.

It would be admitted that only people with a special training ever speak of "introspecting," but in such phrases as "he caught himself wondering how to do so and so," or "when I catch myself getting into a panic, I do such and such," the plain man is expressing at least part of what is meant by the word.

Now supposing, (which it is the negative object of this book to deny,) that there did exist events of the postulated ghostly status, there would still be objections to the initially plausible assumption that there also exists a species of perception capable of having any of these events for its proprietary objects. For one thing, the occurrence of such an act of inner perception would require that the observer could attend to two things at the same time. He would, for example, be both resolving to get up early and concomitantly observing his act of resolving; attending to the programme of rising betimes and perceptually attending to his attending to this programme. This objection is not, perhaps, logically fatal, since it might be argued that some people can, anyhow after practice, combine attention to the control of a car with attention to the conversation. The fact that we speak of undivided attention suggests that the division of attention is a possibility, though some people would describe the division of attention as a rapid to-and-fro switch of attention, rather than as a synchronous distribution of it. But many people who begin by being confident that they do introspect, as introspection is officially described, become dubious that they do so, when they are satisfied that they would have to be attending twice at once in order to do it. They are more sure that they do not attend twice at once than that they do introspect.

However, even if it is claimed that in introspecting we are attending twice at once, it will be allowed that there is some limit to the number of possible synchronous acts of attention, and from this it follows that there must be some mental processes which are unintrospectible, namely those introspections which incorporate the maximum possible number of synchronous acts of attention. The question would then arise for the holders of the theory how these acts would be found occurring, since if this knowledge was not introspectively got, it would follow that a person's knowledge of his own mental processes could not always be based on introspection. But if this knowledge does not always rest on introspection, it is open to question whether it ever does. This objection might be countered by appeal to the other form of Privileged Access; we know that we introspect not by introspecting on our introspections, but from the direct deliverances of consciousness. To the guests of Charybdis, Scylla appears the more hospitable resort.

When psychologists were less cautious than they have since become, they used to maintain that introspection was the main source of empirical information about the workings of minds. They were not unnaturally embarrassed to discover that the empirical facts reported by one psychologist sometimes conflicted with those reported by another. They reproached one another, often justly, with having professed to find by introspection just those mental phenomena which their preconceived theories had led them to expect to find. There still occur disputes which should be finally soluble by introspection, if the joint theories of the inner life and inner perception were true. Theorists dispute, for example, whether there are activities of conscience distinct from those of intellect and distinct from habitual deferences to taboos. Why do they not look and see? Or, if they do so, why do their reports not tally? Again, many people who theorize about human conduct declare that there occur certain processes *sui generis* answering to the description of "volitions"; I have argued that there are no such processes. Why do we argue about the existence of these processes, when the question ought to be as easily decidable as the question whether or not there is a smell of onions in the larder?

There is one last objection to be made against the claims for introspection, that made by Hume. There are some states of mind which cannot be coolly scrutinized, since the fact that we are in those states involves that we are not cool, or the fact that we are cool involves that we are not in those states. No one could introspectively scrutinize the state of panic or fury, since the dispassionateness exercised in scientific observation is, by the definition of "panic" and "fury," not the state of mind of the victim of those turbulences. Similarly, since a convulsion of merriment is not the state of mind of the sober experimentalist, the enjoyment of a joke is also not an introspectible happening. States of mind such as these more or less violent agitations can be examined only in retrospect. Yet nothing disastrous follows from this restriction. We are not shorter of information about panic or amusement than about other states of mind. If retrospection can give us the data we need for our knowledge of some states of mind, there is no reason why it should not do so for all. And this is just what seems to be suggested by the popular phrase "to catch oneself doing so and so." We catch, as we pursue and overtake, what is already running away from us. I catch myself daydreaming about a mountain walk after, perhaps very shortly after, I have begun the daydream; or I catch myself humming a particular air only when the first few notes have already been hummed. Retrospection, prompt or delayed, is a genuine process and one which is exempt from the troubles ensuing from the assumption of multiply divided attention; it is also exempt from the troubles ensuing from the assumption that violent agitations could be the objects of cool, contemporary scrutiny.

Part, then, of what people have in mind, when they speak familiarly of introspecting, is this authentic process of retrospection. But there is nothing intrinsically ghostly about the objects of retrospection. In the same way that I can catch myself daydreaming, I can catch myself scratching; in the same way that I can catch myself engaged in a piece of silent soliloquy, I can catch myself saying something aloud.

It is true and important that what I recall is always something expressible in the form "myself doing so and so." I recall not a clap of thunder but hearing the clap of thunder; or I catch myself swearing, but I do not, in the same sense, catch you swearing. The objects of my retrospections are items in my autobiography. But although personal, they need not be, though they can be, private or silent items of that autobiography. I can recollect seeing things just as much as I can recollect imagining things, my overt acts just as well as my sensations. I can report the calculations that I have been doing in my head, but I can also report the calculations that I have been doing on the blotter.

Retrospection will carry some of the load of which introspection has been nominated for the porter. But it will not carry all of it and in particular it will not carry many of the philosophically precious or fragile parcels. Aside from the fact that even prompt recollection is subject both to evaporations and to dilutions, however accurately I may recollect an action or feeling, I may still fail to recognize its nature. Whether yesterday's twinge which I recall today was a pang of genuine compassion or a twinge of guilt, need not be any the more obvious to me for the fact that my memory of it is vivid. Chronicles are not explanatory of what they record.

The fact that retrospection is autobiographical does not imply that it gives us a Privileged Access to facts of a special status. But of course it does give us a mass of data contributory to our appreciations of our own conduct and qualities of mind. A diary is not a chronicle of ghostly episodes, but it is a valuable source of information about the diarist's character, wits and career.

4. *Self-Knowledge without Privileged Access.*

It has been argued from a number of directions that when we speak of a person's mind, we are not speaking of a second theatre of special-status incidents, but of certain ways in which some of the incidents of his one life are ordered. His life is not a double series of events taking place in two different kinds of stuff; it is one concatenation of events, the differences between some and other classes of which largely consist in the applicability or inapplicability to them of logically different types of law-propositions and law-like propositions. Assertions about a person's mind are therefore assertions of special sorts about that person. So questions about the relations between a person and his mind, like those about the relations between a person's body and his mind are improper questions. They are improper in much the same way as is the question, "What transactions go on between the House of Commons and the British Constitution?"

It follows that it is a logical solecism to speak, as theorists often do, of someone's mind knowing this, or choosing that. The person himself knows this and chooses that, though the fact that he does so can, if desired, be classified as a mental fact about that person. In partly the same way it is improper to speak of my eyes seeing this, or my nose smelling that; we should say, rather, that I see this, or I smell that, and that these assertions carry with them certain facts about my eyes and nose. But the analogy is not exact, for while my eyes and nose are organs of sense, "my mind" does not stand for another organ. It signifies my ability and proneness to do certain sorts of things and not some piece of personal apparatus without which I could or would not do them. Similarly the British Constitution is not another British political institution functioning alongside of the Civil Service, the Judiciary, the Established Church, the Houses of Parliament and the Royal Family. Nor is it the sum of these institutions, or a liaison-staff between them. We can say that Great Britain has gone to the polls; but we cannot say that the British Constitution has gone to the polls, though the fact that Great Britain has gone to the polls might be described as a constitutional fact about Great Britain.

Actually, though it is not always convenient to avoid the practice, there is a considerable logical hazard in using the nouns "mind" and "minds" at all. The idiom makes it too easy to construct logically improper conjunctions, disjunctions and cause-effect propositions such as "so and so took place not in my body but in my mind," "my mind made my hand write," "a person's body and mind interact upon each other" and so on. Where logical candor is required from us, we ought to follow the example set by novelists, biographers and diarists, who speak only of persons doing and undergoing things.

The questions "What knowledge can a person get of the workings of his own mind?" and "How does he get it?" by their very wording suggest absurd answers. They suggest that, for a person to know that he is lazy, or has done a sum carefully, he must have taken a peep into a windowless chamber, illuminated by a very peculiar sort of light, and one to which only he has access. And when the question is construed in this sort of way, the parallel questions, "What knowledge can one person get of the workings of another mind?" and "How does he get it?" by their very wording seem to preclude any answer at all; for they suggest that one person could only know that another person was lazy, or had done a sum carefully, by peering into another secret chamber to which, *ex hypothesi*, he has no access.

In fact the problem is not one of this sort. It is simply the methodological question, how we establish, and how we apply, certain sorts of law-like propositions about the overt and the silent behavior of persons. I come to appreciate the skill and tactics of a chess-player by watching him and others playing chess, and I learn that a certain pupil of mine is lazy, ambitious and witty by following his work, noticing his excuses, listening to his conversation and comparing his performances with those of others. Nor does it make any important difference if I happen myself to be that pupil. I can indeed then listen to more of his conversations, as I am the addressee of his unspoken soliloquies; I notice more of his excuses, as I am never absent, when they are made. On the other hand, my comparison of his performances with those of others is more difficult, since the examiner is himself taking the examination, which makes neutrality hard to preserve and precludes the demeanor of the candidate, when under interrogation, from being in good view.

To repeat a point previously made, the question is not the envelope-question "How do I discover that I or you have a mind?" but the range of specific questions of the pattern, "How do I discover that I am more unselfish than you; that I can do long division well, but differential equations only badly; that you suffer from certain phobias and tend to shirk facing certain sorts of facts; that I am more easily irritated than most people but less subject to panic, vertigo, or morbid conscientiousness?" Besides such pure dispositional questions there is also the range of particular performance questions and occurrence questions of the patterns, "How do I find out that I saw the joke and that you did not; that your action took more courage than mine; that the service I rendered to you was rendered from a sense of duty and not from expectation of kudos; that, though I did not fully understand what was said at the time, I did fully understand it, when I went over it in my head afterwards, while you understood it perfectly from the start; that I was feeling homesick yesterday?" Questions of these sorts offer no mysteries; we know quite well how to set to work to find out the answers to them; and though often we cannot finally solve them and may have to stop short at mere conjecture, yet, even so, we have no doubt what sorts of information would satisfy our requirements, if we could get it; and we know what it would be like to get it. For example, after listening to an argument, you aver that you understand it perfectly; but you may be deceiving yourself, or trying to deceive me. If we then part for a day or two, I am no longer in a position to test whether or not you did understand it perfectly. But still I know what tests would have settled the point. If you had put the argument into your own words, or translated it into French; if you had invented appropriate concrete illustrations of the generalizations and abstractions in the argument; if you had stood up to cross-questioning; if you had correctly drawn further consequences from different stages of the argument and indicated points where the theory was inconsistent with other theories; if you had inferred correctly from the nature of the argument to the qualities of intellect and character of its author and predicted accurately the subsequent development of his theory, then I should have required no further evidence that you understood it perfectly. And exactly the same sorts of tests would satisfy me that I had understood it perfectly; the sole differences would be that I should probably not have voiced aloud the expressions of my deductions, illustrations, etc., but told them to myself more perfunctorily in silent soliloquy; and I should probably have been more easily satisfied of the completeness of my understanding than I was of yours.

In short it is part of the *meaning* of "you understood it" that you could have done so and so and would have done it, if such and such, and the *test* of whether you understood it is a range of performances satisfying the apodoses of these general hypothetical statements. It should be noticed, on the one hand, that there is no single nuclear performance, overt or in your head, which would determine that you had understood the argument. Even if you claimed that you had experienced a flash or click of comprehension and had actually done so, you would still withdraw your other claim to have understood the argument, if you found that you could not paraphrase it, illustrate, expand or recast it; and you would allow someone else to have understood it who could meet all examination questions about it, but reported no click of comprehension. It should also be noticed, on the other hand, that though there is no way of specifying how many or what sub-tests must be satisfied for a person to qualify as having perfectly understood the argument, this does not imply that no finite set of sub-tests is ever enough. To settle whether a boy can do long division, we do not require him to try out his hand on a million, a thousand, or even a hundred different problems in long division. We should not be quite satisfied after one success, but we should not remain dissatisfied after twenty, provided that they were judiciously variegated and that he had not done them before. A good teacher, who not only recorded the boy's correct and incorrect solutions, but also watched his procedure in reaching them, would be satisfied much sooner, and he would be satisfied sooner still if he got the boy to describe and justify the constituent operations that he performed, though of course many boys can do long division sums who cannot describe or justify the operations performed in doing them.

I discover my or your motives in much, though not quite the same way as I discover my or your abilities. The big practical difference is that I cannot put the subject through his paces in my inquiries into his inclinations as I can in my inquiries into his competences. To discover how conceited or patriotic you are, I must still observe your conduct, remarks, demeanor and tones of voice, but I cannot subject you to examination-tests or experiments which you recognize as such. You would have a special motive for responding to such experiments in a particular way. From mere conceit, perhaps, you would try to behave self-effacingly, or from mere modesty you might try to behave conceitedly. None the less, ordinary day to day observation normally serves swiftly to settle such questions. To be conceited is to tend to boast of one's own excellences, to pity or ridicule the deficiencies of others, to daydream about imaginary triumphs, to reminisce about actual triumphs, to weary quickly of conversations which reflect unfavorably upon oneself, to lavish one's society upon distinguished persons and to economize in association with the undistinguished. The tests of whether a person is conceited are the actions he takes and the reactions he manifests in such circumstances. Not many anecdotes, sneers or sycophancies are required from the subject for the ordinary observer to make up his mind, unless the candidate and the examiner happen to be identical.

The ascertainment of a person's mental capacities and propensities is an inductive process, an induction to law-like propositions from observed actions and reactions. Having ascertained these long-term qualities, we explain a particular action or reaction by applying the result of such an induction to the new specimen, save where open avowals let us know the explanation without research. These inductions are not, of course, carried out under laboratory conditions, or with any statistical apparatus, any more than is the shepherd's weather-lore, or the general practitioner's understanding of a particular patient's con-stitution. But they are ordinarily reliable enough. It is a truism to say that the appreciations of character and the explanations of conduct given by critical, unprejudiced and humane observers, who have had a lot of experience and take a lot of interest, tend to be both swift and re-liable; those of inferior judges tend to be slower and less reliable. Simi-larly the marks awarded by practiced and keen examiners who know their subject well and are reasonably sympathetic towards the can-didates tend to be about right; those of inferior examiners tend to scatter more widely from the proper order. The point of these truisms is to remind us that in real life we are quite familiar with the techniques of assessing persons and accounting for their actions, though accord-ing to the standard theory no such techniques could exist.

There is one class of persons whose qualities and frames of mind are specially difficult to appreciate, namely persons who simulate qualities which they lack and dissimulate qualities which they possess. I refer to hypocrites and charlatans, the people who pretend to motives and moods and the people who pretend to abilities; that is, to most of us in some stretches of our lives and to some of us in most stretches of our lives. It is always possible to pretend to motives and abilities other than one's real ones, or to pretend to strengths of motives and levels of ability other than their real strengths and levels. The theatre could not exist, if it was not possible to make such pretences and to make them efficiently. It is, moreover, always possible for a person to take others or himself in by acting a part (as the spectators are not taken in at the theatre, since they have paid to see people act who advertise themselves as actors). At first sight it seems, then, that no one can ever have proper knowledge of his own mind, or of the minds of others, since there is no kind of observable behavior of which we can say, "no one could possibly be putting that on." Certainly we do not ordinarily feel practi-cally embarrassed by this possibility, but some people feel a theoreti-cal embarrassment, since if any particular action or reaction might be a piece of shamming, might not every action or reaction be a piece of

shamming? Might not all our appreciations of the conduct of others
and of ourselves be uniformly deluded? People sometimes feel an
analogous embarrassment about sense perception, for since there is
nothing to prevent any particular sensible appearance from being an
illusion, there seems to be nothing to prevent all of them from being
illusions.

However, the menace of universal shamming is an empty menace.
We know what shamming is. It is deliberately behaving in ways in which
other people behave who are not shamming. To simulate contrition is
to put on gestures, accents, words and deeds like those of people who
are contrite. Both the hypocrite and the people whom he deceives must
therefore know what it is like for someone to be contrite and not merely
to be pretending to be contrite. If we were not usually correct in sizing
up contrite people as contrite, we could not be gulled into thinking
that the hypocrite was really contrite. Furthermore, we know what it is
like to be hypocritical, namely to try to appear actuated by a motive
other than one's real motive. We know the sorts of tricks the hypocrite
must use. We possess, though we cannot always apply, the criteria by
which to judge whether these tricks are being used or not and whether
they are being used cleverly or stupidly. So sometimes we can, and
sometimes we cannot, detect hypocrisies; but even when we cannot,
we know what sorts of extra clues, if we could secure them, would betray the hypocrite. We should, for example, like to see how he would
act if told that the cause for which he professed devotion required half
his fortune or his life. All that we need, though we often cannot get it,
is an *experimentum crucis,* just as the doctor often needs but cannot
get an *experimentum crucis* to decide between two diagnoses. To establish hypocrisy and charlatanry is an inductive task which differs
from the ordinary inductive tasks of assessing motives and capacities
only in being a second order induction. It is trying to discover whether
someone is trying to model his actions on what he and we have in-
ductively discovered to be the behavior of people who are not shamming.
When we and the hypocrite have learned how hypocrisy is exposed, we
might have to cope with the second order hypocrite, the double-
bluffer who has learnt how not to act like a first order hypocrite. There
is no mystery about shamming, though it is a tautology to say that skill-
ful shamming is hard to detect and that successful shamming is un-
detected.

So far we have been considering chiefly those brands of self-knowledge and the knowledge of others which consist in the more or less
judicial assessment of long-term propensities and capacities, together
with the application of those assessments in explanations of partic-

ular episodes. We have been considering how we interpret or understand courses of conduct. But there remains another sense of "know" in which a person is commonly said to know what he is at this moment doing, thinking, feeling, etc., a sense which is nearer to what the phosphorescence-theory of consciousness tried, but failed, to describe. To bring out the force of this sense of "know," we should consider first certain kinds of situations in which a person admits that he did not know at the time what he was doing, although what he was doing was not an automatism but an intelligent operation. A person trying to solve a cross-word puzzle is confronted by an anagram; after a short or long pause he gets the answer, but denies that he was aware of taking any specifiable steps, or following any specifiable method, to get it. He may even say that he was thinking, and knew that he was thinking, about some other part of the puzzle. He is in some degree surprised to find that he has got the answer to the anagram, for he had not been aware of going through any shuffling and reshuffling operations, or considering any of the unsuccessful rearrangements of the letters. Yet his solution is correct and he may repeat his success several times in the course of solving the whole puzzle. Our impromptu witticisms often take us by surprise in the same sort of way.

Now usually we are not surprised to catch ourselves having whistled, planned or imagined something and we say, if asked, that we are not surprised, because we knew we were doing these things, while we were doing them. What sort of a rider are we adding when we say "I did so and so and knew at the time that I was doing it"? The tempting reply is to say "Well, while I was doing the thing, it must have flashed or dawned upon me that I was doing it; or, if the action was a protracted one, it must have kept on flashing or dawning on me that I was doing the thing." Yet these metaphors of flashing and dawning leave us uneasy, for we do not ordinarily recall any such occurrences, even when we are quite sure that we knew what we were doing, while we were doing it. Moreover, if there had occurred any such flashings or dawnings, the same question would arise once more. Did you know that you were getting these lightings-up, when they were on, and that you were not getting them, when they were not on? Did it flash on you that it was flashing on you that you were whistling? Or is your knowing that something is going on not always a matter of something flashing on you?

When a person is described as not being surprised when something takes place, he can also be described as having expected it or having been prepared for it. But we use "expect" in at least two markedly different ways. Sometimes we mean that at a particular moment he considered and accepted the proposition that the event would, or would probably, take place; in this sense, there would be an answer to the question, "Exactly when did you make this forecast?" But sometimes we mean that whether or not he ever went through the process of making such a forecast, he was continuously prepared or ready for the thing to happen. The gardener who, in this sense, expects rain need not be repeatedly switching his attention from gardening tasks to silent or vocal prognostications of rain; he just leaves the watering-can in the tool-shed, keeps his coat handy, beds out more seedlings, and so on. He anticipates the rain not by delivering occasional or incessant verbal presages, but by gardening appropriately. All the afternoon he is ready and making ready for rain. It may be objected, "Oh, but he must be constantly considering the proposition that it will rain. That is what makes him keep his coat handy and the watering-pot in the shed." But the answer to this is easy. "Tell me at which particular moments he told himself or others that it was going to rain, and then tell me whether he was or was not expecting rain in the intervals between those prognostications." He prognosticated rain at this, that and the other moment, because he was all the time expecting rain; and he kept his coat handy and the watering-can in the shed for the same reason. In this sense "expect" is used to signify not an occurrence but a standing condition or frame of mind. He is all the afternoon in the frame of mind to say certain things in the future tense in certain contingencies, as well as to conduct his gardening-operations in certain ways, to keep his coat handy and so on. To expect, in this sense, is to be prepared; and the giving of warnings, private or public, is only one sort of precautionary measure among others. So when we say that the gardener was not taken by surprise by the rain, or that he was sure that it was going to rain, or that he was ready for rain, we are not referring, save *per accidens*, to any internal flashes of foresight, or to any silent or vocal utterances in the future tense. All his afternoon activities, horticultural and verbal, were performed in a rain-expectant frame of mind.

This lesson can be applied to our problem. There are many tasks in which we are from time to time engaged the execution of which requires continued application; doing the second step requires having done the first step. Sometimes the earlier steps stand to the later as means to ends, as we lay the table in order to have a meal. Sometimes the earlier steps stand in some other relation to the later; we do not eat the first course in order to eat the second, or begin to hum a tune in order to finish humming it. Very often an undertaking, though it requires consecutive application, is only artificially divisible into steps or stages, but it still remains significant to say that it might be broken off short, when only about half or about three-quarters accomplished.

Now if the agent is carrying out such a serial operation with any degree of heed, he must at any given stage in it have in mind, in some sense, what is to be done next and what has already been done; he must have kept track of where he has got to and he must be expecting, or even intending, to be getting on to the stages after the present stage. This is sometimes expressed by saying that, in anyhow those serial undertakings that are more or less intelligently performed, the agent must have had from the start a plan or programme of what he is to do and he must continuously consult this plan as he progresses. And this does frequently happen. But it cannot always happen, and even when it does happen, this construction and consultation of programmes is not enough to explain the consecutive and methodical prosecution of the undertaking, since constructing and consulting plans are themselves serial operations intelligently and consecutively prosecuted, and it would be absurd to suggest that an infinite series of serial operations must precede the intelligent performance of any serial operation. Nor can intermittent consultation of a plan explain how we know what to be getting on with between the consultations, how we know which items of the plan to consult at different stages in the task, or how we know that what we are now doing is in accordance with the recently consulted plan.

The prime sense in which a person engaged in a non-sudden task has it in mind what is to be done at later stages is that he is ready to perform step three when the occasion requires, namely when step two is completed; and, what goes with this, that he is ready to tell himself or the world what he would have gone on to do, if he had not been prevented. While engaged in any given step, he is prepared for what should or may follow, and when it does follow, he is not surprised. In this sense he may be alive to what he is doing all the time he is doing it, even though his attention is concentrated on his task and is not divided between the task and any contemplations or chroniclings of his prosecution of it.

In other cases, as when he suddenly makes an unpremeditated witticism, he is surprised to find what he has done and would not describe himself as having known what he was doing, while he did it, or even as having been trying to make a joke. The same thing is true of other sudden acts performed on the spur of the moment. The action may well be the right action to have performed, but the agent does not know how he came to perform it, as he was unprepared for it. His being unprepared for it is not the effect or the cause of his not knowing what he was doing; it is the same thing, differently expressed.

Unlike the man who with surprise catches himself making a good impromptu joke, the man who pursues a new argument is ordinarily alive to what he is doing. He may be surprised by the conclusion at which he arrives, but he is not surprised to find himself arriving at a conclusion. His progressive operation of reasoning was a display of his effort to reach one. So he knew what he was then doing, not in the sense that he had to dilute his consideration of his premises with other acts of considering his consideration of them—he need not have had any such side-issues flash or dawn upon him—but in the sense that he was prepared not only for the steps in reasoning that he was to take, but also for a variety of other eventualities, most of which never occurred, such as being asked what he was doing, what justification he had for taking this rather than that line, and so forth. The phosphorescence-theory of consciousness was in part an attempt to construe concepts of frames of mind like "prepared," "ready," "on the *qui vive*," "bearing in mind," "would not be surprised," "expect," "realize" and "alive to" as concepts of special internal happenings.

The same sort of account holds good of not-forgetting. When a person engaged in conversation reaches the middle of a sentence, he has ordinarily not forgotten how his sentence began. In some sense he keeps continuous track of what he has already said. Yet it would be absurd to suggest that he accompanies every word that he utters with an internal repetition of all its predecessors. Apart from the physical impossibility of reciting the previous seventeen words in the moment when the eighteenth word is just giving place to the nineteenth, the process of repetition is itself a serial operation, the execution of the later parts of which would again require that its author had kept track of its earlier parts. Not-to-have-forgotten cannot be described in terms of the performance of actual reminiscences; on the contrary, reminiscences are only one kind of exercise of the condition of not-having-forgotten. Bearing in mind is not recalling; it is what makes recalling, among other things, possible.

Thus the intelligent conduct of serial operations does entail that the agent is throughout the progress of the operation *au fait* both with what he has completed and with what remains to do, but it does not entail that the performance of such operations is backed up by any second order performance or process of monitoring the first order performance. Of course an agent can, from time to time, if he is prompted to do so, announce to himself or the world "Hallo, here I am whistling 'Home Sweet Home.'" His ability to do so is part of what is meant by saying that he is in that particular frame of mind that we call "being alive to what he is doing." But not only is his actually making such announcements not entailed by the fact that he is concentrating on whistling this tune, but his concentration would be broken each time he produced such a commentary.

I have so far illustrated what I mean by a serial performance by such relatively brief operations as whistling a tune, or uttering a sentence. But in a slightly looser and more elastic sense, an entire conversation may be a serial performance; and so may be the conduct of one's work and recreation during a day or a year. Eating porridge is a non-sudden performance, but so is eating breakfast; giving a lecture is a serial performance, but so is giving a course of lectures.

Now in almost the same way as a person may be, in this sense, alive to what he is doing, he may be alive to what someone else is doing. In the serial operation of listening to a sentence or a lecture delivered by someone else, the listener, like the speaker, does not altogether forget, yet nor does he have constantly to recall the earlier parts of the talk, and he is in some degree prepared for the parts still to come, though he does not have to tell himself how he expects the sentence or lecture to go on. Certainly his frame of mind is considerably different from that of the speaker, since the speaker is, sometimes, creative or inventive, while the listener is passive and receptive; the listener may be frequently surprised to find the speaker saying something, while the speaker is only seldom surprised; the listener may find it hard to keep track of the course taken by the sentences and arguments, while the speaker can do this quite easily. While the speaker intends to say certain fairly specific things, his hearer can anticipate only roughly what sorts of topics are going to be discussed.

But the differences are differences of degree, not of kind. The superiority of the speaker's knowledge of what he is doing over that of the listener does not indicate that he has Privileged Access to facts of a type inevitably inaccessible to the listener, but only that he is in a very good position to know what the listener is often in a very poor position to know. The turns taken by a man's conversation do not startle or perplex his wife as much as they had surprised and puzzled his fiancée, nor do close colleagues have to explain themselves to each other as much as they have to explain themselves to their new pupils.

I have, for expository purposes, treated as separate things the way in which an ordinary person is ordinarily alive to what, at a particular moment, he is occupied with and the ways in which judicially minded persons assess the characters and explain the actions of others and of themselves. There are undoubtedly many big differences. To appraise or examine requires special gifts, interests, training, experience, powers of comparison and generalization, and impartiality; whereas merely to be alive to what one is whistling or where one is walking, is within the capacities of an ordinary child. None the less, the most naive knowledge of what one is doing shades into the most sophisticated appreciations of particular performances, much as the child's interest in the robins on the bird table shades into ornithology. A boy working out an arithmetical problem is alive in the most primitive way to what he is doing; for while he is thinking about numbers (and not about thinking about numbers), he does not forget the earlier stages of his reckoning, he bears in mind the rules of multiplication and he is not surprised to find himself arriving at the solution. But he differs only in degree of alertness, caution and sophistication from the boy who checks his results, from the boy who tries to find out where he has made a mistake, or from the boy who spots and explains the mistakes in the calculations of someone else; this last boy, again, differs only in degree from the cooperative parent, the professional teacher, or the examiner. The boy who is just capable of working out a simple sum is probably not yet able to state precisely what he is doing, or why he takes the steps that he takes; the examiner can evaluate the actual performances of the candidates in a fairly precise and highly formalized system of marks. But here again the inarticulateness of the beginner's knowledge of what he is doing shades by a series of gradations into the examiner's numerical appraisal code.

A person's knowledge about himself and others may be distributed between many roughly distinguishable grades yielding correspondingly numerous roughly distinguishable senses of "knowledge." He may be aware that he is whistling "Tipperary" and not know that he is whistling it in order to give the appearance of a sangfroid which he does not feel. Or, again, he may be aware that he is shamming sangfroid without knowing that the tremors which he is trying to hide derive from the agitation of a guilty conscience. He may know that he has an uneasy conscience and not know that this issues from some specific repression. But in none of the senses in which we ordinarily consider whether a person does or does not know something about himself, is the postulate of a Privileged Access necessary or helpful for the explanation of how he has achieved, or might have achieved, this knowledge. There are respects in which it is easier for me to get such knowledge about myself than to get it about someone else; there are other respects in which it is harder. But these differences of facility do not derive from, or lead to, a difference in kind between a person's knowledge about himself and his knowledge about other people. No metaphysical Iron Curtain exists compelling us to be for ever absolute strangers to one another, though ordinary circumstances, together with some deliberate management, serve to maintain a reasonable aloofness. Similarly no metaphysical looking glass exists compelling us to be for ever completely disclosed and explained to ourselves, though from the everyday conduct of our sociable and unsociable lives we learn to be reasonably conversant with ourselves.

5. Disclosure by Unstudied Talk.

Our knowledge of other people and of ourselves depends upon our noticing how they and we behave. But there is one tract of human behavior on which we preeminently rely. When the person examined has learned to talk and when he talks in a language well known to us, we use part of his talk as the primary source of our information about him, that part, namely, which is spontaneous, frank and unprepared. It is, of course, notorious that people are frequently reticent and keep things back, instead of letting them out. It is notorious, too, that people are frequently insincere and talk in manners calculated to give false impressions. But the very fact that utterances can be guarded and studied implies that unguarded, unstudied utterance is possible. To be reticent is deliberately to refrain from being open, and to be hypocritical is deliberately to refrain from saying what comes to one's lips, while pretending to say frankly things one does not mean. In a certain sense of "natural," the natural thing to do is to speak one's mind, and the sophisticated thing to do is to refrain from doing this, or even to pretend to do this, when one is not really doing so. Furthermore, not only is unstudied talk natural or unsophisticated, it is also the normal way of talking. We have to take special pains to keep things back, only because letting them out is our normal response; and we discover the techniques of insincerity only from familiarity with the modes of unforced conversation that are to be simulated. To say this is not to accord ethical laurels to human nature. Unstudied utterance is not honesty or candor. Honesty is a highly sophisticated disposition, for it is the disposition to abstain from insincerity, just as candor is the disposition to abstain from reticence. A person could not be honest or candid who had never known insincerity or reticence, any more than a person could be insincere or reticent who had never known ingenuous and open utterance.

There are other kinds of studied utterance, some of which will have to be discussed at a later stage, that belong not to normal sociable conversations but only to more serious affairs. The physician, the judge, the preacher, the politician, the astronomer and the geometrician may give their counsels, verdicts, homilies, theories and formulae by word of mouth, but they are then talking not in the sense of "chatting" but in the sense of "pronouncing" or "propounding." Perhaps they prepare, but at least they weigh, their words. They do not say the first things that come to their lips, for their discourse is disciplined. What they say would, unlike spontaneous chat, generally tolerate being written down and even printed. It is not impromptu or spontaneous, let fall or blurted out, but delivered. Their authors are considering what to say and how to say it, in order to produce precisely the right effect. This sort of talk is literally prosy.

We need to contrast normal unstudied talk both with studied conversational talk and with studied nonconversational talk, for it is the basis of both of them. We use unstudied, conversational talk not only before we learn to converse guardedly and insincerely and before we learn to discourse weightily; we also continue to occupy a good part of our talking day in saying the first things that come to our lips. Camouflage and gravity are only intermittent necessities.

It is not only in our unembarrassed, uncalculated colloquies with others that we say the first things that come to our lips; we do so also in the easy, unbuttoned colloquies that we hold, commonly in silence, with ourselves.

In unstudied chat we talk about whatever we are at the moment chiefly interested in. It is not a rival interest. We talk about the garden from the motive that prompts us to inspect and potter in the garden, namely interest in the garden. We chat about our dinner not because we are not interested in our dinner, but because we are. We may talk about our dinner because we are hungry, just as we eat it because we are hungry; and we cannot easily help talking about the steepness of the hill, for the same reason that we cannot easily help our steps flagging as we climb it. Spontaneous utterance is not a collateral, competing interest, it is an exercise auxiliary to the taking of any interest in anything whatsoever.

A person who is annoyed with a knotted shoelace is, if he has learned to talk, also in the mood to use a verbal expression of annoyance with it. He talks about it in a fretful tone of voice. What he says, together with his way of saying it, discloses or lets us know his frame of mind, just because his unstudied using of that expression is one of the things that he is in the frame of mind to do. To tug fretfully at the shoelace might be another. He is sufficiently aggravated by the knot to talk aggravatedly about it.

Unstudied utterances are not, on the one hand, effects of the frames of mind in which they are used, since frames of mind are not incidents; but nor, on the other hand, are they reports about those frames of mind. If the lorry-driver asks urgently, "Which is the road to London?" he discloses his anxiety to find out, but he does not make an autobiographical or psychological pronouncement about it. He says what he says not from a desire to inform us or himself about himself, but from a desire to get on to the right road to London. Unstudied utterances are not self-comments, though, as we shall shortly see, they constitute our primary evidence for making self-comments, when we come to be interested in making them.

Now many unstudied utterances embody explicit interest phrases, or what I have elsewhere been calling "avowals," like "I want," "I hope," "I intend," "I dislike," "I am depressed," "I wonder," "I guess" and "I feel hungry"; and their grammar makes it tempting to misconstrue all the sentences in which they occur as self-descriptions. But in its primary employment "I want . . ." is not used to convey information, but to make a request or demand. It is no more meant as a contribution to general knowledge than "please." To respond with "do you?" or "how do you know?" would be glaringly inappropriate. Nor, in their primary employment, are "I hate . . ." and "I intend . . ." used for the purpose of telling the hearer facts about the speaker; or else we should not be surprised to hear them uttered in the cool, informative tones of voice in which we say "he hates . . ." and "they intend. . . ." We expect them, on the contrary, to be spoken in a revolted and a resolute tone of voice respectively. They are the utterances of persons in revolted and resolute frames of mind. They are things said in detestation and resolution and not things said in order to advance biographical knowledge about detestations and resolutions.

A person who notices the unstudied utterances of a speaker, who may or may not be himself, is, if his interest in the speaker has the appropriate direction and if he knows the language in which the utterances are made, especially well situated to pass comments upon the qualities and frames of mind of their author. While careful observation of the subject's other behavior, such as his other overt actions, his hesitations and his tears and laughter, may tell him much, this behavior is not *ex officio* made easy to witness, or easy to interpret. But speech is *ex officio* made to be heard and made to be construed. Learning to talk is learning to make oneself understood. No sleuth-like powers are required for me to find out from the words and tones of voice of your unstudied talk, or even of my own unstudied talk, the frame of mind of the talker.

When talk is guarded—and often we do not know whether it is so or not, even in the avowals we make to ourselves—sleuth-like qualities do have to be exercised. We now have to infer from what is said and done to what would have been said, if wariness had not been exercised, as well as to the motives of the wariness. Finding out what is on the pages of an open book is a matter of simple reading; finding out what is on the pages of a sealed book requires hypotheses and evidence. But the fact that concealments have to be penetrated does not imply that nonconcealments have to be penetrated.

One of the things often signified by "self-consciousness" is the notice we take of our own unstudied utterances, including our explicit avowals, whether these are spoken aloud, muttered or said in our heads. We eavesdrop on our own voiced utterances and our own silent monologues. In noticing these we are preparing ourselves to do something new, namely to describe the frames of mind which these utterances disclose. But there is nothing intrinsically proprietary about this activity. I can pay heed to what I overhear you saying as well as to what I overhear myself saying, though I cannot overhear your silent colloquies with yourself. Nor can I read your diary, if you write it in cipher, or keep it under lock and key. Indeed, not only is this sort of self-study the same in kind as the study of the unguarded and later also the guarded utterances of others, but we learn to make this study of our own talk from first taking part in the public discussion of anyone's talk as well as from reading novelists' illustrative deployment of their characters' talk, together with their explanatory descriptions of it.

Critical readers may ask why I have refrained from using the verb "to think" instead of such trivial verbs as "talk," "chat," "converse" and "let out," since clearly the utterances which I have been mentioning are, ordinarily, pertinent utterances, the authors of which mean what they say; I have been mentioning significant and intelligible speech and not things like guffaws, babblings or rigmarole. My reasons are two, and are closely connected. First, the utterances I have been considering belong to sociable interchanges of conversation between speakers and hearers, who may be one and the same persons. Their point is a conversational point. Since many of the utterances that constitute a conversation are not in the indicative mood, but are questions, commands, complaints, quips, scoldings, congratulations, etc., we cannot in their case speak of those epistemological darlings the "thoughts," "judgments" or "propositions" expressed by them. Secondly, we tend to reserve the verb "to think" for the uses of those studied and severely drilled utterances which constitute theories and policies. Now we learn to chat in the nursery, but we have to go to school to learn even the rudiments of theorizing. The techniques of theorizing are learned in set lessons, while conversational speech is acquired almost entirely by conversing. So the use of sentences, and particularly of certain sorts of indicative sentences, for the special ends of propounding, i.e. providing premisses and delivering conclusions, is a belated and sophisticated use, and necessarily comes later than the conversational uses of sentences and phrases. When a theory or a bit of a theory is voiced aloud, instead of being conveyed in its proper milieu of print, we hesitate to call the voicing by the name of "talk" and we should flatly refuse to call it "chat" or "conversation." It is meant didactically, not sociably. It is a kind of work, whereas unstudied chat is no kind of work, not even easy or agreeable work.

6. The Self.

Not only theorists but also quite unsophisticated people, including young children, find perplexities in the notion of "I." Children sometimes puzzle their heads with such questions as, "What would it be like if I became you and you became me?" and "Where was I before I began?" Theologians have been exercised over the question "What is it in an individual which is saved or damned?" and philosophers have speculated whether "I" denotes a peculiar and separate substance and in what consists my indivisible and continuing identity. Not all such puzzles arise from the unwitting adoption of the paramechanical hypothesis, and I propose in this section to try to do justice to one particular family of such enigmas, the expounding and solving of which may be of some general theoretical interest.

The enigmas that I have in mind all turn on what I shall call the "systematic elusiveness" of the concept of "I." When a child, like Kim, having no theoretical commitments or equipment, first asks himself, "Who or What am I?" he does not ask it from a desire to know his own surname, age, sex, nationality or position in the form. He knows all his ordinary personalia. He feels that there is something else in the background for which his "I" stands, a something which has still to be described after all his ordinary personalia have been listed. He also feels, very vaguely, that whatever it is that his "I" stands for, it is something very important and quite unique, unique in the sense that neither it, nor anything like it, belongs to anyone else. There *could* only be one of it. Pronouns like "you," "she" and "we" feel quite unmystifying, while "I" feels mystifying. And it feels mystifying, anyhow in part, because the more the child tries to put his finger on what "I" stands for, the less does he succeed in doing so. He can catch only its coattails; it itself is always and obdurately a pace ahead of its coattails. Like the shadow of one's own head, it will not wait to be jumped on. And yet it is never very far ahead; indeed, sometimes it seems not to be ahead of the pursuer at all. It evades capture by lodging itself inside the very muscles of the pursuer. It is too near even to be within arm's reach.

Theorists have found themselves mocked in a similar way by the concept of "I." Even Hume confesses that, when he has tried to sketch all the items of his experience, he has found nothing there to answer to the word "I," and yet he is not satisfied that there does not remain something more and something important, without which his sketch fails to describe his experience.[3]

Other epistemologists have felt similar qualms. Should I, or should I not, put my knowing self down on my list of the sorts of things that I can have knowledge of? If I say "no," it seems to reduce my knowing self to a theoretically infertile mystery, yet if I say "yes," it seems to reduce the fishing net to one of the fishes which it itself catches. It seems hazardous either to allow or to deny that the judge can be put into the dock.

I shall try before long to explain this systematic elusiveness of the notion of "I" and with it the apparent nonparallelism between the notion of "I" and the notions of "you" and "he." But it is expedient first to consider some points which hold good of all personal pronouns alike.

People, including philosophers, tend to raise their questions about what constitutes a self by asking what the words "I" and "you" are the names of. They are familiar with the river of which "Thames" is the name and with the dog called "Fido." They are also familiar with the persons of whom their acquaintances' and their own surnames are the surnames. They then feel vaguely that since "I" and "you" are not public surnames, they must be names of another and queer sort and must in consequence be the names of some extra individuals hidden away behind or inside the persons who are known abroad by their ordinary surnames and Christian names. As pronouns are not registered at Somerset House, their owners must be different, somehow, from the owners of the Christian and surnames which are registered there. But this way of broaching the question is mistaken from the start. Certainly "I" and "you" are not regular proper names like "Fido" and "Thames," but they are not irregular proper names either. They are not proper names, or names at all, any more than "today" is an ephemeral name of the current day. Gratuitous mystification begins from the moment that we start to peer around for the beings named by our pronouns. Sentences containing pronouns do, of course, mention

[3]See Hume selection above, pp. 46–57.—Ed.

identifiable people, but the way in which the people mentioned are identified by pronouns is quite different from the way in which they are identified by proper names.

This difference can be provisionally indicated in the following manner. There is a class of words (which for ease of reference may be called "index words") that indicate to the hearer or reader the particular thing, episode, person, place or moment referred to. Thus "now" is an index word which indicates to the hearer of the sentence "the train is now going over the bridge" the particular moment of the crossing. The word "now" can, of course, be used at any moment of any day or night, but it does not mean what is meant by "at any moment of any day or night." It indicates that particular moment at which the hearer is intended to hear the word "now" being uttered. The moment at which the train crosses the bridge is indicated by the utterance at that moment of the word "now." The moment at which "now" is breathed is the moment which it indicates. In a partly similar way the word "that" is often used to indicate the particular thing at which the speaker's index finger is pointing at the moment when he breathes out the word "that." "Here" indicates, sometimes, that particular place from which the speaker propagates the noise "here" into the surrounding air; and the page indicated by the phrase "this page" is the page of which the printed word "this" occupies a part. Other index words indicate indirectly. "Yesterday" indicates the day before that on which it is uttered, or printed in a newspaper; "then," in certain uses, indicates a moment or period standing in a specified relation with that in which it is heard or read.

Now pronouns like "I" and "you" are, anyhow sometimes, direct index words, while others, like "he" and "they" and, in some uses, "we" are indirect index words. "I" can indicate the particular person from whom the noise "I," or the written mark "I," issues; "you" can indicate the one person who hears me say "you," or it can indicate that person, whoever he is (and there may be several) who reads the "you" that I write, or have printed. In all cases the physical occurrence of an index word is bodily annexed to what the word indicates. Hence "you" is not a queer name that I and others sometimes give you; it is an index word which, in its particular conversational setting, indicates to you just who it is to whom I am addressing my remarks. "I" is not an extra name for an extra being; it indicates, when I say or write it, the same individual who can also be addressed by the proper name "Gilbert Ryle." "I" is not an alias for "Gilbert Ryle"; it indicates the person whom "Gilbert Ryle" names, when Gilbert Ryle uses "I."

But this is far from being the whole story. We have now to notice that we use our pronouns, as well as our proper names, in a wide variety of different ways. Further mystifications have arisen from the detection, without the comprehension of contrasts between such different uses of "I" and, to a lesser extent, of "you" and "he."

In the sentence "I am warming myself before the fire," the word "myself" could be replaced by "my body" without spoiling the sense; but the pronoun "I" could not be replaced by "my body" without making nonsense. Similarly the sentence "Cremate me after I am gone" says nothing self-annihilating, since the "me" and the "I" are being used in different senses. So sometimes we can, and sometimes we cannot, paraphrase the first personal pronoun by "my body." There are even some cases where I can talk about a part of my body, but cannot use "I" or "me" for it. If my hair were scorched in a fire, I could say "I was not scorched; only my hair was," though I could never say "I was not scorched; only my face and hands were." A part of the body which is insensitive and cannot be moved at will is mine, but it is not part of me. Conversely, mechanical auxiliaries to the body, such as motorcars and walking sticks, can be spoken of with "I" and "me"; as in "I collided with the pillar-box," which means the same thing as "the car which I was driving (or which I owned and was having driven for me in my presence) collided with the pillar-box."

Let us now consider some contexts in which "I" and "me" can certainly not be replaced by "my body" or "my leg." If I say "I am annoyed that I was cut in the collision," while I might accept the substitution of "my leg was cut" for "I was cut," I should not allow "I am annoyed" to be reconstructed in any such way. It would be similarly absurd to speak of "my head remembering," "my brain doing long division," or "my body battling with fatigue." Perhaps it is because of the absurdity of such collocations that so many people have felt driven to describe a person as an association between a body and a nonbody.

However, we are not yet at the end of our list of elasticities in the uses of "I" and "me"; for we find further contrasts breaking out between uses of the first personal pronoun in which none can be paraphrased by mere references to the body. It makes perfect sense to say that I caught myself just beginning to dream, but not that I caught my body beginning to dream, or that my body caught me doing so; and it makes sense to say that a child is telling himself a fairy story, but nonsense to make his body either narrator or auditor.

Contrasts of these types, perhaps above all the contrasts advertised in descriptions of exercises of self-control, have induced many preachers and some thinkers to speak as if an ordinary person is really some sort of committee or team of persons, all laced together inside one skin;

as if the thinking and vetoing "I" were one person, and the greedy or lazy "I" were another. But this sort of picture is obviously of no use. Part of what we mean by "person" is someone who is capable of catching himself beginning to dream, of telling himself stories and of curbing his own greed. So the suggested reduction of a person to a team of persons would merely multiply the number of persons without explaining how it is that one and the same person can be both narrator and auditor, or both vigilant and dreamy, both scorched and amazed at being scorched. The beginning of the required explanation is that in such a statement as "I caught myself beginning to dream," the two pronouns are not names of different persons, since they are not names at all, but that they are index words being used in different senses in different sorts of context, just as we saw was the case with the statement "I am warming myself by the fire" (though this is a different difference of sense from the other). In case it seems unplausible to say that inside one sentence the twice used first personal pronoun can both indicate the same person and also have two different senses, it is enough for the moment to point out that the same thing can happen even with ordinary proper names and personal titles. The sentence "after her wedding Miss Jones will no longer be Miss Jones" does not say that the particular woman will cease to be herself, or cease to be the sort of person she now is, but only that she will have changed her name and status; and the sentence "after Napoleon returned to France, he was Napoleon no longer" might mean only that his qualities of generalship had altered, and is obviously analogous to the familiar expression "I am not myself." The statements "I was just beginning to dream" and "I caught myself just beginning to dream" are statements of logically different types, and it follows from their being of different types that the pronoun "I" is being used with a different logical force in the two sentences.

In considering specifically human behavior—behavior, that is, which is unachieved by animals, infants and idiots—we should for several reasons notice the fact that some sorts of actions are in one way or another concerned with, or are operations upon, other actions. When one person retaliates upon another, scoffs at him, replies to him or plays hide-and-seek with him, his actions have to do, in one way or another, with certain actions on the part of the other; in a sense to be specified later, the performance of the former involves the thought of the latter. An action on the part of one agent could not be one of spying or applauding, unless it had to do with the actions of another agent; not could I behave as a customer, unless you or someone else behaved as a seller. One man must give evidence if another is to cross-examine him; some people must be on the stage, if others are to be dramatic critics. It will sometimes be convenient to use the title "higher order actions" to denote those the descriptions of which involve the oblique mention of other actions.

Some, but not all, higher order actions influence the agent dealt with. If I merely comment on your actions behind your back, my comment has to do with your actions in the sense that my performance of my act involves the thought of your performance of yours; but it does not modify your actions. This is especially clear where the commentator or critic is operating after the death of the agent on whose doings he passes his judgments. The historian cannot change Napoleon's conduct of the battle of Waterloo. On the other hand, the moment and the methods of my attacking do affect the timing and the techniques of your defense, and what I sell has a lot to do with what you buy.

Next, when I speak of the actions of one agent having to do with those of another, I do not exclude those actions which are performed under the mistaken impression that the other is doing something which he is not really doing. The child who applauds my skill in pretending to be asleep, though I have in fact really fallen asleep, is doing something which, in the required sense, presupposes that I am pretending; and Robinson Crusoe really is having conversationally to do with his parrot, if he believes, or half believes, that the bird follows what he says, even if this belief is false.

Finally, there are many kinds of dealings which are concerned with subsequent, or even merely possible, or probable, actions. When I bribe you to vote for me, your voting has not yet taken place and may never take place. A reference to your vote enters into the description of my bribe, but the reference must be of the pattern "that you shall vote for me," and not of the pattern "because you did vote," or "because I thought that you did vote for me." In the same way my talking to you presupposes only in this way your understanding and agreeing with me, namely that I talk in order that you may understand and agree with me.

So when John Doe counters, detects, reports, parodies, exploits, applauds, mocks, abets, copies or interprets something done by Richard Roe, any description of his action would have to embody an oblique mention of the thing done, or supposed to be done, by Richard Roe; whereas no such description of John Doe's behavior would have to enter into the description of that of Richard Roe. To talk about John Doe's detection or mockery would involve, but not be involved in, talking about what he had been detecting or mocking, and this is what is meant by saying that John Doe's action is of a higher order than that of Richard Roe. By "higher" I do not mean "loftier." Blackmailing a deserter is of a higher order than his desertion, and advertising is of a higher order than selling. Recollecting the doing of a kindness is not nobler than the doing of it, but it is of a higher order.

It may be hygienic to remember that though the actions of reporting or commenting on the actions of others behind their backs is one species of higher order action, it has no special priority over the other ways of dealing with these actions. Keeping an academic tally of what Richard Roe does is only one way in which John Doe takes steps about Richard Roe's steps. The construction and public or private use of sentences in the indicative is not, as intellectualists love to think, either John Doe's indispensable first move or his Utopian last move. But this point requires us to consider the sense in which performing a higher order action "involves the thought of" the corresponding lower order action. It does not mean that if, for example, I am to mimic your gestures, I must do two things, namely both verbally describe your gestures to myself and produce gestures complying with the terms employed in that description. Telling myself about your gestures would in itself be a higher order performance, and one which would equally involve the thought of your gestures. The phrase "involve the thought of" does not signify a causal transaction, or the concomitance of a process of one sort with a process of another sort. As commenting on your gestures, to be commenting, must itself *be* thinking in a certain way of your gestures, so mimicking them, to be mimicry and not mere replica, must itself *be* thinking in a certain way of your gestures. But of course this is a strained sense of "thinking"; it does not denote any sort of pondering or entail the enunciation of any propositions. It means that I must know what I am doing and, since what I am doing is mimicking, I must know the gestures you made and be using that knowledge, using it in the mimicking way and not in the reporting or commenting way.

Higher order actions are not instinctive. Any one of them can be done efficiently or inefficiently, appropriately or inappropriately, intelligently or stupidly. Children have to learn how to perform them. They have to learn how to resist, parry and retaliate, how to forestall, give way and cooperate, how to exchange and haggle, reward and punish. They have to learn to make jokes against others and to see some jokes against themselves, to obey orders and give them, make requests and grant them, receive marks and award them. They have to learn to compose and follow reports, descriptions and commentaries; to understand and to give criticisms, to accept, reject, correct and compose verdicts, catechise and be catechised. Not least (and also not soonest) they have to learn to keep to themselves things which they are inclined to divulge. Reticence is of a higher order than unreticence. My object in drawing attention to these truisms of the playroom and the schoolroom can now be seen. At a certain stage the child discovers the trick of directing higher order acts upon his own lower order acts. Having been separately victim and author of jokes, coercions, catechisms, criticisms and mimicries in the interpersonal dealings between others and himself, he finds out how to play both roles at once. He has listened to stories before, and he has told stories before, but now he tells stories to his own enthralled ear. He has been detected in insincerities and he has detected the insincerities of others, but now he applies the techniques of detection to his own insincerities. He finds that he can give orders to himself with such authority that he sometimes obeys them, even when reluctant to do so. Self-suasion and self-dissuasion become more or less effective. He learns in adolescence to apply to his own behavior most of those higher order methods of dealing with the young that are regularly practiced by adults. He is then said to be growing up.

Moreover, just as he had earlier acquired not only the ability, but also the inclination to direct higher order acts upon the acts of others, so he now becomes prone, as well as competent, to do the same upon his own behavior; and just as he had earlier learned to cope not only with the particular performances of others, but also with their dispositions to conduct such performances, so he now becomes in some degree both able and ready to take steps, theoretical and practical, about his own habits, motives and abilities. Nor are his own higher order performances, or his dispositions to perform them, in any way exempted from just the same treatment. For any performance of any order, it is always possible that there should be performed a variety of higher order actions about it. If I ridicule something done by you, or by myself, I can, but usually do not go on to pass a verbal comment on my amusement, apologize for it, or let others into the joke; and then I can go on to applaud or reproach myself for doing so, and make a note in my diary that I have done this.

It will be seen that what is here under discussion covers much of both what is ordinarily called "self-consciousness" and what is ordinarily called "self-control," though it covers much more than them. A person can, indeed, and must act sometimes as reporter upon his own doings and sometimes as prefect regulating his own conduct, but these higher order self-dealings are only two out of innumerable brands, just as the corresponding interpersonal dealings are only two out of innumerable brands.

Nor must it be supposed that the reports which a person makes to himself upon his own doings, or the régimes which he imposes upon his own conduct are inevitably free from bias or carelessness. My reports on myself are subject to the same kinds of defects as are my reports on you, and the admonitions, corrections and injunctions which I impose on myself may show me to be as ineffectual or ill-advised as does my disciplining of others. Self-consciousness, if the word is to be used at all, must not be described on the hallowed para-optical model, as a torch that illuminates itself by beams of its own light reflected from a mirror in its own insides. On the contrary it is simply a special case of an ordinary more or less efficient handling of a less or more honest and intelligent witness. Similarly, self-control is not to be likened to the management of a partially disciplined subordinate by a superior of perfect wisdom and authority; it is simply a special case of the management of an ordinary person by an ordinary person, namely where John Doe, say, is taking both parts. The truth is not that there occur some higher order acts which are above criticism, but that any higher order act that occurs can itself be criticized; not that something unimprovable does take place, but that nothing takes place which is not improvable; not that any operation is of the highest order, but that for any operation of any order there can be operations of a higher order.

7. The Systematic Elusiveness of "I."

We are now in a position to account for the systematic elusiveness of the notion of "I," and the partial nonparallelism between it and the notion of "you" or "he." To concern oneself about oneself in any way, theoretical or practical, is to perform a higher order act, just as it is to concern oneself about anybody else. To try, for example, to describe what one has just done, or is now doing, is to comment upon a step which is not itself, save *per accidens*, one of commenting. But the operation which is the commenting is not, and cannot be, the step on which that commentary is being made. Nor can an act of ridiculing be its own butt. A higher order action cannot be the action upon which it is performed. So my commentary on my performances must always be silent about one performance, namely itself, and this performance can be the target only of another commentary. Self-commentary, self-ridicule and self-admonition are logically condemned to eternal penultimacy. Yet nothing that is left out of any particular commentary or admonition is privileged thereby to escape comment or admonition for ever. On the contrary it may be the target of the very next comment or rebuke.

The point may be illustrated in this way. A singing master might criticize the accents or notes of a pupil by mimicking with exaggerations each word that the pupil sang; and if the pupil sang slowly enough, the master could parody each word sung by the pupil before the next came to be uttered. But then, in a mood of humility, the singing master tries to criticize his own singing in the same way, and more than that to mimic with exaggerations each word that he utters, including those that he utters in self-parody. It is at once clear, first, that he can never get beyond the very earliest word of his song and, second, that at any given moment he has uttered one noise which has yet to be mimicked—and it makes no difference how rapidly he chases his notes with mimicries of them. He can, in principle, never catch more than the coattails of the object of his pursuit, since a word cannot be a parody of itself. None the less, there is no word that he sings which remains unparodied; he is always a day late for the fair, but every day he reaches the place of yesterday's fair. He never succeeds in jumping on to the shadow of his own head, yet he is never more than one jump behind.

An ordinary reviewer may review a book, while a second order reviewer criticizes reviews of the book. But the second order review is not a criticism of itself. It can only be criticized in a further third order review. Given complete editorial patience, any review of any order could be published, though at no stage would all the reviews have received critical notices. Nor can every act of a diarist be the topic of a record in his diary; for the last entry made in his diary still demands that the making of it should in its turn be chronicled.

This, I think, explains the feeling that my last year's self, or my yesterday's self, could in principle be exhaustively described and accounted for, and that your past or present self could be exhaustively described and accounted for by me, but that my today's self perpetually slips out of any hold of it that I try to take. It also explains the apparent nonparallelism between the notion of "I" and that of "you," without construing the elusive residuum as any kind of ultimate mystery.

There is another thing which it explains. When people consider the problems of the Freedom of the Will and try to imagine their own careers as analogous to those of clocks or watercourses, they tend to boggle at the idea that their own immediate future is already unalterably fixed and predictable. It seems absurd to suppose that what I am just about to think, feel or do is already preappointed, though people are apt to find no such absurdity in the supposition that the futures of other people are so preappointed. The so-called "feeling of spontaneity" is closely connected with this inability to imagine that what I am going to think or do can already be anticipated. On the other hand, when I consider what I thought and did yesterday, there seems to be no absurdity in supposing that that could have been forecast, before I did it. It is only while I am actually trying to predict my own next move that the task feels like that of a swimmer trying to overtake the waves that he sends ahead of himself.

The solution is as before. A prediction of a deed or a thought is a higher order operation, the performance of which cannot be among the things considered in making the prediction. Yet as the state of mind in which I am just before I do something may make some difference to what I do, it follows that I must overlook at least one of the data relevant to my prediction. Similarly, I can give you the fullest possible advice what to do, but I must omit one piece of counsel, since I cannot in the same breath advise you how to take that advice. There is therefore no paradox in saying that while normally I am not at all surprised to find myself doing or thinking what I do, yet when I try most carefully to anticipate what I shall do or think, then the outcome is likely to falsify my expectation. My process of preenvisaging may divert the course of my ensuing behavior in a direction and degree of which my prognosis cannot take account. One thing that I cannot prepare myself for is the next thought that I am going to think.

The fact that my immediate future is in this way systematically elusive to me has, of course, no tendency to prove that my career is in principle unpredictable to prophets other than myself, or even that it is inexplicable to myself after the heat of the action. I can point to any other thing with my index finger, and other people can point at this finger. But it cannot be the object at which it itself is pointing. Nor can a missile be its own target, though anything else may be thrown at it.

This general conclusion that any performance can be the concern of a higher order performance, but cannot be the concern of itself, is connected with what was said earlier about the special functioning of index words, such as "now," "you" and "I." An "I" sentence indicates whom in particular it is about by being itself uttered or written by someone in particular. "I" indicates the person who utters it. So, when a person utters an "I" sentence, his utterance of it may be part of a higher order performance, namely one, perhaps of self-reporting, self-exhortation or self-commiseration, and this performance itself is not dealt with in the operation which it itself is. Even if the person is, for special speculative purposes, momentarily concentrating on the Problem of the Self, he has failed and knows that he has failed to catch more than the flying coattails of that which he was pursuing. His quarry was the hunter.

To conclude, there is nothing mysterious or occult about the range of higher order acts and attitudes, which are apt to be inadequately covered by the umbrella title "self-consciousness." They are the same in kind as the higher order acts and attitudes exhibited in the dealings of people with one other. Indeed the former are only a special application of the latter and are learned first from them. If I perform the third order operation of commenting on a second order act of laughing at myself for a piece of manual awkwardness, I shall indeed use the first personal pronoun in two different ways. I say to myself, or to the company, "I was laughing at myself for being butter-fingered." But so far from this showing that there are two "Mes" in my skin, not to speak, yet, of the third one which is still commenting on them, it shows only that I am applying the public two-pronoun idiom in which we talk of her laughing at him; and I am applying this linguistic idiom, because I am applying the method of interpersonal transaction which the idiom is ordinarily employed to describe.

Before concluding this chapter, it is worth mentioning that there is one influential difference between the first personal pronoun and all the rest. "I," in my use of it, always indicates me and only indicates me. "You," "she" and "they" indicate different people at different times. "I" is like my own shadow; I can never get away from it, as I can get away from your shadow. There is no mystery about this constancy, but I mention it because it seems to endow "I" with a mystifying uniqueness and adhesiveness. "Now" has something of the same besetting feeling.

8

Norman Malcolm

WITTGENSTEIN'S *PHILOSOPHICAL INVESTIGATIONS*[1]*

*Ein Buch ist ein Spiegel; wenn ein Affe hineinguckt, so kann freilich
kein Apostel heraussehen.*

LICHTENBERG

An attempt to summarize the *Investigations* would be neither successful nor useful. Wittgenstein compressed his thoughts to the point where
further compression is impossible. What is needed is that they be unfolded and the connections between them traced out. A likely first
reaction to the book will be to regard it as a puzzling collection of reflections that are sometimes individually brilliant, but possess no unity,
present no system of ideas. In truth the unity is there, but it cannot be
perceived without strenuous exertion. Within the scope of a review
the connectedness can best be brought out, I think, by concentrating
on some single topic—in spite of the fact that there are no separate
topics, for each of the investigations in the book crisscrosses again
and again with every other one. In the following I center my attention
on Wittgenstein's treatment of the problem of how language is related
to inner experiences—to sensations, feelings, and moods. This is one of
the main inquiries of the book and perhaps the most difficult to understand. I am sufficiently aware of the fact that my presentation of this
subject will certainly fail to portray the subtlety, elegance, and force of
Wittgenstein's thinking and will probably, in addition, contain positive
mistakes.

References to Part I will be by paragraph numbers, e.g., (207), and
to Part II by page numbers, e.g., (p. 207). Quotations will be placed
within double quotation marks.

Private language. Let us see something of how Wittgenstein attacks
what he calls "the idea of a private language." By a "private" language

[1]From *Knowledge and Certainty: Essays and Lectures* by Norman Malcolm, © 1963, with
the permission of Prentice-Hall, Inc., Englewood Cliffs, N.J., and the author. This essay
originally appeared in *Philosophical Review* (1954).
*Ludwig Wittgenstein, *Philosophical Investigations*, German and English on facing pages.
Tr. by G. E. M. Anscombe (New York: The Macmillan Company, 1953).

is meant one that not merely is not but *cannot* be understood by anyone other than the speaker. The reason for this is that the words of this language are supposed to "refer to what can only be known to the person speaking; to his immediate private sensations" (243). What is supposed is that I "*associate* words with sensations and use these names in descriptions" (256). I fix my attention on a sensation and establish a connection between a word and the sensation (258).

It is worth mentioning that the conception that it is possible and even necessary for one to have a private language is not eccentric. Rather it is the view that comes most naturally to anyone who philosophizes on the subject of the relation of words to experiences. The idea of a private language is presupposed by every program of inferring or constructing the 'external world' and 'other minds.' It is contained in the philosophy of Descartes and in the theory of ideas of classical British empiricism, as well as in recent and contemporary phenomenalism and sense-datum theory. At bottom it is the idea that there is only a contingent and not an *essential* connection between a sensation and its outward expression—an idea that appeals to us all. Such thoughts as these are typical expressions of the idea of a private language: that I know only from my *own* case what the word 'pain' means (293, 295); that I can only *believe* that someone else is in pain, but I *know* it if I am (303); that another person cannot have *my* pains (253); that I can undertake to call *this* (pointing inward) 'pain' in the future (263); that when I say 'I am in pain' I am at any rate justified *before myself* (289).

In order to appreciate the depth and power of Wittgenstein's assault upon this idea you must partly be its captive. You must feel the strong grip of it. The passionate intensity of Wittgenstein's treatment of it is due to the fact that he lets this idea take possession of him, drawing out of himself the thoughts and imagery by which it is expressed and defended—and then subjecting those thoughts and pictures to fiercest scrutiny. What is written down represents both a logical investigation and a great philosopher's struggle with his own thoughts. The logical investigation will be understood only by those who duplicate the struggle in themselves.

One consequence to be drawn from the view that I know only from my *own* case what, say, 'tickling' means is that "I know only what *I* call that, not what anyone else does" (347). I have not *learned* what 'tickling' means, I have only called something by that name. Perhaps others use the name differently. This is a regrettable difficulty; but, one may think, the word will still work for me as a name, provided that I apply it consistently to a certain sensation. But how about 'sensation'? Don't I know only from my *own* case what *that* word means?

Perhaps what I call a "sensation" others call by another name? It will not help, says Wittgenstein, to say that although it may be that what I have is not what others call a 'sensation,' at least I have *something*. For don't I know only from my own case what 'having something' is? Perhaps my use of *those* words is contrary to common use. In trying to explain how I gave 'tickling' its meaning, I discover that I do not have the right to use any of the relevant words of our common language. "So in the end when one is doing philosophy one gets to the point where one would like just to emit an inarticulate sound" (261).

Let us suppose that I did fix my attention on a pain as I pronounced the word 'pain' to myself. I think that thereby I established a connection between the word and the sensation. But I did not establish a connection if subsequently I applied that word to sensations other than pain or to things other than sensations, e.g., emotions. My private definition was a success only if it led me to use the word correctly in the future. In the present case, 'correctly' would mean '*consistently* with my own definition'; for the question of whether my use agrees with that of others has been given up as a bad job. Now how is it to be decided whether I have used the word consistently? What will be the difference between my having used it consistently and its *seeming* to me that I have? Or has this distinction vanished? "Whatever is going to seem right to me is right. And that only means that here we can't talk about 'right'" (258). If the distinction between 'correct' and 'seems correct' has disappeared, then so has the concept *correct*. It follows that the 'rules' of my private language are only *impressions* of rules (259). My impression that I follow a rule does not confirm that I follow the rule, unless there can be something that will prove my impression correct. And the something cannot be another impression—for this would be "as if someone were to buy several copies of the morning paper to assure himself that what it said was true" (265). The proof that I am following a rule must appeal to something *independent* of my impression that I am. If in the nature of the case there cannot be such an appeal, then my private language does not have *rules*, for the concept of a rule requires that there be a difference between 'He is following a rule' and 'He is under the impression that he is following a rule'—just as the concept of understanding a word requires that there be a difference between 'He understands this word' and 'He thinks that he understands this word' (cf. 269).

'Even if I cannot prove and cannot know that I am correctly following the rules of my private language,' it might be said, 'still it *may* be that I am. It has *meaning* to say that I am. The supposition makes sense: you and I *understand* it.' Wittgenstein has a reply to this (348-353).

We are inclined to think that we know what it means to say 'It is five o'clock on the sun' or 'This congenital deaf-mute talks to himself inwardly in a vocal language' or 'The stove is in pain.' These sentences produce pictures in our minds, and it *seems* to us that the pictures tell us how to *apply* them—that is, tell us what we have to look for, what we have to do, in order to determine whether what is pictured is the case. But we make a mistake in thinking that the picture contains in itself the instructions as to how we are to apply it. Think of the picture of blindness as a darkness in the soul or in the head of the blind man(424). There is nothing wrong with it *as a picture.* "But *what* is its application?" What shall count for or against its being said that this or that man is blind, that the picture applies to him? The *picture* doesn't say. If you think that you understand the sentence 'I follow the rule that *this* is to be called "pain"' (a rule of your private language), what you have perhaps is a picture of yourself checking off various feelings of yours as either being *this* or not. The picture appears to solve the problem of how you determine whether you have done the 'checking' right. Actually it doesn't give you even a hint in that direction; no more than the picture of blindness provides so much as a hint of *how* it is to be determined that this or that man is blind (348–353, 422–426, p. 184).

One will be inclined to say here that one can simply *remember* this sensation and by remembering it will know that one is making a consistent application of its name. But will it also be possible to have a *false* memory impression? On the private-language hypothesis, what would *show* that your memory impression is false—or true? Another memory impression? Would this imply that memory is a court from which there is no appeal? But, as a matter of fact, that is *not* our concept of memory.

Imagine that you were supposed to paint a particular color "C," which was the color that appeared when the chemical substances X and Y combined.—Suppose that the color struck you as brighter on one day than on another; would you not sometimes say: "I must be wrong, the color is certainly the same as yesterday"? This shows that we do not always resort to what memory tells us as the verdict of the highest court of appeal [56].

There is, indeed, such a thing as checking one memory against another, e.g., I check my recollection of the time of departure of a train by calling up a memory image of how a page of the time-table looked—but "this process has got to produce a memory which is actually *correct.*

If the mental image of the time-table could not itself be *tested* for correctness, how could it confirm the correctness of the first memory?" (265).

If I have a language that is really private (i.e., it is a logical impossibility that anyone else should understand it or should have any basis for knowing whether I am using a particular name consistently), my assertion that my memory tells me so and so will be utterly empty. 'My memory' will not even mean—my memory *impression*. For by a memory impression we understand something that is either accurate or inaccurate; whereas there would not be, in the private language, any *conception* of what would establish a memory impression as correct, any conception of what 'correct' would mean here.

The same. One wants to say, 'Surely there can't be a difficulty in knowing whether a feeling of mine is or isn't the *same* as the feeling I now have. I will call this feeling "pain" and will thereafter call the *same* thing "pain" whenever it occurs. What could be easier than to follow that rule?' To understand Wittgenstein's reply to this attractive proposal we must come closer to his treatment of rules and of what it is to follow a rule. (Here he forges a remarkably illuminating connection between the philosophy of psychology and the philosophy of mathematics.) Consider his example of the pupil who has been taught to write down a cardinal number series of the form 'o, n, 2n, 3n . . .' at an order of the form ' + n,' so that at the order ' + 1' he writes down the series of natural numbers (185). He has successfully done exercises and tests up to the number 1,000. We then ask him to continue the series ' + 2' beyond 1,000; and he writes 1,000, 1,004, 1,008, 1,012. We tell him that this is wrong. His instructive reply is, "But I went on in the same way" (185). There was nothing in the previous explanations, examples and exercises that made it *impossible* for him to regard that as the continuation of the series. Repeating *those* examples and explanations won't help him. One must say to him, in effect, 'That isn't what we *call* going on in the *same* way.' It is a fact, and a fact of the kind whose importance Wittgenstein constantly stresses, that it is *natural* for human beings to continue the series in the manner 1,002, 1,004, 1,006, given the previous training. But that is merely what it is—a fact of human nature.

One is inclined to retort, 'Of course he can misunderstand the instruction and misunderstand the order ' + 2'; but if he *understands* it he must go on in the right way.' And here one has the idea that "The understanding itself is a state which is the *source* of the correct use"

(146)—that the correct continuation of the series, the right application of the rule or formula, springs from one's understanding of the rule. But the question of whether one understands the rule cannot be divorced from the question of whether one will go on in that one particular way that we call 'right.' The correct use is a criterion of understanding. If you say that knowing the formula is a state of the mind and that making this and that application of the formula is merely a *manifestation* of the knowledge, then you are in a difficulty: for you are postulating a mental apparatus that explains the manifestations, and so you ought to have (but do not have) a knowledge of the construction of the apparatus, quite apart from what it does (149). You would like to think that your understanding of the formula determines in advance the steps to be taken, that when you understood or meant the formula in a certain way "your mind as it were flew ahead and took all the steps before you physically arrived at this or that one" (188). But how you meant it is not independent of how in fact you use it. "We say, for instance, to someone who uses a sign unknown to us: 'If by '$x!2$' you mean x^2, then you get *this* value for y, if you mean $2x$, *that* one!—Now ask yourself: how does one *mean* the one thing or the other by '$x!2$'?" (190). The answer is that his putting down *this* value for y shows whether he meant the one thing and not the other: "*That* will be how meaning it can determine the steps in advance" (190). How he meant the formula determines his subsequent use of it, only in the sense that the latter is a criterion of how he meant it.

It is easy to suppose that when you have given a person the order 'Now do the *same* thing,' you have pointed out to him the way to go on. But consider the example of the man who obtains the series 1, 3, 5, 7 . . . by working out the formula $2x + 1$ and then asks himself, "Am I always doing the same thing, or something different every time?" (226). One answer is as good as the other; it doesn't matter which he says, so long as he continues in the right way. If we could not observe his work, his mere remark 'I am going on in the same way' would not tell us what he was doing. If a child writing down a row of 2's obtained '2, 2, 2' from the segment '2, 2' by adding '2' once, he might deny that he had gone on in the *same* way. He might declare that it would be doing the same thing only if he went from '2, 2' to '2, 2, 2, 2' in *one* jump, i.e., only if he *doubled* the original segment (just as it doubled the original single '2'). That could strike one as a *reasonable* use of 'same.' This connects up with Wittgenstein's remark: "If you have to have an intuition in order to develop the series 1 2 3 4 . . . you must also have one in order to develop the series 2 2 2 2 . . ." (214). One is inclined to say of the latter series, 'Why, all that is necessary is that you keep on doing the *same* thing.' But isn't this just as true of the other series? In both cases one has already *decided* what the correct continuation is, and one calls that continuation, and no other, 'doing the same thing.' As Wittgenstein says: "One might say to the person one was training: 'Look, I always do the same thing: I . . .'" (223). And then one proceeds to show him what 'the same' *is*. If the pupil does not acknowledge that what you have shown him is the *same*, and if he is not persuaded by your examples and explanations to carry on as you wish him to—then you have reached bedrock and will be inclined to say "This is simply what I do" (217). You cannot give him more reasons than you yourself have for proceeding in that way. Your reasons will soon give out. And then you will proceed, without reasons (211).

Private rules. All of this argument strikes at the idea that there can be such a thing as my following a rule in my private language—such a thing as naming something of which only I can be aware, 'pain,' and then going on to call the same thing, 'pain,' whenever it occurs. There is a charm about the expression 'same' which makes one think that there cannot be any difficulty or any chance of going wrong in deciding whether *A* is the *same* as *B*—as if one did not have to be *shown* what the 'same' is. This may be, as Wittgenstein suggests, because we are inclined to suppose that we can take the identity of a thing *with itself* as "an infallible paradigm" of the *same* (215). But he destroys this notion with one blow: "Then are two things the same when they are what *one* thing is? And how am I to apply what the *one* thing shows me to the case of two things?" (215).

The point to be made here is that when one has given oneself the private rule 'I will call this same thing "pain" whenever it occurs,' one is then free to do anything or nothing. That 'rule' does not point in any direction. On the private-language hypothesis, no one can teach me what the correct use of 'same' is. I shall be the sole arbiter of whether this is the *same* as that. What I choose to call the 'same' will *be* the same. No restriction whatever will be imposed upon my application of the word. But a sound that I can use *as I please* is not a *word*.

How would you teach someone the meaning of 'same'? By example and practice: you might show him, for instance, collections of the same colors and same shapes and make him find and produce them and perhaps get him to carry on a certain ornamental pattern uniformly (208). Training him to form collections and produce patterns is teaching him what Wittgenstein calls "techniques." Whether he has mastered various techniques determines whether he understands 'same.' The exercise of a technique is what Wittgenstein calls a "practice." Whether your pupil has understood any of the rules that you taught him (e.g., the rule; this is the 'same' color as that) will be shown in his practice. But now there cannot be a 'private' practice, i.e., a practice that cannot be exhibited. For there would then be no distinction between believing that you have that practice and having it. 'Obeying a rule' is itself a practice. "And to *think* one is obeying a rule is not to obey a rule. Hence it is not possible to obey a rule 'privately'; otherwise thinking one was obeying a rule would be the same thing as obeying it" (202. cf. 380).

If I recognize that my mental image is the 'same' as one that I had previously, how am I to know that this public word 'same' describes what I recognize? "Only if I can express my recognition in some other way, and if it is possible for someone else to teach me that 'same' is the correct word here" (378). The notion of the private language doesn't admit of there being 'some other way.' It doesn't allow that my behavior and circumstances can be so related to my utterance of the word that another person, by noting my behavior and circumstances, can discover that my use of the word is correct or incorrect. Can I discover this for myself, and how do I do it? That discovery would presuppose that I have a conception of correct use which comes from outside my private language and against which I measure the latter. If this were admitted, the private language would lose its privacy and its point. So it isn't admitted. But now the notion of 'correct' use that will exist within the private language will be such that if I *believe* that my use is correct then it is correct; the rules will be only impressions of rules; my 'language' will not be a language, but merely the impression of a language. The most that can be said for it is that I *think* I understand it (cf. 269).

Sensations of others. The argument that I have been outlining has the form of *reductio ad absurdum:* postulate a 'private' language; then deduce that it is not *language*. Wittgenstein employs another argument that is an external, not an internal, attack upon private language. What is attacked is the assumption that once I know from my *own* case what pain, tickling, or consciousness is, then I can transfer the ideas of these things to objects outside myself (283). Wittgenstein says:

If one has to imagine someone else's pain on the model of one's own, this is none too easy a thing to do: for I have to imagine pain which I do not feel on the model of the pain which I do feel. That is, what I have to do is not simply to make a transition in imagination from one

*place of pain to another. As, from pain in the hand to pain in the arm.
For I am not to imagine that I feel pain in some region of his body.
(Which would also be possible.)* [302]

The argument that is here adumbrated is, I think, the following: If
I were to learn what pain is from perceiving my own pain then I should,
necessarily, have learned that pain is something that exists only when *I*
feel pain. For the pain that serves as my paradigm of pain (i.e., my own)
has the property of existing only when *I* feel it.[2] That property is essential, not accidental; it is nonsense to suppose that the pain I feel
could exist when I did not feel it. So if I obtain my *conception* of pain
from pain that I experience, then it will be part of my conception of
pain that *I* am the only being that can experience it. For me it will be
a *contradiction* to speak of *another's* pain. This strict solipsism is
the necessary outcome of the notion of private language. I take the
phrase "this is none too easy" to be a sarcasm.

One is tempted at this point to appeal to the 'same' again: "But if
I suppose that someone has a pain, then I am simply supposing that he
has just the same as I have so often had" (350). I will quote Wittgenstein's brilliant counterstroke in full:

> *That gets us no further. It is as if I were to say: "You surely know
> what 'It is 5 o'clock here' means; so you also know what 'It's 5 o'clock
> on the sun' means. It means simply that it is just the same time there*

[2][This is an error. Apparently I fell into the trap of assuming that if two people, A and
B, are in pain, the pain that A feels must be *numerically* different from the pain that B
feels. Far from making this assumption, Wittgenstein attacks it when he says: "In so
far as it makes *sense* to say that my pain is the same as his, it is also possible for us both
to have the same pain" (*op. cit.*, 253). There is not some sense of "same pain" (*numerically*
the same) in which A and B *cannot* have the same pain. "Today I have that same backache that you had last week" is something we say. "Same" means here, answering to
the same description. We attach no meaning to the "question" of whether the backache
you had and the one I have are or are not "numerically" the same.

A more correct account of Wittgenstein's point in sec. 302 is the following: A proponent
of the privacy of sensations rejects circumstances and behavior as a criterion of the sensations of others, this being essential to his viewpoint. He does not need (and could not
have) a criterion for the existence of pain that he feels. But surely he will need a criterion
for the existence of pain that *he* does *not* feel. Yet he cannot have one and still hold to
the privacy of sensation. If he sticks to the latter, he ought to admit that he has not the
faintest idea of what would count for or against the occurrence of sensations that he does
not feel. His conclusion should be, not that it is a contradiction, but that it is unintelligible
to speak of the sensations of others. (There is a short exposition of Wittgenstein's attack
on the idea that we learn what sensation is *from our own case*, in "Knowledge of Other
Minds," see pp. 136-138 of *Knowledge and Certainty*.)

as it is here when it is 5 o'clock."—The explanation by means of identity
*does not work here. For I know well enough that one can call 5 o'clock
here and 5 o'clock there "the same time," but what I do not know is in
what cases one is to speak of its being the same time here and there.*
   *In exactly the same way it is no explanation to say: the supposition
that he has a pain is simply the supposition that he has the same as I.
For* that *part of the grammar is quite clear to me: that is, that one will
say that the stove has the same experience as I,* if *one says: it is in pain
and I am in pain* [350].

Expressions of sensation. Wittgenstein says that he destroys "houses of
cards" ("Luftgebäude": 118) and that his aim is to show one how to
pass from disguised to obvious nonsense (464). But this is not all he
does or thinks he does. For he says that he changes one's *way of looking
at things* (144). What is it that he wishes to substitute for that way of
looking at things that is represented by the idea of private language?
One would *like* to find a continuous exposition of his own thesis, instead of mere hints here and there. But this desire reflects a misunderstanding of Wittgenstein's philosophy. He rejects the assumption that
he should put forward a *thesis* (128). "We may not advance any kind
of theory" (109). A philosophical problem is a certain sort of confusion.
It is like being lost; one can't see one's way (123). Familiar surroundings
suddenly seem strange. We need to command a view of the country,
to get our bearings. The country is well known to us, so we need only
to be *reminded* of our whereabouts. "The work of the philosopher consists in assembling reminders for a particular purpose" (127). "The
problems are solved, not by giving new information, but by arranging
what we have always known" (109). When we describe (remind ourselves of) certain functions of our language, what we do must have a
definite bearing on some particular confusion, some "deep disquietude"
(111), that ensnares us. Otherwise our work is irrelevant—to *philosophy.*
It is philosophically pointless to formulate a general theory of language
or to pile up descriptions for their own sake. "This description gets
its light, that is to say its purpose—from the philosophical problems"
(109). Thus we may not complain at the absence from the *Investigations*
of elaborate theories and classifications.
   Wittgenstein asks the question "How do words *refer* to sensations?"
transforms it into the question "How does a human being learn the
meaning of the names of sensations?" and gives this answer: "Words
are connected with the primitive, the natural expressions of the sensation and used in their place. A child has hurt himself and he cries;

and then the adults talk to him and teach him exclamations and, later, sentences. They teach the child new pain-behavior" (244). Wittgenstein must be talking about how it is that a human being learns to refer with words to his *own* sensations—about how he learns to use 'I am in pain'; not about how he learns to use 'He is in pain.' What Wittgenstein is saying is indeed radically different from the notion that I learn what 'I am in pain' means by fixing my attention on a 'certain' sensation and calling it 'pain.' But is he saying that what I do instead is to fix my attention on my *expressions* of pain and call them 'pain'? Is he saying that the word 'pain' means crying? "On the contrary: the verbal expression of pain replaces crying and does not describe it" (244). My words for sensations are used *in place of* the behavior that is the natural expression of the sensations; they do not *refer* to it.

Wittgenstein does not expand this terse reminder. He repeats at least once that my words for sensations are "tied up with my natural expressions of sensation" (256) and frequently alludes to the importance of the connection between the language for sensations and the behavior which is the expression of sensation (e.g., 288, 271). The following questions and objections will arise:

(1) What shows that a child has made this 'tie up'? I take Wittgenstein to mean that the child's utterances of the word for a sensation must, in the beginning, be frequently concurrent with some nonverbal, natural expression of that sensation. This concomitance serves as the criterion of his understanding the word. Later on, the word can be uttered in the absence of primitive expressions. ('It hurts' can be said without cries or winces.)

(2) In what sense does the verbal expression 'replace' the nonverbal expression? In the sense, I think, that other persons will react to the child's mere words in the same way that they previously reacted to his nonverbal sensation-behavior; they will let the mere words serve as a *new* criterion of his feelings.

(3) I feel inclined to object: 'But has the child *learned* what the words *mean?* Hasn't he merely picked up the *use* of the word from his parents?' My objection probably arises from assimilating the learning of the meaning of words to the labeling of bottles—a tendency that is easily decried but not easily resisted. 'Learning *ought* to consist in attaching the right name to the right object,' I should like to say (cf. 26). The example of 'the beetle in the box' is pertinent here (see 293). The aim of this fantasy is to prove that attending to a private object can have nothing to do with learning words for sensations. Suppose you wanted to teach a child what a tickling feeling is. You tickle him in

the ribs, and he laughs and jerks away. You say to him, 'That's what the feeling of tickling is.' Now imagine he felt something that you can't know anything about. Will this be of any interest to you when you decide from his subsequent use of the word 'tickling' whether he understands it? Others understand the word too. If each one has something that only he can know about, then all the somethings may be different. The something could even be nothing! Whatever it is, it can have no part in determining whether the person who has it understands the word. "If we construe the grammar of the expression of sensation on the model of 'object and name' the object drops out of consideration as irrelevant" (293, cf. 304).

My previous objection could be put like this: the teaching and learning of names of sensations cannot stop at the mere expressions of sensation; the names must be brought *right up* to the sensations themselves, must be applied *directly* to the sensations! Here we can imagine Wittgenstein replying, "Like *what*, e.g.?" as he replies to an analogous objection in a different problem (191). In *what* sense is Wittgenstein denying that names are applied directly to sensations? Do I have a model of what it would be to apply the name 'directly'? No. I have this picture—that learning the meaning of 'pain' is applying the sign 'pain' to pain itself. I have that picture, to be sure, but what does it teach me, what is its "application"? When shall I say that what it pictures has taken place, i.e., that someone has learned the meaning of 'pain'? It doesn't tell me; it is *only* a picture. It cannot conflict with, cannot refute, Wittgenstein's reminder of what it is that determines whether a child has learned the word for a sensation.

(4) Wittgenstein says that the verbal expressions of sensation can take the place of the nonverbal expressions and that in learning the former one learns "new pain-behavior." This seems to mean that the words (and sentences) for sensations are related to sensations in the same way as are the primitive expressions of sensations. I am inclined to object again. I want to say that the words are used to *report* the occurrence of a sensation and to inform others of it. The natural expressions, on the contrary, are not used to inform others; they are not 'used' at all; they have no purpose, no function; they *escape* from one. But I have oversimplified the difference, because (a) a sentence can be forced from one, can escape one's lips ('My God, it hurts!'), and (b) a natural expression of sensation can be used to inform another, e.g., you moan to let the nurse know that your pain is increasing (you would have suppressed the moan if she hadn't entered the room), yet the moan is genuine. Perhaps my objection comes to this: I don't *learn* to moan; I do learn the words. But this is the very distinction that is made by saying that

moaning is a "natural," a "primitive," expression of sensation.

It is a mistake to suppose that Wittgenstein is saying that the utterance 'My leg hurts' is *normally called* an 'expression of sensation.' (Of course it isn't. For that matter, only a facial expression, not a groan, is called an '*expression* of pain.' But this is of no importance.) He is not reporting ordinary usage, but drawing our attention to an *analogy* between the groan of pain and the utterance of those words. The important similarity that he is trying to bring to light (here I may misinterpret him) is that the verbal utterance and the natural pain-behavior are each (as I shall express it) 'incorrigible.'[3] A man cannot be in *error* as to whether he is in pain; he cannot say 'My leg hurts' by mistake, any more than he can groan by mistake. It is senseless to suppose that he has wrongly identified a tickle as pain or that he falsely believes that it is in his leg when in fact it is in his shoulder. True, he may be undecided as to whether it is best described as an 'ache' or a 'pain' (one is often hard put to give satisfactory descriptions of one's feelings); but his very indecision *shows* us what his sensation is, i.e., something between an ache and a pain. His hesitant observation, 'I'm not sure whether it is a pain or an ache,' is itself an *expression* of sensation. What it expresses is an indefinite, an ambiguous sensation. The point about the incorrigibility of the utterance 'I'm in pain' lies behind Wittgenstein's reiterated remark that 'I *know* I'm in pain' and 'I don't know whether I'm in pain' are both senseless (e.g., 246, 408).[4] Wherever it is *meaningless* to speak of 'false belief,' it is also meaningless to speak of 'knowledge'; and wherever you cannot say 'I don't know . . .' you also cannot say 'I know . . . .' Of course, a philosopher can say of me that I *know* I am in pain. But "What is it supposed to mean—except perhaps that I *am* in pain?" (246).[5]

There are many 'psychological' sentences, other than sentences about sensations, that are incorrigible, e.g., the *truthful* report of a dream is a criterion for the occurrence of the dream and, unless some other criterion is introduced, "the question cannot arise" as to

[3][I try to explain the notion of "incorrigibility," as I understand it, in "Direct Perception" (see pp. 77-86 of *Knowledge and Certainty*). I concentrate there on the seeing of after-images, but with appropriate changes the notion carries over to bodily sensations.]

[4]It is interesting to note that as long ago as 1930 Wittgenstein had remarked that it has no sense to speak of *verifying* "I have a toothache." (See G. E. Moore, "Wittgenstein's Lectures in 1930-33," *Mind*, LXIII, January 1954, 14.) [This is reprinted in *Wittgenstein and the Problem of Other Minds*, ed. Harold Morick (McGraw-Hill, 1967), p. 121.]

[5][In "A Definition of Factual Memory," I mention a sense in which an adult person (but not an infant or a dog) can be said to know that he has a pain (see p. 239 of *Knowledge and Certainty*).]

whether the dreamer's memory deceives him (pp. 222-223). If one who has a mental image were asked whom the image is of, "his answer would be decisive," just as it would be if he were asked whom the drawing represents that he has just made (p. 177). When you say 'It will stop soon' and are asked whether you *meant* your pain or the sound of the piano-tuning, your truthful answer *is* the answer (666-684).

When Wittgenstein says that learning the words for sensations is learning "new pain-behavior" and that the words "replace" the natural expressions, he is bringing to light the arresting fact that my sentences about my present sensations have the same logical status as my out-cries and facial expressions. And thus we are helped to "make a radical break with the idea that language always functions in one way, always serves the same purpose: to convey thoughts—which may be about houses, pains, good and evil, or anything else you please" (304).

This is not to deny that first-person sentences about sensations may, in other respects, be more or less like natural expressions of sensation. Wittgenstein's examples of the use of 'I am afraid' (pp. 187-188) show how the utterance of that sentence can be a cry of fear, a comparison, an attempt to tell someone how I feel, a confession, a reflection on my state of mind, or something in between. "A cry is not a description. But there are transitions. And the words 'I am afraid' may approximate more, or less, to being a cry. They may come quite close to this and also be *far* removed from it" (p. 189). The words 'I am in pain' "may be a cry of complaint, and may be something else" (p. 189); and 'it makes me shiver' may be a "shuddering reaction" or may be said "as a piece of information" (p. 174). If we pursue these hints, it is not hard to construct a list of examples of the use of the words 'My head hurts,' in which the variety is as great as in Wittgenstein's list for 'I am afraid.' E.g., compare 'Oh hell, how my head hurts!' with 'If you want to know whether to accept the invitation for tonight then I must tell you that my head hurts again.' In one case the sentence 'My head hurts' be-longs to an exclamation of pain, not in the other. In saying that in *both* cases it is an 'expression' of pain, Wittgenstein stretches or-dinary language and in so doing illuminates the hidden continuity between the utterance of that sentence and—expressions of pain.

Criterion. That the natural pain-behavior and the utterance 'It hurts' are each incorrigible is what makes it possible for each of them to be a criterion of pain. With some reluctance I will undertake to say a little bit about this notion of 'criterion,' a most difficult region in Witt-genstein's philosophy. Perhaps the best way to elucidate it is to bring out its connection with *teaching* and *learning* the use of words. "When

I say the ABC to myself, what is the criterion of my doing the same as
someone else who silently repeats it to himself? It might be found that
the same thing took place in my larynx and in his. (And similarly when
we both think of the same thing, wish the same, and so on.) But then did
we learn the use of the words, 'to say such-and-such to oneself,' by
someone's pointing to a process in the larynx or the brain?" (376).
Of course we did not, and this means that a physiological process
is not our 'criterion' that *A* said such-and-such to himself. Try to imagine, realistically and in detail, how you would teach someone the meaning of 'saying the ABC silently to oneself.' This, you may think, is merely
psychology. But if you have succeeded in bringing to mind what it is
that would show that he *grasped* your teaching, that he *understood* the
use of the words, then you have elicited the 'criterion' for their use—
and that is not psychology. Wittgenstein exhorts us, over and over,
to bethink ourselves of how we learned to use this or that form of
words or of how we should teach it to a child. The purpose of this is
not to bring philosophy down to earth (which it does), but to bring into
view those features of someone's circumstances and behavior that
settle the question of whether the words (e.g., 'He is calculating in
his head') rightly apply to him. Those features constitute the 'criterion'
of calculating in one's head. It is logically possible that someone
should have been born with a knowledge of the use of an expression or
that it should have been produced in him by a drug; that his knowledge
came about by way of the normal process of teaching is not necessary.
What is necessary is that there should be something on the basis of
which we *judge* whether he *has* that knowledge. To undertake to describe this may be called a 'logical' investigation, even though one
should arrive at the description by reflecting on that logically inessen-
tial process of teaching and learning.

If someone says, e.g., 'I feel confident . . . ,' a question can arise
as to whether he understands those words. Once you admit the un-
tenability of 'private ostensive definition' you will see that there must
be a *behavioral* manifestation of the feeling of confidence (579). There
must be behavior against which his words 'I feel confident . . . ,'
can be checked, if it is to be possible to judge that he does not understand them. Even if you picture a feeling of confidence as an "inner
process," still it requires "outward criteria" (580).

Wittgenstein contrasts 'criterion' with 'symptom,' employing both
words somewhat technically. The falling barometer is a 'symptom'
that it is raining; its looking like *that* outdoors (think how you would
teach the word 'rain' to a child) is the 'criterion' of rain (354). A process
in a man's brain or larynx might be a symptom that he has an image of

red; the criterion is "what he says and does" (377, 376). What makes something into a symptom of *y* is that experience teaches that it is always or usually associated with *y*; that so-and-so is the criterion of *y* is a matter, not of experience, but of "definition" (354). The satisfaction of the criterion of *y* establishes the existence of *y* beyond question. The occurrence of a symptom of *y* may also establish the existence of *y* 'beyond question'—but in a different sense. The observation of a brain process may make it certain that a man is in pain—but not in the same way that his pain-behavior makes it certain. Even if physiology has established that a specific event in the brain accompanies bodily pain, still it *could* happen (it makes sense to suppose) that a man was not in pain although that brain event was occurring. But it will not make sense for one to suppose that another person is not in pain if one's criterion of his being in pain is satisfied. (Sometimes, and especially in science, we *change* our criteria: "what to-day counts as an observed concomitant of a phenomenon will to-morrow be used to define it" [79].)

The preceding remarks point up the following question: Do the propositions that describe the criterion of his being in pain *logically imply* the proposition 'He is in pain'? Wittgenstein's answer is clearly in the negative. A criterion is satisfied *only in certain circumstances*. If we come upon a man exhibiting violent pain-behavior, couldn't something show that he is not in pain? Of course. For example, he is rehearsing for a play; or he has been hypnotized and told, 'You will act as if you are in pain, although you won't be in pain,' and when he is released from the hypnotic state he has no recollection of having been in pain; or his pain-behavior suddenly ceases and he reports in apparent bewilderment that it was as if his body had been possessed—for his movements had been entirely involuntary, and during the 'seizure' he had felt no pain; or he has been narrowly missed by a car and as soon as a sum for damages has been pressed into his hand, his pain-behavior ceases and he laughs at the hoax; or . . . , etc. The expressions of pain are a criterion of pain in *certain* "surroundings," not in others (cf. 584).

Now one would like to think that one can still formulate a logical implication by taking a description of his pain-behavior and conjoining it with the negation of every proposition describing one of those circumstances that would count against saying he is in pain. Surely, the conjunction will logically imply 'He is in pain'! But this assumes there is a *totality* of those circumstances such that if none of them were fulfilled, and he was also pain-behaving, then he *could not but* be in pain (cf. 183). There is no totality that can be exhaustively enumerated, as can the letters of the alphabet. It is quite impossible to list six or nine such circumstances and then to say 'That is all of them; no other circumstances can be imagined that would count against his being in pain.' The list of circumstances has no 'all,' in that sense; the list is, not infinite, but *indefinite*. Therefore, entailment-conditions cannot be formulated; there are none.

The above thought is hard to accept. It is not in line with our *ideal* of what language should be. It makes the 'rules' for the use of 'He is in pain' too vague, too loose, not really *rules*. Wittgenstein has deep things to say about the nature of this 'ideal': "We want to say that there can't be any vagueness in logic. The idea now absorbs us, that the ideal *'must'* be found in reality. Meanwhile we do not as yet see *how* it occurs there, nor do we understand the nature of this 'must.' We think it must be in reality; for we think we already see it there" (101). "The strict and clear rules of the logical structure of propositions appear to us as something in the background—hidden in the medium of the understanding" (102). "The more narrowly we examine actual language, the sharper becomes the conflict between it and our requirement. (For the crystalline purity of logic was, of course, not a *result of investigation:* it was a requirement.)" (107). What we need to do is to remove from our noses the logical glasses through which we look at reality (103). We must study our language as it is, without preconceived ideas. One thing this study will teach us is that the criteria for the use of third-person psychological statements are not related to the latter by an entailment-relation.

Wittgenstein suggests that propositions describing the fulfillment of behavioral criteria are related to third-person psychological statements in the way that propositions describing sense-impressions are related to physical-objects statements (compare 486 and p. 180). It does not *follow* from the propositions describing my sense-impressions that there is a chair over there (486). The relation cannot be reduced to a *simple* formula (p. 180). *Why* doesn't it follow? Wittgenstein does not say, but the reason would appear to be of the same sort as in the example of 'He is in pain.' The propositions describing my sense-impressions would have to be conjoined with the proposition that I am not looking in a mirror, or at a painted scenery, or at a movie film, or . . . , etc. Here too there cannot be an exhaustive enumeration of the negative conditions that would have to be added to the description of sense-impressions *if* 'There's a chair over there' *were* to be logically implied.

The puzzling problem now presents itself: if it does not *follow* from his behavior and circumstances that he is in pain, then how can it ever be *certain* that he is in pain? "I can be as *certain* of someone else's sensations as of any fact," says Wittgenstein (p. 224). How can this be so, since there is not a definite set of six or eight conditions (each of which would nullify his pain-behavior) to be checked off as not fulfilled? It *looks* as if the conclusion ought to be that we cannot 'completely verify' that he is in pain. This conclusion is wrong, but it is not easy to see why. I comprehend Wittgenstein's thought here only dimly. He says:

> *A doctor asks: "How is he feeling?" The nurse says: "He is groaning."*
> *A report on his behaviour. But need there be any question for them whether the groaning is really genuine, is really the expression of anything? Might they not, for example, draw the conclusion "If he groans, we must give him more analgesic"—without suppressing a middle term? Isn't the point the service to which they put the description of behaviour [p. 179]?*

One hint that I take from this is that there can be situations of real life in which a question as to whether someone who groans is pretending, or rehearsing, or hypnotized, or . . . , simply does not exist. "Just try—in a real case—to doubt someone else's fear or pain" (303). A doubt, a question, would be rejected as absurd by anyone who knew the actual surroundings. 'But might there not be still further surroundings, unknown to you, that would change the whole aspect of the matter?' Well, we go only *so* far—and then we are certain. "Doubting has an end" (p. 180). Perhaps we can *imagine* a doubt; but we do not take it seriously (cf. 84). Just as it becomes certain to us that there is a chair over there, although we can imagine a *possible* ground of doubt. There is a concept of certainty in these language-games only because we stop short of what is conceivable.

"'But, if you are *certain*, isn't it that you are shutting your eyes in face of doubt?'—They are shut" (p. 224). This striking remark suggests that what we sometimes do is draw a boundary around *this* behavior in *these* circumstances and say 'Any additional circumstances that might come to light will be irrelevant to whether this man is in pain.' Just as we draw a line and say 'No further information will have any bearing on whether there is a chair in the corner—that is settled.' If your friend is struck down by a car and writhes with a broken leg, you do not think: Perhaps it was prearranged in order to alarm me; possibly his leg was anesthetized just before the 'accident' and he isn't suffering at all. Someone *could* have such doubts whenever another person was ostensibly in pain. Similarly: "I can easily imagine someone always doubting before he opened his front door whether an abyss did not yawn behind it; and making sure about it before he went through the door (and he might on some occasion prove to be right)—but that does not make me doubt in the same case" (84).

The man who doubts the other's pain may be neurotic, may 'lack a sense of reality,' but his reasoning is perfectly sound. *If* his doubts are true then the injured man is *not* in pain. His reaction is abnormal but not illogical. The certainty that the injured man is in pain (the normal reaction) ignores the endless doubts that *could* be proposed and investigated.

And it is important to see that the abnormal reaction *must* be the exception and not the rule. For if someone *always* had endless doubts about the genuineness of expressions of pain, it would mean that he was not using *any criterion* of another's being in pain. It would mean that he did not accept anything as an *expression* of pain. So what could it mean to say that he even had the *concept* of another's being in pain? It is senseless to suppose that he has this concept and yet always doubts.

Third-person sensation-sentences. Wittgenstein assimilates first-person, not third-person, sensation-sentences to *expressions* of sensation. I will say one or two things more about his conception of the use of third-person sensation-sentences.

(1) "Only of a living human being and what resembles (behaves like) a living human being can one say: it has sensations; it sees; is blind; hears; is deaf; is conscious or unconscious" (281). The *human* body and *human* behavior are the *paradigm* to which third-person attributions of consciousness, sensations, feelings are related. (The use of first-person sensation-sentences is governed by *no* paradigm.) Thus there cannot occur in ordinary life a question as to whether other human beings ever possess consciousness, and I can have this question when I philosophize only if I forget that I use that paradigm in ordinary life. It is by analogy with the human form and behavior that I attribute consciousness (or unconsciousness) to animals and fish: the more remote the analogy the less sense in the attribution. (Just as it is by analogy with our ordinary language that anything is called 'language') (494). In order to imagine that a pot or a chair has thoughts or sensations one must give it, in imagination, something like a human body, face, and speech (282, 361). A child says that its doll has stomach-ache, but this is a "secondary" use of the concept of pain. "Imagine a case in which people ascribed pain *only* to inanimate things; pitied *only* dolls!" (282; cf. 385, p. 216). Wittgenstein means, I think, that this is an impossible supposition because we should not want to say that those

people *understood* ascriptions of pain. If they did not ever show pity for human beings or animals or expect it for themselves, then their treatment of dolls would not be *pity*.

(2) My criterion of another's being in pain is, first, his behavior and circumstances and, second, his words (after they have been found to be connected in the right way with his behavior and circumstances). Does it follow that my interest is in his behavior and words, not in his pain? Does 'He is in pain' *mean* behavior? In lectures Wittgenstein imagined a tribe of people who had the idea that their slaves had no feelings, no souls—that they were automatons—despite the fact that the slaves had human bodies, behaved like their masters, and even spoke the same language. Wittgenstein undertook to try to give sense to that idea. When a slave injured himself or fell ill or complained of pains, his master would try to heal him. The master would let him rest when he was fatigued, feed him when he was hungry and thirsty, and so on. Furthermore, the masters would apply to the slaves our usual distinctions between genuine complaints and malingering. So what could it mean to say that they had the idea that the slaves were automatons? Well, they would *look* at the slaves in a peculiar way. They would observe and comment on their movements *as if* they were machines. ('Notice how smoothly his limbs move.') They would discard them when they were worn and useless, like machines. If a slave received a mortal injury and twisted and screamed in agony, no master would avert his gaze in horror or prevent his children from observing the scene, any more than he would if the ceiling fell on a printing press. Here is a difference in 'attitude' that is not a matter of believing or expecting different facts.

So in the *Investigations*, Wittgenstein says, "My attitude towards him is an attitude towards a soul. I am not of the *opinion* that he has a soul" (p. 178). I do not *believe* that the man is suffering who writhes before me—for to what facts would a 'belief' be related, such that a change in the facts would lead me to alter it? I *react* to his suffering. I look at him with compassion and try to comfort him. If I complain of headache to someone and he says 'It's not so bad,' does this prove that he believes in something *behind* my outward expression of pain? "His attitude is a proof of his attitude. Imagine not merely the words 'I am in pain' but also the answer 'It's not so bad' replaced by instinctive noises and gestures" (310). The thought that behind someone's pain-behavior is the pain itself does not enter into our use of 'He's in pain,' but what does enter into it is our sympathetic, or unsympathetic, reaction to him. The fact that the latter does enter into our use of that sentence (but might not have) gives sense to saying that the sentence 'He is in pain' does not just *mean* that his behavior, words, and circumstances are such and such—although these are the criteria for its use.

When he groans we do not *assume*, even tacitly, that the groaning expresses pain. We fetch a sedative and try to put him at ease. A totally different way of reacting to his groans would be to make exact records of their volume and frequency—and do nothing to relieve the sufferer! But our reaction of seeking to comfort him does not involve a presupposition, for, "Doesn't a presupposition imply a doubt? And doubt may be entirely lacking" (p. 180).

Form of life. The gestures, facial expressions, words, and activities that constitute pitying and comforting a person or a dog are, I think, a good example of what Wittgenstein means by a "form of life." One could hardly place too much stress on the importance of this latter notion in Wittgenstein's thought. It is intimately related to the notion "language-game." His choice of the latter term is meant to "bring into prominence the fact that the *speaking* of language is part of an activity, or of a form of life" (23; cf. 19). If we want to understand any concept we must obtain a view of the human behavior, the activities, the natural expressions, that surround the words for that concept. What, for example, is the concept of *certainty* as applied to *predictions?* The nature of my certainty that fire will burn me comes out in the fact that "Nothing could induce me to put my hand into a flame" (472). That reaction of mine to fire shows the *meaning* of certainty in this language-game (474). (Of course, it is *different* from the concept of certainty in, e.g., mathematics. "The kind of certainty is the kind of language-game" [p. 124].) But is my certainty justified? Don't I need reasons? Well, I don't normally think of reasons, I can't produce much in the way of reasons, and I don't feel a need of reasons (cf. 477). Whatever was offered in the way of reasons would not strengthen my fear of fire, and if the reasons turned out to be weak I still wouldn't be induced to put my hand on the hot stove.

As far as 'justification' is concerned, "What people accept as a justification—is shewn by how they think and live" (325). If we want to elucidate the concept of justification we must take note of what people *accept* as justified; and it is clearly shown in our lives that we accept as justified both the certainty that fire will burn and the certainty that this man is in pain—even without reasons. Forms of life, embodied in language-games, teach us what justification is. As philosophers we must not attempt to justify the forms of life, to give reasons for *them* —to argue, for example, that we pity the injured man because we believe, assume, presuppose, or know that in addition to the groans and writhing, there is pain. The fact is, we pity him! "What has to be accepted, the given, is—so one could say—*forms of life*" (p. 226). What we should say is: *"This language-game is played"* (654).

From this major theme of Wittgenstein's thought one passes easily to another major theme—that "Philosophy simply puts everything before us, and neither explains nor deduces anything" (126). "It leaves everything as it is" (124).

Strawson's criticism. Mr. Peter Strawson's critical notice[6] of the *Investigations* contains misunderstandings that might obtain currency. To Strawson it appears that, for Wittgenstein, "no word whatever stands for or names a special experience,"[7] "no words name sensations (or 'private experiences'); and in particular the word 'pain' does not."[8] Wittgenstein "has committed himself to the view that one cannot sensibly be said to recognize or identify anything, unless one uses *criteria;* and, as a consequence of this, that one cannot recognize or identify sensations."[9] His "obsession with the *expression* of pain" leads him "to deny that sensations can be recognized and bear names."[10] Wittgenstein is hostile to "the idea of what is not observed (seen, heard, smelt, touched, tasted), and in particular to the idea that what is not observed can in any sense be recognized or described or reported"[11]—although at one place in the book (p. 189) "it looks as if he were almost prepared to acknowledge" that 'I am in pain' "may be just a report of my sensations."[12] His "prejudice against 'the inner'" leads him to deny that it is possible for a person to report the words that went through his mind when he was saying something to himself in his thoughts.[13] Strawson attributes Wittgenstein's errors not only to prejudice and, possibly, to "the old verificationist horror of a claim that cannot be checked,"[14] but also to various confusions and muddles.[15]

It is important to see how very erroneous is this account of Wittgenstein. The latter says, "Don't we talk about sensations every day, and give them names?" and then asks, "How does a human being learn the names of sensations?—of the word 'pain' for example?" (244). So Wittgenstein does not deny that we *name* sensations. It is a howler to accuse Wittgenstein of "hostility to the idea of what is not observed"

---

[6]"Critical Notice: *Philosophical Investigations,*" *Mind,* LXIII, January 1954, 70-99. [Reprinted in *Wittgenstein and the Problem of Other Minds,* ed. Morick, pp. 3–42.] (References to Strawson will be placed in footnotes, references to Wittgenstein will remain in the text.)
[7]P. 83.   [8]P. 84.   [9]P. 86.   [10]P. 87.   [11]P. 90.   [12]P. 94.
[13]P. 91.   [14]P. 92.   [15]See p. 86 and p. 98.

("observed" apparently means 'perceived by one of the five senses') and of "hostility to the idea that what is not observed can in any sense be recognized or described or reported."[16] Dreams and mental pictures are not observed, in Strawson's sense; yet Wittgenstein discusses *reports* of dreams (p. 222; also p. 184) and *descriptions* of mental pictures (e.g., 367). Consider this general remark: "Think how many different kinds of things are called 'description': description of a body's position by means of its co-ordinates; description of a facial expression; *description of a sensation of touch;* of a mood" (24, my italics). And at many places in the *Investigations*, Wittgenstein *gives* descriptions of various sensations, although sensations are not observed, in Strawson's sense. Strawson's belief that Wittgenstein thinks that "one cannot sensibly be said to recognize or identify anything, unless one uses criteria,"[17] is proved false by the remarks about mental images: I have *no* criterion for saying that two images of mine are the same (377); yet there is such a thing as *recognition* here, and a correct use of 'same' (378). How can it be maintained that Wittgenstein has a prejudice against 'the inner' when he allows that in our ordinary language a man *can* write down or give vocal expression to his "inner experiences—his feelings, moods, and the rest—for his private use"? (243). Wittgenstein does not deny that there are *inner* experiences any more than he denies that there are *mental* occurrences. Indeed, he gives examples of things that he calls *"seelische Vorgänge,"* e.g., "a pain's growing more or less," and in contrast with which a thing like *understanding a word* is not, he argues a *"seelischen Vorgang"* (154). Either to deny that such occurrences exist or to claim that they cannot be named, reported, or described is entirely foreign to Wittgenstein's outlook. For what would the denial amount to other than an attempt to "reform language," which is not his concern? It may *look* as if he were trying to reform language, because he is engaged in "giving prominence to distinctions which our ordinary forms of language easily make us overlook" (132). For example, Wittgenstein suggests that when we think about the philosophical problem of sensation the word 'describe' *tricks* us (290). Of course he does not mean that it is a mistake to speak of 'describing' a sensation. He means that the similarity in "surface grammar" (664) between 'I describe my sensations' and 'I describe my room' may mislead, may cause us to fail "to call to mind the differences between the language-games" (290).

Strawson rightly avers, "To deny that 'pain' is the name of a (type of) sensation is comparable to denying that 'red' is the name of a col-

[16]P. 90.   [17]P. 86.

our."[18] I suppose that, conversely, to affirm that 'pain' is the name of a sensation is like affirming that 'red' is the name of a color, and also that '0' is the name of a number. This classification tells us nothing of philosophical interest. What we need to notice is the *difference* between the way that '0' and '2,' say, function, although both are 'names of numbers' (think how easily one may be tempted to deny that 0 is a number), and the difference between the way 'red' and 'pain' function, although both are 'names.' "We call very different things 'names'; the word 'name' is used to characterize many different kinds of use of a word, related to one another in many different ways" (38). To suppose that the uses of 'pain' and 'red,' as *names,* are alike is just the sort of error that Wittgenstein wants to expose. If one thinks this, one will want to by-pass the *expression* of pain and will wonder at Wittgenstein's 'obsession' with it. Not that Strawson does by-pass it, but he seems to attach the wrong significance to it. He appears to think that the fact that there is a characteristic pain-behavior is what makes possible a *common* "language of pain," and he seems to imply that if we did not care to have a *common* language of pain each of us would still be able to name and describe his pains in "a private language-game," even if there were no characteristic pain-behavior.[19] It looks as if he thinks that with his private language he could step between pain and its expression, and apply names to the bare sensations themselves (cf. 245).

For Strawson the conception of a private language possesses no difficulty. A man "might simply be struck by the recurrence of a certain sensation and get into the habit of making a certain mark in a different place every time it occurred. The making of the marks would help to impress the occurrence on his memory."[20] Just as, I suppose, he might utter a certain sound each time a cow appeared. But we need to ask, what makes the latter sound a *word*, and what makes it the word for *cow?* Is there no difficulty here? Is it sufficient that the sound is uttered when and only when a cow is present? Of course not. The sound might refer to anything or nothing. What is necessary is that it should play a part in various activities, in calling, fetching, counting cows, distinguishing cows from other things and pictures of cows from pictures of other things. If the sound has no fixed place in activities ("language-games") of this sort, then it isn't a word for *cow.* To be sure, I can sit in my chair and talk about cows and not be engaged in any of those activities—but what makes my words *refer* to cows is the fact that I have already mastered those activities; they lie in the background.

---

[18]P. 87   [19]See pp. 84-88.   [20]P. 85.

The kind of way that 'cow' refers is the kind of language-game to which it belongs. If a mark or sound is to be a word for a *sensation* it, too, must enter into language-games, although of a very different sort. What sort? Well, such things as showing the location of the sensation, exhibiting different reactions to different intensities of stimulus, seeking or avoiding causes of the sensation, choosing one sensation in preference to another, indicating the duration of the sensation, and so on. Actions and reactions of that sort constitute the sensation-behavior. They are the "outward criteria" (580) with which the sign must be connected if it is to be a sign for a sensation *at all*, not merely if it is to be a sign in a *common* language. In the mere supposition that there is a man who is "struck by the recurrence of a certain sensation" and who gets into the habit of "making a certain mark in a different place every time it occurred," no ground *whatever* has been given for saying that the mark is a sign for a sensation. The necessary surroundings have not been supplied. Strawson sees no problem here. He is surprised that "Wittgenstein gives himself considerable trouble over the question of how a man would *introduce* a name for a sensation into this private language."[21] It is as if Strawson thought: There is no difficulty about it; the man just *makes* the mark refer to a sensation. How the man does it puzzles Strawson so little that he is not even inclined to feel that the connection between the name and the sensation is queer, occult (cf. 38)—which it would be, to say the least, if the name had no fixed place in those activities and reactions that constitute sensation-behavior, for that, and not a magical act of the mind, is what *makes* it refer to a sensation.

The conception of private language that Wittgenstein attacks is not the conception of a language that only the speaker does understand, but of a language that no other person *can* understand (243). Strawson thinks that Wittgenstein has not refuted the conception of a private language but has only shown that certain conditions must be satisfied if a common language is to exist. Strawson appears to believe (I may misunderstand him) that each of us not only can have but does have a private language of sensations, that if we are to understand one another when we speak of our sensations there must be criteria for the use of our sensation-words, and that therefore the words with which we *refer* to our sensations must, in addition, contain "allusions" either to behavior or to material substances that are "associated" with the sensations.[22] The allusions must be to things that can be perceived by us all. By virtue of this the use of sensation-words can be taught and

[21]*Ibid.*   [22]P. 86.

misuses corrected, and so those words will belong to a common language. There is another feature of their use (namely, their reference) that cannot be taught. Thus sensation-words will have both a public and a private meaning. Strawson's view appears to be accurately characterized by Wittgenstein's mock conjecture: "Or is it like this: the word 'red' means something known to everyone; and in addition, for each person, it means something known only to him? (Or perhaps rather: it *refers* to something known only to him.)" (273)

But if my words, *without* these allusions, can refer to my sensations, then what is alluded to is only *contingently* related to the sensations. Adding the "allusions to what can be seen and touched"[23] will not help one little bit in making us understand one another. For the behavior that is, for me, contingently associated with 'the sensation of pain' may be, for you, contingently associated with 'the sensation of tickling'; the piece of matter that produces in you what you call 'a metallic taste' may produce in me what, if you could experience it, you would call 'the taste of onions'; my 'sensation of red' may be your 'sensation of blue'; we do not know and cannot know whether we are talking about the same things; we cannot *learn* the essential thing about one another's use of sensation-words—namely, their reference. The language in which the private referring is done cannot be turned into a common language by having something grafted on to it. Private language cannot be the understructure of the language we all understand. It is as if, in Strawson's conception, the sensation-words were supposed to perform two functions—to refer and to communicate. But if the reference is incommunicable, then the trappings of allusion will not communicate it, and what they do communicate will be irrelevant.

Strawson's idea that expressions like 'jabbing pain,' 'metallic taste,' mean something known to everyone and, in addition, for each person, refer to something known only to him, is responsible, I believe, for his failure to understand Wittgenstein on the topic of recognizing and identifying sensations. There is *a* sense of 'recognize' and 'identify' with respect to which Wittgenstein does deny that we can recognize or identify our own sensations, feelings, images. Consider, for example, that although a man understands the word 'alcohol' he may fail to identify the alcohol in a bottle as alcohol, because the bottle is marked 'gasoline' or because the cork smells of gasoline; or, although he understands 'rabbit' and is familiar with rabbits, he may fail to recognize a rabbit as a rabbit, taking it for a stump instead; or, he may be in doubt and say, 'I don't know whether this is alcohol,' 'I'm not sure whether

[23]*Ibid.*

that is a rabbit or a stump.' But can a man who understands the word 'pain' be in doubt as to whether he has pain? Wittgenstein remarks:

> If anyone said "I do not know if what I have got is a pain or some-thing else," we should think something like, he does not know what the English word "pain" means; and we should explain it to him.—How? Perhaps by means of gestures, or by pricking him with a pin and saying: "See, that's what pain is!" This explanation, like any other, he might understand right, wrong, or not at all. And he will show which he does by his use of the word, in this as in other cases.
>
> If he now said, for example: "Oh, I know what 'pain' means; what I don't know is whether this, that I have now, is pain"—we should merely shake our heads and be forced to regard his words as a queer reaction which we have no idea what to do with [288].

That a man wonders whether what he has is pain can only mean that he does not understand the word 'pain'; he cannot both understand it and have that doubt. Thus there is a sense of 'identify' that has no application to sensations. One who understands the word 'alcohol' may fail to identify *this* as alcohol or may be in doubt as to its identity or may correctly identify it. These possibilities have no meaning in the case of pain. There is not over and above (or underneath) the under-standing of the word 'pain' a further process of correctly identifying or failing to identify *this* as pain. There would be if Strawson's conception was right. But there is not, and this is why "That expression of doubt ['Oh, I know what 'pain' means; what I don't know is whether *this*, that I have now, is pain'] has no place in the language-game" (288). (Strawson does not have, but in consistency should have, an inclination to dispute this last remark of Wittgenstein's.)[24] The fact that there is no *further* process of identifying a particular sensation is a reason why "the object drops out of consideration as irrelevant" when "we con-strue the grammar of the expression of sensation on the model of 'object and name'" (293)—a remark that Strawson misunderstands as the thesis that "no words name sensations."[25] If my use of a sensation-word satisfies the normal outward criteria and if I truthfully declare that I have that sensation, then I *have* it—there is not a further problem of my applying the word right or wrong within myself. If a man used the word 'pain' in accordance with "the usual symptoms and presup-positions of pain" then it would have no sense to suppose that perhaps his memory did not retain *what* the word 'pain' refers to, "so that he

[24]See p. 85. [25]P. 84.

constantly called different things by that name" (271). If my use of the word fits those usual criteria there is not an added problem of whether I accurately pick out the objects to which the word applies. In this sense of 'identify,' the hypothesis that I identify my sensations is "a mere ornament, not connected with the mechanism at all" (270).

It does not follow nor, I think, does Wittgenstein mean to assert that there is *no* proper use of 'identify' or 'recognize' with sensations. He acknowledges a use of 'recognize' with mental images, as previously noted. It would be a natural use of language, I believe, if someone who upon arising complained of an unusual sensation were to say, 'Now I can identify it! It is the same sensation that I have when I go down in an elevator.' Wittgenstein, who has no interest in reforming language, would not dream of calling this an incorrect use of 'identify.' He attacks a philosophical use of the word only, the use that belongs to the notion of the private object. In this example of a non-philosophical use, if the speaker employed the rest of the sensation-language as we all do, and if his behavior in this case was approximately what it was when he was affected by the downward motion of an elevator, then his declaration that he was feeling the elevator-sensation would be decisive; and also his declaration that it was *not* the elevator-sensation would be decisive. It is *out of the question* that he should have made a mistake in identifying the sensation. His identification of his sensation is an *expression* of sensation (in Wittgenstein's extended sense of this phrase). The identification is 'incorrigible.' We have here a radically different use of 'identify' from that illustrated in the examples of alcohol and rabbit.

The philosophical use of 'identify' seems to make possible the committing of *errors* of identification of sensations and inner experiences. The idea is that my sensation or my image is an object that I cannot show to anyone and that I identify it and from it derive its description (374). But if this is so, why cannot my identification and description go wrong, and not just sometimes but always? Here we are in a position to grasp the significance of Wittgenstein's maneuver: "Always get rid of the idea of the private object in this way: assume that it constantly changes, but that you do not notice the change because your memory constantly deceives you" (p. 207). We are meant to see the *senselessness* of this supposition: for what in the world would *show* that I was deceived constantly or even once? Do I look again—and why can't I be deceived that time, too? The supposition is a knob that doesn't turn anything (cf. 270). Understanding this will perhaps remove the temptation to think that I have something that I cannot show to you and from which I derive a knowledge of its identity. This is what Wittgenstein means in saying that when I related to another what I just said to myself in my thoughts " 'what went on within me' is not the point at all" (p. 222). He is not declaring, as Strawson thinks, that I cannot report what words went through my mind.[26] He is saying that it is a report "whose truth is guaranteed by the special criteria of truthfulness" (p. 222). It is *that* kind of report. So it is not a matter of trying faithfully to observe something within myself and of trying to produce a correct account of it, of trying to do something at which I might unwittingly fail.

The influence of the idea of the private object on Strawson's thinking is subtly reflected, I believe, in his declaration that a metallic taste is "quite certainly recognizable and identifiable in itself" and in his remark that "if the question 'What is the criterion of identity here?' is pushed, one can only answer: 'Well, the taste itself' (cf. 'the sensation itself')."[27] Strawson realizes that we don't identify a sensation by means of criteria (e.g., a metallic taste by means of the metallic material that produces it). He is inclined to add that we identify it by 'the sensation itself.' This seems to me to misconstrue the 'grammar' of 'identify' here. It may be to the point to consider again the comparison of colors and sensations. Wittgenstein says, "How do I know that this colour is red?—It would be an answer to say 'I have learned English'" (381). One thing this answer does is to deny that I have *reasons* for saying that this color before me is red. We might put this by saying that I identify it as red by 'the color itself,' not by anything else. The cases of red and pain (or metallic taste) so far run parallel. Equally, I don't have reasons for saying that this color is red or that this sensation is pain. But it *can* happen that I should fail to identify this color correctly, even though I have learned English (e.g., the moonlight alters its appearance). Here the parallel ends. Nothing can alter the 'appearance' of the sensation. Nothing counts as mistaking its identity. If we assimilate identifying sensations to identifying colors, because in neither instance reasons are relevant, we conceal the philosophically more important difference. To insist that the parallel is perfect, that one identifies sensations in the same sense that one identifies colors, is like saying that "there must also be something boiling in the pictured pot" (297). Identifying one's own sensation is nothing that is either in error or *not* in error. It is not, in *that* sense, *identifying*. When I identify my sensation, I do not *find out* its identity, not even from 'the sensation itself.' My identification, one could say, *defines* its identity.

[26]See pp. 90, 91.   [27]P. 86.

We use a man's identification of his sensation as a criterion of what his sensation is. But this is a *dependent* criterion. His verbal reports and identifications would not *be* a criterion unless they were grounded in the primitive sensation-behavior that is the primary and independent criterion of his sensations. If we cut out human behavior from the language-game of sensations (which Strawson does in defending the 'private language-game') one result will be that a man's identifying a sensation as the 'same' that he had a moment before will no longer be a criterion of its being the same. Not only the speaker but *no one* will have a criterion of identity. Consequently, for no one will it have any meaning to speak of a man's being "struck by the *recurrence* of a certain sensation."[28]

---

[28]P. 85, my italics.

9

U. T. Place

IS CONSCIOUSNESS A BRAIN PROCESS?[1]

The thesis that consciousness is a process in the brain is put forward as a reasonable scientific hypothesis, not to be dismissed on logical grounds alone. The conditions under which two sets of observations are treated as observations of the same process, rather than as observations of two independent correlated processes, are discussed. It is suggested that we can identify consciousness with a given pattern of brain activity, if we can explain the subject's introspective observations by reference to the brain processes with which they are correlated. It is argued that the problem of providing a physiological explanation of introspective observations is made to seem more difficult than it really is by the "phenomenological fallacy." the mistaken idea that descriptions of the appearances of things are descriptions of the actual state of affairs in a mysterious internal environment.

1. Introduction

The view that there exists a separate class of events, mental events, which cannot be described in terms of the concepts employed by the physical sciences no longer commands the universal and unquestioning acceptance among philosophers and psychologists which it once did. Modern physicalism, however, unlike the materialism of the seventeenth and eighteenth centuries, is behavioristic. Consciousness on this view is either a special type of behavior, "sampling" or "running-back-and-forth" behavior as Tolman has it,[2] or a disposition to behave in a certain way, an itch for example being a temporary propensity to scratch. In the case of cognitive concepts like "knowing," "believing," "understanding," "remembering," and volitional concepts like "wanting" and "intending," there can be little doubt, I think, that an analysis in terms of dispositions to behave is fundamentally sound.[3] On the other

[1]*British Journal of Psychology*, February, 1956. Reprinted by permission of the author and editor.
[2]E. C. Tolman, *Purposive Behavior in Animals and Men* (Berkeley: University of California Press, 1932).
[3]L. Wittgenstein, *Philosophical Investigations* (Oxford: Blackwell, 1953); [See Malcolm selection above.—Ed.] G. Ryle, *The Concept of Mind* (London: Hutchinson's University Library, 1949). [See Ryle selections above.—Ed.]

hand, there would seem to be an intractable residue of concepts clustering around the notions of consciousness, experience, sensation, and mental imagery, where some sort of inner process story is unavoidable.[4] It is possible, of course, that a satisfactory behavioristic account of this conceptual residuum will ultimately be found. For our present purposes, however, I shall assume that this cannot be done and that statements about pains and twinges, about how things look, sound, and feel, about things dreamed of or pictured in the mind's eye, are statements referring to events and processes which are in some sense private or internal to the individual of whom they are predicated. The question I wish to raise is whether in making this assumption we are inevitably committed to a dualist position in which sensations and mental images form a separate category of processes over and above the physical and physiological processes with which they are known to be correlated. I shall argue that an acceptance of inner processes does not entail dualism and that the thesis that consciousness is a process in the brain cannot be dismissed on logical grounds.

2. The "Is" of Definition and the "Is" of Composition

I want to stress from the outset that in defending the thesis that consciousness is a process in the brain, I am not trying to argue that when we describe our dreams, fantasies, and sensations we are talking about processes in our brains. That is, I am not claiming that statements about sensations and mental images are reducible to or analyzable into statements about brain processes, in the way in which "cognition statements" are analyzable into statements about behavior. To say that statements about consciousness are statements about brain processes is manifestly false. This is shown (a) by the fact that you can describe your sensations and mental imagery without knowing anything about your brain processes or even that such things exist, (b) by the fact that statements about one's consciousness and statements about one's brain processes are verified in entirely different ways, and (c) by the fact that there is nothing self-contradictory about the statement "X has a pain but there is nothing going on in his brain." What I do want to assert, however, is that the statement "Consciousness is a process in the brain," although not necessarily true, is not necessarily false. "Consciousness is a process in the brain," on my view is neither self-contradictory nor self-evident; it is a reasonable scientific hypothesis, in the way that the statement "Lightning is a motion of electric charges" is a reasonable scientific hypothesis.

[4]U. T. Place, "The Concept of Heed," *British Journal of Psychology*, XLV (1954), 243-55.

The all but universally accepted view that an assertion of identity between consciousness and brain processes can be ruled out on logical grounds alone, derives, I suspect, from a failure to distinguish between what we may call the "is" of definition and the "is" of composition. The distinction I have in mind here is the difference between the function of the word "is" in statements like "A square is an equilateral rectangle," "Red is a color," "To understand an instruction is to be able to act appropriately under the appropriate circumstances," and its function in statements like "His table is an old packing case," "Her hat is a bundle of straw tied together with string," "A cloud is a mass of water droplets or other particles in suspension." These two types of "is" statements have one thing in common. In both cases it makes sense to add the qualification "and nothing else." In this they differ from those statements in which the "is" is an "is" of predication; the statements "Toby is 80 years old and nothing else," "Her hat is red and nothing else" or "Giraffes are tall and nothing else," for example, are nonsense. This logical feature may be described by saying that in both cases both the grammatical subject and the grammatical predicate are expressions which provide an adequate characterization of the state of affairs to which they both refer.

In another respect, however, the two groups of statements are strikingly different. Statements like "A square is an equilateral rectangle" are necessary statements which are true by definition. Statements like "His table is an old packing case," on the other hand, are contingent statements which have to be verified by observation. In the case of statements like "A square is an equilateral rectangle" or "Red is a color," there is a relationship between the meaning of the expression forming the grammatical predicate and the meaning of the expression forming the grammatical subject, such that whenever the subject expression is applicable the predicate must also be applicable. If you can describe something as red then you must also be able to describe it as colored. In the case of statements like "His table is an old packing case," on the other hand, there is no such relationship between the meanings of the expressions "his table" and "old packing case"; it merely so happens that in this case both expressions are applicable to and at the same time provide an adequate characterization of the same object. Those who contend that the statement "Consciousness is a brain process" is logically untenable base their claim, I suspect, on the mistaken assumption that if the meanings of two statements or expressions are quite unconnected, they cannot both provide an adequate characterization of the same object or state of affairs: if something is a state of consciousness, it cannot be a brain process, since there is nothing self-contradictory in supposing that someone feels a pain when there is nothing happening inside his skull. By the same token we might be led to conclude that a table cannot be an old packing case, since there is nothing self-contradictory in supposing that someone has a table, but is not in possession of an old packing case.

3. The Logical Independence of Expressions and the Ontological Independence of Entities

There is, of course, an important difference between the table/packing case case and the consciousness/brain process case in that the statement "His table is an old packing case" is a particular proposition which refers only to one particular case, whereas the statement "Consciousness is a process in the brain" is a general or universal proposition applying to all states of consciousness whatever. It is fairly clear, I think, that if we lived in a world in which all tables without exception were packing cases, the concepts of "table" and "packing case" in our language would not have their present logically independent status. In such a world a table would be a species of packing case in much the same way that red is a species of color. It seems to be a rule of language that whenever a given variety of object or state of affairs has two characteristics or sets of characteristics, one of which is unique to the variety of object or state of affairs in question, the expression used to refer to the characteristic or set of characteristics which defines the variety of object or state of affairs in question will always entail the expression used to refer to the other characteristic or set of characteristics. If this rule admitted of no exception it would follow that any expression which is logically independent of another expression which uniquely characterizes a given variety of object or state of affairs, must refer to a characteristic or set of characteristics which is not normally or necessarily associated with the object or state of affairs in question. It is because this rule applies almost universally, I suggest, that we are normally justified in arguing from the logical independence of two expressions to the ontological independence of the states of affairs to which they refer. This would explain both the undoubted force of the argument that consciousness and brain processes must be independent entities because the expressions used to refer to them are logically independent and, in general, the curious phenomenon whereby questions about the furniture of the universe are often fought and not infrequently decided merely on a point of logic.

The argument from the logical independence of two expressions to the ontological independence of the entities to which they refer breaks down in the case of brain processes and consciousness, I believe, because this is one of a relatively small number of cases where the rule stated above does not apply. These exceptions are to be found, I suggest, in those cases where the operations which have to be performed in order to verify the presence of the two sets of characteristics inhering in the object or state of affairs in question can seldom if ever be performed simultaneously. A good example here is the case of the cloud and the mass of droplets or other particles in suspension. A cloud is a large semitransparent mass with a fleecy texture suspended in the atmosphere whose shape is subject to continual and kaleidoscopic change. When observed at close quarters, however, it is found to consist of a mass of tiny particles, usually water droplets, in continuous motion. On the basis of this second observation we conclude that a cloud is a mass of tiny particles and nothing else. But there is no logical connection in our language between a cloud and a mass of tiny particles; there is nothing self-contradictory in talking about a cloud which is not composed of tiny particles in suspension. There is no contradiction involved in supposing that clouds consist of a dense mass of fibrous tissue; indeed, such a consistency seems to be implied by many of the functions performed by clouds in fairy stories and mythology. It is clear from this that the terms "cloud" and "mass of tiny particles in suspension" mean quite different things. Yet we do not conclude from this that there must be two things, the mass of particles in suspension and the cloud. The reason for this, I suggest, is that although the characteristics of being a cloud and being a mass of tiny particles in suspension are invariably associated, we never make the observations necessary to verify the statement "That is a cloud" and those necessary to verify the statement "This is a mass of tiny particles in suspension" at one and the same time. We can observe the microstructure of a cloud only when we are enveloped by it, a condition which effectively prevents us from observing those characteristics which from a distance lead us to describe it as a cloud. Indeed, so disparate are these two experiences that we use different words to describe them. That which is a cloud when we observe it from a distance becomes a fog or mist when we are enveloped by it.

4. When Are Two Sets of Observations Observations of the Same Event?

The example of the cloud and the mass of tiny particles in suspension was chosen because it is one of the few cases of a general proposition involving what I have called the "is" of composition which does not involve us in scientific technicalities. It is useful because it brings out the connection between the ordinary everyday cases of the "is" of composition like the table/packing case example and the more technical cases like "Lightning is a motion of electric charges" where the analogy with the consciousness/brain process case is most marked. The limitation of the cloud/tiny particles in suspension case is that it does not bring out sufficiently clearly the crucial problem of how the identity of the states of affairs referred to by the two expressions is established. In the cloud case the fact that something is a cloud and the fact that something is a mass of tiny particles in suspension are both verified by the normal processes of visual observation. It is arguable, moreover, that the identity of the entities referred to by the two expressions is established by the continuity between the two sets of observations as the observer moves towards or away from the cloud. In the case of brain processes and consciousness there is no such continuity between the two sets of observations involved. A closer introspective scrutiny will never reveal the passage of nerve impulses over a thousand synapses in the way that a closer scrutiny of a cloud will reveal a mass of tiny particles in suspension. The operations required to verify statements about consciousness and statements about brain processes are fundamentally different.

To find a parallel for this feature we must examine other cases where an identity is asserted between something whose occurrence is verified by the ordinary processes of observation and something whose occurrence is established by special scientific procedures. For this purpose I have chosen the case where we say that lightning is a motion of electric charges. As in the case of consciousness, however closely we scrutinize the lightning we shall never be able to observe the electric charges, and just as the operations for determining the nature of one's state of consciousness are radically different from those involved in determining the nature of one's brain processes, so the operations for determining the occurrence of lightning are radically different from those involved in determining the occurrence of a motion of electric charges. What is it, therefore, that leads us to say that the two sets of observations are observations of the same event? It cannot be merely the fact that the two sets of observations are systematically correlated such that whenever there is lightning there is always a motion of electric charges. There are innumerable cases of such correlations where we have no temptation to say that the two sets of observations are observations of the same event. There is a systematic correlation, for example, between the movement of the tides and the stages of the moon, but this does not lead us to say that records of tidal levels are records of the moon's stages or vice versa. We speak rather of a causal connection between two independent events or processes.

The answer here seems to be that we treat the two sets of observations as observations of the same event in those cases where the technical scientific observations set in the context of the appropriate body of scientific theory provide an immediate explanation of the observations made by the man in the street. Thus we conclude that lightning is nothing more than a motion of electric charges, because we know that a motion of electric charges through the atmosphere, such as occurs when lightning is reported, gives rise to the type of visual stimulation which would lead an observer to report a flash of lightning. In the moon /tide case, on the other hand, there is no such direct causal connection between the stages of the moon and the observations made by the man who measures the height of the tide. The causal connection is between the moon and the tides, not between the moon and the measurement of the tides.

5. The Physiological Explanation of Introspection and the Phenomenological Fallacy

If this account is correct, it should follow that in order to establish the identity of consciousness and certain processes in the brain, it would be necessary to show that the introspective observations reported by the subject can be accounted for in terms of processes which are known to have occurred in his brain. In the light of this suggestion it is extremely interesting to find that when a physiologist as distinct from a philosopher finds it difficult to see how consciousness could be a process in the brain, what worries him is not any supposed self-contradiction involved in such an assumption, but the apparent impossibility of accounting for the reports given by the subject of his conscious processes in terms of the known properties of the central nervous system. Sir Charles Sherrington has posed the problem as follows:

The chain of events stretching from the sun's radiation entering the eye to, on the one hand, the contraction of the pupillary muscles, and on the other, to the electrical disturbances in the brain-cortex are all straightforward steps in a sequence of physical "causation," such as, thanks to science, are intelligible. But in the second serial chain there follows on, or attends, the stage of brain-cortex reaction an event or set of events quite inexplicable to us, which both as to themselves and as to the causal tie between them and what preceded them science does not help us; a set of events seemingly incommensurable with any of the events leading up to it. The self "sees" the sun; it senses a two-dimensional disc of brightness, located in the "sky," this last a field of lesser brightness, and overhead shaped as a rather flattened dome, coping

*the self and a hundred other visual things as well. Of hint that this is
within the head there is none. Vision is saturated with this strange
property called "projection," the unargued inference that what it sees
is at a "distance" from the seeing "self." Enough has been said to
stress that in the sequence of events a step is reached where a physical
situation in the brain leads to a psychical, which however contains no
hint of the brain or any other bodily part. . . . The supposition has to
be, it would seem, two continuous series of events, one physicochemical,
the other psychical, and at times interaction between them.*[5]

Just as the physiologist is not likely to be impressed by the philosopher's contention that there is some self-contradiction involved in
supposing consciousness to be a brain process, so the philosopher is
unlikely to be impressed by the considerations which lead Sherrington
to conclude that there are two sets of events, one physicochemical,
the other psychical. Sherrington's argument for all its emotional appeal
depends on a fairly simple logical mistake, which is unfortunately all
too frequently made by psychologists and physiologists and not infrequently in the past by the philosophers themselves. This logical
mistake, which I shall refer to as the "phenomenological fallacy,"
is the mistake of supposing that when the subject describes his experience, when he describes how things look, sound, smell, taste, or
feel to him, he is describing the literal properties of objects and events
on a peculiar sort of internal cinema or television screen, usually referred to in the modern psychological literature as the "phenomenal
field." If we assume, for example, that when a subject reports a green
after-image he is asserting the occurrence inside himself of an object
which is literally green, it is clear that we have on our hands an entity
for which there is no place in the world of physics. In the case of the
green after-image there is no green object in the subject's environment
corresponding to the description that he gives. Nor is there anything
green in his brain; certainly there is nothing which could have emerged
when he reported the appearance of the green after-image. Brain
processes are not the sort of things to which color concepts can be
properly applied.

The phenomenological fallacy on which this argument is based depends on the mistaken assumption that because our ability to describe
things in our environment depends on our consciousness of them, our
descriptions of things are primarily descriptions of our conscious ex-

[5]Sir Charles Sherrington, *The Integrative Action of the Nervous System* (Cambridge:
Cambridge University Press, 1947), pp. xx-xxi.

perience and only secondarily, indirectly, and inferentially descriptions of the objects and events in our environments. It is assumed that because we recognize things in our environment by their look, sound, smell, taste, and feel, we begin by describing their phenomenal properties, i.e., the properties of the looks, sounds, smells, tastes, and feels which they produce in us, and infer their real properties from their phenomenal properties. In fact, the reverse is the case. We begin by learning to recognize the real properties of things in our environment. We learn to recognize them, of course, by their look, sound, smell, taste, and feel; but this does not mean that we have to learn to describe the look, sound, smell, taste, and feel of things before we can describe the things themselves. Indeed, it is only after we have learned to describe the things in our environment that we can learn to describe our consciousness of them. We describe our conscious experience not in terms of the mythological "phenomenal properties" which are supposed to inhere in the mythological "objects" in the mythological "phenomenal field," but by reference to the actual physical properties of the concrete physical objects, events, and processes which normally, though not perhaps in the present instance, give rise to the sort of conscious experience which we are trying to describe. In other words when we describe the after-image as green, we are not saying that there is something, the after-image, which is green; we are saying that we are having the sort of experience which we normally have when, and which we have learned to describe as, looking at a green patch of light.

Once we rid ourselves of the phenomenological fallacy we realize that the problem of explaining introspective observations in terms of brain processes is far from insuperable. We realize that there is nothing that the introspecting subject says about his conscious experiences which is inconsistent with anything the physiologist might want to say about the brain processes which cause him to describe the environment and his consciousness of that environment in the way he does. When the subject describes his experience by saying that a light which is in fact stationary, appears to move, all the physiologist or physiological psychologist has to do in order to explain the subject's introspective observations, is to show that the brain process which is causing the subject to describe his experience in this way, is the sort of process which normally occurs when he is observing an actual moving object and which therefore normally causes him to report the movement of an object in his environment. Once the mechanism whereby the individual describes what is going on in his environment has been worked out, all that is required to explain the individual's capacity to make introspective observations is an explanation of his ability to discriminate between those cases where his normal habits of verbal description are appropriate to the stimulus situation and those cases where they are not and an explanation of how and why, in those cases where the appropriateness of his normal descriptive habits is in doubt, he learns to issue his ordinary descriptive protocols preceded by a qualificatory phrase like "it appears," "seems," "looks," "feels," etc.[6]

[6]I am greatly indebted to my fellow-participants in a series of informal discussions on this topic which took place in the Department of Philosophy, University of Adelaide, in particular to Mr. C. B. Martin for his persistent and searching criticism of my earlier attempts to defend the thesis that consciousness is a brain process, to Prof. D. A. T. Gasking, of the University of Melbourne, for clarifying many of the logical issues involved, and to Prof. J. J. C. Smart for moral support and encouragement in what often seemed a lost cause.

10

P. F. Strawson

PERSONS[1]

1

In the *Tractatus* (5.631-5.641), Wittgenstein writes of the I which occurs
in philosophy, of the philosophical idea of the subject of experiences.
He says first: "The thinking, presenting subject—there is no such
thing." Then, a little later: *"In an important sense* there is no subject."
This is followed by: "The subject does not belong to the world, but is
a limit of the world." And a little later comes the following paragraph:
"There is [therefore] really a sense in which in philosophy we can talk
nonpsychologically of the I. The I occurs in philosophy through the
fact that the 'world is my world.' The philosophical I is not the man,
not the human body, or the human soul of which psychology treats,
but the metaphysical subject, the limit—not a part of the world." These
remarks are impressive, but also puzzling and obscure. Reading them,
one might think: Well, let's settle for the human body and the human
soul of which psychology treats, and which is a part of the world, and
let the metaphysical subject go. But again we might think: No, when
I talk of myself, I do after all talk of that which has all of my experiences,
I do talk of the subject of my experiences—and yet also of something
that is part of the world in that it, but not the world, comes to an end
when I die. The limit of *my* world is not—and is not so thought of by
me—the limit of *the* world. It may be difficult to explain the idea of
something which is both a subject of experiences and a part of the
world. But it is an idea we have: it should be an idea we can explain.

Let us think of some of the ways in which we ordinarily talk of ourselves, of some of the things which we ordinarily ascribe to ourselves.
They are of many kinds. We ascribe to ourselves *actions and intentions*
(I am doing, did, shall do this); *sensations* (I am warm, in pain); *thoughts
and feelings* (I think, wonder, want this, am angry, disappointed, con-
tented); *perceptions and memories* (I see this, hear the other, remember
that). We ascribe to ourselves, in two senses, position: *location* (I am
on the sofa) and *attitude* (I am lying down). And of course we ascribe

[1]From *Minnesota Studies in the Philosophy of Science*, Vol. II, *Concepts, Theories, and
the Mind-Body Problem*, ed. Herbert Feigl, Michael Scriven, and Grover Maxwell (Minneapolis: University of Minnesota Press, 1958). © Copyright 1958 by the University of
Minnesota. Reprinted by permission of the author and publisher.

to ourselves not only temporary conditions, states, and situations, like most of these, but also enduring characteristics, including such physical characteristics as height, coloring, shape, and weight. That is to say, among the things we ascribe to ourselves are things of a kind that we also ascribe to material bodies to which we would not dream of ascribing others of the things that we ascribe to ourselves. Now there seems nothing needing explanation in the fact that the particular height, coloring, and physical position which we ascribe to ourselves, should be ascribed to *something or other;* for that which one calls one's body is, at least, a body, a material thing. It can be picked out from others, identified by ordinary physical criteria and described in ordinary physical terms. But it can seem, and has seemed, to need explanation that one's states of consciousness, one's thoughts and sensations, are ascribed *to the very same thing* as that to which these physical characteristics, this physical situation, is ascribed. Why are one's states of consciousness ascribed to the very same thing as certain corporal characteristics, a certain physical situation, etc.? And once this question is raised, another question follows it, viz.: Why are one's states of consciousness ascribed to (said to be of, or to belong to) anything at all? It is not to be supposed that the answers to these questions will be independent of one another.

It might indeed be thought that an answer to both of them could be found in the unique role which each person's body plays in his experience, particularly his perceptual experience. All philosophers who have concerned themselves with these questions have referred to the uniqueness of this role. (Descartes was well enough aware of its uniqueness: "I am *not* lodged in my body like a pilot in a vessel.")[2] In what does this uniqueness consist? Well, of course, in a great many facts. We may summarize some of these facts by saying that for each person there is one body which occupies a certain *causal* position in relation to that person's perceptual experience, a causal position which is in various ways unique in relation to each of the various kinds of perceptual experience he has; and—as a further consequence—that this body is also unique for him as an *object* of the various kinds of perceptual experience which he has. This complex uniqueness of the single body appears, moreover, to be a contingent matter, or rather a cluster of contingent matters; we can, or it seems that we can, imagine many peculiar combinations of dependence and independence of aspects of our perceptual experience on the physical states or situation of more than one body.

Now I must say, straightaway, that this cluster of apparently contingent facts about the unique role which each person's body plays in his experience does not seem to me to provide, *by itself*, an answer to our questions. Of course these facts explain *something*. They provide a very good reason why a subject of experience should have a *very special regard* for just one body, why he should think of it as unique and perhaps more important than any other. They explain—if I may be permitted to put it so—why I feel *peculiarly attached* to what in fact I call my own body; they even might be said to explain why, granted that I am going to speak of one body as *mine*, I should speak of this body (the body that I do speak of as mine) as mine. But they do not explain why I should have the concept of *myself* at all, why I should ascribe my thoughts and experiences to *anything*. Moreover, even if we were satisfied with some other explanation of why one's states of consciousness (thoughts and feelings and perceptions) were ascribed to *something*, and satisfied that the facts in question sufficed to explain why the "possession" of a particular body should be ascribed to the *same* thing (i.e., to explain why a particular body should be spoken of as standing in some special relation, called "being possessed by" to that thing), yet the facts in question still do not explain why we should, as we do, ascribe certain corporal characteristics not simply to the body standing in this special relation to the thing to which we ascribe thoughts, feelings, etc., but to the thing itself to which we ascribe those thoughts and feelings. (For we say "I am bald" as well as "I am cold," "I am lying on the hearthrug" as well as "I see a spider on the ceiling.") Briefly, the facts in question explain why a subject of experience should pick out one body from others, give it, perhaps, an honored name and ascribe to it whatever characteristics it has; but they do not explain why the experiences should be ascribed to any subject at all; and they do not explain why, if the experiences are to be ascribed to something, they *and* the corporal characteristics which might be truly ascribed to the favored body, should be ascribed to the same thing. So the facts in question do not explain the use that we make of the word "I," or how any word has the use that word has. They do not explain the concept we have of a person.

2

A possible reaction at this point is to say that the concept we have is wrong or confused, or, if we make it a rule not to say that the concepts we have are confused, that the usage we have, whereby we ascribe, or seem to ascribe, such different kinds of predicate to one and the same thing, is confusing, that it conceals the true nature of the concepts involved, or something of this sort. This reaction can be found in two very important types of view about these matters. The first type of view is Cartesian, the view of Descartes and of others who think like him. Over the attribution of the second type of view I am more hesitant; but there is some evidence that it was held, at one period, by Wittgenstein and possibly also by Schlick. On both of these views, one of the questions we are considering, namely "Why do we ascribe our states of consciousness to the very same thing as certain corporal characteristics, etc.?" is a question which does not arise; for on both views it is only a linguistic illusion that both kinds of predicate are properly ascribed to one and the same thing, that there is a common owner, or subject, of both types of predicate. And on the second of these views, the other question we are considering, namely "Why do we ascribe our states of consciousness to anything at all?" is also a question which does not arise; for on this view, it is only a linguistic illusion that one ascribes one's states of consciousness at all, that there is any proper subject of these apparent ascriptions, that states of consciousness belong to, or are states of, anything.

That Descartes held the first of these views is well enough known.[3] When we speak of a person, we are really referring to one or both of two distinct substances (two substances of different types), each of which has its own appropriate type of states and properties; and none of the properties or states of either can be a property or state of the other. States of consciousness belong to one of these substances, and not to the other. I shall say no more about the Cartesian view at the moment—what I have to say about it will emerge later on—except to note again that while it escapes one of our questions, it does not escape, but indeed invites, the other: "Why are one's states of consciousness *ascribed* at all, to *any* subject?"

The second of these views I shall call the "no-ownership" or "no-subject" doctrine of the self. Whether or not anyone has explicitly held this view, it is worth reconstructing, or constructing, in outline.[4] For the errors into which it falls are instructive. The "no-ownership"

---

[3]See Descartes selection above.—Ed.

[4]The evidence that Wittgenstein at one time held such a view is to be found in the third of Moore's articles in *Mind* on "Wittgenstein's Lectures in 1930-33" (*Mind*, 1955, especially pp. 13-14). [This is reprinted in *Wittgenstein and the Problem of Other Minds*, ed. Harold Morick (McGraw-Hill, 1967).] He is reported to have held that the use of "I" was utterly different in the case of "I have a tooth-ache" or "I see a red patch" from its use in the case of "I've got a bad tooth" or "I've got a matchbox." He thought that there were two uses of "I" and that in one of them "I" was replaceable by "this body." So far the view might be Cartesian. But he also said that in the other use (the use exemplified by "I have a tooth-ache" as opposed to "I have a bad tooth"), the "I" *does not denote a possessor*, and that no ego is involved in thinking or in having tooth-ache; and referred with apparent approval to Lichtenberg's dictum that, instead of saying "I think," we (or Descartes!) ought to say "There is a thought" (i.e., "Es denkt").

theorist may be presumed to start his explanations with facts of the sort which illustrate the unique causal position of a certain material body in a person's experience. The theorist maintains that the uniqueness of this body is sufficient to give rise to the idea that one's experiences can be ascribed to some particular individual thing, can be said to be possessed by, or owned by, that thing. This idea, he thinks, though infelicitously and misleadingly expressed in terms of ownership, would have some validity, would make some sort of sense, so long as we thought of this individual thing, the possessor of the experiences, as the body itself. So long as we thought in this way, then to ascribe a particular state of consciousness to this body, this individual thing, would at least be to say something contingent, something that might be, or might have been, false. It might have been a misascription; for the experience in question might be, or might have been, causally dependent on the state of some other body; in the present admissible, though infelicitous, sense of "belong," it might have belonged to some other individual thing. But now, the theorist suggests, one becomes confused: one slides from this admissible, though infelicitous, sense in which one's experiences may be said to belong to, or be possessed by, some particular thing, to a wholly inadmissible and empty sense of these expressions; and in this new and inadmissible sense, the particular thing which is supposed to possess the experiences is not thought of as a body, but as something else, say an ego.

Suppose we call the first type of possession, which is really a certain kind of causal dependence, "having$_1$," and the second type of possession, "having$_2$"; and call the individual of the first type "B" and the supposed individual of the second type "E." Then the difference is that while it is genuinely a contingent matter that *all my experiences*

The attribution of such a view to Schlick would have to rest on his article "Meaning and Verification," Pt. V (*Readings in Philosophical Analysis*, H. Feigl and W. Sellars, eds.). Like Wittgenstein, Schlick quotes Lichtenberg, and then goes on to say: "Thus we see that unless we choose to call our body the owner or bearer of the data [the data of immediate experience]—which seems to be a rather misleading expression—we have to say that the data have no owner or bearer." The full import of Schlick's article is, however, obscure to me, and it is quite likely that a false impression is given by the quotation of a single sentence. I shall say merely that I have drawn on Schlick's article in constructing the case of my hypothetical "no-subject" theorist; but shall not claim to be representing his views.

Lichtenberg's anti-Cartesian dictum is, as the subsequent argument will show, one that I endorse, if properly used. But it seems to have been repeated, without being understood, by many of Descartes' critics.

The evidence that Wittgenstein and Schlick ever held a "no-subject" view seems indecisive, since it is possible that the relevant remarks are intended as criticisms of a Cartesian view rather than as expositions of the true view. [Cf. Harold Morick, "Logically Non-Transferable Ownership and Epistemic Privilege", abs. in *Journal of Philosophy* (1966).—Ed.]

are had₁ by B, it appears as a necessary truth that *all my experiences are had₂ by E*. But the belief in E and in having₂ is an illusion. Only those things whose ownership is logically transferable can be owned at all. So experiences are not owned by anything except in the dubious sense of being causally dependent on the state of a particular body. This is at least a genuine relationship to a thing, in that they might have stood in it to another thing. Since the whole function of E was to own experiences in a logically non-transferable sense of "own," and since experiences are not owned by anything in this sense, for there is no such sense of "own," E must be eliminated from the picture altogether. It only came in because of a confusion.

I think it must be clear that this account of the matter, though it contains *some* of the facts, is not coherent. It is not coherent, in that one who holds it is forced to make use of that sense of possession of which he denies the existence, in presenting his case for the denial. When he tries to state the contingent fact, which he thinks gives rise to the illusion of the "ego," he has to state it in some such form as "All *my* experiences are had₁ by (uniquely dependent on the state of) body B." For any attempt to eliminate the "my," or some other expression with a similar possessive force, would yield something that was not a contingent fact at all. The proposition that *all* experiences are causally dependent on the state of a single body B, for example, is just false. The theorist means to speak of all the experiences *had by a certain person* being contingently so dependent. And the theorist cannot consistently argue that "all the experiences of person P" *means the same thing* as "all experiences contingently dependent on a certain body B"; for then his proposition would not be contingent, as his theory requires, but analytic. He must mean to be speaking of some class of experiences of the members of which it is in fact contingently true that they are all dependent on body B. And the defining characteristic of this class is in fact that they are "*my* experiences" or "the experiences *of* some person," where the sense of "possession" is the one he calls into question.

This internal incoherence is a serious matter when it is a question of denying what prima facie is the case: that is, that one does genuinely ascribe one's states of consciousness to something, viz., oneself, and that this kind of ascription is precisely such as the theorist finds unsatisfactory, i.e., is such that it does not seem to make sense to suggest, for example, that the identical pain which was in fact one's own might have been another's. We do not have to seek far in order to understand the place of this logically non-transferable kind of ownership in our general scheme of thought. For if we think of the requirements

of identifying reference, in speech, to *particular* states of consciousness, or private experiences, we see that such particulars cannot be
thus identifyingly referred to except as the states or experiences *of* some
identified *person*. States, or experiences, one might say, *owe* their
identity as particulars to the identity of the person whose states or
experiences they are. And from this it follows immediately that if they
can be identified as particular states or experiences at all, they must
be possessed or ascribable in just that way which the no-ownership
theorist ridicules, i.e., in such a way that it is logically impossible that
a particular state or experience in fact possessed by someone should
have been possessed by anyone else. The requirements of identity
rule out logical transferability of ownership. So the theorist could maintain his position only by denying that we could ever refer to particular
states or experiences at all. And *this* position is ridiculous.

We may notice, even now, a possible connection between the no-
ownership doctrine and the Cartesian position. The latter is, straight-
forwardly enough, a dualism of two subjects (two types of subject).
The former could, a little paradoxically, be called a dualism too: a
dualism of one subject (the body) and one non-subject. We might sur-
mise that the second dualism, paradoxically so called, arises out of
the first dualism, nonparadoxically so called; in other words, that if
we try to think of that to which one's states of consciousness are ascribed as something utterly different from that to which certain corporeal characteristics are ascribed, then indeed it becomes difficult
to see why states of consciousness should be ascribed, thought of as
belonging to, anything at all. And when we think of this possibility,
we may also think of another: viz., that both the Cartesian and the no-
ownership theorist are profoundly wrong in holding, as each must,
that there are two uses of "I" in one of which it denotes something which
it does not denote in the other.

3

The no-ownership theorist fails to take account of all the facts. He
takes account of some of them. He implies, correctly, that the unique
position or role of a single body in one's experience is not a sufficient
explanation of the fact that one's experiences, or states of consciousness, are ascribed to something which *has* them, with that peculiar
nontransferable kind of possession which is here in question. It may be
a necessary part of the explanation, but it is not, by itself, a sufficient
explanation. The theorist, as we have seen, goes on to suggest that it
is perhaps a sufficient explanation of something else: viz., of our confusedly and mistakenly *thinking* that states of consciousness are to be

ascribed to something in this special way. And this suggestion, as we have seen, is incoherent: for it involves the denial that someone's states of consciousness are anyone's. We avoid the incoherence of this denial, while agreeing that the special role of a single body in someone's experience does not suffice to explain why that experience should be ascribed to anybody. The fact that there is this special role does not, by itself, give a sufficient reason why what we think of as a subject of experience should have any use for the conception of himself as such a subject.

When I say that the no-ownership theorist's account fails through not reckoning with all the facts, I have in mind a very simple but, in this question, a very central, thought: viz., that it is a necessary condition of one's ascribing states of consciousness, experiences, to oneself, in the way one does, that one should also ascribe them (or be prepared to ascribe them) to others who are not oneself.[5] This means not less than it says. It means, for example, that the ascribing phrases should be used in just the same sense when the subject is another, as when the subject is oneself. Of course the thought that this is so gives no trouble to the non-philosopher: the thought, for example, that "in pain" means the same whether one says "I am in pain" or "He is in pain." The dictionaries do not give two sets of meanings for every expression which describes a state of consciousness: a first-person meaning, and a second- and third-person meaning. But to the philosopher this thought has given trouble; indeed it has. How could the sense

---

[5]I can imagine an objection to the unqualified form of this statement, an objection which might be put as follows. Surely the idea of a uniquely applicable predicate (a predicate which *in fact* belongs to only one individual) is not absurd. And, if it is not, then surely the most that can be claimed is that a necessary condition of one's ascribing predicates of a certain class to one individual (oneself) is that one should be prepared, or ready, on appropriate occasions, to ascribe them to other individuals, and hence that one should have a conception of what those appropriate occasions for ascribing them would be; but not, necessarily, that one should actually do so on any occasion.

The shortest way with the objection is to admit it, or at least to refrain from disputing it; for the lesser claim is all that the argument strictly requires, though it is slightly simpler to conduct it on the basis of the larger claim. But it is well to point out further that we are not speaking of a single predicate, or merely of some group or other of predicates, but of the whole of an enormous class of predicates such that the applicability of those predicates or their negations determines a major logical type or category of individuals. To insist, at this level, on the distinction between the lesser and the larger claims is to carry the distinction over from a level at which it is clearly correct to a level at which it may well appear idle or, possibly, senseless.

The main point here is a purely logical one: the idea of a predicate is correlative with that of a range of distinguishable individuals of which the predicate can be significantly, though not necessarily truly, affirmed.

be the same when the method of verification was so different in the two cases—or, rather, when there *was* a method of verification in the one case (the case of others) and not, properly speaking, in the other case (the case of oneself)? Or, again, how can it be right to talk of *ascribing* in the case of oneself? For surely there can be a question of ascribing only if there is or could be a question of identifying that to which the ascription is made? And though there may be a question of identifying the one who is in pain when that one is another, how can there be such a question when that one is oneself? But this last query answers itself as soon as we remember that we speak primarily to others, for the information of others. In one sense, indeed, there is no question of my having to *tell who it is* who is in pain, when I am. In another sense I may have to *tell who it is*, i.e., to let others know who it is.

What I have just said explains, perhaps, how one may properly be said to ascribe states of consciousness to oneself, given that one as-cribes them to others. But how is it that one can ascribe them to others? Well, one thing is certain: that *if* the things one ascribes states of consciousness to, in ascribing them to others, are thought of as a set of Cartesian egos to which *only* private experiences can, in correct logical grammar, be ascribed, *then* this question is unanswerable and this prob-lem insoluble. If, in identifying the things to which states of conscious-ness are to be ascribed, private experiences are to be all one has to go on, then, just for the very same reason as that for which there is, from one's own point of view, no question of telling that a private experience is one's own, there is also no question of telling that a private experience is another's. All private experiences, all states of consciousness, will be mine, i.e., no one's. To put it briefly: one can ascribe states of con-sciousness to oneself only if one can ascribe them to others; one can ascribe them to others only if one can identify other subjects of experi-ence; and one cannot identify others if one can identify them *only* as subjects of experience, possessors of states of consciousness.

It might be objected that this way with Cartesianism is too short. After all, there is no difficulty about distinguishing bodies from one another, no difficulty about identifying bodies. And does not this give us an indirect way of identifying subjects of experience, while preserving the Cartesian mode? Can we not identify such a subject as, for example, "the subject that stands to that body in the same special relation as I stand to this one"; or, in other words, "the subject of those experiences which stand in the same unique causal relation to body N as *my* ex-periences stand to body M"? But this suggestion is useless. It requires me to have noted that *my* experiences stand in a special relation to body M, when it is just the right to speak of *my* experiences at all that is in question. (It requires me to have noted that *my* experiences stand in a special relation to body M; but it requires me to have noted this as a condition of being able to identify other subjects of experience, i.e., as a condition of having the idea of myself as a subject of experience, i.e., as a condition of thinking of any experience as *mine*.) So long as we persist in talking, in the mode of this explanation, of experiences on the one hand, and bodies on the other, the most I may be allowed to have noted is that experiences, *all* experiences, stand in a special relation to body M, that body M is unique in just this way, that this is what makes body M unique among bodies. (This "most" is, perhaps, too much—because of the presence of the word "experiences.") The proffered explanation runs: "Another subject of experience is distinguished and identified as the subject of those experiences which stand in the same unique causal relationship to body N as *my* experiences stand to body M." And the objection is: "But what is the word 'my' doing in this explanation? (It could not get on without it.)"

What we have to acknowledge, in order to begin to free ourselves from these difficulties, is the *primitiveness* of the concept of a person. What I mean by the concept of a person is the concept of a type of entity such that *both* predicates ascribing states of consciousness *and* predicates ascribing corporal characteristics, a physical situation, etc. are equally applicable to a single individual of that single type. And what I mean by saying that this concept is primitive can be put in a number of ways. One way is to return to those two questions I asked earlier: viz., (1) why are states of consciousness ascribed to anything at all? and (2) why are they ascribed to the very same thing as certain corporal characteristics, a certain physical situation, etc.? I remarked at the beginning that it was not to be supposed that the answers to these questions were independent of each other. And now I shall say that they are connected in this way: that a necessary condition of states of consciousness being ascribed at all is that they should be ascribed to the *very same things* as certain corporal characteristics, a certain physical situation, etc. That is to say, states of consciousness could not be ascribed at all, *unless* they were ascribed to persons, in the sense I have claimed for this word. We are tempted to think of a person as a sort of compound of two kinds of subject—a subject of experiences (a pure consciousness, an ego), on the one hand, and a subject of corporal attributes on the other.

Many questions arise when we think in this way. But, in particular, when we ask ourselves how we come to frame, to get a use for, the concept of this compound of two subjects, the picture—if we are honest and careful—is apt to change from the picture of two subjects to the picture of one subject and one non-subject. For it becomes impossible to see how we could come by the idea of different, distinguishable, identifiable subjects of experiences—different consciousnesses—*if this idea is thought of as logically primitive,* as a logical ingredient in the compound idea of a person, the latter being composed of two subjects. For there could never be any question of assigning an experience, as such, to any subject other than oneself; and therefore never any question of assigning it to oneself either, never any question of ascribing it to a subject at all. So the concept of the pure individual consciousness— the pure ego—is a concept that cannot exist; or, at least, cannot exist as a primary concept in terms of which the concept of a person can be explained or analyzed. It can only exist, if at all, as a secondary, non-primitive concept, which itself is to be explained, analyzed, in terms of the concept of a person. It was the entity corresponding to this illusory primary concept of the pure consciousness, the ego-substance, for which Hume was seeking, or ironically pretending to seek, when he looked into himself, and complained that he could never discover himself without a perception and could never discover anything but the perception.[6] More seriously—and this time there was no irony, but a confusion, a Nemesis of confusion for Hume—it was this entity of which Hume vainly sought for the principle of unity, confessing himself perplexed and defeated,[7] sought vainly because there is no principle of unity where there is no principle of differentiation. It was this, too, to which Kant, more perspicacious here than Hume, accorded a purely formal ("analytic") unity: the unity of the "I think" that accompanies all my perceptions and therefore might just as well accompany none.[8] And finally it is this, perhaps, of which Wittgenstein spoke when he said of the subject, first, that there is no such thing, and, second, that it is not a part of the world, but its limit.

So, then, the word "I" never refers to this, the pure subject. But this does not mean, as the no-ownership theorist must think and as Wittgenstein, at least at one period, seemed to think, that "I" in some cases does not refer at all. It refers, because I am a person among others. And the predicates which would, *per impossibile,* belong to the pure subject if it could be referred to, belong properly to the person to which "I" does refer.

The concept of a person is logically prior to that of an individual consciousness. The concept of a person is not to be analyzed as that of an animated body or of an embodied anima. This is not to say that

[6]See Hume selection, p. 47 above.—Ed.
[7]See pp. 55–57 above.—Ed.
[8]See Kant selection above.—Ed.

the concept of a pure individual consciousness might not have a logically secondary existence, if one thinks, or finds, it desirable. We speak of a dead person—a body—and in the same secondary way we might at least think of a disembodied person, retaining the logical benefit of individuality from having been a person.[9]

4

It is important to realize the full extent of the acknowledgment one is making in acknowledging the logical primitiveness of the concept of a person. Let me rehearse briefly the stages of the argument. There would be no question of ascribing one's own states of consciousness, or experiences, to anything, unless one also ascribed states of consciousness, or experiences, to other individual entities of the same logical type as that thing to which one ascribes one's own states of consciousness. The condition of reckoning oneself as a subject of such predicates is that one should also reckon others as subjects of such predicates. The condition, in turn, of this being possible, is that one should be able to distinguish from one another (pick out, identify) different subjects of such predicates, i.e., different individuals of the type concerned. And the condition, in turn, of this being possible is that the individuals concerned, including oneself, should be of a certain unique type: of a type, namely, such that to each individual of that type there *must* be ascribed, or ascribable, *both* states of consciousness and corporal characteristics. But this characterization of the type is still very opaque and does not at all clearly bring out what is involved. To bring this out, I must make a rough division, into two, of the kinds of predicates properly applied to individuals of this type. The first kind of predicate consists of those which are also properly applied to material bodies to which we would not dream of applying predicates ascribing states of consciousness. I will call this first kind M-predicates: and they include things like "weighs 10 stone," "is in the drawing room," and so on. The second kind consists of all the other predicates we apply to persons. These I shall call P-predicates. And P-predicates, of course, will be very various. They will include things like "is smiling," "is going for a walk," as well as things like "is in pain," "is thinking hard," "believes in God," and so on.

So far I have said that the concept of a person is to be understood as the concept of a type of entity such that *both* predicates ascribing states of consciousness *and* predicates ascribing corporal characteris-

---

[9]A little further thought will show how limited this concession is. But I shall not discuss the question now.

tics, a physical situation, etc. are equally applicable to an individual entity of that type. And all I have said about the meaning of saying that this concept is primitive is that it is not to be analyzed in a certain way or ways. We are not, for example, to think of it as a secondary kind of entity in relation to two primary kinds, viz., a particular consciousness and a particular human body. I implied also that the Cartesian error is just a special case of a more general error, present in a different form in theories of the no-ownership type, of thinking of the designations, or apparent designations, of persons as *not* denoting precisely the same thing, or entity, for all kinds of predicate ascribed to the entity designated. That is, if we are to avoid the general form of this error we must *not* think of "I" or "Smith" as suffering from type-ambiguity. (If we want to locate type-ambiguity somewhere, we would do better to locate it in certain predicates like "is in the drawing room," "was hit by a stone," etc., and say they mean one thing when applied to material objects and another when applied to persons.)

This is all I have so far said or implied about the meaning of saying that the concept of a person is primitive. What has to be brought out further is what the implications of saying this are as regards the logical character of those predicates in which we ascribe states of consciousness. And for this purpose we may well consider P-predicates in general. For though not all P-predicates are what we should call "predicates ascribing states of consciousness" (for example, "going for a walk" is not), they may be said to have this in common, that they imply the possession of consciousness on the part of that to which they are ascribed.

What then are the consequences of this view as regards the character of P-predicates? I think they are these. Clearly there is no sense in talking of identifiable individuals of a special type, a type, namely, such that they possess both M-predicates and P-predicates, unless there is in principle some way of telling, with regard to any individual of that type, and any P-predicate, whether that individual possesses that P-predicate. And, in the case of at least some P-predicates, the ways of telling must constitute in some sense logically adequate kinds of criteria for the ascription of the P-predicate. For suppose in no case did these ways of telling constitute logically adequate kinds of criteria. Then we should have to think of the relation between the ways of telling and what the P-predicate ascribes (or a part of what it ascribes) always in the following way: we should have to think of the ways of telling as *signs* of the presence, in the individual concerned, of this different thing (the state of consciousness). But then we could only know that the way of telling was a sign of the presence of the different thing ascribed by the P-predicate, by the observation of correlations between the two. But this observation we could each make only in one case, namely, our own. And now we are back in the position of the defender of Cartesianism, who thought our way with it was too short. For what, now, does "our own case" mean? There is no sense in the idea of ascribing states of consciousness to oneself, or at all, unless the ascriber already knows how to ascribe at least some states of consciousness to others. So he cannot (or cannot generally) argue "from his own case" to conclusions about how to do this; for unless he already knows how to do this, he has no conception of *his own case,* or any *case* (i.e., any subject of experiences). Instead, he just has evidence that pain, etc. may be expected when a certain body is affected in certain ways and not when others are.

The conclusion here is, of course, not new. What I have said is that one ascribes P-predicates to others on the strength of observation of their behavior; and that the behavior criteria one goes on are not just signs of the presence of what is meant by the P-predicate, but are criteria of a logically adequate kind for the ascription of the P-predicate. On behalf of this conclusion, however, I am claiming that it follows from a consideration of the conditions necessary for any ascription of states of consciousness to anything. The point is not that we must accept this conclusion in order to avoid skepticism, but that we must accept it in order to explain the existence of the conceptual scheme in terms of which the skeptical problem is stated. But once the conclusion is accepted, the skeptical problem does not arise. (And so with the generality of skeptical problems: their statement involves the pretended acceptance of a conceptual scheme and at the same time the silent repudiation of one of the conditions of its existence. This is why they are, in the terms in which they are stated, insoluble.) But this is only half the picture about P-predicates.

Now let us turn to the other half. For of course it is true, at least of some important classes of P-predicates, that when one ascribes them to oneself, one does not do so on the strength of observation of those behavior criteria on the strength of which one ascribes them to others. This is not true of all P-predicates. It is not, in general, true of those which carry assessments of character and capability: these, when self-ascribed, are in general ascribed on the same kind of basis as that on which they are ascribed to others. And of those P-predicates of which it is true that one does not generally ascribe them to oneself on the basis of the criteria on the strength of which one ascribes them to others, there are many of which it is also true that their ascription is liable to correction by the self-ascriber on this basis. But there remain many cases in which one has an entirely adequate basis for ascribing a P-predicate to oneself, and yet in which this basis is quite distinct from those on which one ascribes the predicate to another. (Thus one says, reporting a present state of mind or feeling: "I feel tired, am depressed, am in pain.") How can this fact be reconciled with the doctrine that the criteria on the strength of which one ascribes P-predicates to others are criteria of a logically adequate kind for this ascription?

The apparent difficulty of bringing about this reconciliation may tempt us in many directions. It may tempt us, for example, to deny that these self-ascriptions are really ascriptions at all; to *assimilate* first-person ascriptions of states of consciousness to those other forms of behavior which constitute criteria on the basis of which one person ascribes P-predicates to another. This device seems to avoid the difficulty; it is not, in all cases, entirely inappropriate. But it obscures the facts, and is needless. It is merely a sophisticated form of failure to recognize the special character of P-predicates (or at least of a crucial class of P-predicates). For just as there is not (in general) one primary process of learning, or teaching oneself, an inner private meaning for predicates of this class, then another process of learning to apply such predicates to others on the strength of a correlation, noted in one's own case, with certain forms of behavior, so—and equally—there is not (in general) one primary process of learning to apply such predicates to others on the strength of behavior criteria, and then another process of acquiring the secondary technique of exhibiting a new form of behavior, viz., first-person P-utterances. Both these pictures are refusals to acknowledge the unique logical character of the predicates concerned.

Suppose we write 'Px' as the general form of propositional function of such a predicate. Then according to the first picture, the expression which primarily replaces "x" in this form is "I," the first-person singular pronoun; its uses with other replacements are secondary, derivative, and shaky. According to the second picture, on the other hand, the primary replacements of "x" in this form are "he," "that person," etc., and its use with "I" is secondary, peculiar, not a true ascriptive use. But it is essential to the character of these predicates that they have both first- and third-person ascriptive uses, that they are both self-ascribable otherwise than on the basis of observation of the behavior of the subject of them, and other-ascribable on the basis of behavior criteria. To learn their use is to learn both aspects of their use. In order to *have* this type of concept, one must be both a self-ascriber and an other-ascriber of such predicates, and must see every other as a self-ascriber. And in order to *understand* this type of concept, one must acknowledge that there is a kind of predicate which is unambiguously and adequately ascribable *both* on the basis of observation of the subject of the predicate *and* not on this basis (independently of observation of the subject): the second case is the case where the ascriber is also the subject. If there were no concepts answering to the characterization I have just given, we should indeed have no philosophical problem about the soul; but equally we should not have *our* concept of a person.

To put the point—with a certain unavoidable crudity—in terms of one particular concept of this class, say, that of depression, we speak of behaving in a depressed way (of depressed behavior) and also of feeling depressed (of a feeling of depression). One is inclined to argue that feelings can be felt, but not observed, and behavior can be observed, but not felt, and that therefore there must be room here to drive in a logical wedge. But the concept of depression spans the place where one wants to drive it in. We might say, in order for there to be such a concept as that of X's depression, the depression which X has, the concept must cover both what is felt, but not observed, by X and what may be observed, but not felt, by others than X (for all values of X). But it is perhaps better to say: X's depression *is* something, one and the same thing, which is felt but not observed by X and observed but not felt by others than X. (And, of course, what can be observed can also be faked or disguised.) To refuse to accept this is to refuse to accept the structure of the language in which we talk about depression. That is, in a sense, all right. One might give up talking; or devise, perhaps, a different structure in terms of which to soliloquize. What is not all right is simultaneously to pretend to accept that structure and to refuse to accept it; i.e., to couch one's rejection in the language of that structure.

It is in this light that we must see some of the familiar philosophical difficulties in the topic of the mind. For some of them spring from just such a failure to admit, or fully appreciate, the character which I have been claiming for at least some P-predicates. It is not seen that these predicates could not have either aspect of their use (the self-ascriptive and the non-self-ascriptive) without having the other aspect. Instead, one aspect of their use is taken as self-sufficient, which it could not be, and then the other aspect appears as problematical. And so we oscillate between philosophical skepticism and philosophical behaviorism. When we take the self-ascriptive aspect of the use of some P-predicate (say, "depressed") as primary, then a logical gap seems to open between the criteria on the strength of which we say that another is depressed, and the actual state of depression. What we do not realize is that if this logical gap is allowed to open, then it swallows not only his depression, but our depression as well. For if the logical gap exists, then depressed behavior, however much there is of it, is no more than a sign of depression. And it can become a sign of depression only because of an observed correlation between it and depression. But whose depression? Only mine, one is tempted to say. But if *only* mine, then *not* mine at all. The skeptical position customarily represents the crossing of the logical gap as at best a shaky inference. But the point is that not even the syntax of the premises of the inference exists if the gap exists.

If, on the other hand, we take the other-ascriptive uses of these predicates as self-sufficient, we may come to think that all there is in the meaning of these predicates, as predicates, is the criteria on the strength of which we ascribe them to others. Does this not follow from the denial of the logical gap? It does not follow. To think that it does is to forget the self-ascriptive use of these predicates, to forget that we have to do with a class of predicates to the meaning of which it is essential that they should be both self-ascribable and other-ascribable to the same individual, when self-ascriptions are not made on the observational basis on which other-ascriptions are made, but on another basis. It is not that these predicates have two kinds of meaning. Rather, it is essential to the single kind of meaning that they do have that both ways of ascribing them should be perfectly in order.

If one is playing a game of cards, the distinctive markings of a certain card constitute a logically adequate criterion for calling it, say, the Queen of Hearts; but, in calling it this, in the context of the game, one is also ascribing to it properties over and above the possession of those markings. The predicate gets its meaning from the whole structure of the game. So it is with the language which ascribes P-predicates. To say that the criteria on the strength of which we ascribe P-predicates to others are of a logically adequate kind for this ascription is not to say that all there is to the ascriptive meaning of these predicates is these criteria. To say this is to forget that they are P-predicates, to forget the rest of the language-structure to which they belong.

5

Now our perplexities may take a different form, the form of the question "But how can one ascribe to oneself, not on the basis of observation, *the very same thing* that others may have, on the basis of observation, a logically adequate reason for ascribing to one?" And this question may be absorbed in a wider one, which might be phrased: "How are P-predicates possible?" or "How is the concept of a person possible?" This is the question by which we replace those two earlier questions, viz.: "Why are states of consciousness ascribed at all, ascribed to anything?" and "Why are they ascribed to the very same thing as certain corporal characteristics, etc.?" For the answer to these two initial questions is to be found nowhere else but in the admission of the primitiveness of the concept of a person, and hence of the unique character of P-predicates. So residual perplexities have to frame themselves in this new way. For when we have acknowledged the primitiveness of the concept of a person and, with it, the unique character of P-predicates, we may still want to ask what it is in the natural facts that makes it intelligible that we should have this concept, and to ask this in the hope of a non-trivial answer.[10] I do not pretend to be able to satisfy this demand at all fully. But I may mention two very different things which might count as beginnings or fragments of an answer.

And, first, I think a beginning can be made by moving a certain class of P-predicates to a central position in the picture. They are predicates, roughly, which involve doing something, which clearly imply intention or a state of mind or at least consciousness in general, and which indicate a characteristic pattern, or range of patterns, of bodily movement, while not indicating at all precisely any very definite sensation or experience. I mean such things as "going for a walk," "furling a rope," "playing ball," "writing a letter." Such predicates have the interesting characteristic of many P-predicates that one does not, in general, ascribe them to oneself on the strength of observation, whereas one does ascribe them to others on the strength of observation. But, in the case of these predicates, one feels minimal reluctance to concede that what is ascribed in these two different ways is the same. And this is because of the marked dominance of a fairly definite pattern of bodily movement in what they ascribe, and the marked absence of any distinctive experience. They release us from the idea that the only things we can know about without observation, or inference, or both, are private experiences; we can know also, without telling by either of these means, about the present and future movements of a body. Yet bodily movements are certainly also things we can know about by observation and inference.

Among the things that we observe, as opposed to the things we know without observation, are the movements of bodies similar to that about which we have knowledge not based on observation. It is important that we understand such observed movements; they bear on and condition our own. And in fact we understand them, we interpret them,

---

[10]I mean, in the hope of an answer which does not *merely* say: Well, there are people in the world.

only by seeing them as elements in just such plans or schemes of action as those of which we know the present course and future development without observation of the relevant present movements. But this is to say that we see such movements (the observed movements of others) as *actions*, that we interpret them in terms of intention, that we see them as movements of individuals of a type to which also belongs that individual whose present and future movements we know about without observation; that we see others, as self-ascribers, not on the basis of observations, of what we ascribe to them on this basis.

Of course these remarks are not intended to suggest how the "problem of other minds" could be solved, or our beliefs about others given a general philosophical "justification." I have already argued that such a "solution" or "justification" is impossible, that the demand for it cannot be coherently stated. Nor are these remarks intended as a priori genetic psychology. They are simply intended to help to make it seem intelligible to us, at this stage in the history of the philosophy of this subject, that we have the conceptual scheme we have. What I am suggesting is that it is easier to understand how we can see each other (and ourselves) as persons, if we think first of the fact that we act, and act on each other, and act in accordance with a common human nature. "To see each other as persons" is a lot of things; but not a lot of separate and unconnected things. The class of P-predicates that I have moved into the center of the picture are not unconnectedly there, detached from others irrelevant to them. On the contrary, they are inextricably bound up with the others, interwoven with them. The topic of the mind does not divide into unconnected subjects.

I spoke just now of a common human nature. But there is also a sense in which a condition of the existence of the conceptual scheme we have is that human nature should not be common, should not be, that is, a community nature. Philosophers used to discuss the question of whether there was, or could be, such a thing as a "group mind." And for some the idea had a peculiar fascination, while to others it seemed utterly absurd and nonsensical and at the same time, curiously enough, pernicious. It is easy to see why these last found it pernicious: they found something horrible in the thought that people should cease to have toward individual persons the kind of attitudes that they did have, and instead have attitudes in some way analogous to those toward groups; and that they might cease to decide individual courses of action for themselves and instead merely participate in corporate activities. But their finding it pernicious showed that they understood the idea they claimed to be absurd only too well. The fact that we find it natural to individuate as persons the members of a certain class of what might also be individuated as organic bodies does not mean that such a conceptual scheme is inevitable for any class of beings not utterly unlike ourselves.

Might we not construct the idea of a special kind of social world in which the concept of an individual person has no employment, whereas an analogous concept for groups does have employment? Think, to begin with, of certain aspects of actual human existence. Think, for example, of two groups of human beings engaged in some competitive but corporate activity, such as battle, for which they have been exceedingly well trained. We may even suppose that orders are superfluous, though information is passed. It is easy to imagine that, while absorbed in such activity, the members of the groups make no references to individual persons at all, have no use for personal names or pronouns. They do, however, refer to the groups and apply to them predicates analogous to those predicates ascribing purposive activity which we normally apply to individual persons. They may, *in fact*, use in such circumstances the plural forms "we" and "they"; but these are not genuine plurals, they are plurals without a singular, such as we use in sentences like these: "We have taken the citadel," "We have lost the game." They may also refer to elements in the group, to members of the group, but exclusively in terms which get their sense from the parts played by these elements in the corporate activity. (Thus we sometimes refer to what are in fact persons as "stroke" or "tackle.")

When we think of such cases, we see that we ourselves, over a part of our social lives—not, I am thankful to say, a very large part—do operate conceptual schemes in which the idea of the individual person has no place, in which its place is taken, so to speak, by that of a group. But might we not think of communities or groups such that this part of the lives of their members was the dominant part—or was the whole? It sometimes happens, with groups of human beings, that, as *we* say, their members think, feel, and act "as one." The point I wish to make is that a condition for the existence, the use, of the concept of an individual person is that this should happen *only sometimes*.

It is absolutely useless to say, at this point: But all the same, even if this happened all the time, every member of the group would have an individual consciousness, would be an individual subject of experience. The point is, once more, that there is no sense in speaking of the individual consciousness just as such, of the individual subject of experience just as such: for there is no way of identifying such pure entities.[11]

[11]More accurately: their identification is necessarily secondary to the identification of persons.

It is true, of course, that in suggesting this fantasy, I have taken our concept of an individual person as a starting point. It is this fact which makes the useless reaction a natural one. But suppose, instead, I had made the following suggestion: that each part of the human body, each organ and each member, had an individual consciousness, was a separate center of experiences. This, in the same way, but more obviously, would be a useless suggestion. Then imagine all the intermediate cases, for instance these. There is a class of moving natural objects, divided into groups, each group exhibiting the same characteristic pattern of activity. Within each group there are certain differentiations of appearance accompanying differentiations of function, and in particular there is one member of each group with a distinctive appearance. Cannot one imagine different sets of observations which might lead us, in the one case, to think of the particular member as the spokesman of the group, as its mouthpiece; and in the other case to think of him as its mouth, to think of the group as a single *scattered* body? The point is that as soon as we adopt the latter way of thinking then we want to drop the former; we are no longer influenced by the human analogy in its first form, but only in its second; and we no longer want to say: "Perhaps the members have consciousness." To understand the movement of our thought here, we need only remember the startling ambiguity of the phrase "a body and its members."

6

I shall not pursue this attempt at explanation any further. What I have been mainly arguing for is that we should acknowledge the logical primitiveness of the concept of a person and, with this, the unique logical character of certain predicates. Once this is acknowledged, certain traditional philosophical problems are seen not to be problems at all. In particular, the problem that seems to have perplexed Hume[12] does not exist—the problem of the principle of unity, of identity, of the particular consciousness, of the particular subject of "perceptions" (experiences) considered as a primary particular. There is no such problem and no such principle. If there were such a principle, then each of us would have to apply it in order to decide whether any contemporary experience of his was his or someone else's; and there is no sense in this suggestion. (This is not to deny, of course, that one *person* may be unsure of his own identity in some way, may be unsure, for example, whether some particular action, or series of actions, had been performed

[12]Cf. the Appendix to the *Treatise of Human Nature* [second part of Hume selection above. —Ed.].

by him. Then he uses the same methods (the same in principle) to resolve the doubt about himself as anyone else uses to resolve the same doubt about him. And these methods simply involve the application of the ordinary criteria for *personal* identity. There remains the question of what exactly these criteria are, what their relative weights are, etc.; but, once disentangled from spurious questions, this is one of the easier problems in philosophy.)

Where Hume erred, or seems to have erred, both Kant and Wittgenstein had the better insight. Perhaps neither always expressed it in the happiest way. For Kant's doctrine that the "analytic unity of consciousness" neither requires nor entails any principle of unity is not as clear as one could wish. And Wittgenstein's remarks (at one time) to the effect that the data of consciousness are not owned, that "I" as used by Jones, in speaking of his own feelings, etc., does not refer to what "Jones" as used by another refers to, seem needlessly to flout the conceptual scheme we actually employ. It is needlessly paradoxical to deny, or seem to deny, that when Smith says "Jones has a pain" and Jones says "I have a pain," they are talking about the same entity and saying the same thing about it, needlessly paradoxical to deny that Jones can *confirm* that he has a pain. Instead of denying that self-ascribed states of consciousness are really ascribed at all, it is more in harmony with our actual ways of talking to say: For each user of the language, there is just one person in ascribing to whom states of consciousness he does not need to use the criteria of the observed behavior of that person (though he does not necessarily not do so); and that person is himself. This remark at least respects the structure of the conceptual scheme we employ, without precluding further examination of it.

Further Readings

To avoid repetition, this list contains no references to works from which readings have been taken.

Anderson, A. R., ed. *Minds and Machines*. Englewood Cliffs, N.J.: Prentice-Hall, Inc., 1964.

Aune, Bruce. "Feelings, Moods, and Introspection," *Mind*, 1963.

——. "The Problem of Other Minds," *Philosophical Review* 70 1961.

Ayer, A. J. "The Concept of a Person," *The Concept of a Person and Other Essays*. London: Macmillan & Co., Ltd., 1963.

——. "One's Knowledge of Other Minds," *Theoria*, 1953. Reprinted in *Philosophical Essays*. London: Macmillan & Co., Ltd., 1955.

——. "Privacy," *Proceedings of the British Academy*, 1959. Reprinted in *The Concept of a Person and Other Essays*. London: Macmillan & Co., Ltd., 1963.

Blanshard, Brand. *The Nature of Thought*, Vol. 1. London: George Allen & Urwin, Ltd., 1939.

Brain, W. Russell. *Mind, Perception, and Science*. Oxford: B. H. Blackwell, Ltd., 1951.

Broad, C. D. *The Mind and Its Place in Nature*. London: Routledge & Kegan Paul, Ltd., 1925.

Chappell, V. C., ed. *The Philosophy of Mind*. Englewood Cliffs, N.J.: Prentice-Hall, Inc., 1962.

Chisholm, Roderick, ed. *Realism and the Background of Phenomenology*. Glencoe, Ill.: The Free Press of Glencoe, 1960.

Chisholm, R. M., and Sellars, Wilfrid. "Intentionality and the Mental," in H. Feigl *et al*, eds. *Minnesota Studies in the Philosophy of Science*, Vol. 2. Minneapolis: University of Minnesota Press, 1958.

Ducasse, Curt J. *Nature, Mind, and Death*. LaSalle, Ill.: Open Court Publishing Co., 1951. Parts 3 and 4.

Ewing, Alfred C. "Professor Ryle's Attack on Dualism," *Proceedings of the Aristotelian Society*, 1952-1953. Reprinted in H. D. Lewis, ed. *Clarity Is Not Enough*. London: George Allen & Unwin, 1963.

Feigl, Herbert. "The 'Mental' and the 'Physical,'" in H. Feigl *et al.*, eds. *Minnesota Studies in the Philosophy of Science*, Vol. 2. Minneapolis: University of Minnesota Press, 1958. Reprinted separately as *The "Mental" and the "Physical": The Essay and a Postscript*. Minneapolis: University of Minnesota Press, 1967.

Feyerabend, H., and Maxwell, Grover, eds. *Mind, Matter, and Method*. Minneapolis: University of Minnesota Press, 1966.

Flew, Antony, ed. *Body, Mind, and Death*. New York: The Macmillan Co., 1964.

Gustafson, D. F., ed. *Essays in Philosophical Psychology*. Garden City, N.Y.: Doubleday, 1964.

Hampshire, Stuart, ed. *Philosophy of Mind*. New York: Harper & Row, 1966.

Hook, Sidney, ed. *Dimensions of Mind*. New York: New York University Press, 1960.

Kneale, William. *On Having a Mind*. Cambridge: Cambridge University Press, 1962.

Laslett, Peter, ed. *The Physical Basis of Mind*. Oxford: B. H. Blackwell, Ltd., 1951.

Lewis, C. I. "Some Logical Considerations Concerning the Mental," *Journal of Philosophy*, 1941.

Lewis, H. D. "Mind and Body," *Proceedings of the Aristotelian Society*, 1962-1963. Reprinted in *Clarity Is Not Enough*. London: George Allen & Unwin, Ltd., 1963.

Malcolm, Norman. "Knowledge of Other Minds," *Journal of Philosophy*, 1958. Reprinted in *Knowledge and Certainty*. Englewood Cliffs, N.J.: Prentice-Hall, 1963.

Morick, Harold, ed. *Wittgenstein and the Problem of Other Minds*. New York: McGraw-Hill Book Co., 1967.

———. "Cartesian Privilege and the Strictly Mental". *Philosophy and Phenomenological Research*, forthcoming.

Penelhum, Terence. "Personal Identity," in Paul Edwards, ed. *The Encyclopedia of Philosophy*, Vol. 6. New York: The Macmillan Co. & The Free Press, 1967.

Reeves, J. W., ed. *Body and Mind in Western Thought*. Baltimore: Penguin Books, Inc., 1958.

Sartre, Jean-Paul. "Consciousness of Self and Knowledge of Self," in Nathaniel Lawrence and Daniel O'Connor, eds. *Readings in Existential Phenomenology*. Englewood Cliffs, N.J.: Prentice-Hall, Inc., 1967.

————. *Sketch for a Theory of the Emotions.* London: Methuen and Co., Ltd., 1962.

Scriven, Michael. "A Study of Radical Behaviorism," in H. Feigl and M. Scriven, eds. *Minnesota Studies in the Philosophy of Science.* Vol. 1. Minneapolis: University of Minnesota Press, 1956.

Shaffer, Jerome A. *Philosophy of Mind.* Englewood Cliffs, N.J.: Prentice-Hall, Inc., 1968.

Shoemaker, Sydney. *Self-Knowledge and Self-Identity.* Ithaca, N.Y.: Cornell University Press, 1963.

Sluckin, W. *Minds and Machines.* London: Pelican Books, 1954.

Smart, J. J. C. "Sensations and Brain Processes," *Philosophical Review*, 1959.

Strawson, P. F. "Critical Notice of Wittgenstein's *Philosophical Investigations*," *Mind*, 1954. Reprinted in H. Morick, ed. *Wittgenstein and the Problem of Other Minds.* New York: McGraw-Hill Book Co., 1967.

————. *Individuals.* London: Methuen & Co., Ltd., 1959.

Taylor, Richard. *Metaphysics.* Englewood Cliffs, N.J.: Prentice-Hall, Inc., 1963. Chapters 1, 2.

Vesey, G. N. A., ed. *Body and Mind.* London: George Allen & Unwin, Ltd., 1964.

White, Alan R. *The Philosophy of Mind.* New York: Random House, 1967.

Wisdom, John. *Other Minds.* Oxford: Basil Blackwell and Mott, Ltd., 1952.

————. *Problems of Mind and Matter.* London: Cambridge University Press, 1934. Part I.

Wittgenstein, Ludwig. *The Blue and Brown Books.* Oxford: Basil Blackwell & Mott, Ltd., 1958.

————. *Philosophical Investigations.* Oxford: Basil Blackwell & Mott, Ltd., 1953.

Index

Page numbers in *italic* refer to essays in this book.